NEW WORLD ECONOMY

Changing Dimensions of 'Commerce Clause'

Internet as Instrumentality of Commerce and VAT

NEW WORLD ECONOMY

Changing Dimensions of 'Commerce Clause'

Internet as Instrumentality of Commerce and VAT

SWARUPAMA CHATURVEDI

Foreword by

PROF. (DR.) ANIRUDH PRASAD

M.A. (Eng. Lit.), LL.M., Ph.D. (Law)

Head, Department of Law,

D.D.U. Gorakhpur University, Gorakhpur

DEEP & DEEP PUBLICATIONS PVT. LTD.

F-159, Rajouri Garden, New Delhi-110027

NEW WORLD ECONOMY
CHANGING DIMENSIONS OF 'COMMERCE CLAUSE'

ISBN 81-7629-514-0

Typeset by ASHISH TECHNOGRAPHICS,
3190, Mohindra Park, Shakur Basti, Delhi-110034.

Printed in India at MAYUR ENTERPRISES,
WZ Plot No. 3, Gujjar Market, Tihar Village, New Delhi-110018.

Published by DEEP & DEEP PUBLICATIONS PVT. LTD.,
F-159, Rajouri Garden, New Delhi-110027.
Phones : 25435369, 25440916
E-mail: ddpbooks@yahoo.co.in • deep98@del3.vsnl.net.in
Showroom:
2/13, Ansari Road, Daryaganj, New Delhi-110002 • Telefax: 23245122

Contents

Foreword

The worth of a book on *New World Economy: Changing Dimensions of 'Commerce Clause'* is self-evident in the age of globalisation in all walks of life including the new dimensions of commerce clause in federal set-up. Gone are the days when the element of co-ordination and independence between the national government and the federating units were insisted upon. Present is the age of co-operative federalism. It consists of a general approach rather than a specific programme. It visualises the national and state governments as partners in the common function of serving the people.[1]

Commerce clause in a federal system involves three dimensional problems—the problem of citizens' right, the problem of national regulation and the problem of state powers. The federal dimension (national and state) has been very succinctly summarised by Mr. Justice Douglas in these words: "The Commerce-Clause has a negative as well as a positive aspect. The clause not only serves to augment federal authority. By its own force it also cuts down the power of the constituent State in its exercise of what would normally be a part of its residual police power."[2] The curtailment of the economic autarchy of the States was a price for preventing the Balkanization of the economy. As Justice Cardozo put it, "The Constitution was framed upon the theory that the peoples of the several states must sink or swim together, and that in the long-run prosperity and salvation are in Union and not division".[3] That is reason why it is widely recognised principle that free flow of trade, commerce and intercourse within and across inter-state borders is an important pre-requisite for ensuring economic unity, stability and prosperity of a country having a two-tier polity.[4] In *Atiabari Tea Co. v. State of Assam*,[5] The Supreme Court of India took note of this requirement and ruled that free movement and exchange of goods throughout the territory of India is essential for the economy of the nation and for sustaining and improving living standards of the country.[6] It becomes imperative in view of the variegated structure

---

1. M.C. Setalvad, Foreword to the "The Union and the States", National, Delhi, 1972.
2. We the Judges, 222 (1956).
3. *Charles H. Baldwis v G.A.F. Seeling* (1934) 294 U.S. 511 (523).
4. Report of Commission on Centre-State Relations in India, p. 499.
5. A.I.R. 1961 S.C. 232.
6. *Ibid* at p. 247.

of underdeveloped, developing and developed economy of constituent states. As pointed out by the Supreme Court of India in *Automobile Transport Co. Ltd. v. State of Rajasthan.*[7] The framers of the Constitution of India were faced with two problems, "one question was how to achieve a federal economic and fiscal integration so that economic policies affecting the interests of India as a whole could be carried out without putting an ever increasing strain on the Unity of India, particularly in the context of a developing economy. The second question was how to foster the development of areas which were underdeveloped without creating too many preferential or discrimination barriers."[8]

Different federations use different languages with respect to commerce clause. The U.S. Congress has power "to regulate commerce with foreign nations and among the several States and with the Indian Tribes." It does not have a provision analogous to Section 92 of the Australian Constitution with reference to commerce etc. among the States. But similar result has come in U.S.A. through judicial interpretation. The Canadian Parliament's power extends to "the regulation of trade and commerce" which appears to be most extensive. The framers of the Indian Constitution made improvement upon the existing arrangements in different federations. Article 301 Speaks that ". . . trade, commerce and intercourse throughout the territory of India shall be free." The Constitution of India makes the right of trade and commerce most extensive, i.e. inclusive of both inter-state and intra-state trade, commerce and intercourse. But at the same time it empowers Parliament and State Legislatures to regulate such trade, commerce and intercourse.

The present book presents a thorough and in-depth study of the different dimensions of commerce clause in U.S.A., Canada, Australia and India in context of the twenty-first century era of globalization which has demolished trade barriers so that "trade activities are not only restricted to geographical boundaries but cater the markets anywhere in the world." Information technology has destroyed barriers through the use of INTERNET. Cross border trade without setting up business offices in trade countries may invoke new problems of E-Commerce, Cyber regulations and their being free from local regulations. The author rightly observes that American lead to include Internet in commerce would not be sufficient. It may need specific laws and Information Technology Act, 2000 and Communication Convergence Bill, intending to regulate Internet and electronic commerce are moved in right directions.[9]

The book is most informative. It examines in depth the scope of judicial role in view of brevity and details of the constitutional provisions. In U.S.A. and in Canada commerce clause is dealt at one place whereas the Australia Commonwealth Constitution has dealt it at two different

7. A.I.R. 1962 S.C. 1406
8. *Ibid.*
9. Discussed in Chapter 2 of this book.

places. Indian Constitution bears provisions in great detail not leaving even the controversy of inter-state trade and intra-state too. By using the expression "throughout the territory of India", it leaves very little or no scope for judicial speculation. The creativity of judiciary under Indian federation has been crippled by long elaboration. Yet the Judiciary has not failed to keep in mind the requirement and imperative of federal structure with economically and fiscally weak states. The apprehension of threat to the State's fiscal autonomy put by the Constitution Bench decision of the Supreme Court in *Atiabari Tea Co. Case*[10] was removed by the Seven Judge Bench of the Supreme Court in *Automobile Transport (Rajasthan) Ltd.*[11] wherein it unequivocally clarified the direct and immediate effect rule propounded in *Atiabari Tea Co. Case.* In *Automobile Transport (Rajasthan) Ltd. v. State of Rajasthan*[12], the majority of the Supreme Court said that the regulatory measures and measure imposing compensatory taxes does not fall within the purview of Article 301. In fact such measures instead of putting impediment in the way of the free flow of Trade and Commerce help in speeding up the free flow of commerce. The Supreme Court also refused to accept the fair recompense theory evolved by the High Court of Australia while determining the compensatory nature of taxes imposed under section 92 of the Commonwealth of Australia Act. The view of the Supreme Court as to compensatory tax and role of commerce clause in a federal set-up has been heartily accepted by the Commission on Centre-State Relations in India. The author correctly and very aptly remarks, "elucidating the objectives and importance of the Indian "Commerce Clause" for the economic integrity of the Nation, what was stated by the Supreme Court in Automobile Transport[13] was heartily appreciated by the Sarkaria Commission." The second notable decision from the point of view of requirement of states' revenue raising power under a federal set-up is *International Tourist Corporation v. State of Haryana.*[14] Mr. Justice O. Chinnappa Reddy said, "In a federal constitution like ours where there is a division of legislative subjects, but the residuary power is vested in Parliament, such residuary power cannot be so expansively interpreted as to whittle down the power of the State legislature. That might affect and jeopardize the very federal principles. The federal nature of the Constitution demands that an interpretation, which would allow the exercise of legislative power by Parliament pursuant to the residuary power vested in it to trench upon State legislation and which would thereby destroy or belittle State autonomy must be rejected."

The author has appreciated the Supreme Court's view most

10. *Atiabari Tea Co. v. State of Assam*, AIR (1961) SC 232.
11. AIR (1962) SC 1406.
12. *Ibid.*
13. *Ibid.*
14. AIR 1981 SC 774.

particularly in following the *Automobile* formula as to determine the nature of compensatory tax with insisting on *faire recompense.*

The book is thought provoking and full of sparks as it touches many issues which are emerging and are controversial but are becoming most pressing in view of new emerging trends due to globalization. The discussion on INTERNET and E-COMMERCE is not conclusive but is enough for initiation of fruitful dialogue from the federal angle. In U.S.A. Internet has been included within the meaning of commerce. Some attempts have been made to tackle the problem by keeping the regulation of Internet outside the purview of States by enacting The Internet Tax Freedom Act (ITFA) 1998. It had put a moratorium on new discriminatory Sales Tax on E-Commerce and the levying of new Internet access taxes till October 2001. But it has been highly controversial. Congress has not made a comprehensive federal control on Internet and some sort of State regulation would be needed in this regard. In India too it is at the preliminary stage.[15]

The other emerging and imperative issue discussed in the book is VAT (Value Added Tax).[16] It is successfully working in some federations as well as in European countries. In India, States are apprehensive of the erosion of their fiscal autonomy and therefore, they are resisting its implementation. However, in view of emerging Internet culture the need of VAT will be more welcome.

The book is full of information with new ideas and new solutions. The get up is attractive and print without blemish. Keeping in view the crumbling barriers of geographical boundaries in the age of globalization but the need of the federating Units not to depart from regulatory measures on trade and commerce, the book is the need of hour for lawyers, economists, professionals and policy-makers.

I feel proud of writing a Foreword to such an informative, timely and useful work on Commerce Clause in federal set-up and recommend it for study by lawyers, economists, professionals, etc. I wish all success to the book.

Gorakhpur

ANIRUDH PRASAD
Professor & Head, Dept. of Law,
D.D.U. Gorakhpur University

15. Discussed in Chapter 7 of this book.
16. Discussed in Chapter 8 of this book.

Preface

The scintilla of writing on **New World Economy: Changing Dimensions of the 'Commerce Clause'** was put in me by our learned **Prof. Anirudh Prasad**, Head of the Department of Law, D.D.U. Gorakhpur University, Gorakhpur. He gave me an impulse to work on the topic so that a fruitful conclusion may be reached about to be a pointer for the Government, Legislators and the Courts. I deem it my privilege to be vocalic for heart felt sense of gratitude and highest veneration to Laureate Prof. Prasad for his instrumentality in not only undertaking the theme but shaping the work from time to time by valuable constructive suggestions, glaring ideas and laconic academic exchange.

No words would be sufficient to express my extreme indebtedness which I owe to **Prof. Amarendra Kumar Mishra**, Professor, Department of Law, D.D.U. Gorakhpur University, Gorakhpur who has been perennial source of my inspiration. I express profound sense of indebtedness that I owe to Prof. Mishra, for his painstaking indefatigable efforts in going through the manuscript to avoid grammatical errors, which helped me to prune out many crudities of style and diction.

In the present study an attempt has been made to analyse certain aspects of the freedom of trade, commerce and intercourse. It has been the effort to touch some novel aspects of this freedom especially analysing the limitations of federal and state governments to regulate the same in a federal set-up. There has been an attempt to reach at the conclusion how economic equilibrium between the federating units can be attained—whether by making the Centre powerful or the States more powerful? The study has been confined not only to India, but after assessing the position in this regard in America, Canada and Australia, also an attempt has been made to make the study a comparative one and to point out the pitfalls in each of the federal set-up.

There is no doubt that the success of any federalism depends upon economic unity of the nation which includes the economic unity of the federating units and the Centre; therefore, it has been thought necessary to examine the impact of 'Commerce Clause', upon nation's economy of the federal set-up under consideration.

This is a commercial age and the concept of commerce has undergone a radical change almost in every part of the world; the concept of commerce today is not what did Marshall conceive as early as in 1824 in *Gibbon's Case*. Therefore, in the present work it was considered proper to identify the ambit and scope of commerce today. Business through Internet (E-commerce) is now an accepted mode of commerce. With the passage of time there has been a change in instrumentalities of commerce. In this technological era Internet is a new instrumentality of commerce and therefore it has been explored as to what extent the concept of E-commerce can be brought within the scope of the "Commerce Clause" of different countries. The internet like other modes of commerce (i.e. highway and railroad, etc.) has been held as an instrument of inter-state commerce and therefore, it has been analysed accordingly and given proper attention while assessing the ambit of freedom of trade, commerce and intercourse. It can be a separate area of investigation that to what extent The Information Technology Act, 2000 and the proposed Communication Convergence Bill, 2000 can be said as facilitating electronic commerce or restricting the same. Due to paucity of time and limitation of volume as to pages it has not been possible to enter into this area in depth. However, a bird's eye view of some of the basic issues have been touched.

There has been a change in the standard of morals and therefore there has been a shift in the doctrine of *res extra commercium* also. In the present work an attempt has been made to examine whether actually there has been any shift or not. Further, a theory has been developed that there can be electronic *res extra commercium*. Besides these, there are certain activities and transactions like production and insurance, which lie on the fence of commerce. A slight push may bring them within the sphere of commerce or may kick them out of the commercial sphere. Such marginal situations have vigorously been examined.

During the course of study scheme of allocation of powers in the area of trade and commerce freedom has been vigorously examined along with limitations imposed by commerce clauses of different countries having federal set-up. It has also been attempted to analyse whether these limitations are towards creating a balance between the federal authority and the federating unit's authority or not. While discussing the allocation of powers in relation to trade and commerce it has been tried to ascertain as to where the E-commerce would lie. When Constitutions of either of the countries under examination (U.S.A., Canada, Australia and India) were being drafted, the constitution-makers could not have visualised this type of instrumentality of commerce.

In Constitutions, where commerce clause is in general terms, E-commerce has been brought by judicial interpretation within that commerce clause but the real problem arises were the commerce clause has been elaborately drafted and therefore there is less scope for judicial interpretation. In this context it has been examined whether new law would be necessary to cover this type of instrumentality taking recourse to any of the relevant legislative entries or is there any scope for judicial activism in this situation too.

As no freedom can be absolute, the freedom of trade, commerce and intercourse can also not be absolute. It's regulation is an inevitable phenomenon and therefore, it was thought necessary to examine to what extent regulatory measures are permissible in this area and which level of government and to what extent should be given the power to regulate. This regulation is to be reconciled with the autonomy of states. It has also to be reconciled with 'public interest' and 'reasonableness'. There are and can be many modes of regulations but due to paucity of time and constraints regarding volume in terms of pages, only regulation through rate fixing and taxation including the VAT system has been the target of analysis. As said earlier now-a-days E-commerce is a viable means of commerce and therefore, E-commerce can also be regulated in the same manner as the real space commerce. Unlike real space commerce cyber space commerce is not easy to regulate because jurisdictional problem may and do arise. Those jurisdictional problems have been attempted to be identified and sorted out, though peripherally. It is not claimed that there has been a deep analysis of the problem but it is definitely claimed that it would open an arena of further research. It will serve as pointer to further study and food for future thought on this emerging issue.

A study may either be 'Empirical' or 'Doctrinaire'. One cannot deny that there is no scope for empirical research in the area of 'Freedom of Trade Commerce and Intercourse' by collecting data, conducting surveys and interviewing relevant authorities. The impact study of commerce clause is quite possible but that would involve expenditure of money, time, etc. which is not feasible at this stage of study. Therefore, it was preferred to adopt the doctrinaire approach. In this approach, constitutional provisions of the countries under examination, judicial decisions, text of commentaries, law reports, reports of different commissions have been vigorously examined. Attempt has always been to reach up to primary source of information and knowledge, but in cases where the same has not been possible, there is no hesitation in accepting that reliance was placed upon the secondary sources also.

This Book has been divided into *nine* chapters. Chapter 1 is Federalism and Commerce Clause. Chapter 2 deals with Inter-state and Intra-state Commerce: Federal and State Powers. New Dimensions of Commerce Today and its Limits have been discussed in Chapters 3 and 4 respectively. Chapter 5 has been exclusively devoted to the Role of Commerce Clauses in the Country's Economy. As seen above, no freedom is absolute and so Chapters 6, 7 and 8 deals with this aspect of freedom. Chapter 6 deals with Regulation Through Rate Fixing whereas Chapter 7 deals with Permissible Limits of Regulation Through Taxation and Chapter 8 deals with Regulation of Trade, Commerce and Intercourse through VAT System. Lastly, Chapter 9 is Conclusion and Suggestions.

In completing the work, quite a good number of persons have been helpful physically and mentally in their own ways. Being impuissant, the task of a researcher, to acknowledge the deep felt sense of gratitude for emotional, intellectual and otherwise co-operative affinity of all those who manifestly or clandentially, more or less contributed in the work, is Herculean. Neither it is grandiloquence nor sheer lackadaisical narration but an inchoate though honest effort for the redemption of an owed intellectual debt. Even if feeling extreme sense of indebtedness to all of them, the forced partiality is inevitable and the prudential look needs to be not only justified but also excused.

Though adroit, yet I have great pleasure in expressing a great deal of indebtedness to the luminaries of the field of law, few amongst them are Research Professors of the Indian Law Institute, **Prof. S.C. Srivastava, Prof. (Mrs.) S.K. Verma,** Director I.L.I. and **Prof. P.N. Singh**, Ex-Chairman Law Department and Dean Faculty of Law, Delhi University, Delhi. Prof. Singh deserves special thanks for allowing me to consult the library of the department. Prof. Srivastava's thought provoking discussion helped me a lot in generating an insight in the subject, for which I am personally indebted. **Prof. M.P. Singh**, Professor of Law, Delhi University and **Dr. B.N. Mani**, Ex-Legal Advisor, Ministry of Law, presently member-governing council, I.L.I., New Delhi also come within the same line who by constantly keeping eyes over the publication process indebted me. Their generosity and kindness influenced me a lot and I personally owe a debt to them not only for encouraging me to complete the present work but also for provoking me to continue the present aptitude and curiosity for research. The benevolent assistance extended by the authorities and staff members of the libraries of New Delhi like that of the Indian Law Institute and of the Law Department of Delhi University, can not be overlooked. My special thanks are to **Mr. Bhati**, Registrar of the I.L.I. for making arrangements of my stay at the Institute. The contribution of **Mr. Vishwanath, Mrs. Nimmi, Mr. Pankaj** and **Mr. Govind**, all the members of the staff of the library of the I.L.I. can never be forgotten. They deserve special thanks for helping me in searching the material. In the same chain, the assistance afforded by the staff members of the Central Library and Departmental Law Library of D.D.U. Gorakhpur University, can never be ignored.

I would be ungrateful if I do not pay my sincere thanks to **Mr. S.N. Singh**, the senior Advocate and Lecturer of Law Deptt., D.D.U. Gorakhpur University, Gorakhpur who generously allowed me to use his rich library as and when I requested him.

I would be failing in my duties if I miss the opportunity to acknowledge the contribution of my parents **Sri Ved Yyas Chaturvedi** and **Smt. Lalli Rani** who have been constant source of inspiration. My younger brother **Siddhartha**'s contribution is highly appreciable and can not be forgotten.

Unremitting efforts of **Mr. G.S. Bhatia**, the Managing Director of **Deep & Deep Publications Pvt. Ltd.** in bringing the present book to the present shape are specially acknowledged.

I gratefully place on record my deep obligations to all those who by criticising, commenting and putting suggestions upon me provided an opportunity to bring myself up to this stage. All efforts have been made to make the work complete, up-to-date and without any blemish, yet critical searchlight on it and valuable suggestions will always be welcomed graciously.

Gorakhpur SWARUPAMA CHATURVEDI

Abbreviations

A.C.	Appeal Cases
A.I.R.	All India Reporter
A.L.J.	The Australian Law Journal
A.L.J.R.	Australian Law Journal Report
B.C.L.R.	Boston College Law Review
C.A.D.	Constitution Assembly Debates
C.L.R.	Commonwealth Law Reports
Cal. L. Rev.	California Law Review
Cam. L.J.	Cambridge Law Journal
Can. B. Rev.	Canadian Bar Review
Colum. L. Rev.	Columbia Law Review
e.g.	Example gratia (for example)
EC	European Countries
Eco. & Pol. W.	Economic & Political Weekly
E-Commerce	Electronic Commerce
Ed.	Edition
EU	European Union
Ex. L.T.	Excise Law Times
F.C.	Federal Court
F.T. Rev.	Foreign Trade Review
GFSZA	Gun Free School Zones Act
GST	Goods and Services Tax
Harv. L. Rev.	Harward Law Review
HST	Harmonised Sales Tax
i.e.	That is

I.L.I.	Indian Law Institute
I.L. Rev.	Iowa Law Review
I.M.R.B.	Indian Market Research Bureau
I.S.P.	Internet Service Provides
I.T.F.A.	Internet Tax Freedom Act
J.B.C.I.	Journal of Bar Council of India
J.I.L.I.	Journal of the Indian Law Institute
L.Ed.	Lawyer's Edition
L.Q.R.	Law Quarterly Review
Mc. G.L.J.	McGill Law Journal
Mel. Uni. L.R.	Melbourne University Law Review
N.S.W.	New South Wales
Ny. L.J.	New York Law Journal
OECD	Organisation for Economic Co-operation and Development
P.C.	Privy Council
P.E.	Permanent Establishment
Q.S.T.	Quebec Sales Tax
R.S.T.	Retail Sales Tax System
R.I.C.O.	Racketeer Influenced and Corrupt Organization Act
R.S.T.	Retail Sales Tax
S.C.	Supreme Court
S.C.C.	Supreme Court Cases
S.C.R.	Supreme Court Reports (Canada)
S.C.R.	Supreme Court Reports (India)
S.L. Rev.	Sydney Law Review
Stan. L. Rev.	Stanford Law Review
Tex. L. Rev.	Texas Law Review
U.S.	United States (Supreme Court)
U.N.C.I.T.R.A.L.	United Nations Commission on International Trade Law
Uni of A. Ann. L.R.	University of Australia Annual Law Review

Uni. Chi. L. Rev.	University of Chicago Law Review
Uni. Q.L.J.	University of Queensland Law Journal
US	United States
v	Versus
VAT	Value Added Tax
Viz.	(Videlicet) namely
Wheat.	Wheaton's Reports (United States Supreme Court)
Wm & M.L. Rev.	William & Mary Law Review
Y.L.J.	Yale Law Journal

1

Federalism and the Commerce Clause

The rise of modern constitutional set-up, especially after the Second World War has been marked by the establishment of an increasing number of federal schemes. The pattern is so striking that federalism must be considered one of the most important aspects of constitutionalism. Federalism, when spoken of in general discussions, is used rather vaguely to mean any kind of association of autonomous units. The word may therefore refer to league or federation of states, as well as to a federal system, such as the United States. Not only America, but Switzerland, Germany, Canada, Australia, the Union of South Africa, Brazil, Austria, Nigeria, Malaysia, India and many others have evolved a governmental structure of this federal type. The organisation of the world at large into the United Nations points in the same direction, and so does a united Europe, though both are at present loose leagues or federations of states. Many of the more close-knit federal systems developed their structure out of a preceding league.

Federal schemes, generally speaking, seek to combine a measure of unity with a measure of diversity; usually the diversity follows a territorial pattern, such as French spoken in Western Switzerland, German in Eastern Switzerland. Federalism is the form of political organisation suited to communities where this territorially diversified pattern of values, economy interests, and beliefs and traditions can be effectively implemented by joint efforts in the pursuit of common values and interests, and the cultivation of common beliefs and traditions. Whether the particular federal structure is best described as a single federal government, or as a federation of several governments, may sometimes be difficult to determine. The same observation holds true for all territorial divisions of governmental power. When the particularistic local objectives are sufficiently strong and compact to hold together the territorial sub-divisions of the more comprehensive group, sustaining them as or molding them into autonomous groups then the adequate political pattern is federational. On the other hand, the federal organisation comes into existence when conflicting objectives (interests, tradition, values) are not as yet, or are no longer, sufficiently strong to sustain autonomous units. The contrast between the federal and the federational type or organisation should not close our eyes to the great similarities between them. Communities pass readily from one into the other. Thus, federalism must be seen as a dynamic process, and not merely as a static design. Any particular design or pattern of competencies or jurisdictions is merely a phase, a short-run state of continually evolving political reality. This fact has only in recent years become recognised. Classical theory was concerned with the design and tended to juxtapose the several possible designs, and the arguments revolved around the question as to which of these designs was the genuine federal system of government. All this theorising, political and juristic, unfolded, so to speak, the potentialities of the process by discovering the phases of its successive designs or patterns. A sketch, even in outline, of this evolution of federal theory is a rather complicated affair, since this theorising is intertwined with the evolution of general political theory.[1] It runs from Althusius to Proudhon, and includes such illustrious masters of political philosophy as Grotius, Montesquieu, the Federalist, Rousseau, Kant, and de Tocqueville. The earlier thought down to the end of the eighteenth century was preoccupied with the problem of how to safeguard the component units of a federal system against encroachments, and it stressed the contractual nature of the federal bond, as did Proudhon. The great turn comes with the Federalist and the innovations hammered out at the convention in Philadelphia; there and from then on the preoccupation of the theory of federalism is with how to organize an effective unity and thereby allow a federal order to become a "state". It should be added that from the very beginning and throughout its history, federalism has been seen as a concomitant of constitutionalism; indeed, its very first modern theorist, Johannes Althusius, juxtaposed a federal conception of the state as a cooperative association to the unitary and imperial view of Bodin. The theory presented in the Federalist embodies the successful surmounting of the practical difficulties and the beginning of modern federal theory.[2] A federal system should not only be considered statically, i.e., in terms of a fixed pattern of a particular and precise division of powers between governmental levels. Instead, "federalism" seems the most suitable term by which to designate the process of federalising a political community, that is to say, the process by which a number of separate political organisations, be they states or any other kind of associations, enter into arrangements for working out solutions, adopting joint policies, and making joint decisions on joint problems; or, reversely, the process through which a hitherto unitary political community, as it becomes differentiated into a number of separate and distinct political communities, achieves a new organization in which the differentiated communities, now separately organized, become capable of working out separately and on their own those problems they no longer

1. Friedrich, Constitutional Government and Democracy, Tenth Edition, at p. 190.
2. *Ibid.*

have in common. But it is not only a matter of decision-making, but of the entire range of power and its exercise.

Federalism originated in the experience gathered from political experiments that not merely defence but a number of other subjects, such as control of foreign affairs, inter-state and foreign commerce, export and import and the like, are matters of national concern which require to be dealt with by a national organisation, while other matters, such as public order, public health, fire, water and electric supply services, which are the concern of the inhabitants of a particular local area and have problems of their own connected with the exigencies of that particular locality, would be best administered if entrusted to the representatives of that area. Historically, the earlier form of political organisation was not federal but unitary. But it is the pressure of the economic, political and social circumstances, which impelled unitary states (generally monarchical) to enter into alliance with other states for meeting common problems, which initially, related to defence. It is with the adoption of the Constitution of the U.S.A. in 1787 that the concept of a federal state emerged in a definite shape. Subsequently, the adoption of the federal form in Canada, Switzerland and Australia gave a great impetus to federalism and a number of federal Constitutions have cropped up since World Wars I and II, notable amongst which are the U.S.S.R., West Germany, India, Malaysia (1963), Nigeria (1979).

A federation is a compromise between regional autonomy and national integration. But as has been seen, it takes one step in advance of other loose forms of alliances between independent states in that it creates a National Government apart from the State Governments. Both the national and the state Governments owe their existence and derive their powers from the Federal Constitution and both are separate legal entities known to the law. In the words of Prof. Wheare[3]:

> "There is a single independent authority for the whole area in respect of some matters and there are independent regional authorities for other matters."[4]

It is to be noted that even under a unitary system, there are local or municipal authorities who administer such local affairs, by delegation from the Central Government; but in a federation, there are two tiers of regional administration, namely, the state and local authorities. In a federation, the state government is a larger regional unit, which comes between the federal and local authorities.

A federal state is a union of several states into a central or federal government. After the federation is formed, both the federal and the state governments owe their existence to and authority from the Federal

3. Wheare, Federal Government (1963) at p. 35.
4. *Ibid.*

and the state governments which are to be exercised by them, according to the constitutional distribution, independently of each other.

A federation is thus distinguished from a unitary state in that the regional governments in a federal state are not mere sub-divisions, agents or delegates of the Central Government, but possesses independent constitutional powers. A federation, to recall Dicey,[5] seeks union and not unity. It seeks uniformity, but wants to avoid a monopoly of political and economic powers in one Central Government. It allows the state governments to solve and saves the Central Government from being involved in, purely local issues, which have no direct impact on national affairs.

The word 'federal' or 'federation' or the like is not used at all in the American Constitution, the model of federal Constitution, even though the Preamble to the Constitution of 1787 recites that it was "to form a more perfect Union" (i.e., to improve upon the loose form of the Confederation which had been formed in 1777) that the Constitution of the U.S.A. was going to be adopted.

On the other hand, though both the British North America Act, 1867, and the Commonwealth of Australia Constitution Act, 1900, use the word 'Federally United' and 'Federal Commonwealth' in their respective preambles, Australia is regarded as a true federation of the American pattern because it set-up a dual government with 'co-ordinate powers', while Canada, because of its provisions conferring overriding powers upon the Dominion Government to control the provincial governments, is regarded as a modified form of federation having a unitary bias, so much so, that some scholars call it "quasi-federal'.[6]

In all the three classical Constitutions known to be federal, the transformation has been towards centralisation. In the U.S.A., this process of centralisation has been aided by the Supreme Court by way of liberal interpretation of the federal powers of inter-state commerce[7] and general welfare or the supremacy clause in Art. VI (2) or defence [Art. 1, Sec. 8 (1) as well as by inventing the judicial doctrines of 'implied powers'[8] of the Federal Legislature, 'national pre-emption' and judicial recognition of co-operative federalism.

The Australian Constitution Act, 1900 was framed on the model of the American Federal system of grant of enumerated powers to the Union and residuary powers in favour of the states; there being judicial review to maintain this division of powers. Naturally, judicial interpretation of the Australian federation, up to 1920, held the balance in favour of the reserved rights of states, 'the doctrine of mutual immunity of instrumentalities'; the doctrine of 'implied prohibition' being instrumental for that. Since 1920,

5. Dicey, Law of The Constitution (10th Edition 1962), at p. 141.
6. Wheare, Federal Government (1963) at pp. 16-19.
7. *Gibbons v. Ogden* (1824) 22 U.S. 1; *Heart of Atlanta v. U.S.* (1964) 379 U.S. 241.
8. *McCulloch v. Maryland* (1819) 4 Wh. 316.

however the trend has been definitely towards expansion of federal powers[9] by judicial interpretation (as in the U.S.A.). This has been done by:

(i) Rejecting the doctrine of 'implied prohibitions'.
(ii) Expanding the postal power [Sec. 51(v)], or the power relating to inter-state and foreign trade and commerce, by applying the principle of progressive interpretation.
(iii) Expanding the concept of 'inconsistency' is Sec. 109 in favour of the commonwealth by holding that it arose not only where the federal and state laws could not both be obeyed but also where the federal law showed an intention (express or implied) to occupy the entire field exhaustively.

This put an end to the doctrine of 'reserved powers' of the state by holding that the federal Legislature could exclude state jurisdiction by its own act. In 1971, the High Court[10] has itself explained that this liberal interpretation of the Commonwealth powers at the cost of the reversed powers of the states is due to the Court's recognition of the vast changes in the background that have taken place which call for greater national powers:

> "The colonies became components of a federation, the commonwealth of Australia. It became a nation. Its manhood was in course of time to be consolidated in war, by economic and commercial integration by a recognition and acceptance of external interests and obligations. With these developments the position of the Commonwealth, the federal government, waxed; and that of the states waxed."[11]

Conversely, Canadian federalism is no longer of the highly centralised form as it was in 1867, with the power of the states confined to the matters enumerated in Sec. 92 and the residue belonging to the Union (Sec. 91). Judicial interpretation has expanded the powers of the provincial Legislatures, mainly by a liberal interpretation of Sec. 92(13), relating to 'Property and Civil Rights in the Province', and a restricted interpretation of Dominion power under Sec. 91, in order to reconcile Sec. 91 with Sec. 92.

In the Constitution Act of 1867, the only concurrent subject was 'immigration and agriculture' [Sec. 95]. In 1951, to this was added 'old age pensions' by inserting Sec. 94A by amending the Constitution. Apart from this by judicial interpretation of the different subject Sec. 91-92 and the application of doctrine such as 'aspects of legislation', it has been held that though a matter is enumerated in the Dominion list [Sec. 91] a legislation relating to that matter may have a local incidence, which may be

9. Sawer, Australian Federation in the Courts (1967).
10. *Victoria v. Commonwealth* (1971) 122 C.L.R. 353 (395-96).
11. *Ibid.*

concurrently regulated by the provincial Legislature, subject, however, to the doctrine of federal paramountcy in case there is such unavoidable conflict between the two laws that both cannot exist in the same field.

A more balanced view, amongst foreign scholars has been taken by Prof. Neumann who includes Canada as well as India but excludes U.S.S.R from federalism on the ground that there is a division of power between the Union and the states in the former two Constitutions, while in the U.S.S.R. the division of power under the Soviet Constitution is only 'theoretical', being overshadowed by the domination of the same political party.

A real division of power, operating as a constitutional limitation upon both the Union and the state powers is the true test of a federation and both Canada and India have been rightly assessed to be federal, because they both possess this feature in their Constitutions. Of course, there is provision for federal control or domination in certain spheres under these Constitutions; but as will be evident from the present work, other classical federations, including the American, too, have elements of such federal supremacy of control, so that eventually, it becomes a question of degree as between the different modern Federal Constitutions.[12]

In 1824 Lord Macaulay pointed out in England that free trade, one of the greatest blessings which Government can confer on its people, was in almost every country unpopular. Eight years later Henry Clay said, "the call for free trade is unavailing as the cry of a spoiled child for the moon. It never has existed; it never will exist." Our task is to examine how far these observations are valid in India today.[13]

The principle that our economic unit is the Nation, which alone has the gamut of powers necessary to control the economy, including the vital power of erecting customs barriers against foreign competition, has as its corollary that the states are not separable economic units. What is ultimate is the principle that one state in its dealings with another may not place itself in a position of economic isolation

The great problem of any federal structure is to prevent the growth of sectional and local interests which are inimical to the interests of the nation as a whole. The strength of the Union may be achieved only by minimising inter-state barriers as much as possible, so that the people may feel that they are the members of one nation, though they may, for the time being, be residents of particular geographical divisions of the Country. One of the means to achieve this object is to guarantee to every citizen the freedom of movement throughout the territory of the Union, and also to reside and settle in any part thereof.

No less important is the applied freedom of every citizen to trade with any part of the country. On principle, thus, it comprises both inter-state and intra-state freedom of trade, commerce and intercourse. From the federal

12. Neumann, European and Comparative Government (1960) at p. 679.

13. Quoted in Jariwala, Freedom of Inter-state Trade in India, Sterling Publishers (1975), Delhi.

standpoint we are concerned with the former, i.e., freedom of trade, commerce and intercourse as between the several states of the Union, which might raise economic barriers against each other, in the absence of any constitutional prohibitions in this behalf.

Though a federation is formed to preserve or secure regional autonomy that is not done at the cost of national interests. Unless the national interests are safeguarded, the country would be divided into pieces, resulting in a weak government unable to maintain itself from foreign aggression, and would also create economic chaos in an age when apparently local disturbances have a wide repercussion. It is this last mentioned economic strength of the federation which is intended to be ensured by the safeguard for maintaining freedom of trade, commerce and intercourse throughout the federal territory, which safeguard the Union and the states are both enjoined not to violate.[14]

Explaining the need of this freedom, the Privy Council observed in *James v. Commonwealth of Australia*[15]:

> "The idea starts with the admitted fact that Federation in Australia was intended (*interalia*) to abolish the frontiers between different states and create one Australia. The conception involved freedom from customs duties, imposts, border prohibition and restrictions of every kind: the people of Australia were to be free to trade with each other, and to pass to and for among the states, without any burden, hindrance or restriction based merely on the fact that they were not members of the same state."[16]

The progress of the country as a whole also requires free flow of commerce and intercourse as between different parts, without any barrier, so that the economic resources of the various parts may be exploited to the common advantage of the entire nation. This is particularly essential in a federal system.[17] In the beautiful words of Cardazo, J., the American Constitution, thus, "was framed upon the theory that the people of several states must sink or swim together, and that in the long-run prosperity and salvation are in union and not in division. What is ultimate is the principle that one State in its dealing with another may not place itself in a position of economic isolation."[18]

In the same stream in '*Atiabari*'[19] did Gajendragadkar, J., observe:

---

14. *James v. Commonwealth* (1936) A.C. 578; *Atiabari Tea Co. v. State of Assam*, A.I.R. 1961 S.C. 232.
15. (1936) A.C. 630.
16. *Ibid.*
17. Bowie, Studies in Federation, p. 926.
18. *Baldwin v. G.A.F. Inc.*, (1934) 294 U.S. 511.
19. *Atiabari Tea Co. v. State of Assam*, A.I.R. 1961 S.C. 232.

> "In drafting the relevant Articles of Part XIII, the makers of the Constitution were fully conscious that economic unity was absolutely essential for the stability and progress of the federal polity which had been adopted by the Constitution for the governance of the country. It was realised that in course of time . . . local or regional fears or apprehensions raised by local or regional problems may persuade the state legislatures to adopt remedial measures intended solely for the protection of regional interests without due regards to their effect on the economy of the nation as a whole. The object of Part XIII was to avoid such a possibility".[20]

Sarkaria Commission[21] quoted with approval the following observation of the Supreme Court in *Automobile Transport Case,* which it made elucidating the objectives and importance of the constitutional provisions for the economic integrity of the Nation:

> "There were differences of language, religion, etc. Some of the provinces were economically more developed than the others. Even inside the same province there were under-developed, developed, and highly developed areas from the point of view of industries, communications, etc. the problem of economic integration with which the constitution-makers were faced was a problem with many facets. Two questions, however, stood out: one question was how to achieve a federal, economic and fiscal integration, so that economic policies affecting the interests of India as a whole could be carried out without putting an ever-increasing strain on the unity of India, particularly in the context of developing economy. The second question, was how to foster the development of areas which were under-developed without creating too many preferential or discriminative barriers".

However, the Commission was conscious to mention the need for empowering Parliament to place restrictions on trade and commerce even within state. It opined that : "Ours is a vast country with varying economic potentiality and considerable deference in regard to existing levels of development. The Union's responsibility in respect of certain matters may, therefore, entail regulating Trade and Commerce even within a state for achieving national objectives. For example, there is the need to protect the interests of the weaker sections of our community like the tribal people, etc. Indiscriminate exploitation of natural resources in one state, for example, denudation of forests, may have far-reaching implications for other states

20. *Ibid.*
21. The Sarkaria Commission's Report at p. 502.

which may be effected by floods, silting up of reservoirs, etc. Such situations may require imposition of restrictions on trade even within the state. The importance of Parliamentary control over inter-state trade is also significant where centers of production of certain commodities are situated entirely within a state but the centers of consumption are located outside the state".[22]

As economy is the most important source of power and identity in the world of today, the nations or regions that constitute the federation do not want to lose their hold on economic power. Nor do the economically strong states want the economically weak states to become parasites on them. Therefore, an arrangement must be devised which will ensure free flow of trade, encourage for competition and simultaneously remain capable of discouraging and regulating unfair trade practices.

One common arrangement found in all federations in this regard, is the division between the inter-state and intra-state trade and commerce. While the regulation of the former is assigned to the federal authority, the states retain the regulation of the latter. Some federations have gone further and have made inter-state trade free from regulation both by the federal authority as well as the authority of states. Australia is the foremost example of that. India goes one step further than Australia in so far as it makes flow of inter-state as well as intrastate trade free from regulation by the Union as well as the states. However, unlike Australia, after making such a general declaration the Constitution of India gives adequate powers to the Union and the states, particularly to the former, to regulate trade and commerce.[23]

Our constitution-makers designed to promote free flow of trade and commerce in India because they fully realised it as the main sustaining force for the stability and progress of the political and cultural unity of the federal polity. They were of the view that the country should function as one single economic unit without barriers on internal trade. In order to ensure that the state legislatures subjected to local and regional pulls do not create trade barriers in future, Art. 301 was incorporated in the Constitution. According to this provision:

> "Trade, commerce and intercourse throughout the territory of India shall be free".

The legislative power of the Commonwealth Parliament differs from that of both Congress and the Dominion Parliament in Canada. In the United States the power is "to regulate commerce with foreign nations and among the several states and with the Indian Tribes" and there is no express provision corresponding to Sec. 92 of the Australian Constitution with reference to freedom of inter-state commerce, although, a similar (but not identical) result has been deduced by implication. In Canada, the power

22. *Ibid.*
23. Report of The National Commission to Review the Working of The Constitution, Vol. 1, Chapter 8, Part-C.

extends to "the regulation of trade and commerce." In both cases, it will be observed, the Congress is limited to inter-state commerce as in the case of Australia, but the Dominion power is not so limited. The powers of the Dominion, and those of Congress at least so far as matters of commerce of national import are concerned, are exclusive. These differences in language and content in the three countries have led to differences in approach to the general concept of the extent of the constitutional power in each case.

In Canada, besides the verbal differences e.g., the limitation to "regulation" which has been said to imply the continued existence of the thing to be regulated, the non-restriction of the power to inter-provincial or foreign trade and commerce—the presence of the double enumeration of exclusive powers has led the courts into the enquiry in given cases whether a particular law is or is not in "pith and substance" a law on the subject of trade and commerce or a law with respect to a subject confided to the provinces and, as has been seen, aspects of subjects became of more importance in Canada than in Australia. Canadian cases must therefore be read with caution in this as in any other cases where similar but not identical provisions of the two Constitutions are under consideration.

The two Constitutions, although the Australian was largely modelled upon its American counterpart, differ fundamentally in certain respects, it is in the particular field of inter-state commerce that they differ significantly in content and doctrine, although the respective provisions appear to bear a close resemblance. For example, although the power of Congress is nowhere expressly declared to be exclusive, by a process of judicial interpretation the rule became well established that, in so for as the subject of inter-state and foreign commerce was a matter of national concern requiring national treatment the power of Congress was exclusive, even to the extent that the silence of Congress in any particular respect upon the matter was to be taken as an indication that the subject was to be free from restraint by any state action. This doctrine of exclusiveness led to the adoption in the United States of the theory of state "police" powers in order to support state enactments on such matters as health, inspection and the like, which interfered with inter-state commerce, the question in every case being almost invariably whether the State Act was an Act passed in the exercise of the police power or an Act in regulation of commerce. From these doctrine the result was reached that, in most cases, whether the Act impugned was an Act of Congress passed in supposed exercise of the commerce power, or an Act of the state alleged to constitute an interference with inter-state commerce, the question for decision was whether the law was a substantial regulation of commerce. This has meant a greater emphasis on subject matter as such than has been placed upon the interpretation of the power (and the immunity under Sec. 92) in Australia. Moreover, the effects of the incidental power and its operation in relation to the constitutional power and immunity in Australia have been necessarily different in Australia from the results which have flowed from the "Necessary and Proper Clause" in the Constitution of the United States. It follows from these brief considerations that decisions in the United States under the commerce power, although of great assistance in elucidating the meaning of the expression "trade and commerce," and affording illustrations of what the concept includes, are to be applied in the interpretation of the Australian Constitution with considerable care, since for obvious reasons what may be considered to be the extent of an exclusive power in the United Sates may not always be a true or precise measure of the extent of a concurrent power in Australia. American decisions are less helpful in the ascertainment of what is transgression of the prohibition in Sec. 92 of the Australian Constitution, for reasons stated already, the doctrine of "police" powers can have no logical place in view of the mode of distribution of powers in Australia and, moreover, the prohibition against interference with freedom of inter-state trade, commerce and intercourse is, in Australia, express and not implied. Further, tests based upon the "national" character of a specific aspect of trade and commerce between the states can likewise have no place in the course of interpretation in Australia where the course of interpretation has, consistently with the traditional mode of statutory interpretation, been based upon the terms of the Constitution itself and political, economic, the terms of the sociological, and other similar considerations have not been permitted to obtrude themselves into what are legal questions.

It remains to refer to the controversy between the early members of the High Court as to the applicability of the doctrine of state "reserved" powers to the commerce power, the Court adhering to the principle that intra-state and domestic matters were reserved to the states to the absolute exclusion of the Commonwealth as if the power conferred by Sec. 51(i) contained an explicit declaration that such trade and commerce was exempted from Commonwealth legislation, a doctrine rejected since the decision in the *Engineers' Case*. The beginning of any enquiry into the extent of the federal power in this, as in any other field of valid Commonwealth legislation, must be found in the terms of the grant itself without any reference to any supposed state powers in relation to the subject or other implied limitations.

The impact of the present era of globalisation has been to demolish the trade barriers, so that the trade activities are not only restricted to geographical boundaries but cater the markets anywhere in the world. Information technology has been able to close this barrier through the use of Internet services. The contracts at the international level are being now entered into through electronic means, i.e. Internet. A lot of contracts are being entered and finalised through the Internet whereby the parties may conclude a contract by clicking their acceptance. The Internet allows people to enter into extensive transactions with customers anywhere in the world, without actually entering the geographical boundaries of the customer's country or without setting up business offices in those countries.

Electronic commerce needs to be globally facilitated in view of the fact that in the era of globalisation it is the most commonly used mode of entering into business dealings. The legal framework supporting commercial transactions has to be consistent in and predictable regardless of the jurisdiction in which a particular party resides. Private business has always flourished when and wherever there are predictable and widely accepted legal principles supporting commercial transactions. As the use of electronic commerce has increased it has become more and more important and relevant that the evidence of these transactions is available to demonstrate legal rights and obligations that flow from them.

It is in this era of globalisation that cross-border trade is a routine feature and geographical boundaries are no longer viable in an era of E-commerce. The unprecedented popularity of the Internet and its deep penetration into the common man's life brings in the onerous responsibility for the administrators in day-to-day working. To bring order to the use of the Internet by users with no geographical boundaries the governments world over and United Nations took the task of evolving a regime of uniform "Cyber Regulations."

With a view to promote and desire to standardise homogenization of laws in the subjects, the United Nations Commission on International Trade Law (UNCITRAL) has drafted a Model Law that supports the commercial use of international contracts in electronic commerce, known as the UNCITRAL Model Law on Electronic Commerce, 1996. The Model Law establishes rules and norms that validate and recognise contracts entered through electronic mode. The Model Law does not have any force. It merely serves as a model and guide for the member countries for modernisation and updating their laws and practices in the field of communication involving the use of computerised or any other modern techniques.

In United State some courts have described the Internet as an instrumentality of inter-state commerce that should be subject to exclusive federal oversight.[24] The rapid developments of information and communication technologies over the past decade have brought about a change in the way information is communicated. Transactions are now conducted through electronic means, technically known as "Electronic Commerce", with the speed of thought. It has been made possible with the development of Internet technology, which is a latest technology in communications. It came into existence in 1986. Its growth was exponential. Its acceptance and common use were almost instantaneous unlike other preceding technologies. People often compare the growth of the Internet to the historic growth of other technologies, sometimes to suggest that the Internet is just the latest technological advancements and it is quite possible that it may not signal a revolutionary advancement. There are differences between the birth of the Internet and technologies that preceded it. Once the

---

24. *American Libraries Association v. Pataki*, 969 F. Supp. 160, 182 [S.D.NY. (1997)]; ("The Internet like rail and highway traffic requires a cohesive national scheme of regulation to that users of reasonably able to their obligations"): *A.C.L.U. v. Johnson*, 194 F. 3d 1149, 1162 (10th Cir. 1999): ("Certain types of commerce have recognized as requiring national regulation . . . The Internet is surely such a medium.").

Internet was made available to the general public, it took only 4 years for 50 million people to go on-line.[25]

The Internet technology has evoked unparalleled and easier ways of dealing with day-to-day business and trade or personal affairs. Business has been the biggest beneficiary of this technology as Internet offers global communications system though it is inexpensive. It has also been made secure through other technological developments. Thus, the development of Internet technology, including digital networks and services, provides an important tool for the growth of digital network economy, trade and commerce activities, which is represented by on-line shopping and electronic payment transactions.

The Internet has posed new and complex questions for law-makers and the courts. Goldsmith has argued that improvements in technology may alleviate this problem.[26] First-generation Internet thinkers maintain that Internet communications should not be subjected to local regulation[27] as Internet content providers can inexpensively send content via the Internet into every territorial jurisdiction in the world. Territorial governments cannot stop this content at the border and cannot assert regulatory control over the content source located abroad. If governments try to filter content at the border, information can easily be rerouted. And if some government happen to assert regulatory control over a content provider or its assets, the provider can cheaply and easily relocate to a permission jurisdiction and continue sensing content world-wide from there.

As seen above, in United States, electronic commerce has been held well to be included within the Commerce Clause. The American courts have an opportunity to interpret the 'Commerce Clause' when and, as the circumstances require because it is worded in very general terms. This opportunity our courts do not avail because of the fact that ours commerce clause is elaborately worded and there is little scope for judicial innovation apart from adjudging the 'reasonableness' or interpreting the "public interests". Therefore, though the problem has not arisen yet, but if arises in future as to inclusion of electronic commerce within the "commerce clause", the courts instead of looking at the commerce clause could see at various Entries mentioned in the three Lists of the Constitution and would try to cover laws relating to E-Commerce within either of the Entries. Internet definitely is means of communication. Recently, Information Technology Act, 2000 promotes legal infrastructure to the cyber world. It facilitates electronic intercourse in trade and commerce, eliminating barriers that stand in the way of electronic commerce. The proposed Communication Convergence Bill, 2000 is intended to regulate the Internet and thus the electronic commerce.

---

25. Richard L. Doernberg and Luchinnekens: Electronic Commerce and International Taxation (Kluwer Law International) at p. 3, 1999 Edition.
26. Goldsmith, 65 U. Chi. L. Rev. at pp. 1218, 1227.
27. David R. Johnson & David Post, Law and Borders : The Rise of Law in Cyberspace, 48 Stan. L. Rev. (1996) at p. 1367.

2

Inter-State and Intra-State Commerce: Federal and State Powers

I. THE AMERICAN COMMERCE CLAUSE

In the Constitution of the United States there is no express provision guaranteeing freedom of inter-state trade and commerce but Congress is empowered to "regulate commerce among the several states"[1] The Judiciary has interpreted this power of Congress to regulate inter-state commerce as plenary and exclusive.[2] Thus, even the silence of Congress in any particular respect of this matter, by implication, excludes such matter from regulation or restraint by the states.[3]

A. The Reach of Congressional Power over Inter-state Commerce

Harlan, J. in *Adair v. United States*[4] assessing the scope of the congressional power over the regulation of inter-state commerce viewed that the power to regulate inter-state commerce is the power to prescribe rules by which such commerce must be governed. The Learned Judge firmly asserted that Congress has a large discretion in the selection or choice of the means to be employed in the regulation of inter-state commerce, and such discretion is not to be interfered with except where that which is done is in clear violation of the Constitution.

The power of Congress may extend even to intra-state operations, if their control is required to protect inter-state commerce from any injury, which may threaten it from that quarter. This protective power of Congress to ensure the free flow of inter-state commerce without outside restrictions or obstructions is implied in the plenary nature of the grant made to that

1. Art. 1 Sec. 8 Cl. 3.
2. *Brown v. Maryland* (1877) 12 Wh. 419.
3. *Welton v. Missouri* (1875) 91 U.S. 275 (282).
4. (1908) 208 U.S. 161 at pp. 176-77.

authority to regulate such commerce. It has accordingly been held that: (i) Congress can compel the adoption of safety appliances on cars moving intra-state traffic on an inter-state railroad because of the relation to and effect of such appliances upon the safety of inter-state traffic moving over the same railroad,[5] (ii) it may regulate the activities of a local grain exchange shown to have injurious effect on inter-state commerce,[6] (iii) it might legislate against unfair labour practices of a manufacturer who regularly ships his product in inter-state commerce whenever such practices on his part have led or tended to lead to labour disputes which threaten to obstruct his shipments in the channels of inter-state commerce,[7] (iv) it might effectively control combinations and conspiracies to restrain inter-state commerce, or monopolise any part of it, although the conspirators seek to attain their ends by means of intra-state activities,[8] and (v) it may also regulate intra-state rates of inter-state carriers where the former are discriminatory of or burdening inter-state commerce.[9]

The power over inter-state commerce embraces all the instrumentalities by which such commerce may be conducted. Among the instruments and agents to which the power extends are the trains, locomotives, tenders[10] and cars which are employed in inter-state transportation,[11] and all who are in any way engaged in such transportation, whether as common carriers or as their employees.[12] Wharves which are necessary to the delivery of inter-state or foreign commerce, whether owned independently or by land or ocean carriers are instruments of commerce,[13] and so also are terminals owned and operated by independent corporations at a particular place and engaged in the reception, landing and carriage of freight for inter-state railroads under contracts entered into with them,[14] As harbours are essential to commerce, they may be improved by Congress.[15] Congress may also authorise the Secretary of war to establish harbour lines with a view to the preservation and protection of harbours, and to prevent the construction of piers, wharves, bulkheads, and other works beyond those lines.[16]

The power of Congress to regulate inter-state commerce includes the power to prohibit the carriage in such commerce of articles, goods or persons

5. *Southern Railway Co. v. United States* (1911) 222 U. S. 20.
6. *Chicago Board of Trade v. Olsen* (1923) 262 U. S. 1.
7. *National Relation Board v. Fainblatt* (1939) 306 U. S. 60.
8. *Bedford Cut Stone Co. v. Journeymen S.C. Association* (1927) 274 U.S.37.
9. *Houston, East & West Texas Ry. Co. v. United States* (1914) 234 U.S. 342.
10. Small vessel attending on larger one, truck attached to locomotive.
11. *Napier v. Atlantic Coast Line R. Co.* (1926) 272 U.S. 605.
12. *Second Employers' Liability Cases* (1912) 223 U.S. 1.
13. *Southern Pacific Terminal Co. v. Inter-state Commerce Commission* (1911) 219 U.S. 498.
14. *United States v. Brooklyn Eastern District Terminal* (1919) 249 U.S. 296.
15. *Wisconsin v. Duluth* (1878) 96 U.S. 379.
16. *Philadelphia Co. v. Stimson* (1912) 223 U.S. 605.

deemed injurious to the health, welfare, or morals of the public.[17] The broad language employed by the Supreme Court in *United States v. Darby Lumber Co.,*[18] overruling *Hammer v. Dagenhart,*[19] suggests that the power of Congress to prohibit the inter-state transportation of goods or persons is of wide amplitude.

Congress has authority, under its power to regulate commerce among the states, to construct or to authorise individuals or corporations to construct, railroad across the states.[20] As inter-state commerce includes the transmission of the intelligences or signals across state lines by telegraph, telephone or radio the control of Congress extends to these instrumentalities of commerce also. There is no distinction in principle between transmission of telegraph and telephone message across state lines and the communication of radio message of programmes across state lines.[21]

Air navigation across state lines is also inter-state commerce. Transportation by air is in no way different from transportation by land or water. Congress enacted the Civil Aeronautics Act, 1938 and established a Civil Aeronautics Authority to control the regulation and development of civil aeronautics. This Act, whose scope is limited to foreign and inter-state air-borne commerce, has been enacted under the federal commerce power.

The Necessary and Proper Clause embodied in Art. 1, Sec. 8 of the Constitution, which authorises Congress 'to make all laws which shall be necessary and proper for carrying into execution the foregoing powers' has enabled Congress to deal with matters incidental to or necessary for the carrying out of the express powers granted to it. The following illustrations indicate the scope of this principle:

(i) In dealing with common carriers engaged in both inter-state and intra-state commerce, the authority of Congress has been held to embrace the right to control their intra-state operations in all matters having such a close and substantial relation to inter-state traffic.[22]

(ii) Where inter-state and intra-state commerce are served by the same instrumentalities of a common carrier, it is possible that a regulation of the state applied directly to the intra-state business only may in fact burden the inter-state. Where this occurs Congress may remove the burden, since state regulation must yield to its paramount power to assure adequate inter-state service.[23]

---

17. *Champion v. Ames* (1903) 188 U.S. 321; *Hoke v. United States* (1913) 227 U.S. 308.
18. (1941) 312 U.S. 100.
19. (1918) 247 U.S. 251.
20. *California v. Central Pacific Ry. Co.* (1888) 127 U.S. 1.
21. *Fishers Blend Station v. Tax Commission* (1936) 297 U.S. 650.
22. Taft C.J. in *Railroad Commission v. Chicago, B. & Q. R. Co.* (1922) 257 U.S. 563 at p. 588.
23. Brandies J., *Pacific Telephone & Teleg. Co. v. Tax Commission* (1923) 262 U.S. 1.

(iii) Transactions, which are 'not in and of themselves inter-state commerce' and have become 'a constantly recurring burden and obstruction to that commerce', come within the reach of the federal power.[24]

(iv) There are many other instances in which intra-state operations have been subjected to the federal commerce power, as inter-state operations could not be effectively regulated without controlling intra-state operations also, in view of the fact that both operations were inextricably intermingled.[25]

The exercise of the commerce power by Congress is subject to the limitations contained in the Fifth Amendment to the Federal Constitution.[26] So for as inter-state commerce is concerned, Congress has the same power as that enjoyed by the states, in the regulation of prices for the sale of commodities within their internal commerce. In *Nebbia v. New York,*[27] the Supreme Court observed that there can be no doubt that upon proper occasion and by appropriate measures the state may regulate a business in any of its aspect, including the prices to be charged for the products or commodities it sells.

Under the federal commerce power Congress is competent to legislate to provide for the fixing of prices, the proscription of unfair trade practices and the establishment of marketing rules respecting the inter-state sales of a commodity, in order to prevent uncontrolled competition from disrupting the inter-state channels of trade. In *Sunshine Anthracite Coal Co. v. Adkins,*[28] the Supreme Court upheld the regulatory provisions of the Bituminous Coal Act, of 1937 on the ground that Congress had the power to undertake the stabilisation of an inter-state industry through process of price-fixing and the regulation of distribution.

Congress is competent to establish marketing quotas for agricultural products with the object of fostering, protecting and preserving inter-state and foreign commerce, or to prevent the flow of such commerce from working harm to the people of the nation. The constitutionality of Title III of the Agricultural Adjustment Act, 1938, which established marketing quotas for flue-cured tobacco was upheld in *Mulford v. Smith,*[29] on the ground that 'it purports to be solely a regulation of inter-state commerce, which it reaches and affects at the throat where tobacco enters the stream of inter-state commerce, the marketing warehouse.'

---

24. *Board of Trade v. Olsen* (1938) 305 U.S. 197.
25. *Consolidated Edison Co. v. National Labour Relations Board* (1938) 305 U.S. 197; *Currin v. Wallace* (1939) 306 U.S. 1; and *United States v. Rock Royal Co-operative* (1939) 307 U.S. 533.
26. *Monongahela Navigation Co. v. United States* (1893) 148 U.S. 312; *United States v. Carolene Products Co.* (1938) 304 U.S. 144; *Currin v. Wallace* (1939) 306 U.S. 1.
27. (1934) 291 U.S. 502 at p. 537.
28. (1940) 310 U.S. 381.
29. (1939) 307 U.S. 38.

Congress is competent under its commerce power to fix minimum wages and maximum hours for employees engaged in the production of goods for inter-state commerce. Stone, J. upheld the wage and hour requirements of the Fair Labour Standards Act, 1938, in *United States v. Darby Lumber Company.*[30] He also pointed out that independently of the prohibition of shipment or transportation of the proscribed goods, the provision of the Act, for the suppression of their production for inter-state commerce was within the commerce power.

The "Commerce Clause" is in no sense a limitation upon the power of Congress over inter-state and foreign commerce, but is a grant of plenary and supreme authority to Congress over them. Congress is competent to control the activities of insurance companies, which conduct a substantial part of their business across state lines because a business so conducted is inter-state commerce coming within its commerce power.[31] According to *Prudential Insurance Co. v. Benjamin,*[32] it is open to Congress to declare that the business of insurance, though done in inter-state commerce, shall, except as otherwise expressly provided, continue to be regulated by the state.

The Tenth Amendment is not a limitation on the authority of Congress to resort to all measures for the exercise of its granted power over inter-state commerce, which are appropriate.[33]

B. The Power of the States with Regard to Inter-state Commerce

Let us now discuss the extent of the power, which the states can legitimately exercise even with respect to foreign and inter-state activities carried on inside their territories. The Supreme Court in *Cooley v. Board of Port Wardens*[34] pointed out that the application of the principle enunciated in that case to concrete situations has not always been free from difficulty. Nor, indeed, could this be a matter for surprise when one remembers how diverse are the situations which life presents. The doctrine, which Curtis, J. in *Cooley,* formulated on this subject, may be stated in these terms:

> "As the power of regulation over foreign and inter-state commerce embraces a vast field, some imperatively demanding a uniform rule and others as imperatively demanding a diversity of treatment to meet local needs; the states are competent until Congress has actually intervened, to continue to legislate upon all subjects pertaining to such commerce, except in regard to those which are in their nature national or admit of only one uniform system or plan of regulation."

30. (1941) 312 U.S. 100.
31. *United States v. South-Eastern Underwriters Assn.* (1944) 322 U.S. 533.
32. (1946) 328 U.S. 408.
33. *United States v. Darby Lumber Co.* (1941) 312 U.S. 100.
34. (1851) 12 How. 299.

Field, J., upholding the validity of a statute of the legislature of Alabama creating a Board of Commissioners for the improvement of the river, bay and harbour of mobile, in *Mobile Country v. Kimball,*[35] has given an excellent exposition of the rule of selective or partial exclusiveness formulated in the *Colley.*

Some of the cases, in which state statutes and regulations have been declared invalid on the ground that they regulated subjects of inter-state or foreign commerce which were national in nature or admitted of only one system or plan of supervision, although Congress itself had not legislated in regard to them, are being put as under :

In *Hall v. De Cuir,*[36] a coloured woman claimed damages for being refused accommodation on the basis of her colour in a cabin set apart for white persons. The Supreme Court declared that the regulation of commerce upon the Mississippi and its tributaries was clearly a matter of national concern and admitting of one uniform system of regulation and that the states were completely excluded from this domain. Similarly, in *Welton v. Missouri,*[37] the Court ruled that that portion of commerce with foreign countries and among the states, which consists in the transportation, and exchange of commodities is of national importance so as to preclude state action in that sphere even in the absence in the congressional legislation.

If one analyses *Southern Pacific Co. v. Arizona,*[38] he finds a phase of inter-state commerce where the need for national uniformity was so insistent that state regulation was deemed to be precluded by the "Commerce Clause" although Congress itself had not taken any action.

A variety of state regulations affecting inter-state or foreign commerce in the absence of conflicting congressional legislation have been sustained by the Supreme Court upon the principle that they related to matters of a local character requiring diversity of treatment suited to local circumstances. Within this category those regulations come which: sanction obstructions in navigable rivers;[39] require fees for the use of harbors;[40] establish inspection and quarantine laws;[41] require inspection of the seaworthiness of tugs employed in foreign and inter-state commerce;[42] tend to promote safety upon its highways and conservation of their use applicable alike to vehicles moving in inter-state commerce and intra-state commerce;[43] deal with the

35. (1881) 102 U.S. 691.
36. (1878) 95 U.S. 485 and *Morgan v. Virginia* (1946) 328 U.S. 373.
37. (1876) 91 U.S. 275.
38. (1945) 325 U.S. 761.
39. *Wilson v. Blackbird Creek Marsh Co.* (1829) 2 Pet. 245; *Gilman v. Philadelphia* (1865) 3 Wall. 710; *Lade Shore and Michigan Southern Ry. Co. v. Ohio* (1897) 165 U.S. 365.
40. *Clyde Mallory Lines v. Alabama* (1935) 296 U.S. 261.
41. *Patapsco Guano Co. v. Board of Agriculture* (1898) 171 U.S. 345.
42. *Kelly v. Washington* (1937) 302 U.S. 1.
43. *South Carolina State H. Deptt. v. Barnwell Bros.* (1938) 303 U.S.177.

taking or exportation of domestic game;[44] and insist upon railroad companies operating trains engaged in inter-state traffic to stop such trains in all towns within the state containing a population over a certain limit.[45]

C. Implied Limitations Imposed by the Commerce Clause on State Power

Some of the fundamental principles, which govern this subject, may be put as under:

(i) In relation to subjects of inter-state or foreign commerce, which are of a national character or admit of only one system or plan of regulation, the states are debarred from acting, even though Congress itself has not acted and has remained silent.

(ii) The commerce clause also prohibits all state action which, though nominally of local concern, is, in point of fact aimed at inter-state commerce, or which, by its necessary operation is a means of gaining a local advantage by throwing the attendant burdens on those without the state.[46]

(iii) The "Commerce Clause" also operates of its own force to prevent the state taxation of goods imported from foreign countries and still in the original packages. But if the importer has so acted upon the goods imported that they have become part of the common mass of property in the state, then, they become amenable to the taxing laws of the state.[47]

(iv) Fuller, C.J., speaking for the Court in *Postal Telegraph Cable Co. v. Adams*,[48] has observed :

"It is settled that where by way of duties laid on the transportation of the subjects of inter-state commerce, or on the occupation or business of carrying it on, a tax is levied by a state on inter-state commerce, such taxation amounts to a regulation of such commerce and cannot be sustained."

(v) Inspection laws passed under the police power of the states if unduly burdensome to foreign or inter-state commerce or are plainly discriminatory of products arriving from other states would also be repugnant to the "Commerce Clause."[49]

44. *Geer v. Connecticut* (1896) 161 U.S. 519.
45. *Lake Shore and Michigan Southern Railway Company v. Ohio* (1899) 173 U.S. 285.
46. *Robbins v. Shelby County Taxing District* (1887) 120 U.S. 487; *Baldwin v. Selig* (1935) 294 U.S. 511; *Howe Machine Co. v. Gage* (1879) 100 U.S. 676.
47. *Brown v. Maryland* (1827) 12 Wheat. 419.
48. (1895) 155 U.S. 688.
49. *Minnesota v. Barber* (1890) 136 U.S. 313; *Voight v. Wright* (1891) 141 U.S. 62; *D.E. Foote & Co. v. Stanley*; (1914) 232 U.S. 494; *Standard Oil Co. v. Graves* (1919) 249 U.S. 389.

D. State Police Power and the Commerce Clause

In the exercise of their police powers, the states may, therefore, subject to the paramount authority of Congress, regulate the importation of unhealthy swine, or cattle,[50] or adulterated, decayed or noxious foods.[51] It is considered that these are not proper subjects of commerce and, therefore, there is no unreasonable interference when they are inspected and excluded. A state may also protect its inhabitants against the fraudulent substitution by deceptive colouring or otherwise, of one article for another.[52] A state may also adopt measures calculated to promote safety upon its highways.[53] In enacting police regulations, however, a state may not burden or discriminate against foreign or inter-state commerce.[54]

Congress in the exercise of its paramount authority over the regulation of foreign or inter-state commerce may determine how far its regulations may go. It may occupy the whole field or only a part of the field. And, unless the intent is clearly manifested, it should never be held that Congress intends to supersede or suspend by its legislation the exercise of the police power of the states. And when the validity of a state police measure is contested as being in conflict with a congressional statute, it is for the courts to determine whether the conflict is so direct and positive that the two cannot consistently stand together.[55]

E. State Control over its Internal Commerce

It is settled by various decisions of the Supreme Court that the 'Due Process Clause' was no bar to a state or city from engaging in the business of supplying its citizens with articles in daily use, when it is found that they cannot be secured at reasonable process from the private dealers. Thus, a city may, if the local law permits, buy and sell at retail coal and wood.[56] And a state may, if permitted by its own Constitution, build and operate warehouses, elevators, packinghouses, flourmills, or other factories.[57] A state may also set-up a system of control of prices to be charged for a commodity like milk by fixing the minimum selling price to be charged by dealers to consumers and also a minimum buying price to be paid by dealers to producers.[58]

A state, in the exercise of its power to promote the health, safety or morality of its citizens, generally referred to as its police power, may take

50. *Mintz v. Baldwin* (1933) 289 U.S. 346.
51. *Sevage v. Jones* (1912) 255 U.S. 501.
52. *Hygrade Provision Co. v. Sherman* (1925) 266 U.S. 497.
53. *Bradley v. Public Utilities Commission* (1933) 289 U.S. 92.
54. *Hannibel & St. Joseph Co. v. Husen* (1877) 95 U.S. 465; *Voight v. Wright* (1891) 141 U.S.62.
55. *Cloverleaf Butter Co. v. Patterson* (1942) 315 U.S. 148.
56. *Jones v. Portland* (1917) 245 U.S. 217.
57. *Green v. Frazier* (1920) 253 U.S. 233.
58. *Nebbia v. New York* (1934) 292 U.S. 502.

action impinging upon local commerce. In *Mugler v. Kansas*,[59] the Supreme Court upheld the constitutionality of a Kansas statute of 1881, which completely prohibited the manufacture and sale of intoxicating liquors except for medicinal, scientific and mechanical purposes. A state may also enact a minimum wage law for women labourers.[60]

F. Exclusive *versus* Concurrent Power

The "Commerce Clause" has a negative as well as a positive aspect. The Clause not only serves to augment federal authority. By its own force it also cuts down the power of the constituent state in its exercise of what would normally be a part of its residual police power.[61] If there were no "Commerce Clause," each state could shut out the products of other states or admit them only on conditions. It is consequently clear that the "Commerce Clause," in and of itself, affords protection from state legislation inimical to national commerce.

Thus, the "Commerce Clause," by necessary negative inference, limits the authority of the states. In actuality, despite Justice Story's statement to the contrary, the Marshall view of the commerce power was not that of unequivocal federal exclusiveness. In *Gibbons v. Ogden*,[62] referring to the argument that the commerce power was an indivisible whole, vested exclusively in the Congress, it was stated that there is great force in the argument and the court is not satisfied that it has been refuted. But this is only passing a qualified judgment on a point not relevant to the decision in the case. More significant was Marshall's express recognition that the states did, in fact, possess powers, which might be exercised over commerce. As *Gibbons* acknowledged, "Inspection laws, quarantine laws, health laws of every description, as well as laws for regulating the internal commerce of a state, and those which respect turnpike-roads, ferries, etc., are component parts of this mass" i.e., of state legislation which may, in Marshall's words, have a considerable influence on commerce. The *Wilson*[63] opinion indicates that the Marshall interpretation of the negative aspect of the "Commerce Clause" was not as far from that of his successor, Taney, C.J., as is generally believed. Both Marshall and Taney refused to follow the notion of complete exclusiveness of federal power, under which the "Commerce Clause," of its own force, removed from the states any and all power over inter-state and foreign commerce.

In *Gibbons*, Danial Webster had presented to the highest Court a theory, which, like the Marshall approach just discussed, is somewhere in between the notion of complete exclusiveness and concurrent power. In his argument, Webster contended that the power of Congress to regulate

59. (1887) 123 U.S. 623.
60. *West Coast Hotel Co. v. Parrish* (1937) 300 U.S. 379.
61. Schwartz, A Commentary on the Constitution of the United States, Ed. 1977 at p. 238.
62. 9 Wheat. 1 (1824).
63. *Wilson v. Black Bird Creek Marsh Co.*, 2 Pet. 245 U.S. (1829).

commerce was complete and entire, and to a certain extent necessarily exclusive. He meant by this that this proposition was, not that all the commercial powers are exclusive, but that those powers being separated, there are some which are exclusive in their nature.

Cooley v. Board of Port Wardens[64] arose out of a Pennsylvania law requiring vessels using the port of Philadelphia to engage local pilots or pay a fine, amounting to half the pilot age fee, to go to the use of the society for the relief of Distressed and Decayed Pilots. Since there was no federal statute on the subject, the question for the Supreme Court was that of the extent of state regulatory power over commerce where the Congress was silent on the matter. The *Cooley* doctrine was well summarised by Justice Miller as under :

> "That the power to regulate commerce is one which includes many subjects various and quite unlike in their nature; that whenever subjects of this power are in their nature national, or require one uniform system or plan of regulation, they may be justly held to belong to that class over which Congress has the exclusive power of legislation; but that local and limited matters, not national in their character, which are most likely to be wisely provided for by such diverse rules as the localities and the authorities of the different states may deem applicable, may be regulated by the legislatures of those states in the absence of any Act, of Congress upon the same subject. Of course, when Congress does legislate, as it has a right to do, that excludes the legislation of the states and renders it void so far as it may interfere or conflict with the statutes of the United States."[65]

Under the *Cooley* test, it has been emphasised, that extreme notion that the congressional power over commerce must be wholly exclusive is rejected. The scope of the "Commerce Clause's" implied prohibition against state action is not correlative with the scope of the affirmative commerce power given to Congress. *Cooley*, on the contrary, recognises that the states still retain authority over commerce in appropriate cases.

G. Recent Balancing Approach of Judiciary

Recent judicial assessment of American "Commerce Clause" may be put as under :

In *Oregon Waste Sys. v. Deptt. of Env.*,[66] the Court held that the "Commerce Clause" grants Congress plenary authority over inter-state commerce and the degree of differential burden or charge on inter-state commerce. *First*, measures only the extent of the discrimination, and *second* is

64. 12 How. 299 U.S. (1851).
65. Miller, Lectures on the Constitution of the United States, 454-55 (1893).
66. (1994) 128 L.Ed. 2d 13.

of no relevance to the determination whether a state has discriminated against inter-state commerce.

In *General Motors Cor. v. Tracy,*[67] the Court stated that in respect to the "Federal Commerce Clause" under the dormant commerce clause's prohibition of state regulation that imposes an undue burden on inter-state commerce by favouring the products of an in-state entity over those of an out-of-state entity—when the allegedly competing entities provide different products, there is a threshold question whether the entities are similarly situated for constitutional purposes, because: (i) the difference in products may mean that the different entities serve different markets and would continue to do so even if the supposedly discriminatory burden were removed, and (ii) if that should be the case, then elimination the tax of other regulatory differential would not serve the dormant commerce clause's fundamental objective of preserving a national market for competition undisturbed by preferential advantages conferred by a state upon its residents of resident competitors. The dormant commerce clause protects markets and participants in markets, not taxpayers as such.

In *Reno v. Condon,*[68] Supreme Court of United States pointed out that the personal, identifying information, under the Driver's Privacy Protection Act, which generally prohibits any state Department of Motor Vehicles (DMV), or officer, employer, or contractor thereof, from knowingly disclosing or otherwise making available to any person or entity personal information about any individual obtained by the DMV in connection with a motor vehicle record regulates is a thing in inter-state commerce. The sale or release of that information in inter-state commerce is, therefore, a proper subject of congressional regulation.

In *United States v. Morrison,*[69] Supreme Court made a modern and expansive interpretation of the "Commerce Clause". According to this case the modern jurisprudence relating to the "Commerce Clause" identifies three broad categories of activity that Congress may properly regulate and protect under Congress' commerce power. Those categories are: (i) the use of the channels of inter-state commerce, (ii) The instrumentalities of inter-state commerce—or persons or things in inter-state commerce—even though the threat may come only from intra-state activities, and (iii) those activities having a substantial relation to inter-state commerce, that is, those activities that substantially affect inter-state commerce.

In *Associated Industries v. Lohman,*[70] Court gave the effect of state regulation in United States. The Court held that a purely nominal distinction in a state's statutes between the methods of regulation intra-state and inter-state commerce—as long as such distinction is not translated into any difference in the substance of the regulations imposed—does not violate the

67. (1997) 519 U.S. 278.
68. (2000) 528 U.S. 141.
69. (2000) 529 U.S. 598.
70. (1994) 128 L.Ed. 2d 639.

"Commerce Clause", since such distinction cannot be said to provide benefits to intra-state commerce or to impose discriminatory burdens on inter-state trade. For purposes of determining the validity of a state action under the "Commerce Clause" what is required is that the state action—whether through one agency or another or through one enactment or more than one—be consistent with the restrictions of the Constitution; and there is no demand in the Constitution that the state put its requirements in any one statute, and the state may distribute its requirements as it sees fit if the result, taken in its totality, is within the state's constitutional power.

In *Humana Inc. v. Forsyth*,[71] the Court discussed whether the business of 'Insurance' are regulated by state or federal government. In a suit against a health insurer and a hospital in which beneficiaries of group health insurance policies issued by the insurer in a particular state asserted that the insurer and the hospital were engaged in a fraudulent insurance scheme. It allegedly violated through a pattern of fraudulent racketeering activity the Racketeer Influenced and Corrupt Organization Act (RICO). This Act, provided a private right of action, permits treble damages and did not proscribe conduct that the state insurance law permit. The MacCarran Ferguson Act, provided that no federal statute should be construed to invalidate, impair, or supersede any state law enacted·for the purpose of regulating the business of insurance unless the federal statute specifically related to the business of insurance. It did not block RICO's application because even though RICO did not specifically relate to the business of insurance, (i) under the standard definitions of "invalidate" and "supersede". RICO's application to the case would neither invalidate nor supersede state law; and (ii) RICO, in proscribing the same conduct as, but providing materially different remedies from the state laws, did not impair the state law under RICO. It advanced the state's interest in combating insurance fraud, where RICO's private right of action and treble damages provision appear to complement the state's statutory and common law schemes for relief, which, among other matters, (i) provided a private right of action and permitted compensatory and punitive damages, and (ii) specifically provide that an insurer was under a common law duty to negotiate with its insures in good faith, and did not frustrate any articulated state policy or interfered with any state administrative regime, where the state had filed no brief at any stage of the suit urging that application of RICO to the alleged conduct of the insurer and the hospital would constitute such frustration on interference. The Court held that federal law did not directly conflict with state regulation, and when application of the federal law would not frustrate any declared state policy or interfere with a state's administrative regime, the McCarran-Ferguson Act, which provided that no federal statute should be construed to invalidate, impair, or supersede any state law enacted for the purpose of regulating the business of insurance,

71. (1999) 524 U.S. 299.

unless the federal statute specifically related to the business of insurance did not preclude the federal law's application. Because although Congress did not intend a green light for federal regulation whenever the federal law did not collide head on with state regulation, neither did Congress intend to cede the field of insurance regulation to the states, saving only instances in the states, in which Congress orders otherwise, as if Congress intended to generally pre-empt the field for the states or to limit the application of federal legislation in general, or the Racketeer Influenced and Corrupt Organization Act, in particular, to the business of insurance, then Congress could have so stated proscription against construing any federal statute to invalidate, impair, or supersede any state law which imposes a fee or tax upon the business of insurance belies any congressional intent to preclude federal regulation merely because the regulation imposes liability additional to or greater than state law; and this conclusion accords with prior United States Supreme Court Cases.

H. Dormant Commerce Clause and Electronic Commerce in United States

Unsurprisingly, courts have found that the dormant commerce clause applies to the Internet. The Internet, like a highway or railroad, may be an instrument of inter-state commerce and analysed accordingly.[72] They have found that Internet communications, in particular electronically mailed images via the Internet, constitute inter-state commerce.[73] Courts have invalidated state provisions explicitly aimed at regulating content on the Internet.[74] Art. 1 of the Constitution gives Congress the power to regulate commerce "among the several states."[75] Even in the absence of affirmative congressional regulation of inter-state commerce, the Supreme Court has long invoked the dormant commerce clause as a basis for judicial preemption of state law that unduly burdens inter-state commerce. The Court has devised a number of tests to serve this end.

The dormant commerce clause's central prohibition is on protectionist state legislation that discriminates against out-of-states.[76] If a state law discriminates against out-of-states, it is subject to "the strictest scrutiny of any purported legitimate local purpose and of the absence of non-discriminatory alternatives."[77] Discriminatory state regulations rarely satisfy this standard.[78] A second dormant commerce clause test applies when a state law is non-discriminatory on its face but nonetheless impinges on inter-state

72. *American Libraries Association v. Pataki*, 969 F. Supp. 160 (S.D.NY. 1997).
73. *United States v. Thomas*, 519 U.S. 820 (1996).
74. *A.C.L.U. v. Johnson*, 194 F3d 1149 (10th Cir. 1999).
75. U.S. Const. Art. 1, 8, Cl. 3.
76. *CTS Corp. v. Dynamics Corp. of Am.*, 481 U.S. 69, 87 (1987).
77. *Hughes v. Oklahoma*, 441 U.S. 322, 337 (1979).
78. A rare exceptions found in *Maine v. Taylor*, 477 U.S. 131 (1986), which upheld a ban on the importation of bait fish.

commerce. In this context the Court applies a balancing test: "Where the statute regulates evenhandedly to effectuate a legitimate local public interest, and its effects on inter-state commerce are only incidental, it will be upheld unless the burden imposed on such commerce is clearly excessive in relation to the putative local benefits."[79]

The heightened scrutiny test for discriminatory state legislation and the balancing test for neutral state legislation that burdens inter-state commerce form the core of dormant commerce clause jurisprudence. The dormant commerce clause however is also said to prohibit certain state laws that regulate extraterritorially and others that lead to inconsistent regulatory burdens. These aspects of the dormant commerce clause are unsettled and poorly understood, but they play an important role in the Internet cases.[80]

2. THE CANADIAN COMMERCE CLAUSE

Trade and commerce is among those powers of the Dominion Parliament, which are described "exclusive" by the British North America Act. The constitutional grant is an exceptionally broad one, for in addition to being placed solely in the hands of the national government; commerce and trade regulation is not limited by any phrases such as "among the states." In fact, the power is said to include regulation of any kind of commerce wherever it may exist, "notwithstanding anything else in this Act." [81] But from the very beginning, every argument used against the regulatory power in the United States was used in Canada. But the particularists in Canada were to discover an additional weapon in the Canadian Constitution's delegation of power to the provinces. Almost any federal use of the commerce power has been met by the charge that such use invaded the provincial power over "property and civil rights," or that it was a matter of a "merely local or private nature in the provinces."[82]

In Canada, the provinces have been deprived of the power to levy indirect taxes so that they may not be able to create inter-provincial trade barriers. This has been further strengthened by making "regulation of trade and commerce" a central matter. In addition, Sec. 121 of the B.N.A. Act, which provides that "articles of growth, produce or manufacture of any province shall be admitted free into each of the other provinces". It also curtails the provincial power to put restrictions on entry of goods from other provinces.

The Canadian Supreme Court has interpreted this Sec. somewhat narrowly. It has been held that the word 'free' in the Sec. does not mean absolute freedom from any restrictions whatsoever, but only freedom from

79. *Pike v. Bruce Church, Inc.*, 397 U.S. 137, 142 (1970).
80. Jack J. Goldsmith and Alan O. Sykes, The Internet and the Dormant Commerce Clause, *Yale Law Journal*, Vol. 110, No. 5, at p. 789 (2001).
81. The British North America Act, Sec. 91.
82. *Id.*, Sec. 91 (13) and Sec. 91 (16).

any inter-provincial duty, such as customs duty.[83] Thus, the Dominion Parliament is not debarred from prohibiting import of intoxicating liquor from another Province, in aid of temperance legislation.

Parliament of Canada may validly go so far as to expressly prohibit the admission from one Province to another Province, so long as the prohibition does not involve the imposition of a customs duty. Consequently, it would be competent for a province to impose a consumer or use tax on consumers within the province even though such goods were manufactured in or imported from another province.[84] But Sec. 121 will hit a provincial law, which seeks to *prohibit* the movement of goods to or from the province, subject to manifest exceptions as in the case of danger to life or health.[85]

As applied to the Federal Legislature, Sec. 121 only means that it would invalidate a federal law if it seeks to impose customs duty on goods imported into one province from another. It cannot invalidate a law, which *prohibits* the import of liquor from one province to another; or fixes the price of goods imported into one province from another. A wider interpretation was given by Rand, J. in *Murphy*[86] that it prohibits any trade regulation, which is designed to restrict or limit the free flow of commerce across provincial boundaries.

The very next year a Dominion law, imposing jurisdiction on provincial superior courts to settle contested elections to the House of Commons was validated against a charge that the act invaded the civil rights of the provinces. According to Ritchie, C.J. the terms 'property and civil rights' must necessarily be read in a restricted and limited sense, because many matters involving property and civil rights are expressly reserved to the Dominion Parliament.[87] He pointed out trade and commerce are among those Dominion powers that most directly affected property and civil rights.

3. THE AUSTRALIAN COMMERCE CLAUSE

The Australian Constitution goes into more detail regarding trade and commerce than either the American or Canadian Constitutions. Parliament is given power to make laws with respect to "trade and commerce with other countries, and among the states."[88] In addition, Sec. 98 specifically authorises extending this power to navigation and shipping, and to state-owned railways. Parliament is forbidden to give preference to one state over another by such regulation, or to use this power in such a manner as to deny states or residents therein the "reasonable" use of the river waters for conservation or

83. *Gold Seal Ltd. v. Dominion Express Co.* (1921) 62 S.C.R. 424.
84. *Atlantic Smoke Shops v. Conlon* (1941) S.C.R. 670.
85. *Lawson v. Interior Committee* (1931) S.C.R. 357.
86. *Murphy v. A.G. Canada* (1958) S.C.R. 626.
87. *Valin v. Langlois* (1879), 3 S.C.R. 1, at p. 15.
88. Australia, Constitution, Sec. 51(i).

irrigation. In contrast to the American Constitution, the Australian Constitution additionally grants federal legislative power over a number of specific subjects of trade and commerce, such as banking and the incorporation of banks, insurance, foreign corporations, and trading or financial corporations formed within the Commonwealth, the nationalisation of any property for any purpose in respect of which the Parliament has power to legislate, and the conciliation and arbitration of industrial disputes extending beyond the limits of any one state.

Johnston,[89] in this connection rightly points out that this very generous grant of constitutional power to the Commonwealth Parliament has suffered and still suffers from a very restrictive interpretation by the High Court. The Court seems to have discovered at least three ways to deny national power in the field of commercial regulation. The *first* of these ways is to find that the reserved power of the state inhibits (or prohibits) the use of federal power—the practice that in the United States was called "dual federalism". The *second* is through the Court's refusal to use the "Supremacy Clause" of the Constitution to invalidate conflicting state legislation. Number 5 of the "covering clauses" says that this Act, and all laws made by the Parliament of the Commonwealth under the Constitution, shall be binding on the courts, judges, and people of every state and of every part of the Commonwealth, notwithstanding anything in the laws of any state. The *third* method available to the High Court is the result of a very unusual constitutional clause. When the Constitution was written there was much difficulty with state customs duties and inter-state tariff barriers, and a group of constitutional provisions[90] was intended to prevent these state fiscal barriers in the future. Sec. 88 instructs Parliament to institute "uniform duties of customs" within two years after establishment of the new government, and Sec. 92 says that when such uniform duties are imposed, then 'trade, commerce and intercourse among the states, whether by means of internal carriage or ocean navigation, shall be absolutely free.' Thus, under this Sec. there is an express declaration of the freedom of trade, commerce and intercourse but that declaration is also confined to the inter-state aspect of the freedom.[91]

A. Sec. 51(i) Apart from Sec. 92

(A) Activities Essentially Inter-State or Overseas

The hard core of the grant in Sec. 51(i) is easily determined, the periphery is more difficult to ascertain. The main part of the grant confers Commonwealth power over those activities which form an essential, central or basic attribute of the conception, "trade and commerce with other

89. Richard E. Johnston, The Effect of Judicial Review on Federal—State Relations in Australia, Canada, and the United States, at p. 249.
90. Section 86 to 95.
91. *New South Wales v. Commonwealth* (1915) 20 C.L.R. 54.

countries, and among the states", or which have the characteristics or the character of this conception. The distinction between activities essentially within such a concept and activities not forming part of that concept has been worked out in the cases dealing with the constitutional immunity assured by Sec. 92 of the Constitution.[92] Just as the first class of activities that essentially within the notion of inter-state trade and commerce, falls within the immunity preserved by Sec. 92, equally that class of activities falls within the core of the legislative grant for the phrase inter-state[93] trade and commerce and has the same meaning in Sec. 51(i) as it has in Sec. 92.[94] For instance, the operations of loading and discharging cargo on overseas and inter-state ships are variously described as going to something necessarily possessing the characteristics of oversea and inter-state trade and commerce[95] or as essential to the importation or exportation by sea of goods[96] or as an essential part of sea commerce[97] or as work essentially part of trade and commerce with other countries[98] or as work forming part of inter-state and external commerce.[99] Consequently, such operations as loading and discharging of cargo can be controlled by the Commonwealth, acting well within Sec. 51(i).

The object of customs legislation, including the Customs Act, is to obtain revenue and to control trade—both import trade and export trade;[100] and when a customs law regulates trade by means of control over importation and exportation, the law assumes the control of trade and commerce by means which go to the central point of the power over trade and commerce with other countries.[101] The activity of exportation or importation forms part of the concept of trade and commerce with other countries. For the same reason, namely, that the activities in respect of which the Commonwealth law operates 'are part of the concept of trade and commerce with other countries, the Commonwealth has power under Sec. 51(i) to control the sale and disposition of export fruit abroad.[102]

The grant in Sec. 51(i) enables Commonwealth regulation of overseas and inter-state trade and commerce but also allows Commonwealth participation in such trade and commerce. The Commonwealth by itself or

92. *Hospital Provident Fund Pty. Ltd. v. State of Victoria* (1953) 87 C.L.R. 1 at p.17.
93. *Crowe v. Commonwealth* (1935) 54 C.L.R. 69 at p. 93.
94. W. & A. McArthur Ltd. v. *State of Queensland* (1920) 28 C.L.R. 530 at p. 549.
95. *R. v. Foster ; Ex parte Eastern & Australian Steamship Co. Ltd.* (1959) 32 A.L.J.R. 446, at p. 451.
96. *R. v. Wright ; Ex parte Waterside Workers' Federation of Australia* (1955) 93 C.L.R. 528, at p. 544.
97. *Huddart Parker Ltd. v. The Commonwealth* (1931) 44 C.L.R. 492 at p. 515.
98. *Elliot v. The Commonwealth* (1936) 54 C.L.R. 657 at pp. 680-81.
99. *Victorian St. and General Contracting Co. v. Dignan* (1931) 46 C.L.R. 73 at p. 103.
100. *Radio Corp. Pty. Ltd. v. The Commonwealth* (1938) 59 C.L.R. 170 at p. 180.
101. *O' Sullivan v. Noarlunga Meat Ltd.* (1954) 92 C.L.R. 565 at p. 597.
102. *Morgan v. The Commonwealth* (1947) 74 C.L.R. 421 at p. 452.

its agencies can enter into activities forming part of overseas and inter-state trade and commerce. For example, inter-state transportation of goods or persons lies near the Centre of the concept of trade and commerce among the states.[103] Consequently, the Commonwealth can not only regulate inter-state transportation but it can also establish a Commission to engage in overseas and inter-state transportation by air; or the Commonwealth can constitute a board to manage a shipping line for the same purpose of transportation.

(B) Intra-state Activities

Whilst Sec. 51(i) clearly bestows power over matters essential to inter-state and overseas trade and commerce, just as clearly that placitum gives no power with respect to intra-state trade and commerce. By applying the maxim *expressio unius exclusio alterius* to the Sec.,[104] it is seen that the Sec. itself denies power over the internal trade of a states; apart from overseas trade and commerce there are two classes of trade and commerce inter-state and intra-state; the former by Sec. 51(i) is within Commonwealth power, the latter by Sec. 107 is solely within state power.[105]

The Commonwealth cannot rely on the inter-mingling of intra-state shipping, airlines, etc., with inter-state shipping, airlines, etc., as a justification for its control over the former. It might be otherwise 'if in any given case it were established by evidence in respect of a particular subject matter that the inter-mingling of foreign and inter-state trade and commerce were such that it was impossible for the Commonwealth Parliament to regulate the former without also directly regulating the latter'.[106]

But this is not to say that a given transaction which, in itself and in isolation, is a purely intra-state activity may not be subjected to a law under Sec. 51(i); the transaction may be so closely and inseparably associated with an allied inter-state or overseas activity that by context it assumes the character of the overall inter-state or overseas movement.[107]

(C) Peripheral Activities

Now between these two extremes-activities lying at or near the core of the grant in Sec. 51(i) and activities patently intra-state are the peripheral activities; namely, those acts subsequent or antecedent to the essential inter-state or overseas act. In the transportation of cargo by sea, the loading and the discharging of cargo are the terminus *a quo* and the *terminus ad quem* of the inter-state or overseas activity;[108] the guarding of such cargo, the supervision and the direction of loading and unloading activities, the handling and re-handling of cargo are peripheral activities. Whether the

---

103. *Australian National Airways v. The Commonwealth* (1945) 71 C.L.R. 29 at p. 105.
104. *A. G. for N.S.W. v. Brewery Employees' Union* (1908) 6 C.L.R. 469 at p. 503.
105. *Wragg v. New South Wales* (1953) 88 C.L.R. 353 at p. 385-86.
106. *R. v. Burgess ; Ex parte Henry* (1936) 55 C.L.R. 608 at p. 629.
107. *Russel v. Walters* (1957) 96 C.L.R. 177 at p. 183.
108. *Huddart Parker Ltd. v. The Commonwealth* (1931) 44 C.L.R. 492 at p. 515.

reach of Sec. 51(i) extends to such peripheral activities depends upon the fulfilment of the conditions that (i) the activity, though antecedent to or consequent upon an operation essential to the concept of overseas or inter-state trade and commerce, must itself possess the characteristic of "inter-state" or "overseas," and the act must be objectively identifiable as an overseas or inter-state act; it may not be purely an intra-state act; (ii) the act must have a "connection" with overseas or inter-state trade and commerce; and the connection must be of a particular kind; and (iii) the law said to be within Sec. 51(i) and to extend to the peripheral act must be a law with respect to trade and commerce with other countries and among the states, and not a law which outwardly and in form may deal with such trade and commerce but which on scrutiny is disclosed as a law in substance dealing with matters outside Commonwealth power. Of course, when the Court speaks of what an Act, effects "really and in substance", the Court again displays one of its shibboleths, which conceals the determinants of its creative judicial choice. This much is clear that a law outwardly and formally dealing with trade and commerce among the states may not in its strict legal operation reach down into state domestic matters, as, for example, the control of state public health.[109]

When considering the validity of a law allegedly passed under Sec. 51(i), the Court does not concern itself with the motive of the legislature, provided the law is a law with respect to trade and commerce with other countries and among the states. In such a case the motive is irrelevant.[110] For instance, the motive for granting union preference to watersiders may well have been a desire to control industrial relations on the waterfront without regard to the strictness of Sec. 51(xxxv); but since the law securing union preference was found within Sec. 51(i), motive could be, and was disregarded.

B. Sec. 51(i) and Sec. 92

The grant in Sec. 51(i), as with every Commonwealth grant, is plenary. It gives full and ample power over inter-state trade and commerce. By the grant the Commonwealth can regulate and participate in trade and commerce between the States. Yet, Sec. 92 guarantees an absolute freedom to such trade and commerce. At first blush the two sections strike head on. The resolution of the conflict must be found rather in a limitation of the plenitude of the grant than in a denial of the constitutional immunity of Sec. 92;[111] for Sec. 51(i) is expressly stated to be "subject to this Constitution", of which Sec. 92 is part. Accordingly, Sec. 51(i) reads as a grant with respect to *free* trade and commerce among the states. Under Sec. 51(i) Parliament has complete dominion over a free inter-state trade and commerce.[112] A proviso is to be

109. *O' Sullivan v. Noarlunga Meat Ltd.* (1954) 92 C.L.R. 565 at p. 595.
110. *Bank of N.S.W. v. Commonwealth* (1948) 76 C.L.R. 1, at p. 187.
111. *Duncan v. State of Queensland* (1916) 22 C.L.R. 556 at p. 588.
112. *W. & A. McArthur Ltd. v. State of Queensland* (1920) 28 C.L.R. 530 at p. 568.

written into Sec. 51(i), namely, the Commonwealth Parliament has power with respect to trade and commerce between the states 'so long as such laws leave inter-state trade or commerce or intercourse absolutely free'.[113]

There is sameness about Sec. 51(i) and Sec. 92. Both have the characteristic of "trade and commerce", and the meaning of the phrase is the same in both the sections.[114] The use of the term in Sec. 51(i) extends far beyond the mere buying and selling of goods or the mere act of inter-state transportation, the concepts extend to the disposition and handling of goods as part of the inter-state act to intangibles, services, transport and communication in all its forms. The last-named activities are instances of intercourse, which is included in the term commerce. Commerce undoubtedly, is traffic, but it is something more; it is intercourse. Indeed, there is not much covered by the word "intercourse" in Sec. 92 that is not also covered by the word "commerce" in Sec. 51(i). In the former Sec. non-commercial intercourse is included, whilst under the legislative grant non-commercial intercourse is not covered; otherwise, the phrases "trade, commerce and intercourse" in Sec. 92 and "trade and commerce" in Sec. 51(i) are the same. The "dominant", "central" or "essential" content of trade, commerce and intercourse among the states is contained in such expressions as inter-state movement, interchange, communication, traffic, transportation or transfer. The Court has repeatedly emphasised the notion of inter-state movement as an essential element in the concept contained in Sec. 92.[115]

But there is a difference between Sec. 51(i) and Sec. 92, a difference which lies in two features present in Sec. 51(i), absent in Sec. 92. *Firstly*, Sec. 51(i) empowers laws with respect to trade and commerce abroad and among the states; the term 'with respect to' merely requires a certain relevance or connection between the activity sought to be controlled by a law under Sec. 51(i) and some allied inter-state trading or commercial transaction.[116] In contrast, Sec. 92 gives immunity basically to inter-state trade and commerce itself. The spread of that immunity is not made more ample by the addition of such a phrase as 'with respect to'. *Secondly*, Sec. 51(i) is a grant of power, Sec. 92 a restraint on power. A grant of power carries with it power to use all the means necessary to effectuate the object of the grant. In contrast, Sec. 92 restricts power, its circle of immunity does not expand to protect the antecedent conditions of inter-state trade and commerce, or to protect the entire means incidental to such trade and commerce.[117]

113. *R. v. Vizzard; Ex parte Hill* (1933) 50 C.L.R. 30 at p. 88.

114. *James v. The Commonwealth* (1936) 55 C.L.R. 1 at p. 60.

115. P.H. Lane, Trade & Commerce Power : Constitution Sec. 51(i), *The Australian Law Journal*, Vol. 34, 1960, 99 at p. 106.

116. *Crowe v. The Commonwealth* (1935) 54 C.L.R. 69 at p. 90.

117. The principle enunciated by Marshell C.J. in *McCulloch v. State of Maryland* (1819) 4 Wheat. 316 atp. 421, and adopted in reference to Sec. 51(i) in *Grannall v. Marrickville Margarine Pty. Ltd.* (1955) 93 C.L.R. 55 at p. 77.

In the result, the two features peculiar to Sec. 51(i) give that Sec. a wider spread than the compound of freedom set-up by Sec. 92. The area, operation, width, of range of Sec. 51(i) is wider than that of Sec. 92, and this must be so, otherwise the legislative grant would be rendered nugatory by another Sec. in the same instrument.[118] This means that the peripheral activities ancillary or incidental to the central concept of inter-state trade and commerce and within the scope of Sec. 51(i) will not necessarily fall within the area of immunity assured by Sec. 92.

This is the peripheral field of activities on which laws made under Sec. 51(i) may operate untrammeled by the strictures of Sec. 92. It is a field based on features peculiar to Sec. 51(i). There are two other similarly unrestricted areas open to laws under Sec. 51(i).[119] *Firstly*, the freedom proposed by Sec. 92 must be preserved. Consequently, laws may be made under Sec. 51(i) consistently with Sec. 92 to prevent obstruction to that freedom or to facilitate the freedom. *Secondly*, the freedom assured by Sec. 92 was introduced against a background of a law-controlled, orderly society. That freedom is not licence or a cloak for anarchy. It is a qualified freedom.[120] Consequently, laws may be made under Sec. 51(i) consistently with Sec. 92 to safeguard the existence of an orderly society.

Thus, the activities in respect of which a law under Sec. 51(i) operates may be classified into those activities, which form an essential part of the concept of inter-state trade and commerce, and those activities, which do not form such an essential part.

(A) Essential Inter-State and Overseas Activities

As to activities forming an essential part of inter-state trade and commerce, a law made under Sec. 51(i) may, *firstly*, prohibit or interfere with such activities, *secondly*, prevent hindrances to such activities or facilitate such activities or *thirdly*, prohibit such of these activities as affect the continuance of a law-abiding, orderly community. Let us discuss each of them as under:

(i) Prohibitory Laws

Laws may prohibit or interfere with activities essential in inter-state trade and commerce. Since such laws touch on the central concept of inter-state trade and commerce they are *prima facie* within the legislative grant, but if such laws really prohibit or interfere with that central concept they are struck down by Sec. 92 and by that very fact *ultra vires* Sec. 51(i) which is subject, *inter alia*, to Sec. 92. The loading and unloading of cargo is an essential part of the concept of inter-state trade and commerce.[121] But any real

118. *James v. The Commonwealth* (1936) 55 C.L.R. 1 at p. 60.
119. i.e., areas arising out of an element in Sec. 92.
120. *Commonwealth v. Bank of N. S.W.* (1948) 76 C.L.R. 1 at p. 389.
121. *R. v. Foster ; Ex parte Eastern and Australian Steamship Co. Ltd.* (1959) 32 A.L.J.R. 446 at p. 451.

restriction or interference with an essential part of the concept of inter-state trade and commerce infringes Sec. 92. Therefore, any real restriction or interference with the loading and discharging of cargo on ships is contrary to Sec. 92 and accordingly *ultra vires* Sec. 51(i), and equally *ultra vires* Sec. 98.[122]

(ii) Facilitating Laws

Laws may prevent obstructions to or facilitate activities essential in inter-state trade and commerce. The Commonwealth Parliament can under Sec. 51(i) prohibit acts interfering with trade and commerce between the states. The Crimes Act (1914-55), Sec. 30 J, for instance, provides for the prevention of industrial disturbances prejudicing or threatening trade or commerce among the states. So, too, Parliament can enact laws under Sec. 51(i) which facilitate, preserve, encourage or promote inter-state trade and commerce.[123] Laws ensuring safety measures in that trade and commerce are an example of such permitted laws. Thus, the Navigation Act, (1912-58), lays down conditions for safe inter-state and overseas shipping, and these provisions would be supportable under Sec. 51(i), whilst not derogating from the freedom guaranteed by Sec. 92.[124]

(iii) Preserving Laws

Laws may preserve an orderly, law-controlled society. Instances of such laws passed pursuant to the grant of Sec. 51(i) are the Secret Commissions Act, (1905), the Customs Act, (1901-1965), Sec. 112A, and the Navigation Act, (1912-58), Sec. 2(1) and Sec. 164, the Spirits Act, (1906-52), Sec. 9, the Australian Industries Preservation Act, 1906-50.[125]

Therefore, if a purported law under Sec. 51(i) really burdens or prohibits an activity essential in trade and commerce among the states that law will be *ultra vires* Sec. 51(i) because it violates Sec. 92; it will be otherwise if the law prevents obstructions to or promotes inter-state trade and commerce; and it will be equally so if the law preserves the background of the orderly, law-controlled community presumed by Sec. 92.

(b) Non-Essential Inter-State and Overseas Activities

Activities not forming part of inter-state trade and commerce, can be divided into activities which though not essentially part of inter-state trade and commerce, are so closely related or orientated towards that trade and commerce that they form an inseparable whole with the trade and commerce; and activities which are not essential to inter-state trade and commerce but relevant or ancillary thereto the peripheral activities.

122. That Sec. incorporates by reference Sec. 51(i) which is subject to Sec. 92; then Sec. 98, through Sec. 51(i) is subject to Sec. 92.
123. *Duncan v. State of Queensland* (1916) 22 C.L.R. 556, at p. 588.
124. *Kerr v. Pelly* (1957) 97 C.L.R. 310 at p. 321.
125. P.H. Lane, Trade & Commerce Power: Constitution Sec. 51(i), the *Australian Law Journal*, Vol. 34, 1960, 99 at p. 108.

(i) Inseverable Activities

An activity, fact or thing may be so closely related to and essentially inter-state transaction that a law controlling the former must affect the latter. An alleged law under Sec. 51(i) could not seize upon these consequent or antecedent acts as its pivotal point if the inter-state movement was really burdened thereby. A law purporting to be enacted under Sec. 51(i) cannot burden or hinder the necessary instruments of inter-state movement if thereby an inter-state transaction is itself really obstructed.

(ii) Periferal Activities

An activity, fact or thing may not form part of the concept of trade and commerce among the states. It may be merely ancillary or relevant thereto. Now, the constitutional immunity of Sec. 92 extends to those activities, facts or things forming part of the notion 'trade, commerce and intercourse among the states'. On the other hand, the legislative grant in Sec. 51(i), extends beyond those activities, facts or things to activities, facts or things which are relevant or ancillary to the latter. Accordingly, a law made constitutionally under Sec. 51(i) may turn on an activity, fact or thing, which falls within the grant but outside the immunity.

4. THE INDIAN COMMERCE CLAUSE

A. The Historical Perspective

While making distribution of legislative powers between the Union and the constituent states on the topic of trade and commerce, our constitution-makers had before them not only the Australian and American constitutional models on this topic but also the rich storehouse of experience felt by America and to a lesser degree by Australia. Besides this, they had also before them the scheme of the Government of India Act, 1935, relating to freedom of trade, commerce, etc.

The Government of India Act, 1935, through its Sec. 297, provided—

"(1) No provincial Legislature or Government shall—

(a) by virtue of the Entry in the Provincial Legislative list relating to trade and commerce within the Province, or the entry in that list relating to the production, supply, and distribution of commodities, have power to pass any law or take any executive action prohibiting or restricting the entry into, or export from, the province of goods of any class or description;

(b) by virtue of anything in this Act, have power to impose any tax, cess, toll, or due which, as between goods manufactured or produced in the province and similar goods not so manufactured or produced, discriminates in favour of the former, or which, in the case of goods manufactured or produced outside the province discriminates between goods manufactured or produced in one locality and similar goods manufactured or produced in another locality.

(2) Any law passed in contravention of this Sec. shall, to the extent of the contravention, be invalid."

Cl. (a) of the above Sec. may be said to correspond to Art. 301 but the above provision was narrower than Art. 301 of the Constitution in the following respects—

The above Sec. was not concerned with the *intra-state* aspect of freedom of trade and commerce, nor with the freedom of 'intercourse'.

It did not constitute a limitation upon the Central Legislature or Executive but related to the province alone. The reason was that the Central legislature had no legislative power relating to trade and commerce. Item 27 of List II gave to the state legislature power with respect to 'trade and commerce within the province' and there was no Entry regarding inter-state trade and commerce in the Government of India Act, 1935. The limitation regarding the provincial legislature, too, was limited and not general, as in Art. 301. The limitation in Sec. 297 was directed only against those provincial laws, which were made under the entries relating to trade and commerce, or the production, supply and distribution of commodities, i.e., in exercise of the power conferred by item 27 or 29 of List II. If the provincial legislature could point out some other Entry giving them a power to legislate, e.g., item 31 relating to intoxicating liquor, Sec. 297 had no application.

While Cl. (a) of Sec. 297(1) prohibited a provincial legislature from using its 'Commerce' power, Cl. (b) prohibited it from exercising its taxing power so as to raise discriminatory barriers against the movement of goods from or to other provinces. Of these two limitations specified in Cl. (a) and (b) of Sec. 297(1), the first aspect was dealt with generally, in Art. 301-303, while taxation was specially dealt with in Art. 304(a). However, tax laws have also been included within the sweep of Art. 301, by judicial interpretation.

What transpired in the Constituent Assembly has nicely been summarised by Prof. Prasad[126] as under :

"*First*, the framers were conscious that they were conceding to the judiciary power to oversee the working of the provisions. But they were not sure as to how much power they should concedes. Thus, Pt. Thakurdas Bhargava wanted the adjective reasonable to qualify restrictions [127] in the present Art. 302 as well, which confers power on the Parliament to restrict the freedom in public interest. This was intended to enlarge the scope of judicial review. And Sri T.T. Krishnamachari opposed the proposal precisely for this reason. It appears that they did not think that the requirement of the restriction to be in the public interest itself invited judicial intervention.

126. Dr. Anirudh Prasad, Centre-State Relations in India, 1985 at p. 485.
127. Rao, The Framing of India'a Constitution—A Study, 1968 at p. 704.

Secondly, Pt. Thakurdas Bhargava wanted that reference 'By virtue of any Entry relating to trade and commerce in any of the List in the Seventh Schedule' in the present Art. 303 be omitted but this was negatived and Sri A.K. Ayyar said that the intention was not to impair every exercise of power which may trench on trade and commerce but may not bear directly upon trade and commerce.[128]

Thirdly, The assembly negatived an amendment proposed by Sri P.S. Deshmukh, which could take away the powers of a state to impose restriction on the freedom of trade of commerce within that state.[129]

Lastly, Change of 'freedom among the units' into freedom 'throughout the territory of India' is left totally unexplained in the entire discussion on the subject at the drafting stage and one is left to draw his own inferences from the relevant circumstances. It is to be seen what bearing these facts may have on the interpretation of Part XIII of the Constitution.[130]

But before we start a discussion of that, it would be useful, to highlight the general scheme of our Constitution in the matter of trade and commerce.

B. The Allocation of Powers in the Field of Trade and Commerce

With the experience of the working of the American and Australian commerce clauses present to their minds, the Indian draftsmen have kept steadily in view two important considerations in drafting the relevant provisions relating to the allocation of legislative powers between the Centre and the states in the field of trade and commerce. The *first* consideration is, that instead of allowing the component elements of the trade and commerce power to be vested in the Union and the units to be spelled out of a general clause like the commerce clause of the American Constitution read in conjunction with the Tenth Amendment to it, they have incorporated specific heads of power dealing with many of these component parts in the three legislative lists. The *second* consideration which the Indian designers of the Constitution have kept in view is to minimise, if not completely avoid, problems of divided jurisdiction which have confronted the older federations like the United States, Australia and Canada under the distribution of powers made in their constitutions by allotting important heads of power completely to the Union in India instead of restricting the reach of the Union legislative power to the foreign and inter-state phases of the topic sought to be regulated.[131]

Some of the important topics coming either directly within the field of trade, commerce and intercourse or indirectly connected by having close links with it specifically included in the Indian Union legislative list are

---

128. C.A.D., Vol. IX, pp. 1141-42.
129. *Id.* at pp. 1125-33.
130. Dr. Anirudh Prasad, Centre-State Relations in India, 1985 at p. 486.
131. Ramaswamy, Indian Constitutional Provisions Against Barriers to Trade and Commerce Examined in the Light of Australian and American Experience, *J.I.L.I.* (1959-60), Vol. 2, No. 1-4 at p. 328.

railways, highways, declared to be national highways, shipping and navigation, declared to be national waterways, airways, etc.[132] Among the important topics coming in the state trade and commerce field, which find specific mention in the state legislative list, examples are intoxicating liquor; communications; trade and commerce within the state; production, supply and distribution of goods, taxes on the consumption and sale of electricity, etc.[133] And among the more important of the subjects bearing on the trade and commerce arena specifically enumerated in the concurrent list the examples are contracts (including partnership, agency, contracts of carriage, not including contracts relating to agricultural land); economic and social planning.[134]

From these three lists, it is clear that the specific and detailed enumeration of important components of the trade and commerce topic in the three legislative lists necessarily reduces the role of the inter-state commerce power contained in Entry 42 of List I to one of minor importance. The reason being that the appropriate legislation of importance to the country as a whole can be passed by the Union Legislature drawing upon the authority conferred upon it by the relevant entries in the Union and Concurrent lists, while the state legislatures can deal with matters of local importance by invoking the aid of relevant entries in the State and Concurrent lists.

In India, power is given to regulate whole topics instead of restricting the reach of the Union power to the foreign and interstatal phases only of the topics assigned.[135] This avoids many of the problems, which arise from division of authority in the same legislative arena. In the technological age in which we live, where economic relationships are closely intertwined, it would in many cases be difficult, if not impossible, to draw a line between an inter-state and an intra-state activity and base an efficient and workable scheme of allocation of legislative powers between the Union and the states.

For the reasons stated as above, the "Indian Commerce Clause," unlike its American counterpart, is destined to play a relatively minor role in the economic life of India. It is humbly submitted that the constitution-makers have thought of it only as a residuary grant to buttress a wide and impressive category of specific powers given to the Union Legislature under Lists I and III of the Seventh Schedule for that legislature to regulate trade and commerce topics of national import.

132. Mentioned at various Entries of List I.
133. Mentioned at various Entries of List II.
134. Mentioned at various Entries of List III.
135. Ramaswamy, Indian Constitutional Provisions Against Barriers to Trade and Commerce Examined in the Light of Australian and American Experience, *J.I.L.I.* (1959-60), Vol. 2, No. 1-4 at p. 331.

C. Provisions of Part XIII of the Constitution Examined

The framers of the Indian Constitution were fully impressed with the fact that freedom for the free flow of trade and commerce throughout the country was a prime requisite for the successful working of any federal arrangement, which aims at the economic unity, and prosperity of the land. The guarantee for such freedom enshrined in Art. 301 of the Indian Constitution was evidently designed by the constitution-makers with that great objective in view. The group of Arts. contained in Arts. 302 to 305 is the Indian attempt to define and delimit the extent of and the manner in which Central and State legislative powers in the field of trade and commerce could be used to depart from the general freedom guaranteed in Art. 301, if such departure is required in the larger interests of the country.

Having relaxed the restriction in respect of Parliament under Art. 302, a restriction is put upon that relaxation by Art. 303(1) to the effect that Parliament shall not have the power to make any law giving any preference to one state over another or discriminating between one state and another by virtue of any Entry relating to trade and commerce in lists I and III of the Seventh Schedule. Art. 303(1), which places a ban on Parliament against the giving of preference to one state over another or of discriminating between one state and another, also provides that the same kind of ban should be placed upon the state legislature also legislating by virtue of any entry relating to trade and commerce in lists II and III of the Seventh Schedule. Art. 303(2) again carves out an exception to the restriction placed under Art. 303(1) on the powers of Parliament, by providing that nothing in Art. 303(1) shall prevent Parliament from making any law giving preference to one state over another or discriminating between one state and another, if it is necessary to do so for the purpose of dealing with a situation arising from scarcity of goods in any part of the territory of India. It is important to mention here that this exception applies only to Parliament and not to the state legislatures.

Art. 304 comprises two clauses and each clause operates as a proviso to Arts. 301 and 303. Cl. (1) of that Art. provides that the legislature of a state may "impose on goods imported from other states or the union territories any tax to which similar goods manufactured or produced in that state are subject, so, however, as not to discriminate between goods so imported and goods so manufactured or produced." This clause, therefore, permits the levy on goods imported from sister states or other union territories, any tax which similar goods manufactured or produced in that state are subject to under its taxing laws. In other words, goods imported from sister states are placed at par with similar goods manufactured or produced inside the state in regard to state taxation within the state allocated field, and not accorded any special immunity simply because they have been imported from other states. Patanjali Sastri, C.J., delivering the judgment of the Supreme Court in

State of Bombay v. United Motors,[136] has observed in regard to the provision contained in Art. 303(1) :

> "It will be seen that the principle of freedom of inter-state trade and commerce declared in Art. 301 is expressly subordinated to the state power of taxing goods imported from sister states, provided only no discrimination is made in favour of similar goods of local origin."

Clause (b) in Art. 304 provides that notwithstanding anything in Art. 301 or Art. 303, the legislature of a state may by law impose such reasonable restrictions on the freedom of trade, commerce or intercourse with or within that state as may be required in the public interest. There is a proviso to clause (b) that no Bill or amendment for the purposes of clause (b) shall be introduced or moved in the legislature of a state without the previous sanction of the President. This provision is the state analogue to the Union Parliament's authority defined by Art. 302. Leaving aside the pre-requisite of previous Presidential sanction for the validity of state legislation under clause (b) provided in the proviso to Art. 304(b), there are two important differences between Arts. 302 and 304(b), which require special mention. The first is that while the power of Parliament under Art. 302 is subject to the prohibition of preferences and discriminations decreed by Art. 303(1), unless Parliament makes the declaration contained in Art. 303(2), the state's power contained in Art. 304(b) is made expressly free from the prohibition contained in Art. 303(1), because the opening words of Art. 304 contains a *non-obstante* clause both to Art. 301 and Art. 303. By the removal of this prohibition on the exercise of state power it is possible for a state, theoretically speaking, to practice by its legislation, discriminations or preferences as between one state and another. But in practice this danger may not be serious because state legislation under Art. 304(b) has to obtain for its validity prior presidential sanction and such presidential scrutiny may obviate such undesirable features in such legislation. The second difference springs from the fact that while Parliament's power to impose restriction under Art. 302 upon freedom of commerce in the public interest is not subjected to the requirement of reasonableness, the power of states to impose restrictions on the freedom of commerce in the public interest under Art. 304(b) is subject to the condition that they should be reasonable.

(A) *The Applicability of the Protection of Article 301 to Intra-State Commerce Pure and Simple*

The question has been raised whether the protection afforded by Art. 301 extends only to inter-state trade and the intra-state ramifications of that inter-state trade only and not to intra-state trade pure and simple. It will be noticed that Art. 301, which uses broad language to the effect that "trade,

136. (1953) S.C.R. 1069.

commerce and intercourse throughout the territory of India shall be free" unlike Sec.· 92, which uses words of a restricted amplitude namely that "trade, commerce and intercourse among the states, shall be absolutely free," suggests that the protection of Art. 301 would extend to pure intra-state trade and commerce also, that is to say, domestic trade and commerce carried on between two points within a state's border. Venkatrama Aiyar in *Kutti Keya v. The State of Madras*[137] appears to think, that the trade and commerce protected by Art. 301 and 304(b) "would be not intra-state trade pure and simple but inter-state trade in its flow in the state."

The Supreme Court has also made observations in various cases, which, though they may not be strictly binding as *ratio decidendi*, nevertheless, suggest that pure intra-state commerce is also covered by the guarantee embodied in Art. 301. In *Saghir Ahmad v. State of Uttar Pradesh*,[138] Mukherjea, J. delivering the opinion of the Supreme Court observed that Art. 301 corresponds to Sec. 92 of the Australian Constitution and is even wider than the latter inasmuch as the Australian Constitution provides for the freedom of inter-state trade only. The Bombay and Travancore-Cochin High Courts have expressed similar views.[139]

(b) The Powers of Parliament to Interfere with Trade, Commerce and Intercourse

Assuming the widest possible operation of Art. 301 guaranteeing the freedom of trade, commerce and intercourse, it is obvious that many, if not most, of the legislative powers conferred on Parliament by Arts. 245 and 246, and set out in Lists I and III of the Seventh Schedule to the Constitution, could not be exercised so as to interfere with trade, commerce or intercourse.

But Art. 302 would permit any such interference so long as the restriction imposed was "required in the public interest". But this condition is not a burdensome one. Sir Ivor Jennings asked, "Who is going to decide whether it is required in the public interest?" He answered that though the matter is not free from doubt, it would seem that the task must fall upon the courts. Even if that answer be accepted it is submitted that the scope of judicial review under this Article is of comparatively little significance to the ambit of Parliament's powers.

There will be a strong presumption that Parliament's legislation is in the public interest,[140] and, whatever the theory with respect to 'onus' may be, that presumption will force the person challenging the validity of a law of Parliament under Art. 301 to show the court why it is not "required in the public interest". This will be a very difficult task except in some rare cases where the law is seen on its face to have been passed in some private interest; and in any case such a law is likely to offend some more fundamental

137. A.I.R. 1954, Mad. 621 at p. 633.

138. A.I.R. 1954 S.C. 728.

139. *Bapubhai Ratanchand v. State of Bombay*, 57 Bom. L.R. 892 at p. 901; *George v. State of Travancore-Cochin*, A.I.R. 1954 Traven-Cochin 34 at p. 36.

140. *Motilal & others v. U.P.*, A.I.R. 1951 All. 257 at pp. 300-301.

provision of the Constitution such as Art. 14. It is true that the Supreme Court has not yet passed upon this point, but closely analogous cases under other provisions of the Constitution support the view outlined above.

Art. 303, it is true, provides a further qualification of Parliament's powers; but two things limit the importance of that qualification. *Firstly*, if Parliament enacts a law, which makes a declaration satisfying terms of Art. 303, Clause (2), then the qualification is removed altogether. It should be noted that such a declaration appears to be conclusive and not open to question in the courts. *Secondly*, the qualification itself is a restricted one and is framed in such a way as to have limited practical effect if Parliament wishes to ignore the spirit, which inspired it. This is again for two reasons: *firstly*, because the qualification affects only those laws which are made "by virtue of any entry relating to trade and commerce in any of the Lists in the Seventh Schedule", and, *secondly*, because of the interpretation likely to be given to the words "preference to one state over another" and "discrimination between one state and another" in Art. 303, Cl. (2) in the light of Australian cases where the interpretation of similar words in Sec. 51(ii) and Sec. 99 of the Australian Constitution were in issue.[141]

So far as the first reason is concerned, it would seem clear that Parliament's power discovered in Entries 33 of List III and 41, 42, and 92-A of List I are the only ones affected. Any other powers may be used by Parliament to make laws interfering with trade, commerce or intercourse, which do give preferences or do discriminate between the States without offending Art. 303(2).

It can now be seen, therefore, that at the present time, despite Arts. 301 and 303, the powers of the Centre in India, unlike the position in the Australian Federation and more like that in the U.S.A., are wide enough to permit almost any interference with trade, commerce or intercourse whether by regulation, monopoly control or prohibition. And that is so not only with respect to inter-state trade, commerce and intercourse but also with respect to intra-state trade, commerce and intercourse in many of their aspects.

(c) The Powers of the States to Interfere with Trade, Commerce and Intercourse

Once again assuming the widest possible operation of Arts. 301, it is obvious that many, if not most of the legislative powers conferred upon the states by the Constitution could be exercised so as to interfere with trade, commerce or intercourse.

But in its context the clause is curious, to say the least, and it creates real difficulties when a coherent interpretation of all the Arts. of Part XIII of the Constitution are attempted. It is sufficient here to indicate the problem by pointing out that Art. 304(a) appears to assume two things, which may well be mutually inconsistent. The *first* thing is that Arts. 301 and 303 comprehend laws which impose taxes on goods-else why is the necessity for

141. *Elliott v. The Commonwealth* (1936) 54 C.L.R. 657; *W.R. Moran Pty. v. Dep. Federal Commissioner of Taxation* (1941) 63 C.L.R. 338 (P.C.).

the *non-obstante* clause at all ? The *second* thing assumed appears to be that the States have power to impose taxes on goods, which have been produced or manufactured in the taxing state for the power conferred by Art. 304(a), to tax imported goods is conditional on a non-discriminatory tax having been imposed on local goods. But the most common tax on goods is the sales tax. And, by any definition, a sale is an act of trade, or commerce.[142]

Further a tax, which chooses an act of trade, as the criterion for attracting the imposition of the tax is the most obvious example of an interference with the freedom of trade, which by Art. 301 is guaranteed "throughout the territory of India", i.e., in respect of intra-state as well as inter-state trade. How then can the state's power, conferred by Arts. 245 and 246 by reference to the Seventh Schedule, List II, Entry 54, be exercised validly unless the laws imposing the tax are saved either by Art. 304(b) or by Art. 305.

For the present it is enough to note that the ordinary and unambiguous meaning of Art. 304(a) is that, if the states have taxed or do tax goods of local origin then they are not barred by Art. 301 or 303 from imposing the same tax, non-discriminatory, on similar goods imported from other states, whatever theories about inter-state trade may develop or be accepted.[143]

Art. 304 Clause (b) reads :

"Notwithstanding anything in Art. 301 or Art. 303, the Legislature of a state may by law –

(b) impose such reasonable restrictions on the freedom of trade, commerce or intercourse with or within that state as may be required in the public interest.

Provided that no Bill or amendment for the purpose of clause (b) shall be introduced or moved in the Legislature of a state without the previous sanction of the President."

This is of course the state's power, which parallels the power of Parliament permitted by Art. 302. But, even ignoring the proviso for the moment, there are two important differences between this provision and Art. 302, which must be noted. The *first* is that the power of Parliament discovered in Art. 302 is subject to the prohibition of preference and discriminations contained in Art. 303(1) unless Parliament makes the declaration required by Art. 303(2). The state's power permitted by Art. 304(b), in contrast, is expressly free from the prohibition contained in Art. 303 and so may be used to work preferences or discriminations so long as they do not offend other applicable constitutional provisions. The *second* is that the restrictions which the states may impose on the freedom of trade, commerce and intercourse—as may be required in the public interest must

142. *R.M.D. Chamarbaugwala*, A.I.R. (1957) S.C. 699.

143. David P. Derham, Some Constitutional Problems Arising under Part XIII of The Indian Constitution, 1 *J.I.L.I.* 523.

"reasonable", whereas Parliament's power to impose restriction is not subjected to the requirement of reasonableness.

In *State of Bihar v. Bihar Chamber of Commerce,*[144] the Supreme Court, from the circumstances of the case, inferred that the requirement of prior consent of President was satisfied in the case of the impugned Act. The Court held that an additional levy of three percent by virtue of the impugned Act, on tobacco could not be said to be impeding the trade, commerce or intercourse in tobacco products directly and immediately or to any appreciable degree. In this connection, according to Court, it was not irrelevant to take into consideration the harmful nature of tobacco products. The addition of three percent was not considered either, as unreasonable restriction on the freedom of commerce or that it was not required in public interest. Thus, it was said that the requirement of Art. 304(b) had been satisfied and the challenge of the validity of the impugned Act, on the ground of violation of Art. 301 was held not to be tenable.

Making exception on the ground of public interest, our constitution-makers were quite conscious of the fact that public interest may require such freedom to be curbed or curtailed. This was so held by the Supreme Court in *State of Tamil Nadu v. Sanjeetha Trading Co.*[145] Assuming that Art. 301 does comprehend tax laws it is convenient to consider separately the requirement of reasonableness with respect to tax laws and to other laws, for tax laws present some problems peculiar to themselves.

D. Electronic Commerce and Indian Commerce Clause

Indian situation is slightly different. Indian Courts have not to labour much for bringing E-commerce within the ambit of "Commerce". It has not even to depend upon the "Commerce Clause" contained in the Constitution. The simple reason is that various Entries contained in List I of the Constitution give ample opportunity to the judiciary to bring E-commerce within the scope of "Commerce Clause." For example, Entry 31 of List I mentions "posts and telegraphs, telephones, wireless, broadcasting and *other like means of communication*." At Entry 41 of the Union List there is mention of "trade commerce with foreign countries, import and export trade and commerce" and Entry 42 speaks about "inter-state trade and commerce." Internet can safely be interpreted as being included in *other like means of communication* mentioned at Entry 31st of List I. Therefore, there is no reason why the *Parliament* can not *regulate E-commerce* and why the *Judiciary* can not *regulate Parliament* if it crosses the limits prescribed by the Indian Commerce Clause.

The information era is redefining the way we do business and indeed the way we communicate. Technology is shaping the way businessmen and consumers will interact in future. *Commerce has gone electronic.* Internet commerce or the electronic commerce (E-Commerce) is the exchange of

144. A.I.R. (1996) S.C. 2344.
145. A.I.R. (1993) S.C. 237.

goods or services for value on the Internet. It refers to the modern business use of computers for efficient delivery of goods or services. It is defined as transactions conducted over computer networks. It is online shopping. It is based on the electronic processing and transmission of data. *It refers to a wide array of commercial activities carried out through the use of computers, including online trading of goods and services, electronic funds transfers, online trading of financial instruments, electronic data exchanges between and within companies.* E-commerce carried out over the Internet are producing a wide variety of economic activities such as: sale or lease of goods; provision of services (e.g., banking, health care, technical advice); sale or licensing of software; downloading of entertainment (e.g., movies, books, CDs); provision for online information (e.g., Lexis/Nexis data base); provision for advertising; round the clock global trading in all manner of financial instruments, etc.

The electronic commercial activity can be: business-to-customers; business-to-business; inter-business; intra-business.

Business-to-customers refers to market place transactions where customers are directly involved, such as, in shopping, entertainment, health care, personal finance and home banking. *Business-to-business* commerce goes beyond the retail operations. It relate to business-to-business transactions like dealing with the partners, suppliers, bankers for maintaining accounts, inventory, ordering, invoicing, etc. *Inter-business* refers to companies tying of their internal operations together. They link up their operation with offices or across wide geographical areas to do business more efficiently. *Intra-business* electronic commerce makes available group conferring, through bulletin boards where a user can post a message that a group can see, or through interactive audio or video conferring.

Electronic transfer of commercial data from computer to computer using an agreed standard to structure the message [Electronic data interchange (EDI)] has resulted in cutting down on transaction costs and increasing efficiency. Earlier, business transaction such as purchase orders, invoices, acknowledgements, bill of lading and other shipping documents, etc., were to be recorded in writing on paper as a matter of record and communication. The business transactions were thus required to be evidenced by a "document", "writing" and "signature". The volume of the work involved used to consume time and cost expenses. Their movement depended upon postal system, which is inefficient and causes delay. Under the new regime, a properly transmitted message is deemed written and designated code within the message, signature.

5. ELECTRONIC COMMERCE: THE PROBLEM OF JURISDICTION IN A FEDERAL SET-UP

In the United States of America, the dormant commerce clause applies to non-profit organisations, the courts have routinely upheld solicitation statutes despite dormant commerce clause challenges. While the dormant commerce clause applies to the Internet, this does not imply that states have no authority to regulate Internet activities. The federal government has evinced some intent to regulate the Internet exclusively, this intent remains controversial and undecided. States should (and can) legally apply their solicitation (and other) existing laws to the Internet in order to protect their legitimate interests and those of their citizens.

A. Personal Jurisdiction

In order for a state to enforce its laws against online solicitors who do not register, it must be able to obtain jurisdiction over them.[146] While the courts' decisions in this area have not been completely consistent, in all likelihood a state would be able to obtain jurisdiction over online solicitors. Under *International Shoe v. Washington*,[147] for a forum to exercise jurisdiction over a defendant, the defendant must have "minimum contacts" with the forum state such that exercising jurisdiction would not offend "traditional notions of fair play and substantial justice."[148] The Court has elaborated on the personal jurisdiction inquiry further in recent years. Under the purposeful availment test first laid down in *Ashi Metal Industries v. Superior Court*,[149] a threshold inquiry in the determination of personal jurisdiction is whether the defendant has purposefully availed him or herself of the forum state.

Jurisdiction over a soliciting web site may be proper on other bases as well. As one court acknowledged having a web site (whether it raises money or not) may be analogous to having an ad in a national magazine.[150] The Court found that existing jurisdiction solely on this basis would violate the Due Process Clause of the Fourteenth Amendment and the standards set out in *International Shoe*. Nevertheless, the Court explicitly acknowledged that personal jurisdiction might be established in those instances where a defendant actually does business on the Internet or where the user can exchange information with the host web site. This analysis finds support in Supreme Court precedent, as the Court has found that regular circulation of a magazine in the forum state provides jurisdiction in the libel action based on the magazine's content. Similarly, because web sites are regularly available to residents in all states, courts could support personal jurisdiction based on web site accessibility.

B. Commerce Clause and the Internet: Emerging Conventional Wisdom

In United States, state regulation of charities and Internet transactions implicates the dormant commerce clause. However, courts have upheld the application of solicitation statutes in "real space" against dormant commerce

146. Goldsmith, Against Cyberanarchy, 65 U.Chi. L. Rev., 1216-17 (1998).
147. 326, U.S. 310 (1945).
148. *Id*. at p. 316.
149. 480 U.S. 102, at p. 108-09 (1987).
150. *Weber v. Jolly Hotels*, 977 F. Supp. 327, 333 (D.NJ. 1997) : (finding that advertising through a web site did not give the court personal jurisdiction).

clause challenges. Thus, although courts have yet to apply existing state regulations to the Internet, states should be able to regulate online solicitations without violating the dormant commerce clause.

(a) Dormant Commerce Clause and State Control over Charities in "Real Space"

The Supreme Court has found that both the 'Commerce Clause' and the 'Dormant Commerce Clause' apply to non-profit transactions.[151] Accordingly, courts frequently have applied laws that regulate commerce to non-profit organizations.

While state regulation of out-of-state solicitors does result in multiple jurisdictions regulating one charity, courts have found that solicitation ordinances themselves do not violate the 'Commerce Clause' for several reasons. *First,* they do not regulate inter-state commerce wholly outside the state. *Second,* they relate to legitimate government interests in protecting the public from fraud. *Third,* they are not unduly burdensome in relation to their putative local benefits. The Supreme Court has reaffirmed that while solicitation is protected under the First Amendment, states do have a legitimate interest in regulating charities to protect both the charities and the public from fraud as long as the regulation is narrowly tailored. Various solicitation statutes have survived 'Due Process' and 'First Amendment' challenges.

When a state applies its registration requirements to an out-of-state charity in the same way that it applies them to an in-state charity, this does not raise the discriminatory concerns that are a central feature of dormant commerce clause jurisprudence.[152] Given the facial neutrality of mist solicitation statutes, they should be analysed under the *Pike*[153] balancing test.[154] In the state-to-state context, given that not all states regulate fund raising, there may be a concern that this places an undue burden on charities in non-regulating states. However, the concerns are the same as those that exist in real space.

Moreover, charities that obtain the benefits from soliciting in a jurisdiction should have to bear the corresponding burdens. While we may want to encourage the growth of the Internet and online commerce, state regulation has not been preempted in this area and should not be.

This does not imply that no changes are necessary. Further uniformity in registration requirement and co-operation among states can ease the burden on charities while still protecting legitimate state interests.

151. *Camps Newfound/Owatonna Inc. v. Town of Harrison*, 520 U.S. 564, 584 (1997).

152. *Id.* at p. 581 ("Discrimination against out-of-state consumers is at the very core of activities forbidden by the dormant commerce clause").

153. *Pike v. Bruce Churchm Inc.*, 397 U.S. 137 (1970).

154. American Charities, 32 F Supp 2nd at 1315-17 (upholding a Solicitation Ordinance after applying the *Pike* test).

(b) State Laws and the Internet

At least thirteen states have passed new statutes regulating the Internet. These have mainly aimed at content on the Internet, although some have been tax bills. Some attorneys general, such as Mike Hatch of Minnesota, have actively pursued what they consider to be online violations of state law.[155]

However, while the Internet is a new medium, many existing state laws still apply. Advertising laws, both state and federal apply to ads on the Internet.[156] State common law principles, such as trespass to chattels, similarly apply to the Internet.[157]

In United States of America states should equally be able to apply their solicitation laws online. Protection of consumers from fraud, the aim of solicitation statutes, falls under state police powers and is a compelling local interest.[158] The possibilities for fraud are multiplied on the Internet—it is inexpensive to establish a web page and is easy to reach a vast audience. While state regulation of Internet solicitation implicates the dormant commerce clause, such regulation does not violate it and remains justified by important state interests.

C. Federal Assertion of Control over the Internet

Both Congress and the President have evinced intent to control certain aspects of the Internet on a national, rather than a state level. While this indicates that federal regulation may replace state regulatory efforts directed toward the Internet, this is by no means clear. For example, the Communications Decency Act of 1996 sought to regulate pornography on the Internet and to limit the access of minors to such information. Although the Supreme Court struck down provisions of the Act, that prohibited knowing transmittal of obscene, indecent, patently offensive,. or sexual images or descriptions to minors as violative of First Amendment free speech rights,[159] the Court did leave open the possibility of future Internet regulation.[160]

---

155. Burk, Federalism in Cyberspace, 28 Conn. L. Rev. (1996) at p. 1096.

156. David M. Eisenberg, Questions and Answers About Advertising on the Internet, 43 Prac. Law 79, 80 (July 1997).

157. 24 F Supp. 2nd 548, 549-51 (ED Va 1998).

158. Citizens for a Better Government, 444 U.S. at 636.

159. *Reno v. A.C.L.U.*, 521 U.S. 844, 859-79 (1997).

160. *Id.* at p. 863, n. 30 ("According to the District Judge, the Internet's characteristics and the rest of the District Court's findings 'lead to the conclusion the Congress may not regulate indecency on the Internet at all.' Because plaintiffs do not press this argument before this Court, we do not consider it. Plaintiffs also do not dispute that the Government generally has a compelling interest in protecting minors from 'indecent' and 'patently offensive' speech.")

Some courts have described the Internet as an instrument of inter-state commerce that should be subject to exclusive federal oversight.[161] In the past, other new technologies, which transcended geographical boundaries, have confronted the Court. The Court initially saw such technologies as "instruments" of commerce and struck down regulation by the states; however the Court later revised itself and upheld state regulation.[162] Further, other courts have applied existing state laws to the Internet. There is not currently exclusive federal control in this area, and it remains unclear what direction it will take.[163]

D. States' Jurisdiction and the Dormant Commerce Clause

Internet communication involves real people. The concerns that motivate regulation in real space are just as valid in cyber-space. Allowing the federal government to regulate Internet solicitations would expand the federal government's role in all charitable oversight, either through duplicating state efforts or through preempting state regulation. Duplication is administratively burdensome and unnecessary. Preemption is undesirable as the protection of consumers from fraud that motives solicitation laws is a state police power and is closer to the heart of state, rather than the federal government concerns.

(a) Arguments Against a Complete Lack of Public Control

Some American commentators have argued that the absence of traditional geographic boundaries in cyberspace indicates that it is impossible for states to apply territorially-based notions of the law to the Internet and that states should instead defer to self-regulation on-line.[164] However, the Internet still involves "people in real space in one jurisdiction communicating with people in real space in another jurisdiction."[165] There is a need for public regulation of the Internet in addition to private ordering.[166] Absent public ordering, private ordering may arise that is inefficient and not in the public interest.

---

161. *American Libraries Association v. Pataki*, 969 F Supp. 160, 182 (S.D.NY. 1997) ("The Internet, lide rail and highway traffic . . . requires a cohesive national scheme of regulation so that users are reasonably able to determine their obligations"); *ACLU v. Johnson*, 194 F3d 1149, 1162 (10th Cir. 1999) ("Certain types of commerce have been recognized as requiring national regulation . . . The Internet is surely such a medium").

162. James E. Gaylord, Note, State Regulatory Jurisdiction and the Internet: Letting the Dormant Commerce Clause Lie, 52 V and L. Rev. 1095, 1117-21 (1999) (describing the history of the Court's treatment of the telegraph).

163. Melissa G. Liazos, Can States Impose Registration on Online Charitable Solicitors?; The U. Chi. L. Rev. (2000), Vol. 67, 1379 at p.1398.

164. Johnson and Post, Law and Borders—The Rise of Law in Cyberspace, 48 Stan. L. Rev. 1367 (1996).

165. Goldsmith, The Internet and the Abiding Significance of Territorial Sovereignty, 5 Ind. J. Global Legal Studies 475 at p. 476 (1998).

166. Goldsmith, Against Cyberanarchy, 65 U. Chi. L. Rev. 1199 (1998) at pp. 1213-16

States' concerns about fraud being perpetrated against their citizens are no less legitimate in the Internet context than in real space. Such concerns may be even greater on-line given the low start-up costs and the broad audience that a solicitation may reach. Despite the difficulty of locating users geographically on the Internet, it is "feasible and constitutional" for the law to require the altering of the Internet's code to enable identification of users by various criteria,[167] which could include geographic locale.

(B) Arguments against Federal Control over On-Line Solicitation

Allowing federal regulation of Internet solicitations would likely mean expanding the overall federal role in the oversight of charities. Efforts in the past to expand the federal role in this area have proven unsuccessful.

Regulation of solicitation would require the federal government to register charitable solicitors, monitor their solicitations, and track down and punish violators. It would be duplicative and unnecessarily costly for both the state and federal government to do so. The interests in each case (protection of consumers from fraud) remain the same. Nothing would be added by federal regulation. Although there have been past (unsuccessful) recommendations for the federal government to regulate charitable solicitation, at least some of the conditions that prompted these recommendations have changed.[168]

It is also undesirable for federal regulation to preempt state regulation. It is a well-established principle that state police powers encompass the protection of citizens from fraud.[169] While the federal government can regulate inter-state commerce, and non-profit transactions fall under this power, state solicitation and registration statutes still pass the *Pike* balancing test. Thus, state interest in protecting against fraud can outweigh burdens on inter-state commerce.

While the federal government has evinced some intent to control the Internet on the national level, it has never set-up a national supervisory or regulatory agency. And, there are few who believe that another agency with additional resources is a sufficient cure for any social ill.

Some courts have found that the Internet is an instrument of inter-state commerce, and as such should be subject exclusively to federal control.[170] These cases have struck down new laws that were aimed specifically at the Internet. However, the courts have upheld the application of the *existing*

---

167. Lessig, The Law of the Horse : What Cyberlaw Might Teach, 113 Harv. L. Rev. 501, 506 (1999).

168. Commission on Private Philanthropy and Public Needs, Giving in America: Toward a Stronger Voluntary Sector 177 (Treasury Dept. 1975) ; Cited In The U. Chi. L. Rev. (2000) at p. 1400.

169. Don F. Vacarro, Validity and Application of Governmental Limitation on Permissible Amount or Proportion of Fundraising Expenses and Administrative Costs of Charitable Organisations, 15 A.L.R. 4th 1163 (1982).

170. *A.C.L.U. v. Johnson*, 194 F. 3d 1149, at p. 1160-63; *American Libraries Association v. Pataki*, 969 F. Supp. 160, 161 (S.D.NY. 1997).

state laws to the Internet. Arguments that the Internet is national in nature can just as easily be countered by arguments that the Internet is international in nature, and that the United States government should not be able to regulate it either. We are then left with a regime of no regulation, which is unacceptable. Given the broad definition of solicitation and the fact that solicitations can be deemed to occur where they are received, existing state laws can easily encompass Internet solicitation.

(c) Arguments for State Control over Electronic Commerce

The Internet may be an instrument of inter-state commerce, this does not imply that the federal government can or should preempt all state laws that might apply. In fact, "in no case activity characterized by a state interest become an activity devoid of state interest simply because it has been relocated to cyberspace."[171] We live under a federal government of limited powers : "The powers delegated by the Constitution to the federal government are few and defined. Those which remain in the state governments are numerous and indefinite."[172] Despite broad readings of the Commerce Clause power in the past, the Court has recently indicated that in some instances Congress may go too far.[173] While there are concerns that state regulation of Internet solicitation (and Internet communications in general) may lead to overlapping and thus burdensome regulation, "we already live in a world of multiple, overlapping contradictory, and often times contested sovereignties."[174] While the Internet may complicate this, we already deal with the problem in real space and can do so in cyberspace.

One of the principle concerns with the Internet is that entities cannot limit where their cyber-information is accessed, and thus cannot array their conduct in order to avoid regulation. However, on-line solicitors know (or hope) that they will obtain the benefits of raising money in any jurisdiction. Correspondingly, they know that there are burdens that accompany solicitation, given that almost all states require registration. If an organisation obtains the benefits of contacts with residents of the forum state, then it should have to bear the burdens as well.[175] State regulation can be seen as a cost of doing business and obtaining benefits from the forum state, as well as a driving force behind the development of filtering technology.[176] Further, Internet communications are transmitted via telephone and cable lines. States can regulate solicitations that reach their state via these means.

171. Steven R. Salbu, Who Should Govern The Internet? : Monitoring and Supporting a New Frontier, 11 Harv. L.J. & Tech. 429, 451 (1998).
172. *United State v. Lopez*, 514 U.S. 549, 552 (1995).
173. *Id.* at p. 552.
174. Keith Aoki, Considering Multiple And Overlapping Sovereignties : Liberalism, Libertarianism, National Sovereignty, "Global" Intellectual Property, And The Internet, 5 Ind. J. Global Legal Studies, 443 (1998).
175. Goldsmith, The Internet And The Abiding Significance Of Territorial Sovereignty, 5 Ind. J. Global Legal Studies, 475 at p. 485.
176. *Id.* at pp. 489-90.

Professor Steven Salbu has argued that the characteristics of the Internet only require uniform (federal) control if they meet the following three criteria: (i) technological considerations requiring the compatibility of technologies; (ii) the likelihood of serious Internet encumbrance through fractionalised regulation; and (iii) the need for unified federal technologies to support federal policy goals and programmes.[177] State regulation of online solicitation would have no impact on the compatibility of technologies. Further, regulation is not likely to be fractionalised, as states are already quite uniform in their charitable solicitation and reporting requirements. Finally, while the federal government collects information on charities for the purpose of tax exemption, there is no federal programme as such implicated here. The federal policies of encouraging charitable deductions, ensuring that only legitimate charities receive exemptions and requiring financial information to facilitate this will not be implicated by state regulation here. State regulation meets two further standards articulated by Salbu: Internet technology leaves traditional state concerns (such as fraud) intact, and abandonment of local police power could create a serious enforcement gap.[178] In order to facilitate state regulation, states can develop model codes relating to the Internet.[179] The Model Solicitation Act, already in existence could aid such efforts. However, no such problem should arise in India as there is detailed scheme for distribution of powers between Centre and states through three Lists.

---

177. Salbu, Who Should Govern The Internet? : Monitoring And Supporting a New Frontier, 11, Harv. J.L. & Tech 429 at pp. 465-70.
178. *Id.* at pp. 470-71.
179. *Id.* at p. 478.

3

New Dimensions of 'Commerce' Today

I. THE AMBIT OF COMMERCE

A. The English Concept of Commerce

In Britain, "Commerce" means all gainful activities intended for the market place, as distinguished from those undertaken solely for personal or home use, such as growing food for one's family. According to Smith, "Commerce" means producing a surplus of either natural or manufactured goods to sell in the market. Hamilton & Adair make a distinction between "Commercial" articles manufactured for sale in the market and those things made for individual and home consumption. Thus, "Commerce", for a British, includes: (i) the buying and selling of goods;[1] (ii) their procurement or production through agriculture, fishing, forestry, mining or manufacturing;[2] and (iii) related services such as transportation, banking, and insurance.

In his *Plan of the English Commerce*, Daniel Defog described "Commerce" as a general term that contains several branches: the "Making of goods" through 'production' and 'manufacture', "Labouring" (including the work of 'Miners, Diggers, Fishers, . . . Artists, Mechanics and Craftsmen') and "Employment" generally; "Dealing" (buying and selling of goods by "wholesome," "retail", or "barter"); "Banking" (i.e., monetary exchange); "Shipping and Navigation;" and "Consumption of . . . Goods." Other writers such as Adam Smith and Malachy Postlethwayt shared this broad understanding, which also can be found in contemporaneous newspaper articles, pamphlets, and other common sources. "Commerce" was

1. This is the primary definition of "Commerce" contained in virtually every dictionary of English, both old and modern, e.g. Oxford English Dictionary.
2. Hovenkamp, Judicial Restraint and Constitutional Federalism : The Supreme Court's *Lopez* and *Seminole Tribe* Decisions, 96 Colum. L. Rev. 2230.

considered a more comprehensive and elegant word than "traffic" or "trade."[3]

B. The American Understanding

To be sure, "Commerce" sometimes conveyed a narrower sense, referring solely to the buying and selling of goods. It is unlikely that the Constitution incorporated this limited definition, however, because contemporary writers invariably placed the phrase "to regulate" before "Commerce" to signify that the latter word should be given its usual broader scope. Thus, "to regulate commerce" had a specific, standard meaning, to enact rules to govern all gainful activities, including subjects as diverse as *trade, navigation, agriculture, manufacturing, industry, mining, fisheries, building, employment, wages, prices, banking, insurance, accounting, bankruptcy, business associations, securities, and bills of exchange.* Such mercantilist laws furthered the public good by balancing all competing domestic economic interests and by complementing foreign policy, as economic and military warfare went hand in hand. Despite the growing popularity of Adam Smith's 1776 attack on mercantilism and government intervention in the economy, significant commercial regulation endured until the early to mid-1800s.

It should be noted that "Commerce" had a secondary meaning also, i.e. all human interactions ("Intercourse," in eighteenth-century parlance). When used in the context of government regulations, however, "Commerce" included only human activities geared towards the market place.[4]

(a) The Traditional View

Not surprisingly, England's Colonists adopted the prevailing usage of "Commerce" as encompassing not merely the buying and selling of goods, but also antecedent production, labour and wage transactions, and related business services like insurance. Leading Federalists, including James Wilson and Alexander Hamilton shared this understanding.

Wilson used "Commerce" to describe all gainful activities. For example, in asserting the "superiority of separate over common property," he noted the disastrous experiments in the Plymouth Colony, in which "all commerce was carried on in one joint stock," and in Virginia, which adopted a similar system. Wilson used "Commerce" to mean all economic activities carried on in these colonies, including agriculture.[5]

Alexander Hamilton described manufacturies as a species of commerce and banks as engaging in "Commerce."[6] Indeed, some colonists employed the word "Commerce" to denote all transactions involving money,

3. Grant S. Nelson & Robert, J. Pushaw, Jr., Rethinking the Commerce Clause: Applying First Principle to Uphold Federal Commercial Regulations but Preserve State Control Over Social Issues, Iowa Law Review, Vol. 85, No. 1, 1999, at p. 16.

4. *Id.* at p. 19.

5. Cited in Iowa Law Review (1999) at p. 19.

6. *Id.* at p. 20.

including the buying and selling of real property. In *An Address of the House of Delegates of Marylands to their Constituents,*[7] the term "Commerce" was used to refer to the buying and selling of land and houses and virtually all other economic activities within the state, specifically including manufacturing, farming and employment.

(i) Marshall's Organic Concept of Commerce

Marshall, in Justice Frankfurter's phrase, had an organic concept of commerce. The test, in his conception, was not mere movement across state lines, but whether the particular "Commerce" affected more than one state. The genius and character of the whole government, he said, seem to be, that its action is to be applied to all the external concerns of the nation, and to those internal concerns which affect the states generally. But not to those, which are completely within a particular state, which do affect other states, and with which it is not necessary to interfere, for the purpose of executing some of the general powers of the government. Only the completely internal commerce of a state, under the Marshall notion, could be considered as excluded from the reach of the "Commerce Clause."[8]

In *Gibbons v. Ogden,*[9] the counsel for the appelle had argued that "the correct definition of "Commerce" is, the transportation and sale of commodities." The transportation of passengers, he concluded, was not included in the term, which was limited to "the exchange of one thing for another; the interchange of commodities; trade or traffic." Daniel Webster, who led the arguments for Gibbon, denied that the commerce clause was thus limited. Webster urged that, "nothing was more complex than commerce; and in such an age as this, no words embraced a wider field than commercial regulation. Almost all the business and intercourse of life may be connected, incidentally, more or less, with commercial regulations."

Chief Justice Marshall, in his opinion, adopted the wide definition of "Commerce" urged by Webster. In his view, commerce could not be restricted "to traffic, to buying and selling, or the interchange of commodities." "Commerce," instead, covered all intercourse—a conception extensive enough to include within its scope all business dealings. "Commerce", said Marshall, "undoubtedly, is traffic, but it is something more; it is intercourse. It describes the commercial intercourse between nations, and parts of nations, in all its branches." Very clearly, navigation was comprehended in the Marshall's definition.

The mind can scarcely conceive a system for regulating "Commerce" between nations, which shall exclude all laws concerning navigation, which shall be silent on the admission of the vessels of one nation into the ports of the other, and be confined to prescribing rules for the conduct of individuals,

---

7. Jan. 25, 1787.
8. Bernard Swartz, A Commentary On The Constitution of The United States, Ed. (1977) at p. 183.
9. (1824) 9 Wheat. 1.

in the actual employment of buying and selling, or of barter.[10] According to Marshall, then, "Commerce" not only includes traffic (buying and selling) but also intercourse (transportation). And transportation would include navigation.

(ii) Other Dimensions of Commerce

Since Marshall's day the idea that "Commerce" includes transportation has never been questioned. At first the Supreme Court was inclined to hold that only goods and not persons could be the subjects of "Commerce", though they were being transported. This view found favour with the Supreme Court in *Mayor, etc. of The City of New York v. Miln,*[11] where Mr. Justice Barbour speaking for the Court definitely stated that persons could not be the subject of "Commerce". But this position was soon given up. Now *The Passenger Case*[12], *Handerson v. Wickham*[13] and *The Head Money Cases*[14], establish that transportation of persons also constitutes "Commerce". The object transported need not even be a tangible thing. In *Pensacola Telegraph Co. v. Western Union Telegraph Co.,*[15] the transmission of messages by telegraph was held to be "Commerce". The Supreme Court has, in *Public Utilities Com. v. Attleboro Steam & E. Co.*[16], held the transmission of an electric current as "Commerce." Similarly in *State Tax Commission v. Inter-state National Gas Co.*[17] the transportation of gas was described as "Commerce".

So, it is clear that, in the view of the Supreme Court, transportation whether it involves goods, persons, electric current, gas or merely information or signals, constitute "Commerce." And such transportation or transmission if it transcends state lines becomes inter-state "Commerce."

In *Covington and Cincinnati Bridge Co. v. Kentucky*[18] the Supreme Court referring to a bridge between two states observed:

> " . . . The thousands of people who daily pass and repass over this bridge may be truly said to be engaged in "Commerce" as if they were shipping cargoes of merchandise from New York to Liverpool."

This dictum of the Supreme Court would mean that a person who walks across the boundary line between two states is engaged in inter-state "Commerce." Consistency would demand that a citizen engaged in the very

---

10. *Gibbons v. Ogden* (1824) 9 Wheat. 1, at pp. 189-90.
11. (1837) 11 Pet. 102, at p. 136.
12. (1849) How. 283.
13. (1876) 92 U. S. 259.
14. (1884) 112 U. S. 580.
15. (1877) 96 U. S. 1.
16. (1927) 273 U. S. 83.
17. (1931) 284 U. S. 41.
18. (1894) 154 U. S. 204, at pp. 218-19.

prosaic act of walking across a street in his hometown in a state is engaged in intra-state "Commerce." Such a notion would seem very surprising to many people who are accustomed to associate "Commerce" with the idea of traffic in merchandise. But none the less it would be consistent with the view of the Supreme Court that an act of transportation is in itself "Commerce."

(b) The Restrictive Definition

(i) The Negative Approach

The Supreme Court has held that while distribution of journals constitute "Commerce", the making of contracts for advertising in journals is not "Commerce". It was so ruled by the Supreme Court in *Blumenstock Bros. Ad, Agency v. Curtis Publishing Co.*[19]

Mr. Justice Field in delivering the opinion of the Court in *Paul v. Virginia*[20] observed that the insurance was not "Commerce." Mr. Justice McKenna who delivered the opinion of the Supreme Court in *New York L. Ins. Co. v. Deer Lodge Country*[21] made an elaborate example of the contentions put forward and earlier dicta of the Court upon the subject and reaffirmed the view that insurance was not "Commerce." In the same way Court held in *Crescent Oil Co. v. State of Mississippi*[22] that manufacturing is not included in the ambit of "Commerce." In *Oliver Mining Co. v. Lord*[23], mining was not held to constitute "Commerce".

The Court interpreted "Commerce" as distinct from prior productive activities. In *United States v. E.C. Knight Co.*,[24] it ruled that the Sherman Act would be unconstitutional if construed to cover the purchase of four competing sugar refineries by a multi-state corporation, which gave it control over ninety-eight percent of that industry. Chief Justice Fuller reasoned that sugar refining involved "manufacturing," not "Commerce". It succeeds to manufacture, and is not a part of it.

Moreover, distinguishing federal commerce authority from the states' police power was held to be essential to the preservation of the autonomy of the States as required by U.S.A. dual form of government. The Court warned of the "far-reaching" effects of allowing Congress to act "whenever inter-state . . . 'Commerce' may be ultimately affected." Thus, Congress could regulate only contracts to buy, sell, or exchange goods to be transported among the states; the transit and its instrumentalities; and articles traded for purposes of such transportation.[25] The states, on the other hand, had police

19. (1920) 252 U. S. 436.
20. (1868) 8 Wall. 168.
21. (1913) 231 U. S. 495.
22. (1921) 257 U. S. 129.
23. (1923) 262 U. S. 172.
24. 156 U.S. 1 (1895).
25. *E.C. Knight*, 156 U.S. at p. 13; *Addyston Pipe & Steel Co. v. U.S.*, 175 U.S. 211, 226-48 (1899); *Northern Securities Co. v. U.S.* 197 (1904).

power over manufacturing monopolies, even where the product at issue was made for export.[26] Finally, the Court suggested that its holding would apply to all productive activities intended to be the subject of future commercial transactions—including agriculture, mining, and fisheries—as attempts to control prices and wages.

Following *E.C. Knight*, *Hammer v. Dagenhart*[27] the Child Labor Act was invalidated. This Act prohibited the inter-state shipment of goods made at a factory by children. The Court stressed that the "Commerce Clause" did not give Congress "authority to control the states in their exercise of the police power over local trade and manufacture" (including employment matters), even if the articles produced were later shipped in inter-state commerce.[28] Striking down the statute was therefore necessary to preserve the powers reserved to the states.[29]

Finally, *Carter v. Carter Coal Co.*[30] reviewed the Bituminous Coal Conservation Act of 1935 which, based upon detailed findings that coal production directly affected inter-state "Commerce," established local boards to determine coal prices and authorized collective bargaining over employees' wages and hours.[31] Initially, the Court declared:

> "Congress is powerless to regulate anything which is not "Commerce" . . . As used in the Constitution, the word "Commerce" is the equivalent of the phrase "Intercourse for the purpose of trade," and includes transportation, purchase, sale, and exchange of commodities between the citizens of the different states. And the power to regulate commerce embraces the instrument by which "Commerce" is carried on."[32]

Accordingly, the Court invalidated the Act on the ground that mining, like all productive activities, preceded "Commerce" and was not itself "Commerce."[33] Similarly, employment terms and conditions were "intercourse for the purposes of production, not of trade" and thus "purely local."[34]

The Court emphasized that the structure of the Constitution, its drafting and ratification history, and the Tenth Amendment all made clear that the federal government was limited to its enumerated powers.[35] Hence,

---

26. *E. C. Knight*, 156 U.S. at pp. 11-13.
27. 247 U.S. 251 (1918).
28. *Id.* at pp. 272-74.
29. *Id.* at pp. 274-76.
30. 298 U.S. 238 (1936).
31. *Id.* at pp. 278-84.
32. *Id.* at pp. 297-98.
33. *Id.* at pp. 299-304.
34. *Id.* at pp. 303-04.
35. *Carter*, 298 U.S. at pp. 290-96.

Congress could not enact laws simply to promote the general welfare, or else the states eventually would be reduced "to little more than geographical sub-divisions of the national domain."[36] Of special interest here, the Court noted that inconsistencies in important state law areas, such as family relations and negotiable instruments, were being addressed through state-by-state adoption of statutes proposed by the Commission on Uniform State Laws precisely because Congress lacked the power to do so, despite the fact that federal legislation would be more efficient.[37] Thus, the Court's central proposition is that, if a subject is not "Commerce," Congress cannot regulate it, regardless of its impact on inter-state "Commerce."

(ii) Limiting "Commerce" to the Sale of Goods

Justice Thomas correctly argued in *Lopez* that the Court should discard the "substantial effects" analysis and adopt a rule of decision derived from the language and history of the "Commerce Clause."[38] Undoubtedly, his proposed test that Congress can regulate only the sale and transportation of goods between states is not tenable, despite heroic attempts by Richard Epstein and Raoul Berger to defend it.

Most importantly, the Framers and Ratifiers of the Constitution likely did not intend to so restrict "Commerce," but rather sought to include all market-based activities such as production, banking, and insurance. Thomas, Berger, and Epstein, JJ. do not even cite—much less refute—the massive evidence of this broader meaning. Moreover, even if the original understanding was as confined as Thomas, J. and other scholars claim, it could not possibly govern the modern, nationally integrated economy. Finally, adopting this approach would require invalidating nearly every law enacted under the "Commerce Clause" in America, which would be unthinkable.

(c) Recent Trend: The Lopez Counter-revolution

The above is an account of what was not considered as "Commerce" in the early age but at present the position has gradually rolled on and what was not being considered as 'Commerce' is now being brought within the comprehension of 'Commerce'. The whole position may be summarised as under—

First and most obviously, "Commerce" include buying and selling goods. The most important aspect of such regulation is controlling imports and exports.

Second, the core meaning of "Commerce" includes commercial transportation. For instance, the framers expected that Congress would pass Navigation Acts governing both foreign shipping and that between

36. *Id.* at pp. 295-96.
37. *Id.* at pp. 292-93.
38. *Lopez*, 514 U.S., at p. 585-602 (Thomas, J. concurring).

American ports. Such laws would encourage active American trade as well as manufacturing (especially ship-building).

Third, it is unclear whether the "Commerce Clause," as originally conceived, extended to internal improvements such as harbors, land and marine highways, and bridges. On the one hand, if the clause authorised Congress to create corporations, a main reason to do so would be to create and improve infrastructure, thereby facilitating transportation, trade, manufacturing, agriculture, and communication. On the other hand, the delegates specifically rejected the proposal empowering Congress to charter corporations to build canals, which indicates that they intended to leave that specific power to the states. Moreover, during ratification many expressed the understanding that state control extended to roads, bridges, ferries, and the like.

To the extent that internal improvements concerned facilities located wholly within a state that had no appreciable impact on external "Commerce," Congress had no role to play. With regard to improvements that did have such an effect, Congress arguably had such a power, and indeed asserted it fairly early. It is debatable, however, whether the Framers and Ratifiers of the Constitution intended that result.

Fourth, regulations of "Commerce" encompassed market-based productive activities such as staple-crop farming, large-scale fisheries, and manufacturing.[39] The supporters of the Constitution repeatedly argued that Congress could best balance the inter-dependent interests of manufacturers and farmers, especially as they affected the relationship between the Northern and Southern economies. Thus, federal officials would regulate "Commerce" to account for the related interests of merchants, manufacturers, artisans, and farmers.[40]

Finally, no one suggested that "Commerce," as used in Article 1, signified "all human interaction."[41] Indeed, such a comprehensive definition would have rendered any other enumeration of powers unnecessary and contradicted the Federalists' repeated assurances during the Convention and Ratification that Congress could not act solely to promote the general welfare, it could regulate "Commerce" to further not only market activity but also other social or political goals.

In *United States v. Lopez*,[42] the Court invalidated Sec. 922 (q) of the Gun-Free School Zones Act ("GFSZA"), which made it a crime to possess a firearm in a school area. In his majority opinion, Chief Justice Rehnquist,

39. Joseph Story, Commentaries on the Constitution of the United States, 1078-84, 1089 (1833) (demonstating the longstanding understanding in England and America that the power "to regulate commerce" included protecting and encouraging manufacturing, agriculture, fisheries and navigation) ; Robert L. Stern, That Commerce which Concerns More States than One, 47 Harv. L. Rev. 1335, 1341 (1934).

40. The Federalists No. 35, at 216-21 (Hamilton).

41. Charles E. Carpenter & Robert Charles Mardian, What is Commerce , 22 S. Cal. L. Rev. 398, 398- 400 (1949).

42. 514 U.S. 549 (1995).

joined by Justice Scalia, emphasised that even modern cases had "confirmed that the "Commerce power" is subject to outer limits."[43] The Court held that the GFZSA did not fall within the first two "Commerce Clause" categories—"channels" or "instrumentalities"[44] and could not be sustained under the third prong because no "rational basis existed for concluding that the regulated activity sufficiently affected inter-state "Commerce."[45]

The Chief Justice stressed that gun possession in a school zone was not inter-state economic activity that might, through repetition elsewhere, have a substantial effect on inter-state "Commerce." The Court declared :

> "Section 922 (q) is a criminal statute that by its terms has nothing to do with "Commerce" or any sort of economic enterprise, however broadly one might define those terms. Section 922 (q) is not an essential part of a larger regulation of economic activity, in which the regulatory scheme could be undercut unless the intra-state activities were regulated. It cannot, therefore, be sustained under our cases upholding regulations of activities that arise out of or are connected with a commercial transaction, which viewed in the aggregate, substantially affects inter-state "Commerce."

The Court conceded that "a determination whether an intra-state activity is "commercial" or "non-commercial" may in some cases result in legal uncertainty,"[46] but asserted that such grey areas had given the judiciary longstanding role of enforcing the limits of Congress's enumerated powers.[47]

In a separate concurrence, Justice Thomas urged his colleagues to reconsider 'substantial effects' test with an eye toward construing a standard that reflects the text and history of the "Commerce clause" without totally rejecting more recent "Commerce Clause" jurisprudence."[48] Justice Thomas noted that eighteenth-century dictionaries, as well as statements made during the framing and ratification eras, indicated that the meaning of the term "Commerce" was limited to buying, selling, and transporting goods.[49] Moreover, he argued that if the framers had intended for Congress to regulate any activity that "substantially affected" inter-state "Commerce," their careful enumeration of powers in Article 1 would be inexplicable.[50] Indeed, during its first century-and-a-half the Court rejected the notion that matters such as internal state business practices, production of goods, crime,

43. *Lopez*, 514 U.S. at pp. 556-57.
44. *Id.* at pp. 558-59.
45. *Id.* at p. 557.
46. *Id.* at p. 566.
47. *Id.* at p. 566 (citing *McCulloch*, *Gibbons*, and *Murphy* for this proposition).
48. *Lopez*, 514 U.S. at p. 585 (Thomas, J. concurring).
49. *Id.* at 585-87 (Thomas, J., concurring).
50. *Id.* at p. 588-589 (Thomas, J. concurring).

and police powers could be regulated federally simply because they had a significant effect on inter-state commerce; rather, the New Deal Court invented this test and manipulated *Gibbons* and its progeny to disguise this innovation.[51] Finally, Justice Thomas asserted that the "substantial effects" test effectively granted Congress a national police power.[52]

Justice Breyer and three colleagues dissented on the ground that Congress had a rational basis for its conclusion that banning gun possession near schools promoted quality education, which in turn greatly influenced the national economy and thus significantly affected inter-state commerce.[53] He denied that upholding the statute would destroy federalism by enabling Congress to regulate any activity related to economic productivity (such as family matters), although he did not identify any specific limits on the "Commerce authority."

Justice Breyer argued that the majority decision conflicted with the many cases upholding federal statutes that rested on activities that had less significant connections to "Commerce" than school violence.[54] He also rejected the proffered distinction between "commercial" and "non-commercial" transactions as "failing to heed the Court's earlier warning not to turn 'questions of the power of Congress' upon 'formulas' that would give 'controlling force to nomenclature and foreclose consideration of the actual effects of the activity in question upon inter-state commerce'."[55] Thus, after 1937 the Court focussed not on the economic nature of activity regulated, but rather on the overall impact of the activity on inter-state "Commerce."[56] Justice Breyer emphasised that the decision in *Lopez* created uncertainty as to the validity of many statutes enacted under the "Commerce Clause" and as to the ability of Congress to address other threats to the nation's well-being.[57]

Indeed, *Lopez* has triggered an avalanche of litigation in the lower federal courts, which have struggled to ascertain its true meaning and scope. Moreover, Congress has continued to churn out laws that rest upon a remarkably broad reading of the "Commerce Clause." Reorganising the need to clarify *Lopez*, the Court recently granted *certiorari* to review one of the most controversial of these statutes, the Violence Against Women Act.[58]

The Court pointed out that "As one would expect, the term "Commerce" was used in contradiction to productive activities such as manufacturing and agriculture. Alexander Hamilton, for example, repeatedly treated "Commerce," "agriculture," and "manufacturing" of

---

51. *Id.* at pp. 593-99 (Thomas, J., concurring).
52. *Id.* at pp. 599-602 (Thomas, J., concurring).
53. *Id.* at pp. 615-44 (Breyer, J., dissenting).
54. *Id.* at pp. 625-27 (Breyer, J. dissenting), citing *Perez v. United States*, 402 U.S. 146 (1971).
55. *Id.* at pp. 627-28 (Breyer, J., dissenting)., citing *Wickard v. Filburn*, 317 U.S. 111, 120 (1942).
56. *Id.* at p. 628.
57. *Id.* at pp. 630-31 (Breyer, J. dissenting).
58. *Brzonkala v. Virginia Polytechnic Inst.*, 169 F. 3d 820 (4th Cir. 1999).

three separate endeavors." Thomas, J. (concurring) in the same case[59] says that admittedly, Hamilton and others sometimes included "agriculture, commerce, and manufactures" in the same sentence, which would have been superfluous if "Commerce" included prior productive activities.

In sum, the original conception of "Commerce" certainly included in buying, selling and transporting of goods; most likely extended to antecedent productive activities; probably reached the creation of corporation; and possibly encompassed internal improvements.

C. The Canadian Perspective

In Canada, in the beginning there was very thin line of distinction, rather no line of distinction, between "Trade and Commerce." Henry, J. in *Citizen's Insurance Co. v. Parson*[60] explains that "Trade" means the act or business of exchanging commodities by barter, or the business of buying and selling for money. The Learned Justice clarifies that "Commerce" is only another term for the same thing. Delivering dissenting judgment Taschereau, J. after comparision with American situation makes it clear that whilst in the United States Constitution, only the word "Commerce" is used; ours has the words "Trade and Commerce." Some law dictionaries give the word "Trade" as meaning "Internal Commerce," whilst the word "Commerce" would refer to "Foreign intercourse." But, according to the learned Justice, this appears to be a fanciful distinction, not recognised either in common parlance or in legal language. In this connection he says that :

> "Every word of the Act must have its due force and appropriate meaning, and the Imperial Parliament, which, no doubt, whilst creating a federal union among its North American possessions, had before its eyes the Constitution of the United States, must have intended by adding this word "Trade" to the word "Commerce" to give to our federal authority supreme power, not only over the "Commerce," internal as well as external. Of course, we are not called upon to give a general definition of this word "Trade" as used in the Act. In the interpretation of the Constitution, general definitions are to be avoided."

"Marketing" is definitely a part of the "Commerce". The term has been explained by the Canadian Supreme Court, in *re The Farm Products Marketing Act R.S.O. 1950, C. 131 as Amended*[61], as meaning buying, and offering for sale and includes advertising, assembling, financing, packing and shipping for sale or storage and transporting in any manner by any person.

There is a singular dearth of definition of "Trade" or "Commerce" in the Privy Council's decisions, perhaps because that tribunal assumed or

---

59. *United States v. Lopez* (1995) 514 U. S. SCR 131 L. Ed. 2d 626 at p. 653.
60. (1881), 7 App. Cas. 96.
61. (1957) S.C.R. 198, 7 D.L.R. (2d) 257.

came to a considered conclusion that the problems in the area lay not so much in the words used to define the power granted but rather in the feasibility of local or national control of economic activities which belonged as much to the Provinces under Sec. 92(13)(16) of the B.N.A. Act as to the Dominion under Sec. 91(2). *In re Sections 4 and 70 of the Canadian Insurance Act, 1910,*[62] Duff, J. asserted that Sec. 91(2) "does not embrace the regulation of occupations as such", and he "[did] not think that the various kinds of business which are comprehended under the term 'insurance' can be said to be part of the trade and commerce of the country". Anglin, J. was doubtful that the business of insurance could ever be spoken of as a "Trade," and this doubt was, for him, removed by the association of "Trade" with "Commerce" in Sec. 91(2), which made it clear that "Trade" did not cover the business of "insurance". No advertence was made or consideration given to insurance as "Commerce", not even by the dissenting Judges (Fitzpatrick, C.J.C. and Davies, J.), both of whom were of opinion that insurance was a "Trade". In the *Local Prohibition case*[63], Lord Watson referred to the fact that in the *Parson's case*[64], insurance was admitted to be a "Trade." In the *Insurance Reference case*[65], the question whether insurance was a trade for purposes of Sec. 91(2) was lost in a generalised assertion that federal power was unequal to the regulation by licencing of particular trades carried on in the provinces. The matter has remained in this state, qualified only by recent re-examinations of the "Trade and Commerce" power in cases, which were concerned with marketing controls.

True, there have been some utterances such as those of Duff, C.J.C. in *re Alberta Statutes*[66], which suggest consciousness of the "Commerce" side of Sec. 91(2), but the dominant feature of judicial consideration of Sec. 91(2) has been preoccupation with the "civil rights" aspects of business regulation, considered as a matter of local provincial concern and as a badge of provincial autonomy. It is worth noting that in the United States where the federal power is expressed in terms of "Commerce", it has been held that trade in the sense of transactions between different persons is not a prerequisite to exercise of federal power and that inter-state "Commerce" embraces such instrumentalities of that commerce as bills of lading[67]. The *Murphy case*[68], raised, on the level of legislative operation, the question whether inter-provincial movement of goods by a person for his own use was "Trade" (or Commerce), a question similar to that in *United States v.*

62. 48, S.C.R. 260 at p. 302.
63. (1896) A.C. 348, at p. 363.
64. (1881), 7, App. Cas. 96.
65. (1916), 1, A.C. 588, 26 D.L.R. 288.
66. (1938), S.C.R. 100 at p. 121, (1938), 2 D.L.R. 81, at p. 96.
67. *United States v. Hill* (1919), 248 U.S. 420, 39 S. Ct. 143; *United States v. Ferger* (1919), 250 U.S. 199, 39 S. Ct. 445.
68. *Murphy v. C.P.R. and A.G. Canada*, (1958) S.C.R. 626 at p. 320.

Hill[69], and the affirmative answer of the Court at least points the way to a more explicit concern with "Commerce" under Sec. 91(2) than has hitherto been the case.

D. The Australian Vision

In Australia, there has been a tendency to narrow the meaning of the phrase, "The trade and commerce" in order to lesson the destructive effects of interpreting Sec. 92 so that it applies to other than fiscal charges. This has been the view of Australian High Court in *Buck v. Bavone*[70]. In *W. & A. McArthur Ltd. v. State of Queensland*[71] the majority of the High Court said :

> "The terms 'Trade, Commerce and Intercourse' are not terms of Art. They are expressions of the fact, they are terms of common knowledge, as well known to laymen as to lawyers, and better understood in detail by traders and commercial men than by judges. But as judges we are taken to know and do, in fact, in this instance know the general import of the words. The particular instances that may fall within the ambit of the expression depend upon the varying phases and development of 'Trade, Commerce and Intercourse' itself. Aviation and wireless telephony have been lately added to the list of instances, but the essential character of the class remains the same. 'Trade and Commerce' between different countries . . . have never been confined to the mere act of transportation of merchandise over the frontier . . . All the commercial arrangements of which transportation is the direct and necessary result form part of 'trade and commerce.' The mutual communings, the negotiations—verbal and by correspondence, the bargain, the transport and the delivery are all, but not exclusively, parts of the class of relations between mankind which the world calls 'Trade and Commerce.'"[72]

It is true that, as will be seen hereafter, the doctrine of *McArthur's Case* has not been approved by the Privy Council, but a reference to the decision of the Privy Council in the *James Case*,[73] in which *McArthur's Case* was reviewed in company with a number of other decisions, will show that their Lordships did not detract from the foregoing description of Trade, Commerce and Intercourse *per se*.

Indeed, so far from disapproving of the description, the Board said that, for the purposes of Sec. 51(i), the legislative powers of the

69. (1919), 248 U.S. 420, 39 S. Ct. 143.
70. (1976) A.L.J.R. 648 at p. 657.
71. (1920) 28, C.L.R. 530; 4 Austn. Digest 120
72. 28 C.L.R., at p. 546, 547.
73. *James v. The Commonwealth* (1936), 55 C.L.R. 1.

Commonwealth might attach to the whole series of operations which constituted the trade in question, once it had fallen into the category of inter-state trade, although the principle did not apply in relation to the prohibition in Sec. 92.[74] It is conceived that the statement in the forgoing extract is in point when the limits of the power are under consideration and the citation is given because there appears to be no reason to suppose that it is any the less true as a statement of the general nature of "Trade and Commerce" today than in 1920. Indeed, the trend of judicial decision has not been in any way to limit the extent of the power, but rather the reverse. In *Australian National Airways Pty. Ltd. v. The Commonwealth,*[75] it was held by the whole Court that the Commonwealth had power under Sec. 51(i) to create a body corporate to conduct inter-state air services for reward for persons and goods, irrespective of the question whether the persons or goods carried were being or to be carried for the purposes of "Trade and Commerce." It was argued that transportation was not in itself "Commerce," but only a means by which such "Commerce" could be conducted. The argument was rejected. Latham, C.J. said that the conception of 'trade and commerce among the states' was quite inseparable from movement of goods and persons and that airline services which were conducted for profit were, in the ordinary sense of the word, commercial enterprises of an inter-state character and that the providers of such a service were themselves engaged in inter-State trade and commerce:[76] Ritche, J. said that the phrase "Trade and Commerce" was wide enough to include, not only the sale and disposition of goods, but the transport of goods and persons, not only incidentally to the disposition of goods, but such transport as an end in itself. Dixon, J., while considering that, as in the United State, actual movement of persons and goods among the states would be regarded as enough to attract the power, said that this view was part of a more general understanding of the conception according to which the place given to transportation was "anything but subsidiary." From the beginning, the doctrine prevailing in the United States has been that transportation occupied a central place in the conception of "Commerce" as a subject of the power. These remarks were addressed to the argument that transportation was not in itself "Trade and Commerce." In the *Banking case,*[77] it was sought to show that "Trade and Commerce" was limited to the buying and selling of goods and that, in consequence, banking was not and could not be within the concept (for the purposes of Sec. 92). This argument was not accepted. Justice Dixon in the course of his judgment said that it was part of the purpose of Sec. 92 to remove from the possibility of legislative and governmental restriction activities conducted across State boundaries and to do so rather because of their inter-state character than of any special claim to immunity from

74. 55 C.L.R. at pp. 57, 60.
75. (1945) 71 C.L.R. 29.
76. 71 C.L.R., at pp. 56, 57.
77. *Bank of New South Wales v. The Commonwealth* (1948) 76 C.L.R. 1.

interference that particular activities might have except their inter-state character. To say figuratively that the purpose was to enable Australians to disregard state boundaries and not simply to give immunity from interference to buying, selling and journeying make clear the point, even if the statement may be inadequate and open to objection otherwise. Those who introduced Sec. 92 into the Australian Constitution did so in the full light of American experience. In Sec. 51(i) they coupled the word "Trade" with the word "Commerce," which stood alone in the United States Constitution to define the subject matter of the power of Congress to regulate "Commerce" with foreign nations and among the several states. Not content with the expression "Trade and Commerce" for the purposes of Sec. 92, they there added the word "Intercourse."

It has been said that "Trade" strictly means the buying and selling of goods. That, however, is a specialised meaning of the word. The present primary meaning is much wider, covering the pursuit of a calling or handicraft, and its history emphasises rather use, regularity and course of conduct, than is concerned with commodities. "Intercourse" was doubtlessly added because of the view, now no longer open in the United States, that "Commerce" might not extend to "Intercourse" that was not concerned with business profit or pecuniary gain and because of the degree to which the right of the citizen to access to every constituent part of the Union had been rested on implication. It cannot be thought that the essential content of the expression "Trade, Commerce and Intercourse" in Sec. 92 is any less than is included in the conception of "Commerce" in the modern American view of the "Commerce power." One is not speaking of the spread of that power over an immense field of activities that are incident to "Commerce." It is the central conception expressed in the word to which reference has been made.

The words "Trade, Commerce and Intercourse" are not naturally susceptible of such a reactionary interpretation. The very manner in which they are combined would carry, even to a mind unfamiliar with their background, an intention to include all forms and variety of inter-state transaction whether by way of commercial dealing or of personal converse or passage. An understanding of what lies behind the choice of expression confirms the natural impression produced by the language itself.

In the course of his judgment on this point, Dixon, J., whose description of the concept has been accepted and adopted by the Privy Council in the *Hughes and Vale Case,*[78] said that it covers intangibles as well as the movement of goods and persons. The supply of gas and the transmission of electric current may be considered only an obvious extension of the movement of physical goods. But it covers communication. The telegraph, the telephone, the wireless may be the means employed. It includes broadcasting and, no doubt, it will take in television. In principle there is no reason to exclude visual signals. The conception covers, in the United States,

78. (1954) 93 C.L.R. 1.

the business of press agencies and the transmission of all intelligence, whether for gain or not. Transportation, traffic, movement, transfer, interchange, communication, are words, which perhaps together embrace an idea which is dominant in the conception of what the "Commerce Clause" requires. But to confine the subject matter to physical things and persons would be quite out of keeping with all modern developments. The essential attributes, which belong to the conception, should determine the field of human activities to which it applies. To place among the essential attributes the requirement that there should be goods for sale or delivery or a man upon a journey, is to mistake the particular for the general, the concrete example for the abstract definition, and to yield to habits of thought inherited from a more primitive organisation of society.

Adding that the words in Sec. 92 were not capable of such a reactionary interpretation. His Honour said that the very manner in which they had been combined would carry an intention to include "all forms and variety of inter-State transaction, whether by way of commercial dealing or of personal converse or passage" and this natural impression was confirmed by an understanding of what lay behind the choice of expression. The argument, that a transmission of money or credit involved no movement, was a substitution of an analysis of doubtful accuracy belonging to monetary theory for the common understanding of business and the complexion placed upon it by the law. Whether the banking transactions important as inter-state "trade", "commerce" and "intercourse" were regarded as "falling under the category of cause, of result or of accompanying circumstance, nevertheless, as between the parties to them," they continued to possess "the characteristics which give them the complexion of trade, commerce and intercourse among the states."[79]

E. The Indian Approach

The Indian Judiciary has not felt that difficulty, as the American, in ascertaining the ambit of "Commerce" because most of the activities which were included within the scope of "Commerce" by judicial interpretation in America have been specifically enumerated in the Union List giving Parliament exclusive power to legislate with respect to them.[80] Prof. Prasad,[81] in this connection rightly observes that:

> "We have seen that in the United States of America term "Commerce" was given a wide meaning and this helped in enlarging the powers of the Congress over national economy and commerce. In Australia, on the other hand, Section 92 was

79. 76, C.L.R. at pp. 381-83.
80. For example, posts and telegraphs, telephones, wireless, broadcasting and other like forms of communication have been mentioned at Entry List 31, List I. Similarly, inter-state quarantine has been mentioned at Entry 81, List I.
81. Prof. Anirudh Prasad: Centre-State Relations In India, 1985 at p. 498.

> partly used as a guarantee to an individual in matters of trade and business. *These compulsions do not exist in India . . .* Parliament has the exclusive power to legislate on 'posts and telegraphs, telephones, wireless, broadcasting and other like forms of communication'. . . Thus, the guarantee of freedom of trade, commerce and intercourse has to be interpreted in the context of the above provisions of the Constitution."

Thus, it is clear that the term "Commerce" needs to be interpreted and has been interpreted in such a manner as not to create duplication or contradiction with other express provisions of our Constitution (as indicated above). Because of this reason "Commerce" in India comes to be a narrower concept. However, in *Atiabari Tea Co. Ltd. v. The State of Assam and Others*[82] Shah, J. was in favour of giving wide connotation to the word commerce. He was of the view that:

> "Trade and commerce do not mean merely traffic in goods, i.e., exchange of commodities for money or other commodities. In the complexities of modern conditions, in their wide sweep are included carriage of persons and goods by road, rail, air and waterways, contracts, banking, insurance, transactions in stock exchanges and forward markets, communication of information, supply of energy, postal and telegraphic services and many more activities—too numerous to be exhaustively enumerated—which may be called commercial intercourse. Movement of goods from place to place may in some instances be an important ingredient of effective commercial intercourse, but movement is not an essential ingredient thereof. Dealings in goods and other commercial activities, which do not import a concept of movement, are as much part of trade and commerce as transaction involving movement of goods. The guarantee of freedom of trade and commerce is not addressed merely against prohibitions, complete or partial; it is addressed to tariffs, licencing, marketing regulations, price control, nationalisation, economic or social planning, discriminatory tariffs, compulsory appropriation of goods, freezing or standstill orders and similar other impediments operating directly and immediately on the freedom of commercial intercourse as well. Every sequence in the series of operations which constitutes trade or commerce is an act of trade or commerce and burdens or impediments imposed on any such step are restrictions on the freedom of trade, commerce and intercourse. What is guaranteed is

82. A I R (1961) S.C. 232..

freedom in its widest amplitude—freedom from prohibition, control, burden or impediment in commercial intercourse."[83]

But other judges did not support Justice Shah. For example, Sinha, C.J. and Gajendragadkar, J. in the same case emphasised upon *'free flow of goods'* rather than labouring for *'defining commerce or trade'*. Thus, they centered themselves round the *'movement part of trade and commerce'* instead of their conceptual meaning. Even the majority in *Automobile Transport Ltd. v. State of Rajasthan*[84] did not appreciate Shah, J.'s wider concept of commerce. However, Das, J. opined that the terms "Trade", "Commerce", "Intercourse" should not be given a meaning which would have the effect of making the entire legislative power given to the states subservient to the will of the Union Executive. In this connection the Learned Judge observed that:

> "If the widest view is accepted, then there would be for all practical purposes, an end of state autonomy even within the fields allotted that to them under the distribution of powers envisaged by our Constitution."

Recently, in *M/s B.R. Enterprises v. State of U.P.*[85] the Supreme Court quoted with approval the concept of "Trade" as propounded in *May v. Sloan*[86] and *People v. Polar Vent of America*[87] wherein it was observed that "Trade" is an act or the "Business" of buying and selling for money; traffic, barter. "Trade" is not a technical word and is ordinarily used in three senses : *firstly*, in that of exchanging goods or commodities by barter or by buying and selling for money; *secondly*, in that of business, occupation generally; and *thirdly*, in that of a mechanical employment in contradiction to the learned professions, agriculture or the liberal arts.

COMMERCIAL ELEMENT—HOW FAR NECESSARY TO CONSTITUTE "COMMERCE"

One generally associates commerce with the idea of pecuniary gain. But the Supreme Court evidently has held that in cases where there is transportation, the element of profit is not necessary in order to constitute commerce. *United States v. Hill*,[88] which arose under the Reed Amendment of March 3, 1917, also makes it clear that the element of pecuniary gain is not necessary to constitute "Commerce." Whenever there is transportation, there is "Commerce."

---

83. *Ibid*. at pp. 259, 260.
84. A.I.R. (1962) S.C. 1406.
85. A.I.R. (1999) S.C. 1867 at p. 1902.
86. (1878-79) 101 U.S. 231, 25 L. Ed. 797.
87. 174, N.Y.S. 2d 789, 793.
88. (1919) 248 U. S. 420.

At first glance, an affirmative answer to the problem appears obvious. Since the authority conferred by the "Commerce Clause" is that to regulate commerce, one may not unnaturally conclude that for an activity to be brought within the Congressional power there would have to be involved at some point a commercial element, i.e., one of trade or exchange of goods or services made or rendered for profit. The Supreme Court has, nevertheless, held in a number of cases that a commercial element may not actually be necessary for the commerce power to become operative.

The starting point here, as in so much of "Commerce Clause" jurisprudence, is the opinion in *Gibbons v. Ogden*[89]. In it Chief Justice Marshall rejected the contention that "Commerce" was limited to traffic in commodities. Instead, said he, "Commerce" is something much broader: it is intercourse.

It can hardly be claimed that Marshall, wide though his concept of "Commerce" was, intended to say that all intercourse, whether carried on for purposes of gain or not, was "Commerce". His definition clearly was limited to commercial or business intercourse carried on for financial profit. In more recent cases, however, the High Court has tended to modify this limitation. While retaining the Marshall identification between "Commerce" and "Intercourse," the Court has removed the requirement that inter-state intercourse must be of a commercial character for the "Commerce Clause" to apply. If there are any activities carried on across state lines, i.e., if any inter-state intercourse occurs, the commerce power is operative, even though the activities in question lack a commercial element.

It is, in the first place, settled that all forms of inter-state transportation come within the "Commerce Clause," regardless of whether or not those being transported have any purpose of trade or business. This result is clear if a carrier for hire is involved whatever may be the purpose for which the persons or commodities involved are carried. In such cases, the transportation itself is being carried on for purposes of financial gain.

In *Covington Bridge Co. v. Kentucky,*[90] the question was whether a company, which operated a bridge between two states, was engaged in inter-state commerce. The Supreme Court held that it was, saying that 'Commerce' was 'Intercourse,' and the thousands of people who daily pass and repass over this bridge may be as truly said to be engaged in commerce as if they were shipping cargoes of merchandise from New York to Liverpool. This reasoning would not, it is true, apply to those who used the bridge for non-commercial purposes. Yet, even here the commercial element was not wholly lacking, since the bridge itself was maintained and operated for purposes of pecuniary gain.

From this case, it is a short step to extension of the "Commerce Clause" to all forms of inter-state transit, whether or not engaged in for

89. 22 U.S. (9 Wheat) 1 (1824).

90. 154 U.S. 204 (1894).

purposes of profit. This step was taken in *United States v. Simpson,*[91] where a federal law prohibiting the transportation of liquor in inter-state commerce was applied to the carrying across a state line of five quarts of whisky by their owner in his own automobile and for his personal consumption. "That the liquor was intended for the personal use of the person transporting it is not material," said the Court, so long as there was transportation across state lines. In other words, the emphasis has shifted from commercial intercourse to any transportation between states, whether or not for business purposes. Justice Clarke, who dissented in *Simpson,* stressed this. As he saw it, "The grant of power to Congress is over "Commerce"—not over isolated movements of small amounts of private property, by private persons for their personal use."

The *Simpson* holding is really based upon the proposition that the "Commerce Clause" covers every species of inter-state movement, *whether for profit or not*. Once state lines are crossed, federal power attaches, regardless of the presence or absence of any commercial element.

The cases, which show most clearly that such is in fact the prevailing rule of law, are those arising under the Mann Act. That statute, commonly known as the White Slave Traffic Act, makes it a crime to transport or cause to be transported in inter-state commerce any female for the purpose of prostitution, debauchery, or any other immoral purpose. Of course, no one could seriously contest the application of this law to commercialise vice across state lines, where the transportation of the women concerned is for purposes of gain. Such commercial traffic in women is patently within the "Commerce Clause."

In *Caminetti v. United States,*[92] on the other hand, the Mann Act was held applicable to a case where defendant was charged with transporting a woman across a state line for purposes of personal debauchery. Defendant there had paid for the travel of a woman from California to Nevada, with the intent that she should become his mistress in the latter state. Despite the fact that no commercial motive was present, the high Court ruled that the mere fact of inter-state transportation for an immoral purpose was enough to bring the case within the congressional prohibition. The Congress can keep the channels of commerce free from immoral use, even though there is no mercenary element involved.

It may, nevertheless, be contended that, in Caminetti, a commercial element was present comparable to that in the already-discussed *Covington Bridge case,*[93] since, though defendant did not have any business motive, the transportation was by a carrier engaged for profit in inter-state commerce. In other cases, however, the Supreme Court has held the Mann Act applicable even though there was no transportation for hire involved. The Supreme Court has stated that "the prohibition is not in terms confined to

91. 252 U.S. 465 (1920).
92. 242 U.S. 470 (1917).
93. 154 U.S. 204 (1894).

transportation by common carrier, nor need such a limitation be implied in order to sustain the constitutionality of the enactment."

In *Cleveland v. United States*[94], the Court went so far as to apply the Mann Act to the inter-state transportation of a plural wife by a member of a Mormon sect which practiced polygamy. The Act, reads the opinion there, "while primarily aimed at the use of inter-state commerce for the purposes of commercialised sex, is not restricted to that end." The power of Congress over what crosses state lines is plenary. It may be used to defeat what are deemed to be immoral practices, even in a case like this, where even the remotest commercial element is lacking.

The Mann Act decisions demonstrate plainly that non-commercial intercourse may be treated as commerce for constitutional purposes. As long as there is inter-state movement of goods or the activity in question contemplates or necessarily involves such movement, the congressional power attaches, regardless of whether any commercial element is involved.

If there is movement across state lines, the movement itself, the instrumentalities by which it is effected, the transactions which gave rise to it, and those engaged in both the movement and the transactions are subject to the commerce power. The 'why' and the 'how' of such movement are immaterial, so far as the question of federal authority is concerned. The Supreme Court in 1944 said that "many transactions be commerce though non-commercial; they may be commerce though illegal and sporadic, and though they do not utilize common carriers or concern the flow of anything more tangible than electrons and information."

Yet, even stated so broadly, what has just been said does not exhaust the reach of the commerce power over non-commercial activities. Even where such activities do not involve any movement across state lines, they may be subject to Congressional authority under the present broad approach to the "effect upon commerce" test. Under it, any activities, which can be said to affect inter-state commerce, comes within the radius of the Commerce Clause. And, given the breadth of the recent decisions on the subject, if there is the requisite effect, it should make no difference whether the given activity is commercial in character or not.

That such is, in truth, the law today is made clear by the already-referred-to decision in *Wickard v. Filburn.*[95] In that case, the high bench upheld the exertion of federal regulatory power over the production of wheat, even though the particular wheat was produced and consumed entirely on the farm of the individual concerned. Homegrown wheat, the Supreme Court reasoned, competes with wheat in commerce. As such, it may be said to have an effect upon commerce. This is, of course, all that is needed for the commerce power to attach. Hence, even though the activity involved "may not be regarded as commerce, it may still, whatever its nature, be reached by Congress" under the "effect upon commerce" test.

94. 323 U.S. 329 (1945).
95. 317 U. S. 111 (1942).

The above case indicates plainly that the application of the "effect upon commerce" test does not at all turn upon the presence or absence of a commercial element in the activity over which Congressional authority is asserted. Wickard may be said to go even further. In it, there was, not only no "commercial intercourse", but no "intercourse" at all, in the sense in which that term is commonly used. Consequently, it may be asserted that any activity which has an effect upon inter-state commerce is subject to the commerce power, whatever may be its character and even though it involves no crossing of state lines at all.

The problem posed in the beginning must thus be answered in the negative. Whenever there is movement across state lines (regardless of its nature) or effect upon commerce (in the broad sense in which that term is now used), the commerce power may be employed. The scope of the Commerce Clause is not at all limited to "Commerce".

G. The Doctrine of "Stream of Commerce"

Commentators on the law often err in assuming that legal developments unfold in a strictly consistent fashion, with one Supreme Court decision leading inexorably to its logical successor in the high tribunal's jurisprudence. Perhaps the tendency referred to is due more to a desire to simplify than to mere error, for only by presenting its work in terms of a logically unfolding pattern can the mass of Supreme Court decisions be rendered meaningful.[96]

At the same time, it should be recognised that a picture of the law developing in terms of a completely consistent evolution is bound to be some what distorted. Of course, if one analyses the case law of a tribunal like the highest bench on any subject, he finds a basic stream of jurisprudence. Within it, however, he will note inconsistent currents, at variance with, and even at cross-purposes to, the underlying drift of the stream.

The Supreme Court after Marshall interpreted the Commerce Clause in a much more restricted manner than the great Chief Justice had done. Earlier, it has seen how the Court's narrow conception of commerce culminated in the New Deal cases like *Carter v. Carter Coal Co.,*[97] under which the post-Marshall approach was carried to its logical extreme. Conveniently simple though it is, nevertheless, to treat the cases after Marshall's day as complete repudiations of his expansive view of commerce, it is not entirely accurate. This is true because, contemporary with the post-Marshall decision were cases whose decisions were entirely consistent with the broad Marshall conception. It was these cases, indeed, which laid the basis for the rejection of the restricted view of commerce discussed in the two prior sections and an expansion of the commerce power along the lines laid down in *Gibbons v. Ogden.*[98]

---

96. Schwartz : A Commentary on the Constitution of the United States, Ed. (1977) at p. 189.
97. 298 U. S. 238 (1936).
98. 22 U. S. (9 Wheat.) 1 (1824).

As already emphasised, the Marshall conception of commerce was an organic one. It was plainly that notion of commerce as an organic whole, which served as the foundation for the 1905 decision in *Swift & Co. v. United States.*[99] Defendants there were stockyard firms in Chicago and other cities who had been charged with violating the Sherman Anti-Trust Act by conspiring to monopolise the sale and distribution of fresh meat in the nation's stockyards. Defendants urged that the buying and selling of livestock in a stockyard was not commerce among the states. The Supreme Court rejected this contention, holding that the local activities involved were part and parcel of an integrated commercial whole. As Justice Holmes put it in the key passage of his opinion :

> "Commerce among the States is not a technical legal conception, but a practical one, drawn from the course of business. When cattle are sent from a place in one state, with the expectation that they will end their transit, after purchase, in another, and when in effect they do so, with only the interruption necessary to find a purchaser at the stockyards, and when this is a typical, constantly recurring course, the current thus existing is a current of commerce among the States, and the purchase of the cattle is a part and incident of such commerce."

The Swift reasoning was applied in *Stafford v. Wallace*[100] to uphold the Packers and Stockyards Act, under which the business of commission men and livestock dealers in the nation's stockyards was subjected to federal supervision. There, too, the highest Court emphasized that the sales at the stockyards were not merely local transactions: "The stockyards and the sales are necessary factors in the middle of this current of commerce." A similar approach was used to sustain the Grain Futures Act, regulating transactions on grain exchanges. In the Court's view, the sales on a particular grain exchange were just as indispensable to the continuity of the flow of wheat from the West to the flow of livestock toward the slaughter and packing houses of the East. In both cases, the sales were part of a great inter-state movement or current of commerce. As such they could not be treated as purely local incidents, beyond the reach of the commerce power.

Chief Justice Taft has characterized the *Swift* decision as a milestone in the interpretation of the Commerce Clause, which "drew again the dividing line between inter-state and intra-state commerce where the Constitution intended it to be." Implicit in Taft's language is the assumption that the "Current of Commerce" doctrine enunciated in *Swift* was a return to the Marshall conception of commerce. With commerce treated as an organic whole, the local incidents of a great inter-state movement, which taken alone are intra-state, cannot be permitted to characterize the movement as such.

---

99. 196 U. S. 375 (1905).
100. (1922) 258 U.S. 495 at p. 190.

are intra-state, cannot be permitted to characterize the movement as such. The total movement must be viewed as an entity, and every phase of it considered as subject to the commerce power. Hence, in the words of Justice Frankfurter, "while the now familiar conception of the 'Stream of commerce' was not in terms expressed by Marshall, the phases of commerce embraced by that doctrine were plainly covered by his philosophy."

However, the Indian Judiciary has not taken the pain of going into such a conceptual analysis for reasons as stated earlier.

H. Distinction between 'Trade,' 'Commerce,' 'Intercourse' and 'Business'

In the American "Commerce Clause" the word "Intercourse" is missing; but by way of judicial interpretation it has been held to be falling within 'Commerce'. In the words of Marshall C.J. "Commerce" undoubtedly is traffic, but it is something more; it is Intercourse."[101]

In Australia, however, Sec. 92 of the Constitution mentions "Intercourse" in addition to the word "Trade and Commerce". It has been easy, therefore, to interpret "Intercourse" to mean "non-commercial intercourse",[102] as distinguished from "commercial intercourse" which is included in the expression "Trade or Commerce". "Intercourse", thus, includes travelling between one state and another by tourists, in short, to include all migration or movement of persons from one state to another.[103]

(a) Basu v. Seervai

Examining the Indian position, Basu concludes that he is unable to agree that "Intercourse" in Art. 301 means "Commercial Intercourse". Reason for such a conclusion according to him is that since "Intercourse" has been separately mentioned in Art. 301 of our Constitution, in *justaposition* with the word "Commerce", as in Sec. 92 of the Australian Constitution, it would refer to "non-commercial intercourse. Referring to a Privy Council decision[104], the Learned writer rightly argues that the case refers to the "Freedom of an individual" to cross the barriers and have dealings with the citizens of another part of the Country, irrespective of the movement of goods or merchandise. And, as the American Supreme Court has held, the medium of such dealings may be speech, music, radio-television and the like. He further opines that freedom of inter-state intercourse also includes the freedom of importation of goods for *personal use.*

On the other hand Seervai[105] says that "Intercourse" means "commercial intercourse" and is comprised in "Commerce"[106]. The strongest

101. *Gibbon v. Ogden*, 22 (9 Wheat.) 1824.
102. *R. v. Smithers* (1912) 16 C.L.R. 99 at p. 113; *Duncan v. State of Queens Land* (1916) 22 C.L.R. 556 at p. 636.
103. *Gartwick v. Johnson*, (1945) 70 C.L.R. 1.
104. *Commonwealth v. Bank of New South Wales*, (1949) 2 All E.R. 755 at p. 769.
105. H.M. Seervai, The Freedom of Trade and Commerce in The Indian Constitution (The Atiabari Case And After), *Cambridge Law Journal* (1963) 54 at p. 76.

support for this opinion, according to Seervai, is found in the fact that though "Trade and Commerce" are heads of legislative power in all the Legislative Lists, "Intercourse", as a separate head of power, is not found in any of the Legislative Lists, *and this omission could hardly be inadvertent*. Further, as regards the states, a fetter on their power to interfere with the freedom of "Intercourse" *would be meaningless if "Intercourse" were a separate head of Legislative power, for them the states would lack Legislative competence in respect of "Intercourse"*.

Basu criticises Seervai's above conclusion. In support of his criticism he cites an example. He says that if Parliament enacts a law providing that the citizen of one state shall not use his telephone to talk to a citizen in another state, there is little doubt that the aggrieved persons may challenge such law as violative of Art. 301 and, then, Parliament can maintain the validity of such law only if the public interest in such restriction is demonstrated under Art. 302. In support of his view, Basu cites *Distt. Collector v. Ibrahim*[107] which states that ". . . under Art. 301 . . . that freedom is declared in the widest terms and applies to all forms of "Trade, Commerce and Intercourse" the Learned writer also charges Seervai for overlooking this decision.[108]

It is humbly submitted that Basu is correct in his assertion.

(b) Business and Trade

In *State of Bombay v. R.M.D. Chamarbaugwala*,[109] it was observed that the words "Trade" or "Business" or "Commerce" should not be read in their widest amplitude as meaning any activity which is undertaken or carried on with a view to earning profit. There are certain activities, which can under no circumstance be regarded as trade or business or commerce although the usual forms and instruments are employed therein. To exclude those activities from the meaning of those words is not to cut down their meaning at all but to say only that they are not within the true meaning of those words.

Recently in *M/S B.R. Enterprises v. State of U.P.*[110] a distinction was made between "Trade and Commerce" on the one hand and "Business" on the other hand. 'Business' may be of varying activities, may or may not be for profit, but it necessarily includes within its ambit 'Trade and Commerce'. So sometimes it may be synonymous but its field stretches beyond 'trade and commerce'.

106. The words "Trade, Commerce and Intercourse" are taken from Sec. 92 of the Australian Constitution, which in its turn took them from American decisions on the "Commerce Clause". In interpreting that clause in *Gibbons* Marshall, C.J. said that "Commerce" describes the "commercial intercourse" between nations in all its branches.

107. A.I.R. (1970) S.C. 1275 para 12.

108. Basu, Commentary On The Constitution of India, Vol. L at p. 236.

109. A.I.R. (1957) S.C. 699 at p. 718.

110. A.I.R. (1999) S.C. 1867 at p. 1902.

"Business" has a more extensive meaning than the word "Trade".[111] It is a wider term than "trade", and not synonymous with it and means almost anything which is an occupation as distinguished from a pleasure[112]. However, the term must be construed according to its context[113].

'Business' includes a professional practice and includes any activity carried on by a body of persons, whether corporate or unincorporate[114]. 'Business' includes a profession and the activities of any Government department (including a Northern Ireland department) or local or public authority.[115] "The word business is of large significance, and in its broadest sense includes nearly all the affairs in which either an individual or a corporation can be actors."[116] Referring to *re A Debtor,*[117] Venkataswami and Misra, JJ. observed that:

> ". . . There may, however, be a "Business" without pecuniary profit being at all contemplated. In such a connection, "Business" is a very much larger word than "Trade" and the word "Business" is employed in order to include occupations which would not strictly come within the meaning of the word "Trade". The words "Trade" and "Business" do not mean the same thing . . . The word "Trade" is often confined to buying and selling commodities. Where to draw the line between what is a profession and what is a "trade" is a matter, which it is not possible to deal with any general definition. "Business" is a much wider term than trade. The word "Business" at least covers a continuous occupation involving liabilities to others".[118]

All this clearly indicates, the word 'Business' is wider than the words 'Trade and Commerce'.

2. INSTRUMENTALITIES OF COMMERCE

An outstanding characteristic of the commerce power is its flexible character. This has enabled it to serve as the basis for governmental regulation of an economy whose dominant feature has been the geometric pace of its unfolding.

---

111. Stroud's Judicial Dictionary 5th Ed.
112. Words and Phrases, Butterworths, 3rd Ed.
113. 47 Halsbury's Laws 4th Ed. para 2.
114. Medicines Act, 1968, Sec. 132(i).
115. Sale of Goods Act, 1979, Sec. 61(i).
116. Law Lexicon 1997 Ed.
117. (1927) 1 Ch. 9 : 96 L J (Ch) 28 (CA).
118. *M/S B.R. Enterprises v. State of U.P.*, A.I.R. (1999) S.C. 1867 at p. 1902

The adaptable nature of the "Commerce Clause" was perceived as early as *Gibbons v. Ogden*[119], when Marshall recognised that, "in the process of things", the instruments of commerce will change. In this case itself, the Supreme Court dealt with an instrument of commerce wholly unknown when the organic document was drawn up, namely, the steamboat. Yet, it was clear that the "Commerce Clause" applied as much to such vessels as "if they were wafted on their voyage by the winds, instead of being propelled by the agency of fire."

The classic statement of the nonstatic quality of the commerce power is that of Chief Justice Waite in *Pensacola Telegraph Co. v. Western Union Co.*[120] The Learned C.J. stated that:

> "Powers granted by the 'Commerce Clause' are not confined to the instrumentalities of commerce . . . known or in use when the Constitution was adopted, but they keep pace with the progress of the country, and adapt themselves to the new developments of times and circumstances. They extend from the horse with its rider to the stage-coach, from the sailing-vessel to the steamboat, from the coach and the steamboat to the railroad, and from the railroad to the telegraph, as these new agencies are successively brought into use to meet the demands of increasing population and wealth. They were intended for the government of the business to which they relate, at all times and under all circumstances."

Justice Frankfurter has described the *Pensacola* decision itself as an adaptation of abstract doctrine to the changing national economy. Issue in it was the authority of the Congress to regulate telegraph companies. The High Court recognised, of course, that communication by wire was a form of commerce utterly unknown to the Framers. At the same time, it could hardly be disputed that the telegraph had, since its invention, become one of the necessities of commerce. In the phrase of the *Pensacola* opinion, "*The electric telegraph marks an epoch in the progress of time*". The Commerce Clause is construed so as to keep pace with such progress. As new instrumentalities of commerce are devised, they fall within the scope of congressional authority. This was as true of the telegraph in the *Pensacola* case as it was of the steamboat in *Gibbons v. Ogden.*[121] In sanctioning the power, which Congress exercised, by the Act of 1866, Justice Frankfurter informs us, "[Waite] is loyal to the framers, for he recognised, in the language of one of his colleagues, that the Constitution 'was made for an undefined and expanding future'."

As the stagecoach gave way to the railroad and telegraph, so in our own day, the railroad has given way to the motor vehicle and airplane and

119. 22 U.S. (9 Wheat.) 1 (1824).
120. 96 U.S. 1 (1878).
121. 22 U.S. (9 Wheat.) 1 (1824).

the telegraph to the telephone and radio-television. As these new instrumentalities of commerce have made their appearance, the congressional power has attached. Comprehensive federal regulatory laws have been enacted with regard to each of them. As far as motor vehicles and airplanes have been concerned, there has been no question, since their invention that they have been at least as much subject to the commerce power as the railroads have been. Regulation of inter-state communication by telephone has likewise presented no problem, since it involves basically the same type of transmission by wire as does the telegraph. Indeed, the Supreme Court has gone so far as to state that, "Inter-state communication of a business nature, whatever the means of such communication, is inter-state commerce regulable by Congress."

Such a broad approach made it easy for the high tribunal to deal with the newer means of communication by wireless, when federal regulation of them was at issue. In its essentials, said the Court when the question arose, radio does not refer from the sending of telegraph or telephone messages:

> "In each, transmission is effected by means of energy manifestations produced at the point of reception in one state which are generated and controlled at the sending point in another. Whether the transmission is effected by the aid of wires, or through a perhaps less well-understood medium, 'the ether,' is immaterial, in the light of those practical considerations which have dictated the conclusion that the transmission of information inter-state is a form of 'Intercourse,' which is 'Commerce'."

The "Commerce Clause" consequently comprehends all forms of economic activity—"commercial intercourse in all its branches," to use Marshall's expression. It is immaterial that the particular instrumentality is one that was not even within the comprehension of the men who drafted the Constitution. Because of this, the commerce power has proved adequate to the needs of the Industrial Revolution, from the age of steam to that of the atom. The mind can, in truth, scarcely conceive of a mode of economic activity, which will not be covered by the Commerce Clause. Whatever the economic needs of the moment, the clause can be construed so as to vest in the nation authority sufficient to deal with them.

A. Instrumentalities of Inter-state Commerce

Commercial transportation, which the Court continued to treat with special deference, easily passed this test. For example, in *Southern Railway v. United States,*[122] the Justices unanimously upheld the Federal Safety Appliance Act, which regulated certain equipment on railroad cars,

122. 222 U.S., 20 (1911).

including those running exclusively within a state.[123] Conceptualising railroad transportation as an interdependent unit,[124] the Court ruled that the Commerce Clause power "may be exerted to secure the safety of the persons and property transported [on railroads] and of those who are employed in such transportation, no matter what may be the source of the dangers which threaten it. Such safety concerns likewise justified a statute setting maximum working hours for railway employees,[125] despite the Court's general hostility to employment regulation.

The Court applied such reasoning to federal laws designed to prevent not merely physical injuries, but also economic harms. For example, in the *Shreveport Rate Case*,[126] it upheld an ICC order requiring Texas-based inter-state railroads to charge the same rates for shipments within the state, whether originating from another place in Texas or from Louisiana.[127] The Court concluded that unjust rates which discriminated against out-of-state carriers had a direct and significant effect on inter-state commerce:

> "Congress, in the exercise of its paramount power, may prevent the common instrumentalities of inter-state and intra-state commercial intercourse from being used in their intra-state operations to the injury of inter-state commerce . . . [Congress] does possess the power to foster and protect inter-state commerce, and to take all measures necessary or appropriate to that end, although intra-state transactions of inter-state carriers may thereby be controlled . . . Congress is entitled to keep the highways of inter-state communication open to inter-state traffic upon fair and equal terms."[128]

The Court struck down only those federal railroad laws that did not concern the conduct, safety, or efficiency of the business, but rather promoted "the social welfare of the worker, and therefore were remote from any regulation of commerce.[129] Examples included congressional attempts to give inter-state railway workers a retirement and pension system[130] and the right to union membership.[131]

---

123. *Id.* at pp. 23-27.
124. *Id.* at pp. 26-27.
125. *Baltimore & Ohio R. R. Co. v. I.C.C*, 353 U.S. 325 (1957).
126. *Houston, E & W. Tex. Ry. Co. v. United States*, 234 U.S. 342 (1914).
127. *Id.* at pp. 345-55.
128. *Railroad Comm'n of Wis. v. Chicago, Burlington & Quincy R.R. Co.*, 257 U.S. 563, 585-90 (1922); *The Pipeline Cases*, 234 U.S. 548 (1914); *I.C.C. v. Goodrich Transit Co.*, 224 U.S. 194 (1912).
129. *Railroad Retirement Bd. v. Alton R.R. Co.*, 295 U.S. 330, 368 (1935).
130. *Id.* at pp. 362-68.
131. *Adair v. United States*, 208 U.S. 161, 178 (1908).

B. The Channels of Inter-state Commerce

The Court applied the reasoning of the foregoing "instrumentalities" cases in upholding congressional regulations aimed at protecting the "channels" of inter-state commerce from illicit and harmful things. For example, *Brooks v. United States,*[132] upheld the National Motor Vehicle Theft Act,[133] which prohibited the knowing transportation of a stolen motor vehicle across state lines or involvement with it afterwards. Other laws that addressed threats to public health and safety were also fairly easy to defend. For instance, the Court sustained federal statutes intended to exclude from inter-state commercial channels, diseased cattle[134] and impure or misbranded food and drugs.[135]

More problematic was legislation designed to prevent the use of inter-state channels for objectives that Congress deemed "immoral". The seminal *Lottery Case* (*Champion v. Ames*)[136] involved a federal law prohibiting the inter-state shipment of lottery tickets.[137] The Court stressed that its review was confined to ascertaining whether or not the statute concerned inter-state commerce; if it did, Congress's power was plenary and subject only to political control.[138] The Court determined that lottery tickets (1) were articles of "commerce" because they were bought and sold on the market and (2) were being carried "among the States".[139] Hence, Congress had complete regulatory authority and could prohibit the inter-state transportation of lottery tickets, even to protect "public morals".[140] Indeed, this legislation merely supplemented the states' exercise of their police power to suppress lotteries.[141]

Although *Champion's* holding is sensible,[142] the case quickly came to stand for the proposition that Congress had plenary Commerce Clause power over all inter-state transportation—whether of property or people, and whether for commercial purposes or not.[143] For example, in *Hoke v. United States,*[144] the Court declared :

132. 267 U.S. 432 (1925).
133. *Brooks*, 267 U.S. at p. 438.
134. *Reid v. Colorado*, 187 U.S. 137 (1902).
135. *Hipolite Egg Co. v. United States*, 220 U.S. 45, 54-58 (1911); *McDermott v. Wisconsin*, 228 U.S. 115, 128-35 (1913).
136. 188 U.S. 321 (1903).
137. *Id.* at pp. 353-64.
138. *Id.* at pp. 356-58, 362-63.
139. *Id.* at pp. 353-55, 363. The Court also suggested that the matter regulated was "commercial" in that it involved private companies who were carrying lottery tickets for a fee. *Id.* at pp. 345, 353-55.
140. *Clark Distilling Co. v. Western Md. Ry.*, 242 U.S. 311, 325-32 (1917); *In re Rapier*, 143 U.S. 110,134 (1892).
141. *The Lottery Case*, 188 U.S. at 356-57; *Brooks v. United States*, 267 U.S. 432, 436 (1925).
142. *The Lottery Case*, 188 U.S. at 353-64.
143. *Id.* at p. 371 (Fuller, C.J., dissenting)
144. 227 U.S. 308 (1913).

"The principle established by the cases [e.g., *Champion* and *Hipolite*] is the simple one . . . that Congress has power over transportation "among the several States", that the power is complete in itself, and that Congress, as an incident to it, may adopt not only means necessary but convenient to its exercise, and the means may have the quality of police regulations."[145]

Accordingly, the Court upheld the Mann Act provisions that made it a crime to take a woman across state lines "for the purpose of prostitution."[146] *Caminetti v. United States*[147] sustained another part of this Act, which prohibited inter-state transportation of a woman for "an immoral purpose", as enforced against men who took their mistresses from California to Nevada.[148] The Court concluded that the statute's failure to require any monetary gain did not affect its validity :

"The transportation of passengers in inter-state commerce, it has long been settled, is within the regulatory power of Congress, under the commerce clause of the Constitution, and the authority of Congress to keep the channels of inter-state commerce free from immoral and injurious uses has been frequently sustained, and is no longer open to question."[149]

The Court ignores that prior cases involved either passengers on commercial ships and railroads (not private vehicles) or goods being transported for economic reasons. Moreover, as three dissenters argued, the Mann Act should have been read to effectuate the intent of Congress to halt forced inter-state prostitution, not immoral behaviour between adults who crossed state lines for convenience rather than commercial gain.[150]

C. Legal Instruments used to Facilitate Commerce

Just as Congress can regulate the physical vehicles of inter-state commerce (such as railroads), so too should it be able to ensure uniformity in the legal documents that are the intangible—yet equally essential—instruments of the national economy. For example, bills of exchange, letters of credit, insurance of contracts and corporate securities are so intertwined with the sale and exchange of property and services that they should be treated as "Commerce," and they obviously facilitate commerce among the states. Thus, we would uphold federal regulation of such items.

145. *Id.* at p. 323.
146. *Id.* at pp. 320-323.
147. 242 U.S. 470 (1917).
148. *Id.* at pp. 482-92.
149. *Id.* at p. 491.
150. *Id.* at pp. 496-503 (McKenna, J., dissenting); *United States v. Simpson*, 252 U.S. 465 (1920).

Thus, the Court also broadened the concept of "instrumentalities of inter-state commerce" in two ways. First, this phrase now encompasses documents that facilitate multistate trade, such as bills of lading.[151] Second, the Court analogised certain business facilities to national utilities that handled the flow of commerce.[152]

D. Electronic Media: Modern Instrumentality of Commerce: The Internet

As stated above, there was a time when horse with its rider, sailing vessels, coach and steamboat, railroads, etc. were treated as different instrumentalities of commerce in different eras. But one should not feel stranged if it is said that even these instrumentalities also have become outdated in this modern "high-tech-era".

In America, the "Commerce Clause" has been drafted not much comprehensively and therefore, there has been much scope for judicial interpretation. In its interpretative process, as early as 1878, the American Judiciary in *Pensacola* opined that 'the communication by wire was a form of commerce utterly unknown to the Framers.' It was observed that it could hardly be disputed that the telegraph had, since its invention, become one of the necessities of commerce. The electric telegraph marks an epoch in the progress of time. The "Commerce Clause" was construed so as to keep pace with such progress. As new instrumentalities of commerce are devised, they fall within the scope of congressional authority. This was as true of the telegraph in the *Pensacola* case as it was of the steamboat in *Gibbons v. Ogden.*[153] Further in *Fisher's Blend Station v. Tax Commission of Washington,*[154] Justice Stone pointed out that transmission is effected by means of energy manifestations produced at the point of reception in one state which are generated and controlled at the sending point in another.

Thus, if by process of interpretation telegraph can be held as an instrumentality of commerce why not the modern Internet system ? One should not disagree with the affirmative answer to this question, if two things are kept into mind. One, that the E-commerce is processed through Internet system which is based upon *telephone line, cable lines, wireless connection,* etc. which have been judicially held as instrumentalities of commerce. Two, the Internet can function not only within a state (intra-state) or between states (inter-state), rather it can function at global level also facilitating export and import (international trade). Thus, there is no reason not to include E-commerce within the "Commerce Clause".

In United States, unsurprisingly, courts have found that the dormant "Commerce Clause" applies to the "Internet." The *Internet, like a highway or railroad, may be an instrument of inter-state commerce* and analysed

---

151. *United States v. Ferger,* 250 U.S. 199, 203-206 (1919).
152. *Swift & Co. v. United States,* 196 U.S. 375, 390-402 (1905).
153. 22 U.S. (9 Wheat.) 1 (1824).
154. (1936) 297 U.S. 650.

accordingly.[155] Courts have found that Internet communication, in particular electronically mailed images via the Internet, constitutes inter-state commerce.[156] Courts have invalidated state provisions explicitly aimed at regulating content on the Internet.[157] The business transactions which, perform via Internet are commonly known as electronic commerce.

In Australia, in *Bank of New South Wales v. The Commonwealth*[158] Dixon, J.'s observation is worth quoting in this connection which leads to the conclusion that E-commerce can well be brought within the ambit of "Commerce". The Learned Judge was of the view that "the supply of gas and the transmission of electric current may be considered only an obvious extension of the movement of physical goods. But it covers communication. The telegraph, the telephone, the wireless may be the means implied. It includes broadcasting and, no doubt, it will take in television." On this analogy it can be argued that the Internet can be put along with the aforesaid means of communication through which "Commerce" gets concluded.

However, Indian situation is slightly different. Indian Courts have not to labour much for bringing E-commerce within the ambit of "Commerce". It has not even to depend upon the "Commerce Clause" contained in the Constitution. The simple reason is that various Entries contained in List I of the Constitution give ample opportunity to the judiciary to bring E-commerce within the scope of "Commerce Clause." For example, Entry 31 of List I mentions "posts and telegraphs, telephones wireless, broadcasting and *other like means of communication.*" At Entry 41 of the Union List there is mention of "trade commerce with foreign countries, import and export trade and commerce" and Entry 42 speaks about "inter-state trade and commerce." Internet can safely be interpreted as being included in *other like means of communication* mentioned at Entry 31st of List I. Therefore, there is no reason why the *Parliament* can not *regulate E-commerce* and why the *Judiciary* can not *regulate Parliament* if it crosses the limits prescribed by the Indian Commerce Clause.

No one would doubt that the use of modern means of communication such as electronic mail and Electronic Data Interchange (EDI) for the conduct of international trade has been increasing rapidly. Electronic commerce offers significant advantage over the traditional methods of doing business. It requires new skills, strategies and technologies. It is new business, and not new way of doing old things. However, the communication of legally significant information in the form of paperless messages may be hindered by legal obstacles to the use of such messages, or by uncertainty to their legal effect and validity. The purpose of the Information Technology Act, 2000 is to remove such obstacles. This would lead to create a more secured legal environment for what has now become known as "electronic commerce".

155. *American Libraries Association v. Pataki*, 969 F.Supp. 160, 161 (S.D.NY. 1997).
156. *United States v. Thomas*, 519 U.S. 820 (1996).
157. *A.C.L.U. v. Johnson*, 194 F 3d 1149 (10th Cir. 1999).
158. (1948) 76 C.L.R., 1; on appeal to the Privy Council (1949) 79 C.L.R. 497.

Electronic commerce refers to the business transacted electronically. In common usage, the term usually includes the sale of goods and provisions of services over the Internet. It includes an on-line approach to conducting business with customers including advertising, marketing, order entry and processing, payment, and customer support. In a traditional way of doing business, the transacting parties are known and bound by the terms of contracts. Transactions between them are confidential. The Internet is an open system and the users are hardly traceable. Internet communication is only possible with cryptographic schemes, including public-key encryption and key certification authorities. A message bearing digital signature verified by the public key listed in the digital certificate is as valid, effective and enforceable as if that message has been written on paper. For international contracts for sale of goods, writing is not required. Important features of electronic business are; electronic signature, cryptography, authentication, and certification. Applications of electronic commerce are many and varied. They include the paperless exchange of business information, electronic mail (e-mail), electronic bulletin board, electronic funds transfers, etc.

4

Some Marginal Situations and the Limits of 'Commerce' Today

I. MARGINAL SITUATIONS

A. Productive Activities

While discussing the ambit of "Commerce", it would be unjust if one does not consider the problem whether productive activities like *manufacturing, mining and agriculture* are included within the same or not. The American classification of activities as "Production" and "Trade" is a verbal device. Prior to 1936, the decisions in the United States had proved sufficient to postulate verbal distinctions between "Manufacture" and "Commerce".[1] This simple distinction provided the basis for invalidating the National Industrial Recovery Act, and the regulation of coal mining in the Guffey Act. But the reversal of prevailing conception was neither long delayed nor ambiguous in its expression. Steel production, tobacco growing, wheat production and ultimately coal mining were brought within the "flow or course of inter-state commerce." Thus, the conception of inter-state commerce was pushed back in its origin to the production of these elements. However, there are certain decisions which throw doubt as to inclusion of these activities within the ambit of "Commerce" and that is why they may be termed as "marginal situations." But one thing is clear, i.e., there is a *leaning* towards inclusion, within the ambit of "Commerce" of those activities, which were initially not included within the same.

Let us start with *Kidd v. Pearson.*[2] In this case the constitutionality of a State Statute, which prohibited the manufacture of intoxicating liquors, even though they were made for sale outside the state was challenged. Such law was upheld on the ground that it involved the regulation, not of commerce,

---

1. Robert L. Stern, The Commerce Clause and National Economy, 1933-46 (1946) 59 Harv. L. Rev. 645, at p. 883.
2. 128 U.S. 1(1888).

but of manufacturing. "No distinction," declared the Highest Court, "is more popular to the common mind, or more clearly expressed in economic and political literature, than that between 'Manufactures and commerce'. 'Manufacture' is transformation—the fashioning of raw materials into a change of form for use. The functions of commerce are different. The buying and selling and the transportation incidental thereto constitute commerce."

The power to regulate commerce, according to *Kidd v. Pearson*,[3] does not include any authority over manufacturing, even though the products made are intended to be the subject of commercial transactions in the future. To hold otherwise, the Court asserted, would be to vest in the Congress control over all productive industries. "The result," it said, "would be that Congress would be invested, to the exclusion of the states, with the power to regulate, not only manufacture, but also agriculture, horticulture, stock-raising, domestic fisheries, mining, in short, every branch of human industry."

United States v. E.C. Knight Co.,[4] more popularly styled as the *Sugar Trust Case*, arose out of the first important prosecution brought by the Government under the Sherman Anti-Trust Act. The defendant was a company, which had obtained a virtual monopoly over the manufacture of refined sugar in the country. The complaint charged that defendant had violated the Sherman Act, by acquisition of the stock of its principal competitors, several sugar refining companies in Pennsylvania. The Supreme Court held, however, that such acquisition could not be reached by the federal commerce power. The monopolistic acts related only to manufacturing, which under *Kidd* were not within the scope of the 'Commerce Clause'. In the Court's words, "The fact that an article is manufactured for export to another state does not of itself make it an article of inter-state commerce."

The *Knight* decision, like that in *Kidd* upon which it was based, was a logical consequence of the post-Marshall approach to "Commerce". Once the Marshall conception of commerce as an organic whole gave way to the crossing of state lines as the criterion of Congressional power, the *Kidd-Knight* view followed naturally. The result was the artificial and mechanical separation of "Manufacturing" from "Commerce," without regard to their economic continuity or the effects of the former upon the latter. Manufacture itself was treated as a "purely local" activity and hence beyond the compass of the Commerce Clause.

The *Jones & Laughlin*[5] decision marks a definite break with the restricted view that productive industries are beyond the scope of the "Commerce Clause." In *Jones & Laughlin*, the Supreme Court held squarely that "Manufacturing" as such was not automatically excluded from the range of federal power. Precedents like *Carter*, on which the ink was still

3. *Ibid*.
4. 156 U.S. 1 (1895).
5. *N.L.R.B. v. Jones & Laughlin Steel Corp.*, 301 U.S., 1 (1937).

hardly dry, had held the other way. These precedents were not followed. These cases describe the *Jones & Laughlin* opinion. The High Court restored to the commerce power the broad sweep it had in Marshall's day. Factories, mines, and mills, whose activities had been deemed "local" and hence immune from federal regulation were, under the *Jones & Laughlin* rationale, held to affect inter-state commerce directly enough to justify Congressional control.

Jones & Laughlin[6] itself removed the immunity from the commerce power which manufacture had come to enjoy. But the Supreme Court soon extended the *Jones & Laughlin* approach to other productive industries. In *Sunshine Anthracite Coal Co. v. Adkins,*[7] the Court upheld a 1937 Congressional Act, regulating the Bituminous Coal Industry, similar in many ways to that which had been annulled in the *Carter*. The opinion delivered by Justice Douglas indicates plainly that the high bench was no longer of the view that coal mining must be considered immune from the commerce power. "The regulatory provisions," reads the opinion, "are clearly within the power of Congress under the 'Commerce clause'." The congressional authority permits it to undertake economic stabilisation of a productive industry like mining, which constitutes such an important segment of the economy. "Congress under the 'Commerce Clause'," states Justice Douglas, "is not impotent to deal with what it considers to be dire consequences of *laissez-faire.*"

In *Mulford v. Smith,*[8] the high tribunal held valid the Agricultural Adjustment Act, of 1938, whose basic features were not unlike those of the law of the same name which had been condemned in *United States v. Butler.*[9] The *Butler* decision had been based upon the proposition that agricultural production, as such, was not "Commerce" and hence not subjects to the direct regulatory power of the Congress. The *Mulford* rests upon a rejection of this reasoning. It is true that the *Mulford* opinion did not expressly overrule *Butler* on the point under discussion and holds squarely that "agriculture" came within the definition of "Commerce." This omission led a lower federal court as late as 1954 to assert that "agriculture is not commerce nor does agriculture affect such commerce in a constitutional sense." Hence, concluded the court, "Federal regulation of agriculture invades the reserved rights of the states." The Supreme Court itself quickly laid to rest this ghost of the *Butler*, declaring categorically, in reversing the lower-court decision referred to, that the regulation of agriculture was within the federal commerce power.

It is thus clear that, under the view that has prevailed in the Highest Court since the *Jones & Laughlin*, productive industries such as manufacture and agriculture are no longer removed from the reach of the commerce

6. *Ibid.*
7. (1940) 310 U.S. 381.
8. (1939) 307 U.S. 38.
9. (1936) 297 U.S. 1.

power. No longer must production be treated as a purely "local" activity, immune from congressional control regardless of the impact, which it may have upon the commerce of the country. Instead, we have come back to the Marshall conception of commerce as an organic whole, with the "Commerce Clause" embracing all commerce, which concerns more than one state. Under such conception, the federal power is not limited to commerce, which actually moves across state lines. It includes all activities, which affect inter-state commerce, though such activities, taken alone, might be considered "local." The whole point about the post-*Jones & Laughlin* approach is that they can no longer be considered alone. If they have an effect upon inter-state commerce, they concern more than one state and come within the radius of the "Commerce Clause."

What was true of "manufacturing" was also true of all other forms of "production". "Commerce," stated the High Court in *Knight*, "succeeds to manufacture, and is not a part of it." The same can be said of agriculture, mining, and every other means by which goods are produced. In *Oliver Iron Co. v. Lord,*[10] the Court expressly applied the *Kidd-Knight* approach to the mining of iron ore. The Court said, "Mining, is not inter-state commerce, but like manufacturing, is a local business, subject to local regulation and taxation."

Later cases applied the same reasoning to agriculture, oil production, generation of electric power, and other productive industries. All of these activities were held beyond the reach of the congressional "Commerce power," although they, together with manufacturing, constituted the heart of the economic life of the country. The basic consideration in all of these cases was that articulated in the *Knight* opinion:

> "Slight reflection will show that if the national power extends to all contracts and combinations in manufacture, agriculture, mining, and other productive industries, whose ultimate result may affect external commerce, comparatively little of business operations and affairs would be left for state control."

The question of federal power today cannot be decided simply by finding the activity in question to be "production," nor can consideration of its effect upon commerce be foreclosed by calling such effect merely "indirect." Whether the subject of regulation is "production" is no longer material for purposes of determining the existence of congressional power. In the words of the *Jones & Laughlin* opinion:

> "It is thus apparent that the fact that the employees here concerned were engaged in production is not determinative.

10. 262 U.S. 172 (1923).

The question remains as to the effect upon inter-state commerce."

In *Carter v. Carter Coal Co.,*[11] it was pointed out that "Commerce succeed to manufacture and is not part of it; similarly, mining brings the subject matter of "Commerce" into existence, "Commerce" disposes of it. In *Wickard v. Filburn*[12] it was pointed out by the court that "production", "manufacturing" and "mining" were within the province of state governments, and thus were beyond the power of Congress under the "Commerce Clause".

The only pertinent question in a "Commerce Clause" case is—does the subject of regulation affect inter-state commerce? An affirmative answer compels the conclusion that it is within the scope of federal power. Mines and mills, factories and farms—all engaged in production, rather than commerce in the literal sense—are brought within the sweep of the Commerce Clause, provided only that they exert some economic effect upon inter-state commerce.

In Canada, examining the vires of Sec. 5 (a) of the Dairy Industry Act, in *Re Validity of Section 5(a) of The Dairy Industry Act,*[13] Estey, J. held that the prohibition of the manufacture and sale in section 5(a) directly interferes with the freedom of individuals and corporate bodies to engage in the business of manufacturing or selling the specified food products, including oleomargarine and margarine. Corry points out that :

> "Grading, packaging and marketing provisions must be enforced at the point where the producer makes contact with the dealer or processor. However, at this point, it is very often impossible to say whether the particular lots being graded will remain in provincial trade or will ultimately be drawn into inter-provincial or export trade. Yet, even if the sole purpose were to grade surpluses in order to ensure their access to export markets, there are strong reasons for grading at this point. If grading is postponed until the product reaches an export warehouse, the uncertainty as to grade must constantly hamper movement into export channels."[14]

To what extent can the Dominion legislature regulate the manufacture and wholesale vending of spirituous liquors was discussed by Lord Haldane in *Great Vest Saddlery Co. v. The King*[15] as under :

---

11. 298 U.S. 238,304, 80 L.Ed. 1160, 56 S. Ct. 855 (1936).
12. 317 U.S. 111, 121, 87 L.Ed. 122, 63 S.Ct. 82 (1942).
13. (1949) 1 D.L.R. 433.
14. Corry, Diffuculties of Divided Jurisdiction (Royal Commission Study Appendix 7) at p. 11.
15. (1921) 58 D.L.R. 1.

> "The only other decision to which their Lordships desire to make reference is *Brewers and Maltsters' Association v. A.G. for Ontario*,[16] there the Dominion Legislature had previously and validly regulated the manufacture and wholesale vending of spirituous liquors, and provided for the issue of licences for such manufacture and sale . . ."

This passage sit with the position taken in the *Margarine* case, "While manufacturing is not of itself inter-state commerce the shipment of manufactured goods inter-state is such commerce and the prohibition of such shipment by Congress is indubitably a regulation of the commerce."

If one goes through *Re The Farm Products Marketing Act, R.S.O. 1950, C. 131, as Amended*[17], one can safely conclude that judicial leaning is towards the inclusion of "assembling" being included within the concept of marketing which in turn is included within the ambit of "Commerce". Rand, J., in so many words says, "Marketing means buying, selling, assembling . . ."

The definitive statement of the scope of dominion and provincial jurisdiction made by Duff, C.J.C. in *re Natural Products Marketing Act*,[18] is worth appreciating. The regulation of particular trade confined to the Provinces lies exclusively with the Legislature subject. It may be to Dominion general regulation affecting trade, and to such incidental intrusion by the Dominion as may be necessary to prevent the defeat of Dominion regulation; inter-provincial and foreign trade as correspondingly the exclusion concern of Parliament. That statement is to be read with the judgment of court in *The King v. Eastern Terminal Elevator Co.*,[19] approved by the Judicial Committee in *A.G. B.C. v. A.G. Can.*,[20] to the effect that Dominion regulation cannot embrace local trade merely because in undifferentiated subject-matter the external interest is dominant. But neither the original statement nor its approval furnishes a clear guide to the demarcation of the two classes when we approach as here the origination, the first stages of trade, including certain aspects of manufacture and production.

That demarcation must observe this rule, that if in a trade activity, including manufacture or production, there is involved a matter of extra-provincial interest or concern its regulation thereafter in the aspect of trade is by that fact put beyond provincial power. This is exemplified in *Lawson v. Interior Tree Fruit & Vegetable Committee*,[21] where the Province purported to regulate the time and quantity of shipment, the shippers, the price and the transportation of fruit and vegetables in both unsegregated and segregated local and inter-provincial trade movements.

---

16. (1897) A.C. 231.
17. (1957) 7 D.L.R. (2d) 257.
18. (1936) 3 D.L.R. 622 at p. 633.
19. (1925) 3 D.L.R. 1.
20. (1937) 1 D.L.R. 691 at p. 693.
21. (1931) 2 D.L.R. 193 at p. 200.

A producer is entitled to dispose of his products beyond the Province without reference to a provincial marketing agency or price, shipping or other trade regulation; and an outside purchaser is entitled with equal freedom to purchase and export. Processing is one of a number of trade services that may be given products in the course of reaching the consumer: milling, sorting, packing, slaughtering, dressing, storing, transporting, etc. The producer or purchaser may desire to process to product either within or beyond the Province and if he engages for that with a local undertaking, such as packing plant—and it would apply to any sort of servicing. He takes that service as he finds it but free from such provincial impositions as are strictly trade regulations such as prices or the specification of standards, which could no more, be imposed than provincial trademarks. Regulation of that nature could directly nullify external trade vital to the economy of the country. Trade arrangements reaching the dimensions of world agreements are now a commonplace; inter-provincial trade, in which the Dominion is a single market, is of similar importance, and equally vital to the economic functioning of the country as a whole. The dominion power implies responsibility for promoting and maintaining the vigour and growth of trade beyond provincial confines, and the discharge of this duty must remain unembarrassed by local trade impediments. If the proceeding is restricted to external trade, it becomes an instrumentality of that trade and its control as to prices, movements, standards, etc., by the Dominion follows : *re Validity of Industrial Relations and Disputes Investigation Act.*[22] The licencing of processing plants by the provinces, as a trade regulation is thus limited to their operations in local trade. Likewise the licencing of shippers, whether producers or purchasers, and the fixing of the terms and conditions of shipment, including prices, as trade regulation, where the goods are destined beyond the Province; would be beyond provincial power.

The reaches of trade may extend to aspects of manufacture. In *A.G. Ont. v. A.G. Dom.,*[23] the judicial committee dealt with the question whether the province could prohibit the manufacture within the Province of intoxicating liquor, to which the answer was given that, in the absence of conflicting legislation of Parliament, there would be jurisdiction to that effect if it were shown that the manufacture was carried on under such circumstances and conditions as to make its prohibition a merely local matter in the province. This involves a limitation of the power of the Province to interdict as a trade matter, the manufacture or production of articles destined for external trade.

In Australia, the court has consistently held that production, even when earmarked for inter-state trade is not a part of inter-state trade and commerce. To support this conclusion reference may be made to *Beal v. Marrickville Margarine Pty. Ltd.*[24] and *Barter's Enterprises v.*

22. (1955) 3 D.L.R. at p. 721.
23. (1896) A.C. 348.
24. (1966) 114 C.L.R. at p. 283.

Todd[25]. Inter-state trade in manufactured products only begins, the Court has said, with the inter-state movement of the products; *the production is a mere inter-state preparation for a proposed act of inter-state trade in manufactured goods and is not itself a part of inter-state trade.*[26] However, production or manufacturing when linked with an export market comes within the ambit of "Commerce". For example in *O'Sullivan v. Noarlunga Meat Ltd.*[27] Fullagar, J. opined that "all matters which may affect beneficially or adversely the export trade of Australia in any commodity produced or manufactured in Australia must be the legitimate concern of the Commonwealth. Such matters include not only grade and quality of goods *but* packing, getup, description, labelling, handling, and anything at all that may reasonably be considered likely to affect an export market by developing it or impairing it." But the reasons of Fullagar, J. in *Noarlunga* do raise some difficult questions. The Commonwealth Regulations were valid because they dealt with production or preparation for export. They dealt with an activity which was clearly indemnifiable as part of the chain of activities which made up the export trade in meat. It was indemnifiable as part of that chain because of some clear objective features of the activity, not because of the subjective intention of the processor or producer. The facts of this case were that Noarlunga Meat Ltd. operated a slaughterhouse and abattoirs at Noarlunga in South Australia. The company's premises were registered under the "Commerce" (meat export) Regulations. The Metropolitan and Export Abattoirs Act, 1936 provided that no person should use any premises for the purpose of slaughtering stock for export unless that person held a licence from the State Minister of Agriculture. The company did not hold such a licence. On 27 November 1953 the company slaughtered and froze 152 lambs for export. All of these carcasses were sold and delivered to the Australian Meat Board (an agency of the Commonwealth Government) and exported to the United Kingdom on 13 December 1953. The company was charged (on a complaint made by an inspector of the South Australian Agriculture Department) with using premises on 27 November 1953 to slaughter meat for export, contrary to Sec. 52A of the *Metropolitan and Export Abattoirs Act, 1936* (SA). The company pleaded that the State legislation was inconsistent with the Commonwealth Regulations and therefore invalid.

In *Swift Australian Co. Pty Ltd v. Boyd-Parkinson*[28], Swift operated a poultry killing and processing plant in Queensland. About five per cent of the plant's output was exported from Australia, the balance being sold in Queensland or inter-state. Swift's plant was registered under the *Commerce (Meat Export) Regulations* (which laid down detailed standards for the processing of meat for export) but not under the Poultry Industry Acts, 1946-59, which prohibited the slaughter of poultry for human consumption on

25. (1978) 139 C.L.R. at p. 499.
26. (1966) 114 C.L.R. at pp. 304-05.
27. (1954) 92 C.L.R. 565.
28. (1962) 108 C.L.R. at p. 189.

premises not licenced under the Queensland Acts. Swift was prosecuted for a breach of the *Poultry Industry Acts* and argued, in its defence, that the Queensland legislation was invalid because it was inconsistent with the *Commerce (Meat Export) Regulations*. This argument depended on the conclusion that; (a) the Commonwealth had intended, in the Regulations, to regulate all meat processing in plants where only a part of the processed meat was to be exported, and (b) the trade and commerce power would support such an intention. A majority of the High Court, Dixon, C.J. McTiernan, Kitto, Taylor, Windeyer and Menzies, JJ. held that the Regulations were only intended to regulate the processing of that poultry which was intended for export : the Regulations left the control of the other processing to State legislation. Of the majority justices, Dixon, C.J., Kitto and Windeyer, JJ. did not refer to the constitutional issue. McTiernan, Taylor, Menzies and Owen, JJ. did. The basis of the argument for Commonwealth power was that the organisation of Swift's plant made necessary Commonwealth control over all the processing at the plant. At the time of slaughter, treatment, packing or storage, no one could predict which birds would be exported and which would be sold on the domestic market: if export standards were to be maintained, the whole of the processing had to be conducted according to those standards. McTiernan, J. rejected this submission, citing the assertion of Latham, C.J. in *Burgess* that the constitutional distinction between intra-state and other trade and commerce "must be fully recognized".[29] On the other hand, Menzies, J. said that it was :

> ". . . within the power of the Commonwealth to prohibit slaughtering for home consumption in premises registered for slaughtering for export . . . or to regulate, in an establishment where slaughtering for export is carried on in the interests of overseas trade, operations not directly concerned with preparing goods for that trade."[30]

Taylor, J. made a similar concession.[31] Owen, J., who dissented, found Commonwealth intention and competence to regulate all meat processing on premises where animals were killed and prepared for export. He said :

> "I think it is undeniable that the trade and commerce power is wide enough to enable this to be done. To begin with it is difficult to imagine a state of affairs in which slaughter, treatment, storage and packing of meat for export is carried on in an establishment and the whole of the meat products resulting from those operations is ultimately exported. There must inevitably be some meat which, for a diversity of reasons,

29. *Id.* at p. 203.
30. *Id.* at p. 220.
31. *Id.* at p. 213.

> may be rejected for export yet be entirely suitable for home consumption. Again, as the facts in the present case show, it may be impossible to predicate at the time of slaughter, treatment, storage or packing whether any particular carcass or any particular part of a carcass will ultimately be exported or whether it will go into home consumption."[32]

Redfern v. Dunlop Rubber Australian Ltd.[33] involved the recognition that some commercial activities have a composite character and cannot easily be broken down or segregated into their intra-state, inter-state and international aspects. This composite or integrated, character may be a result of the way in which a trader or traders chose to conduct business. In *Redfern*, it was alleged that the manufacturers had elected to make a single agreement, with effect on inter-state and intra-state trade. If they had made two distinct agreements; (i) not to supply the Victorian retailers from their inter-state factories, and (ii) not to supply those retailers from their Victorian factories, the Commonwealth could have regulated the former agreement but not the latter. This is essentially the reasoning which lies behind Owen, J's approach in *Swift Australian Co. Pty. Ltd. v. Boyd-Parkinson*[34], the organisation of Swift's processing plant inextricably mixed its export and domestic trade processes. To regulate the former, the Commonwealth was justified in regulating the whole.

The Indian position in this respect is quite different from that of other federations. We have an elaborate Constitution containing the "Commerce Code" instead of the "Commerce Clause". Our "Commerce Code" may be described as comprising Art. 19(1)(g), Part XIII, Art. 286 and other like Constitutional provisions dealing with trade, commerce, etc. Indian judiciary has not faced the problem whether production, mining, manufacturing or other like operations comes within the ambit of "Commerce" or not. This is, as said above, because of detailed provisions made under the Constitution. Constitution through three Lists demarcates the legislative competence of Central and State Legislatures. Manufacture, mining, agriculture and other productive activities have been mentioned at one Entry or the other in any of the three lists. For example, Entry 33 of the Concurrent List mentions: "trade and commerce in, and the *production*, supply and distribution of . . ."; Entry 23 of the State List talks about "regulation of mines and mineral development subject to the provisions of List I with respect to regulation and development under the control of the Union"; at Entry 26 "trade and commerce within the state subject to the provisions of Entry 33 of List III" is mentioned. Entry 27 of the same List refers to "production, supply and distribution of goods subject to the provisions of Entry 33 of List III". "Agriculture . . ." are mentioned at Entry 14 of the State List. Similarly,

32. *Id.* at p. 226.
33. (1964) 110, C.L.R. at p. 194.
34. (1962) 108 C.L.R. 189 at p. 226.

Entries 58 and 59 of the Union List talk about "cultivation, manufacture, etc. of different products". The purpose of saying all this is to show that in India, unlike other federations, fields are clearly allocated and the Centre or the states have not to agitate for taking the recourse of a clause like "Commerce Clauses" of other countries. Not only this, if one goes through Art. 304(a) it can be seen that words "manufactured" or "produced" are there. This strengthens the view that manufacturing is definitely an aspect of "Commerce". This dimension of argument gets support from different judicial decisions[35] which though not directly involving the issue whether manufacturing is comprised in "Commerce" or not, yet talk about manufacturing in the perspective of the "Commerce Code".

B. Insurance

"Insurance" lies on the fence and may be described as a marginal situation so for as its inclusion within the ambit of "Commerce" is concerned. The situation may be argued both ways.

A field where the effect of economic changes upon the operation of the "Commerce Clause" is clearly shown is that of the regulation of insurance. Until the Supreme Court gave its decision on June 5, 1944, in *United States v. Underwriters Association,*[36] the Court in a series of cases commencing from *Paul v. Virginia*[37] had consistently maintained the view that insurance was not "Commerce".

In *Paul v. Virginia,*[38] it has been decided that insurance was not "Commerce" and was, as such subject only to state regulation. Contracts of insurance, said the Supreme Court there are not articles of "Commerce" in any proper meaning of the word. They are purely local transactions. A state law regulating insurance companies was sustained because issuing a policy of insurance is not a transaction of "Commerce".

When *Paul* was decided, the insurance business was stilling its virtual infancy. In the three-quarters of a century that followed, it has grown to such an extent that the Supreme Court could characterise it in 1944 as a business, which "holds a commanding position in the trade and commerce of the Nation. Built upon the sale of contracts of indemnity, it has become one of the largest and most important branches of commerce."[39] It involves a

35. *India Copper Corp. Ltd. v. State of Bihar*, A.I.R. (1961) S.C., 347; *M/S Chhotabhai v. Union of India*, A.I.R. (1962) S.C. 1006; *State of M.P. v. Bhailal Bhai*, A.I.R. (1964) S.C. 1006; *Bhawani Cotton Mills v. State of Punjab*, A.I.R. (1967) S.C. 1616; *M/S Chhotabhai v. State of M.P.*, A.I.R. (1968) M.P. 127; *Vrajmal M. & Co. v. State of M.P.*, A.I.R. (1970) S.C. 129; *S.I. Syndicate Ltd. v. Union of India*, A.I.R. (1975) S.C. 460; *State of Maharashtra v. C.P. Manganese Ore*, A.I.R. (1977) S.C. 879; *Prag Ice & Oil Mills v. Union of India*, A.I.R. (1978) S.C. 1296.
36. (1944) 322 U.S. 533.
37. (1868) 8 Wall. 168.
38. *Id.* at p. 183.
39. *United States v. South-Eastern Underwriters' Association*, 322 U.S. 533, (1944) at pp. 539-40.

continuous stream of intercourse among the states composed of collections of premiums, payments of policy obligations, and the countless documents and communications essential to the negotiation and execution of policy contracts. "Insurance," said the 1944 opinion referred to, "touches the home, the family, and the occupation or the business of almost every person in the United States."[40]

The insurance business had thus developed into an inter-state commercial enterprise of gigantic proportions. Under *Paul* its constitutional status remained that of a purely local activity subject only to state control.

In *Hooper v. California*,[41] White, J. drew a distinction between "Inter-state commerce and an instrumentality" thereof on the one side and the "mere incidents which may attend the carrying on of such commerce" on the other. In this case it was held that the making of a contract of insurance was not an instrumentality of commerce but was a mere incident of commercial intercourse.[42] The Learned judge stated that if the power to regulate inter-state commerce applied to all the incidents to which such commerce might give rise then that power would embrace the entire sphere of mercantile activity in any way connected with trade between the states. This would exclude state control over many contracts purely domestic in nature.[43] This case related to a contract of marine insurance. It was held that there was no distinction in principle between insurance against risks of fire and insurance against the perils of the sea.

The Supreme Court in *New York L. Inc. Co. v. Deer Lodge County*[44] was called upon again to decide the question whether insurance constituted "Commerce". The plaintiff, a New York insurance corporation, with its home office in New York City, was carrying on an extensive life insurance business not only in every one of the forty-eight states in the Union but also in many foreign countries. The company was accustomed to transact its business through agents, who solicited insurance, collected the first premium, and also delivered the insurance policy, which was prepared and sent from the home office for such purpose. It was contended for the insurance company that the transactions of insurance conducted by it across state lines constituted inter-state commerce and the taxation of such a business infringed the "Commerce Clause". McKenna, J. who delivered the opinion of the Supreme Court in this case made an elaborate examination of the contentions put forward and earlier dicta of the Court upon the subject and reaffirmed the view that insurance was not "Commerce".

This anomalous situation was removed in 1944 by *United States v. South-Eastern Underwriters' Association*.[45] In it, the highest Court overruled

40. *Id.* at p. 540.
41. (1895) 155, U.S. 648.
42. *Id.* at p. 655.
43. *Ibid.*
44. (1913) 231 U.S. 495.
45. 322 U.S. 533 (1944).

Paul and held that "Insurance is Commerce". Hence, an association of underwriters could be prosecuted under the Sherman Act, for a conspiracy to fix rates and to monopolise trade and commerce. A commercial enterprise like insurance, which conducts its activities across state lines, can not be held beyond the regulatory power of the Congress.

Even the dissenting Justices in the *South-Eastern Underwriters,* did not deny that insurance had in fact become "Commerce," as that term had been interpreted. They urged, nevertheless, that in contemplation of law insurance had acquired an established doctrinal status not based on present day facts, which the Court should not now disturb. Relying upon *Paul,* the states had established an elaborate structure of regulation and taxation of the insurance business. This state system, the dissenters claimed, would be needlessly upset by the majority decision, with no congressional policy or scheme of regulation to take its place. The only result of overturning *Paul,* in their view, would be the loosing of a flood of litigation and legislation, in order to establish a new boundary between state and national power in the insurance field.

The dire consequences foreseen by the dissenters did not, however, ensue. This was true because the Congress, within less than a year after the *South-Eastern Underwriters'* decision, enacted a law expressly authorising state regulation and taxation of insurance, whether inter-state or local. This 1945 law, the Supreme Court has ruled relinquished federal jurisdiction over insurance to the states. In the Court's words, "Obviously Congress' purpose was broadly to give support to the existing and future state systems for regulating and taxing the business of insurance."[46] In effect, the law in question returned the situation to what it was before the *South-Eastern,* at least so far as basic regulatory authority over insurance was concerned.

But the *South-Eastern* ruling that insurance is commerce subject to Congressional power still remains good law. The Congress may, whenever it chooses, itself assume the regulatory authority yielded to the states by the 1945 statute. Indeed, even under the statute, certain aspects of the business are even now subject to federal regulation. Thus, the Securities and Exchange Commission has held variable annuity policies sold across state lines subject to regulation.[47] Advertising materials mailed into other states by a health insurance company have been held subject to regulation by the Federal Trade Commission, at least to the extent that such advertising matter is unregulated by the laws of the state into which it is sent.[48] These holdings were based upon the high Court's interpretation of the terms of the 1945 Statute and other relevant laws.

To put it another way, the Supreme Court, in *South-Eastern Underwriters,* removed the supposed constitutional basis for exemption of insurance from the "Commerce Clause." It is, at the same time, wholly up to

46. *Prudential Insurance Co. v. Benjamin,* 328 U.S. 408, (1946) at p. 429.
47. *Securities and Exchange Commission v. Variable Annuity Co.,* 359 U.S. (1959) at p. 65.
48. *Federal Trade Commission v. Travellers Health Association,* 362 U.S. 293 (1960).

the Congress to determine whether and to what extent its commerce power over insurance will be exercised.

The holding of the Supreme Court in *Underwriters' Association* that the business of insurance conducted across state lines constitutes inter-state commerce would have created grave dislocation in an important segment of the national economy but for passing of the McCarran Act, by Congress. The Supreme Court in *Prudential Insurance Co. v. Benjamin*[49] upheld the constitutionality of the Act. The object of the McCarran Act was broadly to give support to the existing and future state systems for the regulating as well as the taxing of the business of the insurance. The Act, provides as follows:

> ". . .business of insurance is in public interest, and that silence on the part of the Congress shall not be construed to impose any barrier to the regulation or taxation of such business by the several states."

McCarran Act, had put the full weight of its power behind existing and future regulatory and taxing state laws by declaring expressly and affirmatively that the continued state regulation and taxation of insurance was in accord with the public interest.

In *Robertson v. California*[50] the McCarran Act, was not directly considered as the appellant's violation of the penal provision of a California statute had been committed before that Act, had come into effect. The appellant was an agent of Arizona Insurance Corporation, who had challenged the legality of the conviction on the main ground that insurance business conducted across state lines was inter-state commerce as held in the *Underwriters' Association*. Rutledge, J., delivering the opinion of the Court held that the licencing provisions of the state law was primarily designed and adopted to protect the public from fraud, misrepresentation, incompetence and sharp practice. A measure so designed, which applied uniformly without discrimination to agents of local and foreign companies operating in California, did not contravene the "Commerce Clause". In this case, cession of congressional power in favour of state control was regarded as sufficient to entitle a state to impose a tax on foreign companies doing business in the state, although no such tax was imposed on local companies. But in *State Board of Insurance v. Todd Shipyards Corp.,*[51] a state premium tax was invalidated as a violation of due process where paid out of state on out of state insurance although on property within the state.

In Canada, in *Attorney-General for Canada v. Attorney-General for Alberta,*[52] it was decided that it was not competent to the Dominion to

49. (1946) 328 U.S. 408.
50. (1946) 328 U.S. 440.
51. (1962) 370 U.S. 451.
52. (1896) A.C. 348.

regulate generally the business of insurance in such a way as to interfere with the exercise of civil rights in the Provinces.

In *re Sections 4 and 70 of The Canadian Insurance, 1910*,[53] Duff, J. asserted that Sec. 91(2) "does not embrace the regulation of occupations as such", and he "did not think that the various kinds of businesses which are comprehended under the term 'insurance' . . . can be said to be part of the trade and commerce of the country". Angil, J. was doubtful that the business of insurance could ever be spoken of as a trade, and this doubt was, for him, removed by the association of "Trade" with "Commerce" in Sec. 91(2), which made it clear that "trade" did not cover the business of "insurance". No advertence was made or consideration given to insurance as "Commerce", not even by the dissenting Judges,[54] they were of opinion that insurance was a "trade". In the *Local Prohibition* case[55] Lord Watson referred to the fact that in the *Parson's* case[56] insurance was admitted to be a trade. In the *Insurance Reference* case[57] the question whether insurance was a trade for purposes of Sec. 91(2) was lost in a generalised assertion that federal power was unequal to the regulation by licencing of particular trades carried on in the provinces.

In Australia, insurance is not considered as a part of inter-state trade. The point that production was not part of inter-state trade, is an echo of the rationale for the decision in *Hospital Provident Fund Pty. Ltd. v. State of Victoria*,[58] that the making of insurance contracts was not part of inter-state trade and commerce. But this was not because insurance contracts were outside trade and commerce but because they had no inter-state character. Fullager and Taylor, JJ., expressly held and Dixon, C.J. did not deny that insurance was trade and commerce. In this case the hospital provident fund business which was in the nature of insurance was held as not falling within inter-state trade.

In India "Insurance" is mentioned at Entry 47, List I and thus Parliament has power to make laws including regulation regarding insurance. Therefore, in India it should not be a debatable issue whether insurance is included within "trade and commerce" or not. Again, in Australia as seen above the basis for insurance not to be included within inter-state trade is that the whole transaction of insurance is concluded within the boundaries of a state; there is no crossing of borders. (One should bear into mind that in Australia "freedom of trade, commerce and intercourse" is only inter-state not intrastate). The Indian position is not similar to that of Australia. Assuming that transactions in insurance are concluded at one place, it would make no difference for the Indian Judiciary. Also, it is humbly submitted that though in most of the insurance transaction

53. (1913) 48 S.C.R. 260 at p. 302-5.
54. (Fitzpatrick, C.J.C. and Davies, J.).
55. (1896) A.C. 348 at p. 363.
56. (1881) 7 App. Cas. 96.
57. (1961) 1 A.C. 588, 26 D.L.R. 288.
58. (1953) 88 C.L.R. 1.

the philosophy is of social security and the element of gain is either zero or negligible, the same may be put within the ambit of intercourse.

2. THE LIMITS OF COMMERCE: DOCTRINE OF RES EXTRA COMMERCIUM

The words "Trade" and "Commerce" are not words of art and therefore they lack any precise definition. What constitutes "Trade" and "Commerce" is a question of fact to be determined in the light of contemporary social values and practices.[59] In the words of McTiernan, J. whether an activity is trade or commerce "is a matter of social opinion rather than jurisprudence."[60] Ordinarily, organised activities with a view to earning profits are termed trade or commerce.[61] But certainly all kinds of organised activities with a view to earning profits cannot *ipso facto* acquire the status of "Trade" or "Commerce." For example, activities like hiring out goondas to commit crime, selling obscene pictures or literature or trafficking in human beings or making counterfeit coins or smuggling[62] or dealing in adulterated food[63] would not be regarded, at least in the contemporary Indian society, as trade or commerce even if they are organised with a motive to earn profits. So also sale or purchase of slaves, which was once a recognised trade, has now lost that character. Thus, only legitimate profit-oriented activities can acquire the status of trade and commerce. What activities are legitimate is a question to be answered in terms of social opinion, values and realities. In India, the *doctrine res of extra-commercium*, which took birth in *State of Bombay v. R.M.D. Chamarbaugwala*,[64] has been applied in the areas of gambling, lottery and money-lending. Here, an attempt is being made to analyse judicial response towards the applicability of the doctrine in these areas in prevailing Indian social perspective and also to analyse judicial reactions, if any, in other federal systems.

---

59. M.P. Singh : Is Money Lending Extra Commercium? Some Thoughts on *Fatehchand v. State of Maharastra*, 1978, 3 S.C.C. 1.

60. *The King v. Connare*, 61 C.L.R. 596, 631 (1939).

61. In *Narain Soadeshi Weaving Mills v. The Commissioner of Execss Profits Tax*, A.I.R. 1955 S.C. 176 at p. 181, Das, J., said that business connotes some real, substantial and systematic or organised course of activity or conduct with a set purpose. Quoting this statement for defining the word "trade" in Article 19(1) (g) Subba Rao, C.J. in *Drishan Dumar v. F.& D. State*, A.I.R. 1967 S.C. 1368, at 1371, said : "Though the word 'business' is ordinarily more comprehensive than the word 'trade', one is used a synonymous with the other."

62. *Boota Singh v. State*, A.I.R. 1961 Punj. 21.

63. *U.P. v. Kartar Singh*, A.I.R. 1964 S.C. 1135 and *A.P. Grain and Seed Merchants' Assn. v. Union of India*, 1970 S.C.C. 71.

64. A.I.R. 1957 S.C. 699.

A. Extra Commerciality of Lottery and Gambling

The first case concerning lottery to come before the American Court was *Champion v. Ames*[65]. In this case lottery was held as being well covered in the "Commerce Clause". This case involved the Act of 1895 for the suppression of lottery. An earlier Act, excluding lottery tickets from the mails had been upheld *in re Rapier,*[66] on the proposition that Congress clearly had the power to see that the very facilities furnished by it were not put to bad uses. But in the case of "Commerce" the facilities are not ordinarily furnished by the National Government, and the right to engage in foreign and inter-state commerce comes from the Constitution itself, or is anterior to it. In the *Lottery's case*, Harlan, J.'s opinion may be summarised as under :

> "The appellant insists that the carrying of lottery tickets from one state to another state by an express company engaged in carrying freight and packages from State to State, although such tickets may be contained in a box or package, does not constitute, and cannot by any act of Congress be legally made to constitute, "Commerce" among the States within the meaning of the Clause of the Constitution of the United States providing that Congress shall have power, "to regulate commerce with foreign nations, and among the several States, and with the Indian tribes;" consequently, that Congress cannot make it an offense to cause such tickets to be carried from one State to another. The Government insists that express companies, when engaged, for hire, in the business of transportation, from one State to another, are instrumentalities of commerce among the States; that the carrying of lottery tickets from one State to another is commerce which Congress may regulate; and that as a means of executive the power to regulate inter-state commerce Congress may make it an offense against the United States to cause lottery tickets to be carried from one State to another . . . It was said in argument that lottery tickets are not of any real or substantial value in themselves, and therefore are not subjects of commerce. If that were conceded to be the only legal test as to what are to be deemed subjects of the "Commerce" that may be regulated by Congress, we cannot accept as accurate the board statement that such tickets are of no value . . . *We are of opinion that lottery tickets are subjects of traffic, and therefore are subjects of "Commerce", and the regulation of the carriage of such tickets from State to State, at least by independent carriers, is a regulation of commerce among the several states."*

65. *The Lottery Case*, 188 U.S. 321 (1902).
66. 143 U.S. 110 (1892).

From the above it is clear that in America, dealing in lotteries is well within the scope of the "Commerce Clause".

In Australia, the following principle was laid down in the *Mansell v. Beck*[67]:

One of the provisions of the New South Wales Act, held valid in this case made it an offence to accept money for the purchase of the ticket in lottery conducted in another state. McTiernan and Taylor, JJ. were content to say that acts involved in conducting lottery were not trade, commerce and intercourse and that therefore Sec. 92 had no application. On the other hand, Williams, J. regarded inter-state traffic in lottery tickets as forming part of inter-state intercourse and as such entitled to protection by Sec. 92. Kitto, J. was not prepared to take an extensive view. He regarded the acceptance of money as part and parcel of inter-state transaction and since he regarded the transaction as one of the inter-state intercourse, he held the provision invalid. Dixon, C.J. and Webb, J. conceded that the acceptance of the money in the circumstances was part of a transaction of inter-state intercourse.

The principle of the *Lotteries case*,[68] is difficult to grasp and may be difficult to apply with any certainty, as is indicated by Kitto, J.'s dissent from the decision in spite of his acceptance of the principle. The difficulty lies in identifying the characteristic of a transaction, which the particular law selects as the basis of its operation. For example, could it not have been truly said in *Fergusson v. Stevenson*,[69] that the basis of the operation of the law there in question was the conservation of native fauna, and that the possession of kangaroo skins was prohibited not in consequence of any characteristic of inter-state trade or of any connection between the possession and inter-state trade, but by virtue of the character of the skins as native fauna? How is it that, according to the view of Dixon, C.J. and Webb, J., Sec. 92 would not prevent the Federal Parliament from prohibiting inter-State dealings in lottery tickets, but Sec. 92 does prevent the New South Wales Parliament from prohibiting inter-State dealings in kangaroo skins? The difference cannot lie merely in a judicial evaluation of legislative policy, and yet in the *Lotteries Case* there is repeated reference to the long history in Britain and Australia of Anti-Lottery Legislation, while in *Fergusson's Case*,[70] it was thought relevant to point out there was no such history in respect of kangaroo skins and that they were legitimate articles of commerce in Queensland, the State of origin of the skins in question. Would the result in *Fergusson's Case* have been different if Queensland had also put kangaroo skins *extra commercium*? If so, what is it that enables two or more States together to take an activity out of the protection of Sec. 92 in a way which is not open to one State acting alone? There is a suggestion here of evaluation

67. *Mansell v. Beck*, (*The Lotteries case*)1956, 95 C.L.R. 550.
68. *Mansell v. Beck*, 1956, 95 C.L.R. 550.
69. (1951), 84 C.L.R., 421.
70. *Ibid.*

of legislative policy, the criteria being history and the extent of the particular restrictive legislation.

However, that may be, the principle of the *Lotteries Case* does narrow, the scope of Sec. 92 to some unclearly defined extent. It is submitted that it provides the true explanation of the important "exceptions", and which, could be explained only by means of the truism that "Sec 92 was enacted against the background of a law-controlled orderly society which must persist despite the strictures of Sec. 92". If certain classes of people can be excluded from inter-State trade by reason of incompetence, infancy, or incapacity; if injurious things or things *extra commercium* can be excluded from inter-State movement, if individuals can be excluded from inter-state transport in the interests of public safety in terms of Dixon, C.J.'s test it is because the restriction operates in consequence of some feature of the particular activity which does not belong to the concept of inter-State trade, commerce, or intercourse. The incompetence, infancy, or incapacity of the persons concerned; the injurious nature of the things; the prejudice to public safety in the acts of individuals in the circumstances—these must be indemnifiable as the features in consequence of which the restrictions are imposed. It is presupposed of course that the law must be of a general nature dealing with those features, or at least be readily connectable with other laws concerned with the same subject, and it must not specifically select, the occasion of movement inter-State as the occasion for imposition of the restriction.[71]

The *Lotteries Case* suggests that certain other familiar kinds of prohibitory or regulatory legislation are valid even in their application to inter-state transactions, such as prohibition of the sale of stolen goods, or of forged passports, or of counterfeit money, to take examples given by Taylor, J.[72] Might one add noxious drugs, obscene literature? Clearly there must be something more than a mere prohibition of sales, since sale itself is of the essence of inter-State trade.[73] But what additional factors must be present to enable one to identify some feature outside inter-state trade, commerce or intercourse, as the real basis of operation of the law is a problem yet to be elucidated.

But in India, the situation is quite different and the Supreme Court in *Chamarbaugwala* propounding the doctrine of *res extra commercium* took the opposite view.

In *Chamarbaugwala*,[74] the Court derived the doctrine of *res extra commercium* from the observations in certain *Australian* cases, in preference to

71. Dixon, C.J., has consistently regarded the decision of statutory majority of the High Court in *Ex parte Nelson (No. 1)*, 1928, 42 C.L.R., 209, as wrong : see *Gilpin's Case*, 1935, 52 C.L.R., at p. 208-9.

72. 1956, 95 C.L.R. 594.

73. Dixon, J.'s example of the mixing of Straw Chaff and Hay Chaff in *Gilpin's Case* (1935), 52 C.L.R. at p. 206 also *Cam & Sons Pty. Ltd. v. Chief Secretary (N.S.W.)* (1951), 84 C.L.R. 442.

74. *State of Bombay v. Chamarbaugwala*, A.I.R. 1975 S.C. 699 at pp. 718-21.

American decisions in which even deleterious activities in course of inter-state trade were held to be included within the ambit of the "Commerce Clause", but they were subject to regulation which could go to the extent of prohibition in more dangerous cases, e.g. importation of adulterated food[75]; inter-state transportation of women for immoral purposes.[76]

The American view was discarded on the ground that there was nothing in the American Constitution corresponding to Sec. 92 of the Australian Constitution and the only relevant provision in this behalf was the "Commerce Power" of Congress[77] so that unless every activity of inter-state trading or intercourse were brought within the ambit of this power, no Legislature would be competent to control or suppress such inherently dangerous activities.[78]

Recently, the doctrine of *res extra commercium* was discussed at length by the Supreme Court in *M/S. B.R. Enterprises v. State of U.P.*[79] In this case the Supreme Court, comparing with the American and Australian position discussed the nature of lottery and held it as *res extra commercium.*

The Supreme Court considered the issues of great importance, namely, the nature and character of lotteries, whether they by their very nature even if legitimised could be classified as commercium hence trade and business at the common parlance? Or it was distinct class by it self legalised for a limited purpose, for achieving specialised objectives to be used for a temporary period. Thus, the Court had to consider what was the reason for gambling to be legitimised, if in a given situation it had to be for a wider and purposeful objectives which led to imposing conditions to reduce its evil consequences as suggested by the Supreme Court through *Suman Enterprises,*[80] adopted through Section 4 of the impugned Act. Thus, the Court had to consider whether it lost its original character of being pernicious. Even if it could be said to have diluted it, could it still be classified as commercium and equated with every other form of trade and commerce? While disposing of these issues the Court opined that "its effect on its citizens has been cause of concern, which had drawn attention of the kings and his subject since ancient time, the Government, and the courts of various countries including ours. On the one hand, sometimes justifying for the benevolent and good cause like charitable purpose and public benefit but later reiterating even from this stand on account of its pernicious effect on the public at large and on account of its condemnation to such a magnitude that it resulted into complete banning of such lotteries. Justification, as in the present case, is for the

75. *Hipolite v. U.S.* (1911) 220 U.S. 45.
76. *Hoke v. U.S.* (1913) 227 U.S. 308.
77. American Constitution, Article I, Section 8, Cl. 3.
78. As Das, C.J. observed in *Chamarbaugwala's case,* A.I.R. 1957 S.C. 699, the American Congress would have no power to control gambling and like spurious transactions under its power over 'inter-state commerce' if they were not held to be 'commerce'.
79. A.I.R. 1999 S.C. 1867.
80. 1994 (4) S.C.C. 217.

augmentation of public revenue, which swell through voluntary contributions contrary to the exaction through compulsion as in the cases of taxes. "This scenario was in the past and is going on not only in this country but other countries of the world also," the Court added.

The Court considered at length two important questions namely, *first*, what is the nature and character of the lotteries? And *second*, what changes, if any, is brought in when lottery becomes State lottery? So far as lotteries are concerned, the Court held that it could neither be denied nor had been denied that lotteries are a form of gambling. 'The lotteries as such are pernicious in nature cannot be denied,' the Court said. However, the submission is, when it cloaks itself with the linen of state authority and is presented as State organised lottery, it loses its pernicious character. For this assertion the Court, in the light of previously decided case and ancient texts, proceeded to explain what is trade and business, and what is lottery?

The Constitution Bench decision of the Supreme Court in the *R.M.D.C.*,[81] was firstly discussed at length. In this case it had been held that gambling activities are in its very nature and essence extra commercium. They were considered to be a sinful and pernicious vice by the ancient seers and Law-givers of India. It also records that even the laws of England, Scotland, United States of America and Australia have deprecated it. In support, it quoted what seers and Law-givers of India in ancient time looked upon gambling.

A reference was made of *Rigveda*,[82] which proclaims the demerits of gambling.[83] It referred to *Mahabharata*, which deprecates gambling by depicting the woeful conditions of the Pandavas who had gambled away their kingdom. *Manu* advises the king to exclude from his realm gambling and betting, since these two vices cause the destruction of the kingdom of princes. He describes a gambler as secret thieves who constantly harass the good subject by their forbidden practices. He also referred to the gambling as a vice causing great enmity and advised wise men not to practice it even for amusement.[84] As in the present case, even in the ancient time, inspite of condemnation of gambling, *Yajnavalkya* permitted it under state control. *Vrihaspati* on this subject records that gambling had been totally prohibited by *Manu* because it destroys truth, honesty and wealth while some other Law-givers permitted it when conducted under the control of the state so as to allow the king a share of every stake.

After discussing the aforesaid versions of ancient Indian Thinkers the Court referred to certain American and Australian cases in which series *Paul v. Virginia*,[85] was the first. The Court made the following observations from this case to make the discussion useful :

81. A.I.R. 1957 S.C. 699.
82. Hymn XXXIV of the *Rigveda*.
83. *Id.* verses 7, 10 and 13.
84. Verses 221, 226, 227.
85. 1850, 49 U.S. 163 ; 12 L. Ed. 1030, 1033.

> "Experience has shown that the common forms of gambling are comparatively innocuous when placed in contrast with widespread pestilence of lotteries. The former is confined to a few persons and places, but the latter infests the whole community; it enters every dwelling; it reaches every class: it preys upon the hard earnings of the poor, it plunders the ignorant and the simple."

The observations were quoted, with approval in *Douglas v. Kentucky.*[86] After quoting the passage from *Paul* judgment proceeded:

> "Is the state forbidden by the supreme law of the land from protecting its people at all times from practices which it conceives to be attended by such ruinous results? Can the Legislature of a State contract away its power to establish such regulations as are reasonably necessary from time to time to protect the public morals against the evils of lotteries?"

In the said decisions, a reference was made to the decision of Australian High Court in The *King v. Connare,*[87] Evatt, J. did not think that lottery tickets can be regarded as goods or commodities entitled for protection of Sec. 21 of the Commonwealth of Australian Constitution Act:

> "If they are goods or commodities they belong to a very special category, so special in the interests of its citizens that the State may legitimately exile them from the realm of trade, commerce or business. The indiscriminate sale of such tickets may be regarded as causing business disturbance and loss which, on general grounds of policy, the State is entitled to prevent or at least minimize."[88]

In the same decision, McTiernan, J. held:

> "Some trades are more adventurous or speculative than others, but trade or commerce as a branch of human activity belongs to an order entirely different from gaming or gambling. Whether a particular activity falls within the one or the other order is a matter of social opinion rather than jurisprudence . . . It is gambling to buy a ticket or share in a lottery. Such a transaction does not belong to the commercial business of the country. The purchaser stades money in a scheme for distributing prizes by chance. He is a gamester."

---

86. 1897, 168 U.S. 488.
87. 1939, 51 C.L.R. 596.
88. *Id.* at p. 628

McTiernan, J. reiterated his view in another case, *King v. Connare*[89]:

"It is important to observe the distinction that gambling is not trade, commerce and intercourse within the meaning of Sec. 92 otherwise the control of gambling in Australia would be attended with constitutional difficulties."

In the same decision the view of Taylor, J. is also quoted as under :

"No simple legislative expedient purporting to transmute trade and commerce into something else will remove it from the ambit of Sec. 92. But whilst asserting the width of the field in which Sec. 92 may operate it is necessary to observe that not every transaction which employs the forms of trade and commerce will, as trade and commerce, invoke its protection."

With reference to the history of lotteries in England, the learned Judge quoted:

"The foregoing observation give some indication of the attitude of the law for over two and a half centuries towards the carrying on of lotteries. But they show also that, in this country, lotteries were, from the moment of its first settlement, common and public nuisances and that, in general, it was impossible to conduct them except in violation of the law. Indeed it was impracticable for any person to conduct a lottery without achieving the status of a rogue and a vagabond."

The Supreme Court held that it is significant that American Congress, faced with the difficulty to include gambling activity within the "Commerce Clause" of Article 1, Section 8, Clause 3 of the Constitution of the United States in the interests of controlling its activity including ban or penalising a person, interpreted the "Commerce Clause" to include gambling activity. The relevant portion as recorded in *R.M.D.C.*[90] was quoted by the Court as under[91]:

"Congress having made law regulating gambling activities which extended across the State borders, the question arose whether the making of the law was within the legislative competence of the Congress, that is to say whether it could be brought within the "Commerce Clause." The question depended for its answer on the further question whether the

89. 1938, 61 C.L.R. 596.

90. A.I.R. 1957 S.C. 699.

91. *M/s B.R. Enterprises v. State of U.P.*, A.I.R. 1999 S.C. 1867 at p. 1890.

> gambling activities could be said to be commerce amongst the States. If it could, then it was open to Congress to make the law in exercise of its legislative powers under the "Commerce Clause." More often than not gambling activities extend from State to State and in view of the "Commerce Clause," no state Legislature can make a law for regulating inter-State activities in the nature of trade. If betting and gambling does not fall within the ambit of the "Commerce Clause", then neither the Congress nor the State Legislature can in any way control the same. In such circumstances, the Supreme Court of America thought it right to give a wide meaning to the word 'Commerce' so as to include gambling within the commerce clause and thereby enable the Congress to regulate and control the same. Thus, in *Champion v. Ames*[92] the carriage of lottery tickets from one State to another by an express company was held to be inter-State commerce and the Court upheld the law made by Congress which made such carriage an offence."

The Court summarised the relevant portions of the various decisions given by the Australian, American and English Courts to show how they have received the lotteries in their countries, its nature, impact on public at large, their concern about its regulation and control. There can be no doubt, on the perusal of the said decisions that the courts considered lottery as gambling and even where such lotteries were permitted under the regulating power of the State but were not given the status of 'trade and commerce' as understood at common parlance. It is significant, within the fertile and exclusive zone of interpretation, when situation arose, to interpret the word 'Commerce' which normally would not have included 'gambling' within it, in the wider public interest as to bring jurisdiction to the legislature to control or restrict 'betting and gambling', the Court interpreted this also to come within "Commerce Clause." This wider definition to the "Commerce Clause" was given by the American Court with an objective to control such lotteries rather giving absolute freedom to trade in it.

Thus, the law in *Champion*[93] penalising even carriage of lottery tickets from one state to another was upheld. In cases *United States v. Kahriger*,[94] and *Lewis v. United States*,[95] the Supreme Court of United States held that there is no constitutional right to gambling.

In addition to some of the quotations in ancient *Dharmasastra* as referred in *R.M.D.C.*,[96] the Supreme Court give few more of the views in

92. 1902, 188 U.S. 321.
93. *Ibid.*
94. 1953, 345 U.S. 22; 97 L.Ed. 754.
95. 1955, 348 U.S. 419; 99 L.Ed. 475.
96. A.I.R. 1957 S.C. 699.

Dharmasastera on the point in issue. *Kautilya* in *Dyutasamahvaya*,[97] allowed gambling in a central place under States supervision as it led to the detection of thieves. According to the view of some others it was also allowed to be carried in the presence of master of the gambling hall and provided it yielded revenue to the king. If they indulge in gambling openly but give to the king share in the stakes then such a person does not incur in punishment. *Rigveda* records that "gambling is one of the most ancient vices."[98] *Brahmapurna* condemns it in the strong language. It says that the gambler's wife is always in distress and the gambler on seeing the condition of his wife is also worried.

Some of the historical background of the lottery was further cited by the Court as under:

> "Lottery a scheme for the distribution of prizes to be determined by chance, was reputedly an invention of the Romans . . . Lottery in the modern sense originated in Italy during the middle ages spreading to France, Germany and Austria where rulers used them to raise revenue . . . First English lottery was drawn in 1569 . . . However, lotteries encouraged mass gambling and fraudulent drawing and after they had been attacked . . . Parliament provided for their discontinuance in 1823. Thereafter large scale lotteries contrived to inhibit prosecution by giving large sums to charities . . . A century later following agitation for legalised lotteries, the Betting and Lotteries Act, 1934, adopted the recommendation of royal commission and continued the prohibition on all lotteries."[99]

Misra, J., explaining the American perception of lotteries and gambling cited the following observations[100]:

> "Two hundred years ago, government-sanctioned lotteries were common throughout America. Lacking a strong Central Government and burdened with a weak tax base, early Americans viewed lotteries as legitimate vehicles for raising revenue. Lottery proceeds were used to build cities, establish universities, and even to help finance the Revolutionary War. They were gradually abandoned throughout the 1800s as Governments developed better forms of taxation. Lottery fraud became a concern and social problems stemming from excessive gambling developed. In 1893, the Liberarian of Congress wrote of 'a general public conviction that lotteries are to be regarded,

97. III-20 referred to in Chapter 26 of the Dyutasamahvaya.
98. Chapter X Verse 34.
99. Encyclopedia Britannica, 1980 Ed. at pp. 327-28.
100. *M/S B.R. Enterprises v. State of U.P.*, 1999 S.C. 1867 at p. 1892.

> in direct proportion to their extension, as among the most dangerous and prolific sources of human misery'. Soon thereafter, federal legislation brought an end to the last remaining legal American lottery.[101] . . . From 1709 until 1826, the English Government conducted annual lotteries to raise revenue. These were so popular that they soon became a matter of concern. English lotteries were attacked for 'weakening the habits of industry,' diminishing 'permanent sources of the public revenue,' encouraging other forms of gambling, and being 'injurious in the highest degree, to the morals of the people . . . Finally, in 1823, at about the same time that lotteries were beginning to be phased out in America, England abolished lotteries in that country.[102] . . . Until the early 1800s, there was little opposition to State conducted lotteries, State regulation, including bonding of operators and supervision of receipts, quieted opponents. Churches usually benefited from lotteries were not quick to condemn. As the country's dependency on lotteries increased, however, so did the opportunity for abuse. Serious lottery opposition began to mount in the early to mid-1800s as part of general social reform that included movements for temperance, peace, women's rights, educational reform, prison reform and abolition of slavery.[103] . . . Because legalized gambling leads to increased illegal gambling state-sponsored lotteries inevitably increase crime. Legalized gambling's impact on criminal behaviour, however, is not limited to an increase in illegal gambling. Perhaps the most serious concern is that legal gambling creates problem gamblers, and problem gamblers often turn to more serious criminal activity to support their habits."[104]

From the references from *Dharmasastra,* opinions of distinguished authors, references in the Encyclopedia of Britannica and Boston Law Review and others, it may be concluded that lottery remains in the realm of gambling. Even where it is state sponsored still it was looked down as an evil. Right from ancient time till the day all expressed concern to eliminate this, even where it was legalised for raising revenue, either by the king or in the modern times by the State. Even this legitimisation was for the sole purpose of raising revenue, was also for a limited period, since this received condemnation even for this limited purpose. All this gives clear picture of the nature and character of lottery as perceived through the conscience of the

---

101. The Lotteries, Revenues and Social Costs: A historical examination of State-Sponsored gambling, it records in Boston College Law Review, Vol. 34:11 at p. 12.
102. *Id.* at p. 22.
103. *Id.* at p. 32.
104. *Id.* at p. 70.

people, as revealed through ancient scriptures, also by various Courts of the countries. It is in this background that the Court proceeded to examine, if lotteries are goods, could a contract for sale of such goods be conferred the status of trade and commerce as used in Chapter XIII of our Constitution.

The Supreme Court concentrated itself to the questions—what are lottery tickets? What are the ingredients of contract of sale of lottery tickets? Whether does an ingredient constitute it to be trade and to be such trade as receive protection under our Constitution? In other words, could such trade qualify to be a fundamental right or a right conferred by a Statute? If it is a right out of creature of a Statute could it not be regulated curtailed or banned by the same Statute? Whether a right spoken of "free trade" under Article 301 speaks about fundamental right or does it include trade of the nature one is concerned? Whether mere legalisation of a transaction by itself becomes 'commercium' of the nature as to qualify to be a trade as understood under Article 301.

What is 'lottery'?, what would be the ingredients in the sale of lottery tickets'? Can it be equated with other forms of contract pertaining to trade and commerce?, whether there is striking difference between the two?, all these questions were answered by the Supreme Court as under :

> "A lottery is a species of gambling.[105] The lottery statutes were enacted to suppress the widespread evil of gambling in lotteries and to allay and curb the gambling spirit of the public and thus prevent waste of money needed for more substantial purposes, the term 'lottery' as popularly and generally used referring to a gambling scheme in which chances are sold or disposed of for value and the sums thus paid are hazarded in the hope of winning a much larger sum, a scheme for the distribution of prizes by chance.[106] . . . The term lottery in law is of wide signification. In *Horner v. United States,*[107] Blatchford discussed various definitions of lottery and among others approved that found in Worcester's Dictionary, in which it is defined to be "game of hazard in which small sums are ventured with the chance of obtaining a large value, either in money or other articles.[108] The term "tickets" when speaking of the sale of lottery tickets, is equivalent to chances. In a general sense, lottery tickets are more in the nature of chooses in action than merchandise, being in some respects memoranda of conditional promises to pay."[109]

---

105. In Words and Phrases (Permanent Edn.), Vol. 25A at p. 439.
106. *Id.* at p. 444.
107. 409, U.S. 449, 37 L. Ed. 237.
108. In Words and Phrases, Vol. 25A at p. 445.
109. *Id.* at p. 491.

The Court further said that, generally to constitute lottery there must be a prize awarded by chance for a consideration with no infusion of skill.[110] An artifice, no matter how new is within the condemnation of the law against lottery if it, in effect, embodies the principle of a lottery and operates as such.[111] The term lottery has not technical meaning in the law distinct from its popular signification. A lottery is a scheme for the distribution of prizes by chance.[112] A lottery has been described as a scheme for distributing prizes by lot or chance. It must not be entirely forgotten in the construction of these Acts of Parliament (See now the lotteries and Amusement Act, 1976) that the evil which the lottery law has seen to prevent was the evil which existed where poor people with only a few pence to feed their children would go and put these few pence into a lottery and lose them, and this sociologically was a bad thing.[113] It is a chance for a prize for a price. It is a scheme for the distribution of the prize or prizes by lot or chance, the number and value of which is determined by the operator or lottery.[114]

Thus, the Court found three ingredients in the sale of lottery tickets namely: (i) prize, (ii) chance, and (iii) consideration. So when one purchases a lottery ticket, he purchases for a prize, which is by chance and the consideration is price of the ticket. The holder of such ticket knows the consideration, which he has paid, may be for receiving nothing. However, there are few who may be lucky to receive the prize, which is just by chance. *The question is such transaction be termed as trade or commerce*? Part XIII of our Constitution deals with trade, commerce and intercourse within the territory of India. It does not define trade and commerce. Trade is an exchange in any Articles either by Barter or for money or for service rendered. In other words, it is exchange between two parties, one who tenders the consideration and the other who returns for this consideration good, money, service or such other things. Party paying consideration in any trade is aware for what he is paying the consideration. It is neither hypothetical nor it is a contract for any unascertained thing. In any case there is no element or ingredient of chance under any trade. This element of chance makes the lottery a gambling. On the other hand an absence of chance inherently attached to any contract coupled with some skill makes it to be a trade. So trade is always associated with some skill while in lottery there is absence of skill predominantly and essentially with the ingredient of chance. Thus, in nutshell in lottery there is no skill and element of chance, in trade it is for exchange of something for consideration where there is absence of chance and inherently with element of skill.

During the course of its judgment the Supreme Court referred to the opinion of Evatt, McTiernan and Taylor, JJ., which they expressed while

110. *State v. Mabrey* , 60 N.W. 2d 889, 893.

111. *Commonwealth v. Luad,* 15 A 2d 839, 840, 841, 843, 845.

112. Law Lexicon, P. Ramanatha Ayiar,1997, Edn., at p. 1151.

113. Words and Pharases, Buterworths, 3rd Edn. at p. 71.

114. Black's law Dictionary, 6th Edn., at p. 947.

deciding the validity of Section 21 of a New South Wales Statute. The opinion of the Learned Judges was quoted with approval as under :

> "If they are goods or commodities they belong to a very special category, so special that in the interests of its citizens the State may legitimately exile them from the realm of trade, commerce or business . . . [115] It is gambling to buy a ticket or share in a lottery. Such a transaction does not belong to the commercial business of the country . . . [116] But whilst asserting the width of the filed in which Section 92 may operate it is necessary to observe that not every transaction which employs the forms of trade and commerce will as trade and commerce invoke its protection . . ."[117]

The Learned counsel for the State challenging the validity of the Act, submitted that there is marked difference between our Constitution and the Australian Constitution or the Constitution of the United States of America, hence one should not apply the principles of the decision of those courts. It was argued that there is nothing in the American Constitution corresponding to Art. 19(1)(g) or Art. 301 as in our Constitution. Similarly in the Australian Constitution there is no provision as we have in our Art. 19(6) or Art. 302, 304, in contrast Sec. 92 of the Australian Constitution is free without any such limitations. This submission was taken note by the Supreme Court in *R.M.D.C.*[118] The Court pointed out that the reference of the judgments of foreign courts were only to take the stock of the view as to with what vision they judged and what they meant and understood while dealing with the sale of lottery tickets. It was said that these decisions were referred not for interpreting the provisions of our Constitution but only to know the nature and character of lotteries as understood in those countries, as there is no difference with that what is understood in our country. The Court said that it is in this background that the Supreme Court in *R.M.D.C.*,[119] after recording the activities of lotteries which is condemned in this country from the ancient times and also taking note of views of the courts of other countries, found that they equally condemned, discouraged and looked it down with disfavour, viz. in England, Scotland, the United States of America and in Australia.

The purpose of Art. 19(1)(g) and 301 could not possibly have been to guarantee freedom of gambling. To dissolve principle laid down in *R.M.D.C.*,[120] on behalf of the states challenging the validity of the Act, it is

115. Evatt, J.
116. McTiernan, J.
117. Taylor, J.
118. A.I.R. 1957 S.C. 699.
119. *Ibid.*
120. *Ibid.*

submitted that the *R.M.D.C.*,[121] was concerned with the lotteries covered by Entry 34 List II and not the lotteries organised by the state which is covered by Entry 40 List I, hence it would have no application. The Court pointed out that this decision has not diluted the law laid down with respect to the finding that gambling would not fall within the meaning of the word 'trade' under Art. 301 of the Constitution or to have diluted that such transaction would not get protection under Art. 19(1)(g). What is said to that moral prohibitions in Hindu Law text against gambling were not legally enforced. It is true within the moral format, in a strict sense, if it was to be legally enforced there could not have been any legalised gambling. But it can not be doubted and it is recognised by all the countries that gambling by its very nature promises to make poor man a rich man, to quench the thirst of a man in dire economic distress or to a man with bursting desire to become wealthy overnight draws them into the magnetic field of lotteries with crippling effect. More often than not, such hopes with very remote chance encourages the spirit of reckless prosperity in him, running him and his family. This encouraging hope with the magnitude of prize money never dwindles. Losses and failures in lotteries instead of discouragement increase the craze with intoxicating hope, nit only to erase the losses but to fill his imaginative coffer. When this chance mixes with this utopian hope he goes into a chronic state of indebtedness. In this context, it is said that how the Constitution-makers could ever have conceived to give protection to gambling under Art. 19(1)(g) or Art. 301 of our Constitution.

Next, the Court examined why lotteries have been held to be pernicious or gambling and what elements, which constitute it, to be so is filtered out to take it out of gambling jacket. It held that the historical background was mentioned to distinguish between two forms of lotteries. The State lotteries are not penal offence, which has been understood and recognised so since 1870 when section 294-A, I.P.C. was brought into the Indian Penal Code, 1860. This distinction has also been recognised even in the Government of India Act, 1935 where the State lotteries have been separately placed under Entry 48, List I but other form of lotteries were placed under Entry 34, List II, and the same continues even in our Constitution when state lotteries fall under Entry 40, List I while other lotteries fall under Entry 34, List II. Thus, it is submitted that the state lotteries are a distinct class, and it run under the authority of law hence could neither be pernicious nor *res extra commercium*.

It was pointed out that the difference between gambling and the trade is that a *gambling inherently contains a chance with no skill, while trade contains skill with no chance*. What makes lottery a pernicious is its gambling nature. The Court questioned that can it be said that in the State organised lotteries this element of gambling is excluded? There could possibly be no two opinions that even in the State lotteries the same element of chance remains

---

121. *Ibid.*

with no skill. It remains within the boundaries of gambling. The stringent measures and the conditions imposed under the State lotteries are only to inculcate faith to the participant of such lottery, that it is being conducted fairly with no possibility of fraud, misappropriation or deceit and assure the hopeful recipients of high prizes that all is fair and safe. That assurance is from stage one to the last with full transparency. No doubt, holding of the State lotteries for public revenue has been authorised, legalised and once this having been done it is expected from the State to take such measure to see that people at large, faithfully and hopefully participate in larger number for the greater yield of its revenue with no fear in their mind. The Act, further ensures by virtue of section 4(d) that proceeds of the sale of such lottery tickets are credited to the public accounts of the state. This is to give clear message to the participants that the proceeds is not in the hands of individual group or association but is ensured to be credited in the state accounts. However, the Court said that this by itself would not take it outside the realm of gambling. It remains within the same realm. In this regard, there is no difference between lotteries under Entry 34 List II and a lottery organised by the State under Entry 40, List I. When character of both the state organised lotteries and other lotteries remains the same by merely placing the apparel of the State with authority of law, would not make any difference, it remains gambling as element of chance persist with no element of skill. Even other lotteries under Entry 34, List II could only be run under the authority of the State or the law of the State. Only difference is in one case, authority is that of state and in other, the Parliament. That is why, what is excluded from the penal consequences under section 294-A, I.P.C. is the lotteries authorised by the state, not merely lotteries organised by the state. So on the reasoning as put forward even lotteries under Entry 34, List II cannot be said to be pernicious. The lotteries authorised by the state also have a sanction in law. The Court said that a gambling may be taxed and may be authorised for a specified purpose, but it would not attain the status of trade like other trades or become *res commercium.* No gambling could be *commercium* hence in Court's considered opinion the principle of *R.M.D.C.*[122] would equally be applicable even to the state organised lottery. The Constitution-makers could never have conceived to give protection to gambling either under Article 19(1)(g) or it as a trade under Article 301 of the Constitution.

So for as *Anraj case II*[123] was concerned, the Court held, the 'lottery tickets' to be 'goods' and thus subject to sales tax.

It was pointed out that there may be certain transactions of commodity, which are goods, and subject to sales tax but still it would not qualify to be 'trade'. For this reason, the Court felt no hesitation to hold that sale of lottery tickets organised by the state could not be construed to be trade and commerce and even if it could be construed to be so, it cannot be

122. A.I.R. 1957 S.C. 699.

123. A.I.R. 1986 S.C. 63.

raised to the status of 'trade and commerce' as understood at common parlance or 'trade and commerce' as used under Article 301. Hence, question of violation of either Articles 301 and 303 does not arise. Strong reliance was placed on *Khazan Singh's case.*[124] The Court held that if a state has a power to carry on trade in its own state it can carryon the same in every part of India.

Thus, holding lotteries organised by a state was held to be gambling in nature. Accordingly, the principle laid down in *R.M.D.C.* was held equally to be applicable to the case of state lotteries i.e., State lotteries were be construed not to be a 'trade and commerce' within the meaning of Articles 301 to 303 of the Constitution of India.

B. Extra Commerciality of Money Lending: Some Basic Issues

Money lending has always been accepted as a legitimate trade activity in our society, of course like any other activity, subject to regulations relating to rate of interest or other terms.[125] However, a potent problem arises as to how can a money-lender calculate that his activity will lose its legitimacy if by chance the borrower happens to be a man of means below a point to be fixed by the state in future.[126] Answer to this question becomes more difficult when the state has licenced the money-lender to lend money. Logically one fails to understand as to how an activity which is not only tolerated but expressly permitted, loses its legitimacy if the Legislature suddenly decides to derecognise only past transactions without prohibiting its continuance in future.[127]

Though, the Court in *Fatehchand v. State of Maharashtra,*[128] has again and again emphasised that it was excluding only exploitative money-lending from the category of trade, but in fact it has failed to make any effort to distinguish the exploitative from non-exploitative money-lending. No guidelines for the future were laid down. Prof. Singh argues that *Fatehchand* was not a proper occasion to apply the concept of *extra commercium* unless the Court was performing the role of a moral preacher. He argues that it was not a good occasion even to preach morals in so far as it lays down double standards of morality, one for individual money-lenders and another for institutionalised money-lenders such as cooperative societies, banks, etc. He felt that all kinds of profit-oriented organised activities may not claim the status of "trade or commerce" protected under Article 19(1)(g) or 301. An

124. A.I.R. 1974 S.C. 669.

125. N.C. Sen Gupta, Evolution of Ancient Indian Law (1953) 239-40. For the rule of *Damdupat*, according to which the amount of interest should at no one time exceed principal amount, D.F. Mulla, Principals of Hindu Law, (14th ed., 1974, 629 ff.). The Hindu Law has always recongnise an obligation to pay not only one's own debts but also the debts incurred by the one's father. For debts in Muslim Law, The Hedaya, Book XIX.

126. W. Murphy *et al*, Law and Poverty, 212 ff. (1973).

127. M.P. Singh, Is Moneylending Extra Commercium? *Some Thoughts on Fatehchand v. State of Maharashtra*; 1978, 3 S.C.C. 1. at p. 10.

128. 1977, 2 S.C.C., 670.

effort to discourage anti-social or socially harmful activities may be justified on this ground, but at the same time the concept of *extra-commercium* should not be made use of too lightly as it would put the individual in a state of utter confusion in regard to the exercise of his rights. More so when the Constitution expressly permits widest possible restraints on these rights leaving very little or no scope to read implied limitations through definitional technique.

The facts of this case were that the constitutionality of the Maharashtra Debt Relief Act, 1975 was challenged. The Act, in pursuance of the guidelines issued by the Government of India to all the State Governments in July 1975, provided relief in the form of one year's moratorium on all debts in case of small farmers and workers the value of whose immovable property exceeded Rs. 20,000 but did not exceed Rs. 40,000 and liquidation of all debts in respect of a worker whose immovable property did not exceed Rs. 20,000 in market value and also in the case of other debtors like the marginal farmer, the rural labourer and the rural artisan whose total income from all sources did not exceed Rs. 2,400 during the year immediately before August 1, 1975. The provision relating to liquidation of debts was also applicable in the case of workers whose income did exceed Rs. 6,000 during the said period if he was living in an Urban area, or Rs. 4,800 if he was living else where. The petitioner-appellants alleged, *inter alia*, that these provisions of the Act, violated their right to carry on the trade of money-lending protected by Article 301 of the Constitution which provides that "trade, commerce and intercourse throughout the territory of India shall be free". In defence the State contended that money-lending affected by the Act, was not a "trade or commerce" protected by Art. 301 and even if it were so, the Act, imposed only a reasonable restriction on it permissible under Art. 304(b).

In *Fatehchand* the Court has performed a very significant role by paving the path for approaching the Constitution in the broader Indian social perspective. Pursuing that path the Court, in a subsequent decision,[129] has gone to the extent of saying that in a Constitution which is wedded to a social pattern of society the vested interest group must be presumed to have the knowledge that any social legislation for the good of a particular community or the people in general can be brought forward by Parliament at any time. Thus, the privileged groups of the society in their dealings with the under-privileged ones must proceed with caution because if their dealings are found exploitative, or inconsistent with the idea of socialistic pattern of society, a retrospective invalidation of these dealings cannot be said to be unconstitutional or unjust even though the concept of exploitation and socialistic pattern may be debatable and obscure.

The Court, however can only encourage or uphold social measures taken by the legislature or the executive; it cannot initiate them. Heavy burden, therefore, lies on the Legislature and the executive to look at all the

129. Fazal Ali, J. in *Pathumma v. State of Kerala*, 1978, 2, S.C.C. 1, 22 (para 36).

pros and cons of the proposed action to ensure maximum advantage to the beneficiary group with minimum of disadvantage to the losing group. A fine balancing of conflicting interests may be impossibility but an optimum point may be achieved. It seems that the Maharashtra Legislature did not make serious efforts to look for that optimum point. It made a general law without looking into the purpose of the debt or the individual's paying capacity. It also did not draw a distinction between the licenced and unlicenced money-lenders. Nor did it distinguish a transaction involving reasonable rate of interest from the one where unreasonably high rate of interest was charged. It made no arrangements for the large numbers of money-lenders who themselves had borrowed from bigger money-lender and had lent the entire amount to persons whose debts were discharged by the Act.[130] The legislature did not assess the need of the poor to obtain loans, nor did it provide any infrastructure for future loan needs. The institutionalised money-lending agencies do not lend money for consumption purposes, particularly in rural area, and non-institutionalised agencies because of the Act, would not lend except at very extortionate terms.

Definitely the Act, raptured one of the cardinal principles of human justice, *'pacta sunt servanda,'* i.e., a moral and legal obligation to pay off one's debts and also the normal expectation of the parties, particularly of the creditor to get back his money with interest. Legislations of that kind, it is submitted, should also consider the desirability of recompensing the creditor from the public exchequer particularly when the creditor is also likely to be ruined as a direct and immediate result of the legislation. The creditor alone should not be required to bear the entire burden of improving the lot of the poor. Though it gave some relief to the debtors but it also created difficulties for them to obtain credit in future. It did not say that money-lending was so bad that it was outlawed and prohibited forever or even for a short period. Satisfaction would have been if it had done so because an exploitative practice would have been rooted out from this land and also the habits and attitudes of the people in regard to their loan requirements would have changed. But the Act did not do that. It can therefore be called only a palliative and not a serious attack on poverty or a measure of social change.

Some of these criticisms were brought to the notice of the Court in testing the reasonableness of the restrictions under Art. 304(b). They are not directed at discouraging this kind of measures. They are also not directed at stopping all attempts to solve social problems till answers are found to all possible objections. However, the Court had no choice but to uphold or invalidate it, and in our submission, it was perfectly right in upholding it because on any view of the Constitution, the Act could be upheld.

---

130. According to one of the memorandum of appeals decided with *Fatehchand/Pannolla Kesharchand Bathia v. The State of Maharashtra*, Civil appeal No. 645 of 1976—out of the total loaned amount of Rs. 5,51,000, Rs. 4,85,000 had been borrowed from financiers or bigger money-lenders.

In *M/S B.R. Enterprises,*[131] a submission was made that "*Fatehchand*, decision on 'money-lending business' had held that there are 'aspects of business or trade', which in one sense may be noxious when conducted by a given class of persons but when entrusted to another who are well organised it is rationalised and is no more noxious. Just as all 'money-lenders and money-lending' would not necessarily be noxious or pernicious so also all items falling under betting and gambling would not be pernicious." This submission, in view of the Supreme Court, was misconceived. The Court was of the view that this case referred to the village-based, age-old feudal pattern of money-lending given to the labourer, the marginal tiller and the broken farmer, etc. with unvouched usurious interest, which brought such persons into perpetual labour, hereditary service, etc. of the lender. It is because of this it was said to be a pernicious species of money-lending flourishing in the rural and industrial areas of our country. In contrast, it was held that money-lending when through recognised financial institutions, banks, etc., it is legitimate and valid commercial credit and financial dealing which could not be said to be pernicious species of money-lending. The Supreme Court in *B.R. Enterprises*, said that the *Fatehchand* decision referred to about pernicious species of money-lending. It confined this adjective to a limited class of persons, but it did not hold, the business of money-lending as such to be pernicious in nature; it held that pernicious because some class of money-lenders made the poor artisan, bonded labourer, etc., i.e. a perpetual debtors.

C. Extra Commerciality of "Liquor"

Before discussing commerciality or extra commerciality of liquor in India it appears proper to have the American background. In United States the original package doctrine made its debut in *Brown v. Maryland,*[132] where it was applied to remove imports from abroad which were still in the hands of the importer in the original package, out of the reach of the State's taxing power. This rule the Court, overriding a dictum in Marshall's opinion in *Brown v. Maryland,*[133] rejected outright after the Civil War as to imports from sister states.[134]

However, when in the late eighties and early nineties statewide Prohibition laws began making their appearance, the Court seized on the rejected dictum. It began applying it as a brake on the operation of such laws with respect to inter-state commerce in intoxicants, which the Court denominated "legitimate articles of commerce." It held that a State was

131. A.I.R. 1999 S.C. 1867 at p. 1898.
132. 12 Wheat. 419 (1827).
133. *Ibid*. 449.
134. *Woofruff v. Parham*, 8 Wall. 123 (1869). There were later some departures from the rule, apparently due to inattention, in cases involving oil. See *Standard Oil v. Graves*, 249 U.S. 389 (1919); *Askren v. Continental Oil Co.*, 252 U.S. 444 (1920); *Bowman v. Continental Oil Co.*, 256 U.S. 642 (1921) and *Texas Co. v. Brown*, 258 U.S. 466 (1922). These cases were "qualified," and in fact disavowed in *Sonneborn Bros. v. Cureton*, 262 U.S. 506, 520 (1923).

entitled to prohibit the manufacture and sale within its limits of intoxicants,[135]even for an outside market–manufacture being no part of commerce.[136] But it contemporaneously laid down the rule, in *Bowman v. Chicago and Northwestern Railroad Co.*,[137] that so long as Congress remained silent in the matter, a State lacked the power. It lacked power even as part and parcel of a programme of statewide prohibition of the traffic in intoxicants, to prevent the shipment into it of intoxicants from a sister state.

The above holding was soon followed by another to the effect that, so long as Congress remained silent, a State had no power to prevent the sale in the original package of liquors introduced from another state.[138] The effect of the later decision was soon overcome by an Act, of Congress, the so-called Wilson Act, repealing its alleged silence.[139] But the *Bowman* decision still stood, the Act, in question being interpreted by the Court not to subject liquors from sister States to local authority until their arrival in the hands of the person to whom consigned.[140] Not till 1913 was the effect of the decision in the *Bowman* case fully nullified by the Webb-Kenyon Act,[141] which placed intoxicants entering a state from another state under the control of the former for all purposes whatsoever.

In India in *Krishan Kumar Narula v. State of Jammu & Kashmir*,[142] the submission was that potable liquor is noxious and dangerous to the community and subversive of its moral. With reference to potable liquor a challenge was made, the Court held:

> " . . . dealing in noxious and dangerous goods like liquor was dangerous to the community and subversive of its morals . . . such an approach leads to incoherence in thought and expression. Standard of morality can offer guidance to impose restrictions, but cannot limit the scope of right."[143]

Interpreting *Narula's* ruling, *Nashirwar's case*[144] holds as follows:

> "It is not correct to read in the decision of *Narula's case* that there is a fundamental right to do business in liquor. The decision is that dealing in liquor is business and a citizen has a right to do

135. *Mugler v. Kansas*, 123 U.S. 623 (1887).
136. *Kidd v. Pearson*, 128 U.S. 1 (1888).
137. 125 U.S. 465 (1888).
138. *Leisy & Co. v. Hardin*, 135 U.S. 100 (1890).
139. 26 Stat. 313 (1890); sustained in *In re Rahrer*, 140 U.S. 545 (1891).
140. *Rhodes v. Iowa*, 170 U.S, 412 (1898).
141. 37 Stat. 699 (1913); sustained in *Clark Distilling Co. v. Western Md. Ry. Co.*, 242 U.S. 311 (1917).
142. A.I.R. 1967, S. C. 1368.
143. *Id.* at p 1371.
144. A.I.R. 1975, S.C. 360.

business in that commodity and the State can impose reasonable restrictions on the right in public interest. If the State can prohibit business in liquor as is held in *State of Bombay v. F.N. Balsara,*[145] this establishes that the State has exclusive right of privilege of manufacture, possession sale of intoxicating liquor and therefore the state grants such a right of privilege to persons in the shape of licence or lease."

In reaching this conclusion the Supreme Court took note of the decision in *Bharucha's case,*[146] that there was no inherent right in a citizen to sale intoxicating liquors by retail, and that it is not a privilege of a citizen of the State, and observed that as *Bharucha,* was a Constitution Bench decision like *Narula,* the latter could not be said to have overruled the former. As has been stated, the matter again came up for consideration in *Har Shankar's case,*[147] with specific reference to *Narula* and it was reiterated that "there is no fundamental right to do trade or business in intoxicants" and that "in all these manifestations, these rights are vested in the State and indeed without such vesting there can be no effective regulation of various forms of activities in relation to intoxicants." The contrary view of the High Court in the impugned judgments is incorrect and must be set aside, the Court observed.

The Court gave reasons for taking a contrary view with reference to the decision in *Nashirwar*[148] and *Har Shankar.*[149] It views that the state has the exclusive right or privilege to manufacture, store and sale liquor and to grant that right to its licence holders on payment of considerations, with such conditions and restrictions for its regulation as may be necessary in the public interest. The argument to the contrary is futile and is rejected.

Thus, the Court held that right to trade in liquor was business. However, in *Khoday Distilleries,*[150] it reversed the decision of *Narula,* by holding that right to trade in liquor was not constitutionally protected. However, the Court in this case clearly made three exceptions: (a) trade in alcohol is not *per se* prohibited for medicinal and industrial uses; (b) even though trade in potable alcohol was *res extra commercium* the state itself may sale potable alcohol, set-up a monopoly business for that purpose and maximise its revenue by any mode of sale; and (c) the State may on a non-discriminatory basis permit sale of alcohol through private parties. In *Khoday Distilleries,* the Supreme Court held:

"The right to practice any profession or to carry on any occupation, trade or business does not extend to practicing

145. A.I.R. 1951, S.C. 318.
146. A.I.R. 1954, S.C. 220.
147. A.I.R. 1975, S.C. 1121.
148. A.I.R. 1975, S.C. 360.
149. A.I.R. 1975, S.C. 1121.
150. A.I.R. 1996, S.C. 911.

> profession or carrying on an occupation, trade or business which is inherently vicious and pernicious, and is, condemned by all civilised societies. It does not entitle citizens to çarry on trade or business in Activities, which are immoral and criminal, and in articles or goods which are obnoxious and injurious to health, safety and welfare of the general public, i.e. *res extra commercium* (outside commerce). There cannot be business in crime."

Potable liquor as a beverage is an intoxicating and depressant drink which is dangerous and injurious to health and is therefore, an article which is *res extra commercium* being inherently harmful. A citizen has, therefore *no fundamental right to do trade or business in liquor*. Hence the trade or business in liquor can be completely prohibited.

For the same reason, again, the State can impose limitations and restrictions on the trade or business in potable liquor as a beverage which restrictions are in nature different from those imposed on the trade or business in legitimate activities and goods and articles which are *res commercium*. The restrictions and limitations on the trade and business in potable liquor can again be both under Art. 19(6) or otherwise. The restriction and limitations can extend to the State carrying on the trade or business itself to the exclusion or an elimination of others and to preserving to itself the right to sale licences to do trade or business in the same, to others.

The state can carry on trade or business in potable liquor notwithstanding that it is an intoxicating drink and Art. 47 enjoins it to prohibit its consumption. When the state carries on such business, it does so to restrict and regulate production, supply and consumption of liquor, which is also an aspect of reasonable restriction in the interest of general public. The state cannot on that account be said to be carrying on an illegitimate business. It carries on business in products which are not declared illegal by completely prohibiting their production but in products the manufacture, possession and supply of which is regulated in the interest of the health, morals and welfare of people. It does so also in the interests of the general public under Art. 19(6).

The mere fact that the state levies taxes or fees on the productions, sale and income is legitimate or illegitimate, does not make the state a party to the said activities. The power of the state to raise revenue by levying taxes and fees should not be confused with the power of the state to prohibit or regulate the trade or business in question. The state exercises its two different powers on such occasions. Hence, the mere fact that the State levies taxes and fees on trade or business in liquor or derives income from it does not make the right to carry on trade or business in liquor a fundamental right, or even a legal right when such trade or business is completely prohibited.

This decision clearly lays down and demonstrates that manufacture, sale, purchase of potable liquor, which State carries on at common parlance is trade and is a goods still held to be an article different from goods and articles which are *res commercium*. This holds further that transactions in potable liquor by sale, in spite of levy of taxes and fees on this trade or business, should be held to be *res extra commercium*.

D. Electronic Res Extra Commercium

Some so-called Internet regulations do not in fact necessitate any Internet-specific analysis. Let us consider three recent dormant Commerce Clause challenges to state bans on cross-border sales via the Internet. In *Swedenburg v. Kelly*[151] wine-makers who wanted to sell directly to consumers over the Internet challenged state requirements that restricted the sources—both in states and out-of-state—from which out-of-state wine could be bought. In *Ford Motor Co. v. Tex. Dep't of Transp.*,[152] Automakers who wanted to sell cars directly to consumers via the Internet challenged state laws that prohibited manufacturers from selling cars directly to consumers. And in *Santa Fe Natural Tobacco Co. v. Spitzer*,[153]a cigarette manufacturer challenged a New York regulation that effectively precluded the sale of cigarette via the Internet by prohibiting inter-state cigarette shipments directly to consumers.

These state regulations might or might not violate the dormant commerce clause, depending on whether they discriminate against inter-state commerce or fail the balancing test. (The wine cases are especially complex because of the Twenty-First Amendment.[154]) But the fact that the communications before sale take place over the Internet does not mean that any unusual problems are presented under the dormant Commerce Clause. This is because these cases involve the sale and delivery of real-space goods. Unlike cases involving the transmission of digital goods over the Internet, the out-of-state provider of real-space goods knows the real-space location of the recipient and can take steps to keep the offending goods out of the regulating jurisdiction. To be sure, these steps impose costs. The content provider must determine where the goods are going and research and comply with local regulations. But these are the same costs faced by the out-of-state seller when orders are placed by mail or telephone. As we made clear above, these costs are commonplace in our federal system and do not usually implicate dormant commerce clause scrutiny.

Here one can draw a general lesson. Concerns about the cross-border costs of state Internet regulation are heightened when the sale and transmission of digital goods as opposed to real-space goods are at issue. The Pornography and Spam cases are harder than the wine, automobile, and cigarette cases precisely because in the former context it appears more costly

151. No. 00 Civ. 0778, 2000 WL 1264285 (S.D.N.Y. Sept. 5, 2000).
152. 106 F. Supp. 2nd 905 (W.D. Tex. 2000).
153. No. 00 Civ. 7274, 2000 WL 1694307 (S.D.N.Y. Nov. 13, 2000).
154. *Bridenbaugh v. Freeman-Wilson*, 227 F.3d 848 (7th Cir. 2000).

for out-of-state regulated entities to identify and filter their communications and deliveries by geography.

There are other laws besides the Porn and Spam statutes that implicate the concerns of *American Libraries Ass'n*. Let us consider *Consolidated Cigar Co. v. Reilly.*[155] The district court read a Massachusetts cigar advertising law not to apply to Internet advertising, reasoning that such regulation of the Internet "would likely run into significant difficulty . . . "[156] The First Circuit rejected the district court's narrower reading but agreed, with no analysis, that the regulation as applied to the Internet violated the dormant Commerce Clause.[157]

One does not know why the court reached this conclusion, but presumably it did so because of the out-of-state burdens of the advertising regulation, and especially because of the difficulty out-of-state web advertisers would have in keeping offending content out of Massachusetts. Understood this way, the tobacco advertising regulation is like the Porn and Spam statutes and unlike the wine, automobile, and cigarette regulations in the sense that out-of-state persons face the special difficulties of identifying and controlling the flow of digital information. The same is true for state regulations of web gambling, attorney advertising, marketing disclosure, auctions, lotteries, and securities—all of which involve the delivery of digital goods, all of which will become subjects of dormant commerce clause challenge.[158]

Similarly, in cases of gambling on the Internet, courts have found the gambling to occur where the bet is placed rather than where the web site is hosted, and to be illegal under state law.[159] The Internet's status as a new medium does not alter the basic features of a solicitation, i.e. a request by a real-space organisation for money that is received by a real-space state resident.

This Part does not argue that there should be no national policy or regulation of the Internet. However, the arguments for state regulation of solicitation remain as strong in cyberspace as they are in real space, and there is no good reason for the federal government to abrogate this or the many other state consumer protection (and criminal) laws that should legitimately apply online.

Both state and federal governments have applied their existing laws to gambling on the Internet in order to protect their legitimate interests. There is no indication that federal law will preempt state law in the online gambling context.

155. 218 F. 3d 30 (1st Cir. 2000).

156. *Lorillard Tobacco Co. v Reilly*, 84 F. Supp. 2d 180, 204 n. 19 (D. Mass. 2000).

157. *Consol. Cigar*, 218 F. 3d at pp. 55-57.

158. H. Joseph Hameline & William Miles, The Dormant Commerce Clause Meets The Internet, 41 Boston B.J. 8, 8 (1997).

159. *People v. World Interactive Gaming Corp.*, 1999 NY. Misc.

On a normative level, re-empowering the states would serve the goals of competitive federalism. The federalism concern that has most compromised state regulatory jurisdiction is "exit"; if Internet actors could be regulated merely because their communications were accessible from a particular forum, then these actors could avoid regulation only by quitting cyberspace altogether.[160] But if states could regulate actors with a substantial connection to state interests, a cyberspace enterprise could exit simply by severing its relationship with a particular state. The possibility of exit would encourage states to experiment with cyberlaw to provide attractive packages of goods and services to their citizens. In this on-line equivalent of the laboratory of the states,[161] a "competition among rule-sets" would ensure that only the most effective and desirable regulations would survive. Perhaps most importantly, the nexus requirement would help preserve the sovereignty of the states in the new electronic frontier. There, as in the physical world, a diffusion of power will better secure liberty.

The above is a brief account of the American position regarding prohibitions of business through Internet in certain spheres. America is definitely a developed and most advanced country wherein on-line business transactions are frequently done now-a-days. The above analysis shows that the doctrine of *res extra commercium* equally applies in relation to on-line transactions. The situation in Australia and Canada is similar to that of America. However, the Indian situation is different from these countries, as it is a developing country from the point of view of on-line transactions. The reasons for such backwardness is lack of proper commercial and legal system for conducting e-business, lack of infrastructure, lack of secured payment structure, inconsistent taxation laws, etc. There is no judicial decision in India regarding issues in this area as arose in America or Australia and therefore nothing can be predicted at present. However, there is no reason why our Supreme Court should not follow the American Judicial attitude because Internet is a global device.

160. James E. Gaylord State Regulatory Jurisdiction and the Internet: Letting the Dormant Commerce Clause Lie. *Vanderbilt Law Review*, Vol. 52, 1999, pp. 1095-1130.

161. *New State Ice Co. v. Liebmann*, 285 U.S. 262, 311 (1932) (Brandeis, J., dissenting) (describing the states as laboratories of democracy).

5

The Commerce Clauses and its Role in the Country's Economy

I. GENERAL

The economic unity of a federal polity is as much significant as its political unity.[1] The former provides a sustaining force to the latter. And therefore, one of the major factors in the movement toward federation in the United States, Canada, Australia and India was the desire to deprive the individual states of the power to do economic harm to each other and thus to the nation.[2] Economic unity despite political, at the national as well as international plane, is the demand of the day and is projected as a necessary condition for peace, progress and good life. The GATT, UNCTAD, EEC, etc., are some of the manifestations of international efforts to fulfil that condition. In countries where the totality of national resources and powers is divided between the central and regional governments the requisite economic unity consistent with regional claims and interests is sought be achieved by some arrangement in the national Constitution.[3] Normally, every federal country has an even economy. Its constituent units may be either agricultural or industrial or a combination of both. Some of them may produce raw materials while the processing and manufacturing industries may be located in others because of several favourable factors, like availability of cheap labour or electric energy. This creates the possibility that the constituent units, in their interest, may create trade barriers by restricting the flow of commodities either from outside or to other units. Creation of such regional trade barriers may prejudicially affect national interests. This may hamper

1. *Atiabari Tea Co. v. State of Assam*, A.I.R. (1961), S.C. 232, (Gajendragadkar, J.)
2. Johnston, The Effect of Judicial Review on Federal-State Relations in Australia, Canada and United States, 1969, at p. 215.
3. M.P. Singh, Some Reflections on Jariwala's Freedom of Inter-state Trade in India, J.B.C.I., 1977, at p. 26.

the economic growth of the country as a whole, which may be disadvantageous to all the units in the long-run. Besides, the resources and industries of the units may be complementary to each other. "An attempt has, therefore, been made in all federations, through adoption of suitable constitutional formulae, to create and preserve a national economic fabric, transcending, state boundaries, to minimise the possibility of emergence of local economic barriers, to remove impediments in the way of inter-state trade and commerce and thus help in welding the whole country into one single economic unit so that the economic resources of all the various regions may be exploited, harnessed and pooled to the common advantage and prosperity of all."[4]

Thus, one big common internal market and an economic area irrespective of state boundaries is the essence of modern federalism. "Commerce Clause" is the most significant provision in the U.S.A. for this purpose. It provides that the Congress shall have power to regulate commerce among the several states.[5] However, this clause does not restrict state protectionism. By a process of judicial interpretation, it has come to have a restrictive effect on the States in those matters in which the Supreme Court considers that uniformity is necessary to national economic well-being. Thus, the capacity of the states to interfere with inter-state commerce has been very much restricted.[6] The "Commerce Clause" has also bestowed on the Central Government necessary power to regulate the country's economy. The courts have interpreted the words 'inter-state commerce' in a broad sense, and have held that the Congress can regulate not only inter-state commerce but even those inter-state activities which so effect inter-state commerce as to make their regulation appropriate."[7]

To avoid inter provincial trade barriers; in Canada the Provinces have been deprived of the power to levy indirect taxes. This has been further strengthened by making, "regulation of trade and commerce" a central matter. But this central power has not played much meaningful role so far. Sec. 121 of the B.N.A. Act, providing that "articles of growth, produce or manufacture of any province shall be admitted free into each of the other provinces", also curtails the provincial power to put restrictions on entry of goods from other provinces.

In Australia, the states have been debarred from levying excises with an object to promote the economic unity of the country, and thus, to discourage the states from raising trade barriers. Sec. 92 of the Australian Constitution is the cardinal provision, which may be referred to in this connection. According to this section trade, commerce and intercourse among the states shall be absolutely free. The clause applies only to inter-

4. Bowie, Studies in Federalism, 296-357 (1954).
5. Art 1, Section 8, Clause 3 of the U.S. Constitution.
6. *Southern Pacifiç Co. v. Arizona*, 325, U.S. 761 (1945).
7. M.P. Jain, Indian Constitutional Law (1999) at p. 403.

state and not to intra-state commerce, but restricts both the states and the Centre from interfering with trade and commerce.

If one goes through wordings only, the scope of Sec. 92 would appear unlimited and unqualified, but courts have evolved some limitations on this freedom as no freedom can be absolute. It has therefore been laid down that if some regulation of inter-state trade, commerce and intercourse is incompatible with its absolute freedom then Sec. 92 is violated only when a legislative or executive act operates to restrict inter-state trade, commerce and intercourse directly and immediately. If "some indirect or inconsequential impediment which may fairly be regarded as remote,"[8] is imposed then Sec. 92 is not violated.

However, in *North Eastern Dairy Co. v. Dairy Industry Authority,*[9] the High Court of Australia reverted to the test laid down in *Bank of New South Wales*[10] and held that economic consequences of a law operative upon inter-state trade and commerce can not be ignored. The assertion that the economic result produced by an Act is not within its direct operation is not valid. Definitely, economic result produced by any Act is relevant in determining whether the Act leaves trade and commerce free. The courts have also propounded the thesis that inter-state commerce must pay for the facilities it uses, such as bridges, aerodromes, highways, waterways, etc.

In India our constitution-makers fully realised that as the economic unity and integration of the country provide the main sustaining force for the stability and progress of the political and cultural unity of the federal polity, the country should function as one single economic unit without barriers on internal trade.[11] In order to ensure that the state Legislatures subjected to local and regional pulls do not create trade barriers in future, Art. 301 was incorporated in the Constitution. According to this provision, "trade, commerce and intercourse throughout the territory of India shall be free". The exceptions to Art. 301 have been laid down in Arts. 302-305. Total impact of these exceptions is to make the position in India quite different from that of other federal countries in the area of freedom of trade and commerce.

---

8. *Commonwealth of Australia v. Bank of New South Wales,* 1950 A.C. 235 also *Permewan Wright Consolidated Pty. Ltd. v. Trewhitt,* 27 A.L.J.R, 182.
9. *North Eastern Dairy Co. v. Dairy Industry Authority,* 50 A.L.J.R., 121, 129 (1976).
10. (1950) A.C. 235.
11. Derham : Some Constitutional problems arising under Part XIII of the Indian Constitution, 1, J.I.LI., 523, 551; Rice, Division of Powers to control commerce, 1, J.I.L.I., 151 (1959); Ramaswamy, Indian Constitutional Provisions against Barriers to Trade and Commerce, 2, J.I.L.I., 320 (1960); Ebb, Inter-state Barriers in India and American Constitutional Experience, 11, Stan, L. Rev., 37 (1958-59); S.N. Jain, Freedom of Trade, Commerce and Restraints on the State Power to Tax sale in the course of Inter-state Trade and Commerce, 10, J.I.L.I., 547 (1968); M.P. Singh, Prohibition against preference on Discrimination in Trade, Commerce and Intercourse in India: A Reappraisal of Constitutional Problems, 14, J.I.L.I., 39 (1972).

In Australia, as the studies have shown, the "Commerce Clause" has hampered the governments in pursuing many economic programmes so very essential in a modern country for promotion and expansion of the economy. "India steers clear of such difficulties, as the scope of the freedom of trade and commerce can by and large be adjusted by legislative action. Besides Art. 301, the concept of economic unity is also strengthened by the scheme of allocation of powers between the centre and the states. The Centre has been given broad powers in the economic field".[12]

2. THE INFLUENCE OF THE AMERICAN "COMMERCE CLAUSE" ON THE ECONOMIC DOMAIN

The most important of the provisions bearing upon the subject of commerce is the one contained in the "Commerce Clause". Not even the 'Constitution-builders' of America could have visualised the reserves of power latent in the clause to respond to the needs of a great and growing community in the domain of economic affairs in the coming years. Vesting of the power of regulation of foreign commerce in the federal government makes that government the sole spokesman of the people of the United States in the matters of international Commerce. The advantages accruing to the people by the manipulation of the threads of control over foreign commerce by a central authority are definitely immeasurable. The operation of that unified control, whether in the form of the regulation of uniform tariffs, or the negotiation of commercial treaties in the best interests of the whole country, or the control of navigation, or the regulation of immigration, forms a fascinating theme and cells for careful study. Professor Edwin R.A. Seligman has rightly observed that :

> "Then came the powers granted to the union to control the economic relations among the states. This was really the motive force in the original efforts of Hamilton to revive the business life of the nation: Federal control over inter-state commerce is the basis and secret of our economic prosperity. What we did was in effect to create a national market for local productions—a market untrammeled by any restrictions or limitations. That is precisely what they are trying to do in Europe today. It is the one great thing than has made this country what it is".[13]

The operation of the "Commerce Clause" with respect to foreign and inter-state commerce has been noticeable in two important directions. The Supreme Court has interpreted the "Commerce Clause" as operating a

12. M.P. Jain, Indian Constitutional Law (1999), at p. 407.
13. Annuals of the American Academy of Political Science : Federal *versus* State Jurisdiction in American life; Vol. CXXIX, January 1927, at p. 2 as referred in the book of Ramaswamy : The Commerce Clause in the Constitution of U.S.A.

restraint upon the powers of the states, whether taxing or regulatory, which in any way burdened or obstructed the freedom of foreign or inter-state commerce. The second direction in which the "Commerce Clause" has been allowed to operate is the steadily increasing supervisory control assumed by the national government over wide areas of economic enterprise.

A. One Face of the Coin

The Constitution of the U.S.A. empowers Congress to regulate, "*commerce among the several states*". For exactly one hundred years after that superficially simple phrase first appeared in the proposed national charter of 1787. Congress made no substantial use of the authority granted to it. The nation was growing, geographically and economically, there was adequate opportunity for men with initiative and ability without the assistance of government, and there was little demand by the public for the intrusion of government—state or federal—into the world of business and commerce. The *laissez-faire* philosophy embodied in legislation—or the lack of it and judicial decision was a reflection rather than the generating source of the popular feeling that the least government was the best government.

Whether or not it is true as to lawyers and judges, philosophy and economic theory succumb to facts in so far as the public is concerned. When the people began to suffer as a result of the unstrained freedom of enterprise, they called for help from the only peaceful protestive organisation at their command, their Government. Their call was addressed to the national government rather than to the states, since the problems of an integrated nationwide economy were obviously not remediable by state action. When the protests became sufficiently loud to arouse enough of the people's legislative representatives, Congress acted.

The Sherman Act in 1800 and the Inter-state Commerce Act in 1887 were the first manifestations of this demand that business, and particularly big business, be subjected to regulation in the interest of the public. Other statutes were passed to meet specific abuses, including the Federal Trade Commission Act of 1914 and various Acts relating to the railroads. But apart from the anti-trust laws and the regulation of public utilities, few of the statutes imposed substantial restraints upon the operation of business enterprises. The failure of Congress to act in this field did not mean, of course, that the American economy was idyllic, Labour in particular had reason to feel oppressed. But during a period in which most men were making at least a tolerable living, the proportion of the public, which was dissatisfied, and, even more important, the intensity of the dissatisfaction, was not sufficient to overcome the inertia and other obstacles, including judicial, to affirmative legislative relief.

The economic depression of the early 1930's produced a popular reaction strong enough, at least when led by President Roosevelt, to induce Congress to exercise its authority to the fullest extent. The problems were economic, and the "Commerce Clause" was the enumerated power most directly concerned with business and economic or commercial matters.

Consequently, although other powers, particularly the fiscal and appropriative,[14] were brought into play, it was upon the "Commerce Clause" that the legislation directed at controlling many aspects of the national economic system was principally predicated.

The commerce power had previously been exerted mainly in connection with inter-state transportation, although the Sherman Act was exceptional in this respect. The conditions responsible for the business depression, although they had affected the railroads as much as any other industry, were considerably more deep-seated. Unemployment, the purchasing power of workers and farmers, prices in business and agriculture, unsellable surpluses which overhung the markets and the quantity of goods produced and grown—these were the elements with which it was necessary to deal. Could the "Commerce Clause" bear the load?

Although these ingredients of the economic crisis often preceded the movement of goods across state lines and occurred national consequence because the products of the national economy were distributed throughout a national market. The channels of inter-state commerce were the arteries through which the impact of these forces affected the nation. Because of the nation-wide market, and the constitutional impediment placed by the "Commerce Clause" itself in the way of regulation by the states, the state governments were unable to cope with economic problems affecting the nation as a whole. Obviously affected inter-state commerce in the most elementary sense, since it greatly reduced the quantity of products to be transported across state lines.

Nevertheless there could be no assurance that federal legislation directed at the economic causes of the depression would be constitutional. For that depended on what the Supreme Court thought. And there was ample authority in the Supreme Court opinions looking both ways.

B. The Other Face of the Coin

The dormant "Commerce Clause" is a constitutional law doctrine that says Congress's power to "regulate Commerce" among the several States[15] implicitly restricts state power over the same area.[16] In general, the "Commerce Clause" places two main restrictions on state power. *First*, Congress can preempt state law merely by exercising its "Commerce Clause" power. *Second*, the "Commerce Clause" itself restricts state power, the grant of federal power implies a corresponding restriction of state power.[17] This second limitation has come to be known as the dormant "Commerce Clause"

14. *United States v. Butler*, 297 U.S. 1 (1936).
15. U.S. Constitution, Article 1, Sec. 8, Cl. 3.
16. *Camps Newfound/Owatonna, Inc. v. Town of Harrison*, 117 S. Ct. 1590, 1596 (1997); *Wyoming v. Oklahoma*, 502 U.S. 437, 454 (1992); *Hunt v. Washington State Apple Adver. Comm'n*, 432 U.S. 333, 350 (1977).
17. Laurence H. Tribe, American Constitutional Law, 6-2, at p. 403 (2nd Ed. 1988).

because it restricts state power even though Congress's commerce power lies dormant.[18]

Generally, the "Dormant Commerce Clause Doctrine" prohibits states from unduly interfering with inter-state commerce. The Court has developed the tests to determine when state regulation has gone too far. Under one test, the Court balances the burden on inter-state commerce against the state's interest in its regulation.[19] Under the second test, states are prohibited generally from enacting laws that discriminate against inter-state commerce.[20] Over the last two decades, the dormant "Commerce Clause" has received much scholarly attention, with commentators either proposing refinements to the balancing test[21] or challenging the constitutional basis for the doctrine as a whole.[22] The commentators, however, generally have been kind to the anti-discrimination test of the dormant "Commerce Clause". Indeed, even Justice Antonin Scalia, who has argued vigorously (in dissent) that the Court should abandon the dormant "Commerce Clause",[23] applies the anti-discrimination principle.

Justice Scalia applies the anti-discrimination test, but nevertheless refuses to apply the balancing test of the dormant "Commerce Clause", except in rare cases and then only on *stare decisis* grounds.[24] A state statute is invalid under the "Commerce Clause" if, and only if, it accords discriminatory treatment to inter-state commerce in a respect not required to achieve a lawful purpose. When such a validating purpose exists, it is for Congress and not the judges to determine. It is not significant enough to justify the burden on commerce.

Swimming against this tide, this may be argued that the Court's application of the anti-discrimination test is, in some cases, in conflict with the underlying purpose of the "Commerce Clause": to protect the national economic market from opportunistic behaviour by the states.[25] The Court has never held that discrimination between in-state and out-of-state commerce, without more, violates the dormant "Commerce Clause," rather, the Court

18. Julian N. Eule, Laying the Dormant Commerce Clause to Rest, 91 Yale L.J. 425, n. 1 (1982).
19. *Kassel v. Consolidated Freightways Corp.*, 450 U.S. 662, 670-71 (1981); *Raymond Motor Transp., Inc. v. Rice*, 434 U.S. 429, 441-42 (1978); *Pike v. Bruce Church, Inc.*, 397 U.S. 137, 142 (1970); *Southern Pac. Co. v. Arizona*, 325 U.S. 761, 768-71 (1945).
20. *City of Philadelphia v. New Jersey*, 437 U.S. 617 (1978).
21. Mark Tushnet, Rethinking the Dormant Commerce Clause, 1979 Wis . L. Rev. 125; see also Michael E. Smith, State Discriminations Against Inter-state Commerce, 74 Cal. L. Rev. 1203 (1986).
22. Thomas K. Anson and P.M. Schenkhan, Federalism, the Dormant Commerce Clause, and State-Owned Resources, 59 Tex. L. Rev. 71, 78-80 (1980);
23. *Bendix Autolite Corp. v. Midwesco Enters., Inc.*, 486 U.S. 888, 895-98 (1988); *Tyler Pipae Indus,. Inc. v. Washington State Deptt. of Revenue*, 483 U.S. 232, 259-65 (1987).
24. *Bendix Autolite Corp.*, 486 U.S. at p. 897.
25. *New Energy Co. v. Limbach*, 486 U.S. 269, 273-74 (1988) ("This 'negative' aspect of the Commerce Clause prohibits economic protectionism—that is, regulatory measures designed to benefit in-state economic interests by burdening out-of-state competitors.").

has explained that the dormant "Commerce Clause" is concerned with state laws which (i) discriminate between in-state and out-of-state actors that compete with one another, and (ii) harm the welfare of the national economy.[26] Thus, a discriminatory state law that harms the national economy is permissible if in-state and out-of-state commerce do not compete.[27] Conversely, a state law that discriminates between in-state and out-of-state competitors is permissible if it does not harm the national economy.

The Court has been careless in applying the anti-discrimination test; in many cases, neither of the two requirements—inter-state competition or harm to the national economy—is ever mentioned.[28] As the court stated just last term, these requirements have "more often than not remained dormant in this Court's opinion on the state discrimination subject to review under the dormant 'Commerce Clause'." The reason the first requirement, competition between in-state and out-of-state actors, goes unstated is fairly obvious—in most cases (all except two before the Supreme Court), it is clear that in-state and out-of-state actors compete in the same market.[29] The Court's silence merely reflects the frequency with which the issue arises.

The reason the second requirement, harm to the national economy, goes unstated is more complex. It is humbly to say that the Court has neglected this requirement not because it is rarely an issue, but rather because the Court assumes that discrimination between in-state and out-of-state competitors necessarily harms the welfare of the national economy, making the second requirement superfluous. In making this assumption, the Court implicitly has adopted a neoclassical view of economics—that free competition among rational economic actors will necessarily improve the national economy. Thus, the Court's dormant "Commerce Clause" analysis assumes that neoclassical economics best describes the position of states regulating inter-state commerce.

Game theory offers an alternate view of economics and alternate set of economic assumptions that may better model the position of states regulating inter-state commerce. As a close cousin of economics, game theory assumes that individuals act rationally; to economists, this means people try to maximize their personal welfare.[30] Using this assumption, game theory

26. Anson and Schenkhan, Federalism, The Dormant Commerce Clause, and State Owned Resources, 59 Tex. L. Rev. 71 (1980).

27. *General Motors Corp. v. Tracy*, 117 S. Ct. 811, 824-26 (1997).

28. *Hughes v. Oklahoma*, 441 U.S. 322 (1979).

29. *New Energy Co. v. Limbach*, 486 U.S. 269, 272 (1988); *Maine v. Taylor*, 477 U.S. 131 (1986); *Bacchus Imports Ltd. v. Dias*, 468 U.S. 263, 268-69 (1984); *Lewis v. Bt Inv. Managers, Inc.*, 447 U.S. 27, 38-39 (1980); *Hughes*, 441 U.S. at p. 324; *City of Philadelphia v. New Jersey*, 437 U.S. 617, 618-19 (1978); *Great Atl. and Pac. Tea Co. v. Cottrell*, 424 U.S. 366, 367 (1976); *H.P. Hood and Sons, Inc. v. Du Mond*, 336 U.S. 525, 526 (1949); *Baldwin v. G.A.F. Seelig, Inc.*, 294 U.S. 511, 518-19 (1935).

30. David M. Kreps, Game Theory And Economic Modelling 26, n. 8 (1990); A. Mitchell Polinsdy, An Introduction To Law And Economics 10 (2d ed. 1989) (noting that economics assumes that rational individuals seek to "maximize their benefits less their costs"); Richard A. Posner, Economic Analysis of Law, 3 (5th ed. 1998).

models strategic behaviour-situations where "two or more individuals interact and each individual's decision turns on what that individual expects the others to do.[31] Game theory tries to predict how rational people will behave in strategic behaviour situations.[32] Conversely, neoclassical economics assumes that rational people decide how to act based on prevailing market conditions such as price, supply, and demand, independent of expectations about how others will act.

Two examples from the commercial context illustrate the difference between neoclassical and game theory. *First,* consider the situation of a consumer who goes to the grocery store to buy a loaf of bread. Presumably, the consumer will evaluate the information readily available in the marketplace; she will compare the prices of the different brands along with her perception of the quality of the different brands. Based on this analysis, the consumer will decide which brand to purchase. Price and quality are impersonal forces set by the market, independent of any expectations about others' future behaviour. In this first example, the consumer does not act strategically, her decision is independent of any future behaviour of the grocery store or the bread supplier.

Second, consider the purchasing agent for the grocery store who places orders with suppliers to stock the grocery store's shelves. In addition to price and quality, the purchasing agent will consider the future behaviour of the supplier. For example, the purchasing agent will want to know whether the supplier is likely to breach a contract to supply the grocery store; such a breach would result in empty shelves and lost sales. If the purchasing agent expects a supplier to breach, then she may refuse to deal with the supplier regardless of price or quality. The purchasing agent will act strategically by considering how she expects the other party, the supplier, to act.

Neoclassical economics has a blind spot for strategic behaviour; the theory does not address cases in which people anticipate one another's future actions. Game theory tries to bridge this gap by using models—known as "games"—to predict strategic behaviour. These games reveal that strategic behaviour may lead the rational, freely competing actors of neoclassical economics to nonetheless act inefficiently.[33] Neoclassical economics assumes that free competition among rational actors will be efficient; game theory shows that the existence of strategic behaviour undermines that assumption.

Game theory can be used to predict strategic behaviour in response to legal rules.[34] In doing so, law-makers can assess the economic wisdom of different legal rules. To illustrate this point, consider the situation of a

31. Douglas G. Baird Et Al., Game Theory and the Law, 1 (1994); see also Eric Rasmusen, Games, and Information : An Introduction to Game Theory 9 (2d ed., 1994). Mark Seidenfeld, Microeconomic Predicates to Law and Economics, 85 (1996).
32. Kreps, Game Theory and Economic Modelling at p. 5 (1990).
33. Ian Ayres, Playing Games with the Law, 42 Stan. L. Rev. 1291, 1315-17 (1990).
34. Baird *et. al.*, Game Theory and the Law, 1 (1994).

pedestrian and a motorist approaching an inter-section that has four stop signs. Both the pedestrian and the motorist will act strategically. Each will want to know how the other will, or is likely to, act at the inter-section before deciding how to act. If the pedestrian knows that the motorist is likely to run the stop sign, then the pedestrian will allow the motorist to pass before crossing the street. The pedestrian's prediction about the motorist's likely behaviour, in turn, will be affected by the legal rules that govern the situation. For example, if the prevailing legal rules make motorists strictly liable for all injuries to pedestrians, then the pedestrian may predict that the motorist will exercise care, by stopping at all stop signs, to avoid the cost of an accident.[35] The pedestrian's decision therefore will depend on her prediction about the conduct of another person, the motorist, and the prediction is influenced by the prevailing legal rules. Game theory allows us to model such behaviour. It also explains how legal rules affect that behaviour.

Here the game theory has been used to test the neoclassical economic assumption implicit in the Court's dormant "Commerce Clause" anti-discrimination test. The discrimination between in-state and out-of-state competitors necessarily harms the welfare of the national market. If, in some cases, states act strategically, that is, if states act in response to the anticipated behaviour of other states, then the Court is wrong to build neoclassical economic assumptions into its dormant "Commerce Clause" anti-discrimination test. In these cases, state discrimination between in-state and out-of-state competitors may improve national welfare. We have to determine whether, in some cases, states act strategically; if so, game theory better describes their behaviour in those cases.

The states may not burden unduly the free flow of commerce except with the consent of Congress. 'Burden' in this context means more than discrimination; it is essentially an economic concept. That is to say, the court has no preconceived ideas as to what constitutes a burden; but judges solely by the impact which legislation imposing duties or imposts makes on inter-state trade and traders.[36]

In doing so the Court has returned to the aim which was common to both Hamilton and Madison: the preservation of a free trade area from particularistic or eccentric State policies. The national economy today is more sophisticated than it was in 1787, and such policies are no longer confined to the imposition of custom tariffs and embargoes, but as in 1787 the protection of the "Commerce Clause" is essentially a protection of the individual trader.

---

35. Carrying the strategic behaviour further, if a strict liability rule makes pedestrians less careful, then motorists might respond by taking even more care to avoid careless pedestrians. P.E. McGreal, The Flawed Economics of the Dormant Commerce Clause : Wm. and Mary L. Rev., 39, No. 4, at p. 1199 (1998).

36. *Bibb. v. Navajo Freight Lines*, 359 U.S. 520; *Huron Portland Cement Co. v. Detroit*, 362 U.S. 440 (1960); *Colorado Anti-Discrimination Commission v. Continental Airlines*, 372 U.S. 714, 719 (1963); *American Oil Co. v. Neill*, 380 U.S. 451 (1965).

Thus, in *Parker v. Brown*[37], the question was not whether the California marketing scheme interfered with the freedom of the producers of raisins to sell their crop inter-state. Rather the question was whether the scheme operated 'without substantially impairing the national interest in the regulation of commerce by a single authority and without materially obstructing the free flow of commerce.'[38]

The interpretation of the "Commerce Clause" had come a long way since the *Railroad Retirement* and *Carter* cases in 1935 and 1936. In the latter, Mr. Justice Sutherland had even resurrected the old *Sugar Trust* case, which had been considered buried in 1911. But within a year the *Carter* case had joined the *Sugar Trust* case in repose. By the end of the decade, every decision, which had invalidated a congressional exercise of the commerce power, had been disapproved, or distinguished to death.[39] The Tenth Amendment had been restored to its proper place in the constitutional scheme; again it meant only what it said. The theory that the mere existence of state governments limits the scope of the enumerated powers of Congress had been abandoned as a constitutional doctrine, though some members of the Court, notably Mr. Justice Frankfurter, now invoked the same principle as a guide to the construction of federal legislation.[40]

The "Commerce Clause" was now recognised as a grant of authority permitting Congress to allow inter-state commerce to take place on whatever terms it may consider in the interest of the national well-being, subject only to other constitutional limitations, such as the Due Process Clause.[41] The constitutional grant of power over commerce was now interpreted as enabling Congress to enact all appropriate laws for the protection and advancement of commerce among the states,[42] whatever measures Congress might reasonably think adapted to that end,[43] without regard for whether particular regulated acts themselves were inter-state or intra-state. No mechanical formula any longer excluded matters, which might be called "local" from the application of these principles.

In our present-day economy the inter-state and intra-state aspects of American business are inseparable. The sale, shipment, and transportation of commodities across state lines, which constitute inter-state commerce, cannot be segregated economically from "production". Each of these departments of

37. 317 U.S. 341.

38. Peter Nygh, Freedom of Inter-state Trade in Australia, The University of Queensland Law Journal, 1967.

39. *Wickard v. Filburn*, 317 U.S. 111, 122 (1942).

40. E.g., *St. Building, Inc. v. Callus*, 325 U.S. 578 (1945); *F.T.C. v. Bunte Bros.*, 312 U.S. 349 (1941); *A.B. Kirschbaum Co. v. Walling*, 316 U,S. 517, 520-22 (1942); *Connecticut Light and Power Co. v. F.P.C.*, 324 U.S. 515, 530 (1945).

41. *United States v. Varolene Products Co.*, 304 U.S. 144, 148-51 (1938); *United States v. Darby*, 312 U.S. 100, 125-26 (1941).

42. *E.g., N.L.R.B. v. Jones and Laughlin Steel Corp.*, 301 U.S. 1 (1937).

43. *United States v. Darby*, 312 U.S. 100 (1941); *United States v. Wrightwood Dairy Co.*, 315 U.S. 110 (1942).

an industry or business enterprise has an immediate and substantial impact upon the others.

The reinvigoration of the "Commerce Clause" only restores to complete potency of a legislative power. The capacity to exercise that power is affirmatively vested by the Constitution in the representatives of the people. The opinions of the Court since the judicial revolution of 1937 indicate that any attempt in good faith by Congress to cope with a national economic problem will be respected. But the broader interpretation of the "Commerce Clause" does not compel Congress to act; it merely places fewer impediments in the way of the democratic process.

Thus, the Court's dormant "Commerce Clause" cases make assumptions about how states act. The game theory has been used to test the Court's assumptions. After reviewing the history and case law of the dormant "Commerce Clause" and the economic assumptions of both, we are left with three points to guide a new dormant "Commerce Clause" anti-discrimination test :

(a) The Court should continue to ask whether the state law discriminates between in-state and out-of-state actors who are in competition. If so :
(b) The Court should ask whether state law discrimination makes the national economy worse-off than if states did not discriminate.
(c) If the answer to either question requires the resolution of reasonably contested factual or economic contentions, the Court must defer to the states and uphold the challenged law.

If the Court takes federalism seriously, and is truly concerned about protecting states from federal interference, then it should back away when what was once clear has been shown to be uncertain. The anti-discrimination rule of *City of Philadelphia* and its progeny is one such area, and should be discarded in favour of a rule constructed on dormant "Commerce Clause" first principles and the lessons of economic reasoning.

C. Evaluation of the Recent Judicial Trend in the Perspective of the National Economy

On the basis of some of the recently delivered judgments of the Supreme Court, the following case-wise inferences may be drawn :

(a) Oregon Waste Systems, Inc. v. *Department of Environmental Quality of the State of Oregon*[44]

If a state restriction on commerce is discriminatory in the sense of a differential treatment of in-state and out-of-state economic interests that benefits the former and burdens the latter, then the restriction is virtually *per*

44. (1994) 128 L. Ed. 2d 13 at p. 15.

se invalid under the Federal Constitution's "Commerce Clause".[45] It must be invalidated unless the state can show that the restriction advances a legitimate local purpose that cannot be adequately served by reasonable non-discriminatory alternatives.

(b) Oklahoma Tax Commission v. Jefferson Lines, Inc.[46]

The federal Constitution's "Commerce Clause"[47] reflects a central concern of the framers that in order to succeed, the new union would have to avoid the tendencies toward economic balkanization that had plagued relations among the colonies and later among the states under the Articles of Confederation.

(c) United States v. Lopez[48]

Where economic activity substantially affects inter-state commerce, legislation regulating that activity will be sustained.[49] In sum, a holding that the particular Statute falls within the commerce power would not expand the scope of that Clause. Rather it simply would apply pre-existing law to changing economic circumstances. In today's economic world gun-related violence near the classroom makes a significance difference to economic, as well as our social, well-being. In accordance with well-accepted precedent such a holding would permit Congress to act in terms of economic realities. It would interpret the Commerce power as an affirmative power commensurate with the National needs and would acknowledge that the Commerce power does not operate so as to make the Nation powerless to defend itself against economic forces.

In recent years the link between the secondary education and business has strengthened. Increasing global competition also has made primary and secondary education economically more important. The portion of the American economy attributable to International trade nearly tripled between 1950 and 1980, and more than 70 percent of American made goods now compete with imports. Yet, lagging worker productivity has contributed to negative trade balances and to real hourly compensation that has fallen below wages in ten other industrialised nations. At least some significant Part of this serious productivity problem is attributable to students who immerge from classrooms without the reading or mathematical skills necessary to compete with their European or Asian counterparts.[50]

45. Art. I, Sec. 8, Cl 3.
46. (1995) 131 L. Ed. 2d 261.
47. Art. I, Sec. 8, Cl 3.
48. (1995) 131 L.Ed.2d 626.
49. *Id.* at 638.
50. *United States v. Lopez,* 514 U.S. 131 L. Ed. 2d 626 at p. 677.

(d) United States v. Morison[51]

(i) Economic activity that substantially affects inter-state commerce is to be regulated.
(ii) The statute contains an express jurisdictional element, which might limit the statute's reach to explicitly connect with, or affect, inter-state commerce.
(iii) The statute or the statute's legislative history contains express congressional findings regarding the effects upon inter-state commerce.

The link between the regulated conduct and a substantial effect on inter-state commerce is attenuated; where economic activity substantially affects inter-state commerce, legislation regulating that activity will be sustained.

3. THE INFLUENCE OF THE CANADIAN "COMMERCE CLAUSE" ON THE ECONOMIC DOMAIN

A. The Background of Canadian Economic Federalism

Although the two North American Federations are culturally very similar and economically much interconnected, their federal systems are substantially different. The Canadian States (Province) are few, but they differ greatly in size and wealth.[52] Constitutionally they are similarly placed. They all have charge of their local governments, and some are very interested in this side of their responsibilities. Ontario has pioneered the reorganisation of Toronto into a metropolitan area and thickly settled areas are regionally organised. The objective of the latter arrangement is not quite clear.

However, Canada faces one very difficult federal fiscal problem in the cleavage between French Canada (Quebec) and the rest. During recent years the cleavage has deepened, owing to a number of causes, largely unavoidable. One of the most important, although it is partly political, is the relative loss of wealth and status of Quebec in the face of the development of the west. The cleavage implies that in all fiscal legislation special arrangements have been made to suit Quebec.

Because of the great diversity of the provinces and their narrow tax bases, Canada has all along been interested not only in general assistance to correct the inherent federal or provincial imbalance, but also in a policy of discriminating aid to the poorer provinces. A new fiscal Equalisation Programme was launched in 1972, subject to quinquennial review. The first review took place in 1976 and new legislation, the Provincial Fiscal Arrangements Act, came into force in 1977. This introduced some rather

51. (2000) 529 U.S. 598, 146 L. Ed. 2d 658.
52. Wealth is from Ontario to Prince Edward Island.

important changes, although the system remained basically that of 1972. In Canada, all federal fiscal adjustments have been subject to prolonged arguments and negotiations with the provinces. These, unlike many of the American states, are very definite and self-conscious personalities.[53] There were sizable provincial debts, even though the prevailing *laissez-faire* attitudes prevented much government expenditure for social services. The greatest needs in Canada at that time were in the transport fields, and while government regulation of the economy was limited to providing a favourable legal framework for the operation of private enterprise, this did not deter provincial governments from subsidizing the construction of roads, railways, and canals. The existence of this debt and the use of customs and excises for 'provincial tax base' were to be of great importance in the discussions that led to federation.

The primary purpose of Canadian federation was to create a national economy in which free trade would stimulate business by making internal markets available. This meant that customs and excise duties would have to be given to the federal government, but it also meant that the provinces would lose eighty percent of their available source of revenue.[54]

B. The Impressive Monument of 'Dual Federalism'

The list of Dominion social and economic legislation passed under the commerce power, but invalidated as encroaching on provincial rights is an impressive monument to "dual federalism". In Canada, it includes the following:

(a) Legislation for the abolition of the liquor traffic,
(b) Regulation of "through traffic" over provincial and Dominion railways,
(c) Prohibition of monopolies,
(d) Fixing of maximum prices of commodities,
(e) Regulation of the grain trade and of the business of grain dealers, regulating egg sales and deliveries within a province,
(f) Regulating market transactions in natural products,
(g) Validation of agreements between persons in industry as to competition in trade within a province,
(h) Regulating the licencing of fish canneries and fish processing,
(i) Regulation of the business of non-Dominion insurance companies,
(j) Regulations to prevent strikes and lockouts and for settlement of industrial disputes, and

53. Hicks, Federalism Failure and Success, at p. 188.
54. Johnston, The Effect of Judicial Review on Federal—State Relations in Australia, Canada, and the United States, at pp. 121-22 (1969).

(k) Regulations relating to minimum wages and limitations of hours of Labour.[55]

There is no evidence that the Canadian Parliament's trade and commerce power has been significantly expanded in the almost thirty years since it met its most severe test in the great depression and was found wanting. World economic collapse was not sufficient to convince the Court and the Privy Council, and so it was hardly to be expected that the passage of time would do so. There were those who thought that the passage of time would do so. There were those who thought that the abolition of appeals to the Privy Council in 1949 would finally give the Supreme Court an opportunity to return to the large and generous view of the Dominion power it held before 1896. There is little evidence that this was anything but wishful thinking.

C. The Judicial Reaction in Different Fields

The board sweep given to the federal "trade and commerce" power, as an exclusive power in early judgments of the Supreme Court, is indicated by *Severn v. The Queen*[56] and *Fredericton v. The Queen*[57]. The latter case was considerably attenuated by the different approach taken in *Russel v. The Queen*[58], and the authority of the *Severn* case was finally demolished in *Bank of Toronto v. Lambe*[59]. Statement *in re Prohibitory Liquor Laws*[60] shows that the Supreme Court's views on the scope of the trade and commerce power died hard.

In recent years Canada has faced many of the problems relating to agriculture that Australia and the United States have experienced. The production of regionally grown surpluses and the resultant glutted markets necessitated a number of marketing schemes as in Australia. Such schemes, regulating local and extra-provincial exchanges, were held to be invalid when attempted by provincial legislation, and also by the Dominion Parliament. In both instances the Court insisted that each jurisdiction was absolutely bound by its own territorial limits regardless of the intermingling of the real market in that particular product.[61]

To some extent this difficulty has been solved by cooperative schemes between Dominion and provinces, with inter-delegation of powers to marketing boards. Such schemes as the Agricultural Products Marketing Act of 1949 have worked well. The Court has invalidated direct inter-

---

55. *Attorney General for Ontario v. Attorney General for Dominion* (1896), A.C. 348.
56. (1878), 2 S.C.R. 70.
57. (1880), 3 S.C.R. 505.
58. (1882), 7 App. Cas. 829.
59. (1887), 12 App. Cas. 575, at p. 586.
60. (1894), 24 S.C.R. 170.
61. *Lawson v. Interior Tree Fruit Committee and Attorney General for Canada* (1931), S.C.R. 357; *Attorney General of British Columbia v. Attorney General for Canada* (1937), A.C. 377.

parliamentary delegation, but has upheld delegation to boards or agencies of the other government.[62] This amounts to control by a single board jointly appointed by the Dominion and the province involved. Such delegation is by consent only and is often very difficult to obtain from the provinces. Recent decisions have upheld a comprehensive Dominion Wheat Board Act regulating the activities that all grain entering inter provincial or foreign trade must be marketed through the Board exclusively.[63] These cases indicate a possible relaxation of the rigid delineation of jurisdiction that the Court has insisted on maintaining in the past.

Among the least illumined areas of constitutional adjudication is that concerned with the scope of the concurrent power in relation to agriculture, given by Sec. 95 of the B.N.A. Act. There, as much as, if not more than anywhere else in the Act, was an invitation to a working federalism by which problems in the field, if not adequately serviced by provincial legislation, could be taken up or solved through national legislative policies. The possibilities represented by Sec. 95 have, so far, foundered on a construction of the agriculture power that has drained it of substance, both as a source of provincial legislation and of federal legislation. Neither the Privy Council nor the Supreme Court of Canada had any occasion to consider the "agriculture" power during the first half century following confederation. Such lower court decisions as were given on the matter during this period touched what may be reasonably termed as the periphery of that class of subject. Clement[64], stated that "'agriculture' has been given a very wide interpretation"; but his extension of this proposition shown the narrow range of the problems arising thereunder. It covered "all matters connected with the farm, such as the care and improvement of stock, horse breeding, dairying and kindred matters. As properly falling under this head the federal Animal Contagious Diseases Act has been upheld. And a Provincial Act which provided a penalty for fraud in entering horses in a wrong class at race meetings of agricultural associations was considered as competent legislation under this head, there being no federal legislation to which it was repugnant." When opportunity arose for a wider assessment of agriculture as the potent force that it was and is in the Canadian economy, there was a curious refusal to square legislative power with legislative fact. None of the considerations, which moved the Courts to a narrow view of both the general power and the trade and commerce power, was operable in respect of Sec. 95. Yet the resulting construction of the "agriculture" power, juxtaposed to that of the "trade and commerce" power, created a definite hiatus in regulatory possibilities. On the one hand, the former would not support regulation of trade in natural products (although it might support control at the production stage) while the later could not embrace production

62. *Prince Edward Island Potato Marketing Board v. H.B. Willis Inc., and the Attorney General for Canada* (1952), 2 S.C.R. 392.
63. *Murphy v. Canadian Pacific Railway Co.* (1958), S.C.R., 626.
64. Clements, Law of the Canadian Constitution, 3rd edition, 1916.

and was limited, in respect of trade regulation to inter-provincial and export aspects in their strict sense. The expansion of the trade and commerce power, of which evidence is slowly accumulating, may very well make it unnecessary to rely on revitalisation of the "agriculture" power to support national marketing policies respecting products of the soil. If this happens, it will provide another instance of a rather unnecessary reduction, not to say obliteration, of an express power.

Whether or not one accepts the "collocation" argument in the *Parsons case* or the "provincial autonomy" argument in *Montreal v. Montreal Street Ry.*,[65] it is undeniable that they both produced the same inflexibility in measuring the scope of the federal trade and commerce power. This result was produced by decisions measuring the scope of the federal general power. In both situations, the inflexibility led to extravagance of statement by Lord Haldane in the *Snider case*, and in respect of both there has been a retreat that is still in progress. It will be useful to chart the path of the retreat and to attempt some assessment of its consequences.

There is need to reconcile the power to make laws for the peace, order and good government in relation to the regulation of trade and commerce with the powers reposed in the Provinces. It cannot be lastingly met by imprisoning either the former or the latter within pre-determined limits taking no account of social and economic change. Lord Porter remarked in *Commonwealth of Australia v. Bank of New South Wales*,[66] in reference to an issue of validity raised by competing claims of legislative power that the problem to be solved will often be not so much legal as political, social or economic, yet it must be solved by a Court of Law. Such an admission, rare in Australian cases in the Privy Council, is even rarer in the Canadian cases. But it is a commonplace of constitutional adjudication in the Supreme Court of United States; and nowhere has it been more emphatically considered than in examination of the scope of congressional power over inter-state commerce.[67] The federal commerce power is as broad as the economic needs of the nation.[68]

The refusal of the Court to permit any Dominion economic planning has not left a total vacuum, for the court has permitted some provincial regulation of a number of fields under the doctrine that this is a matter of property and civil rights in the province.[69] Of course, it has proven impossible to obtain provincial consent to uniform Labour law for the nation as a whole. It would be very difficult today to refute Professor Bora Laskin's

65. (1912) A.C. 333, 343.
66. (1950) A.C. 235, at p. 310.
67. Murphy, J. in *American Power and Light Co. v. Securities and Exchange Commission* (1946), 329 U.S. 90, at p. 104, 67.
68. Stern, The Commerce Clause and the National Economy (1946), 59 Harv. L. Rev. 645, 883; Abel, The Commerce Clause in the Constitutional Convention and in Contemporary Comment (1941), 25 Minn. L. Rev. 432.
69. *Crawford et. al. v. Attorney General for British Columbia* (1960), 22 D.L.R.

charge that the trade and commerce decisions of the Privy Council and the Supreme Court indicate a conscious and deliberate choice of a policy that required for its advancement manipulations.[70] However, this may be represented as an ordinary judicial technique.

4. THE INFLUENCE OF THE AUSTRALIAN "COMMERCE CLAUSE" ON THE ECONOMIC DOMAIN

A. Aspirations of the Founding Fathers

When the Australian Founding Fathers assembled in the 1890's to draft a Federal Constitution for Australia, it was to be expected that they would be guided by American experience. Like their United States counterparts they were anxious to create one economic unit. Unlike their American predecessors, however, they intended to be specific about it.[71] That is why Section 92 of the constitution provided that:

> "On the imposition of uniform duties of customs, trade, commerce and intercourse among the states, whether by means of internal carriage or ocean navigation, shall be absolutely free."

These words were deliberately left vague and untechnical, "a little bit of laymen's language" as they were described by Sir George Reid[72] at the close of the proceedings in Melbourne when final attempts by lawyer members of the convention to give the clause a more precise wording, were defeated. As a result, the clause is as helpful as is the vague understanding, which existed at the American Convention of 1787 that there should be some sort of economic unity. It does not tell us how that unity is to be achieved and to what extent it should be enforced.

The impression one derives from reading the Debates of the convention is that the Founding Fathers had a Madisonian concept of their handiwork. They were not prepared to surrender the internal autonomy of the states any further than was strictly necessary. To that purpose Section 92 was only to have a relatively limited effect. In the same fashion the federal commerce power bestowed by Sec. 51(i) was to be read in conjunction with Section 92 to which it was clearly subordinate.[73] Hence the power of Federal

---

70. Laskin, "Peace, Order and Good Government Re-examined", 1086.
71. Peter Nygh, Freedom of Inter-state Trade in Australia, University of Queensland Law Journal, 1966-67, at p. 333.
72. Record of the Debates of the Federal Convention, Third Session, Melbourne, 1898, at 2367. (Referred by Peter Nygh in Freedom of Inter-state Trade in Australia, Uni. Ql.I.J., 1966-67, at p. 333).
73. Professor F.R. Beasley, The Commonwealth Constitution; Section 92, Its History in the Federal Conventions (1948) 1 Uni. of West Austr. Ann. L. Rev. 97 at pp. 280-81; Sherwood L. Rev., Section 92 in the Federal Conventions—A Fresh Appraisal (1958) 1 Melb. Uni. L. Rev. 331.

Parliament was to encourage inter-state communication, not to restrain it. Barton said in Melbourne that "the trade and "Commerce Clause" is for the purpose of permitting the Commonwealth, by legislation, to secure those things which are secured by way of declaration in clause 89 (now Section 92), namely, *uninterrupted trade and commerce.* "This he concludes to be the fullest extent of the strength and construction of trade and 'Commerce Clause'."

What the Founding Fathers had in mind was the creation of one economic unit through which trade would flow without regard to frontiers, but subject to non-discriminatory regulation on the Part of the States whose powers in the commercial field were to remain paramount. There is also no doubt that the Founders anticipated the possibility of 'indirect' fiscal protection by methods other than border tariffs and differential excises, and accordingly desired their guarantee of fiscal free trade between the states to be stated with some generality and to be capable of some flexibility of application. But all the same the governing idea is that of fiscal control.[74]

The flood of litigation involving the interpretation of Section 92 really started only after the close of the First World War. The economic dislocations, which followed as aftermath of this war, brought serious economic problems in their train, problems whose handling required the promulgation of legislative controls which brought them into a head on collision with private economic interests. The interests adversely affected by the imposition of such controls sought to escape from their impact by calling the aid of the courts taking their stand upon Section 92 of the Constitution.[75]

B. The Judicial Hobnobbing

'Trade and commerce' seem to describe sectors of the economy which, though forming portion of the whole, have a distinguishable character in contrast with other comparable but contrasted sectors such as "manufacturing", "mining" or "primary production." Thus, in the *Banking Case,*[76] it was contended that banking should be allocated to "finance" as a co-ordinate sector with but not Part of "trade and commerce". Actually the problem was to determine whether banking was "trade, commerce or intercourse." An affirmative answer might amount to nothing more than the assertion that it was at least one of the three. This seems to have been the method of Starke, J., with perhaps a slight preference for intercourse ("commercial intercourse") as the appropriate choice. Again McTiernan, J. was satisfied to assert the inapplicability of each of the three. It is in the judgment of Dixon, J. that there is to be found any elucidation of the fundamental issue as to the nature and content of the "commerce power." In

74. Lord Wright of Durby, Sec. 92 : A Problem Piece, The Sydney Law Rev., Vol. 1, No. 2, Jan. 1954, at p. 167.

75. M. Ramaswamy, Indian Constitutional Provisions Against Barrier to Trade and Commerce Examined in the Light of Australian and American Experience, J.I.L.I., Vol. 2, 1959-60, at p. 340.

76. *Bank of New South Wales v. The Commonwealth* (1948) 76 C.L.R 1, at p. 305.

this judgment it is not thought sufficient to treat banking as "involving" intercourse and therefore within the constitutional conception. Probably it was thought that what was "involved" is not really to the point. It is "trade" or "commerce" which is made free and it is this "entity" which must be identified. The American conception in its modern form and its previous expression is meticulously examined, but rare, it would appear, to give fundamental basis to the inquiry than to provide mechanical examples as "authority." The alternative view of the nature of banking, it had been argued, arose from its function "in providing and regulating the medium of exchange chiefly employed in the Anglo-American world." It is then decided that the transactions, which produce the function, may be cause, result or concomitant but themselves are capable of, and indeed require legal classification and "possess the characteristics, which give them the complexion of trade, commerce and intercourse." Moreover, an earlier passage makes it clear that this sentence can stand as authority without the last two words. It is not necessary to comment upon the perception of the economic facts, which they are adjusted in the solution of the legal problem presented. But it is intriguing to speculate as to the "characteristics" which give to "transaction" the "complexion of commerce." Thus, it is not too speculative to contemplate that, as the economy continues to reach towards maturity so also may the view of the court. It would involve too wide and speculative an inquiry, and of too abstract a nature, to attempt to consider the applicability of the American conception in the Australian Constitutional division of powers. The similarities and differences in the degree of integration of the national economy are singularly elusive and provide justification for the essential empirilism of the lawyer's approach. But, disregard is not a well-founded empirical attitude. It is perhaps permissible to add two comments. When the problem arises for solution the American experience will at least suggest that classification of activities as "production" rather than "trade" is a verbal device. It may provide a justification for a solution reached for unexpressed or perhaps barely perceived reasons. It is not a genuine source of decision. Further, at bottom, history and economic evolution tend to achieve expression sooner or later in the interpretation of the Constitution. This is not an excuse for abdicating, but challenge to exercise the function of judgment and selection. It is an indication of the difficulties involved. The assessment of the trends in broad and complex economic phenomena may appear an unenviable task, but the choice will ultimately be between conscious and unconscious performance of it. The conception of inter-state trade as a "flow" characterised by commercial features rather than legal formalities may be observed in certain views expressed in *The Queen v. Wilkinson.*[77]

Returning to the earlier problem noted, namely, the fixing of the beginning and ending of the course of inter-state commerce the Australian

77. (1952) 85 C.L.R. 467.

judgments are not entirely silent upon this matter, though crucial issues have not as yet demanded solution. The American precedents broadly have divided into two classes. In the earlier cases the court was concerned with determining whether a State Statutory regulation of some business or economic activity reached "into" inter-State commerce so as to be unconstitutional. More recently the problem has related to the validity of Congressional Legislation, which embraced activities prefatory to the more normally recognized phenomena of inter-state Commerce.

The decision in *Malcolm's Case*[78] widened the commerce power by its enunciation of the nature of the necessitated "connection" with the defined subject matter. But, whilst the foundation was thus firmly laid, the building has been slow in arising. This no doubt is an accurate reflection in the legislative sphere of the relatively non-integrated nature of the Australian economy, at all events until recent years.

C. The Economic Dimension of Section 92

In the absence of Commonwealth legislation to fill up the vacuum a slow retreat took place towards a constitutional position comparable with that occupied by the concurrent state power over matters of local concern in United States Jurisprudence. The ambiguity of judicial expression in the American cases helped this development along. As had been pointed out by a learned American commentator,[79] the Supreme Court has often used the term 'State regulation of inter-state commerce' in the narrow sense of State trespass on the area covered by the exclusive power of Congress whilst at the same time the expression has been used to refer to the permissible regulation of local aspects of inter-state commerce by the States. It is the distinction, which in the United States is sometimes summed up in the words 'direct' and 'indirect'. This distinction was adopted by the High Court in *Roughly v. New South Wales, ex parte Beavis.*[80] In themselves the words are innocuous and Isaacs, J. himself had spoken of laws 'directed at commerce', but in the context in which they were used by the majority they required an investigation into the 'object' or purpose of the legislation. Thus, in *ex parte Nelson (no. 1),*[81] a State statute was upheld because 'in truth, the object and scope of the provisions are to protect the large flocks and herds of New South Wales against contagious and infectious disease' 'Issacs, J. in accordance in his absolutist views dissented.'

By manipulating the distinction between 'direct' and 'indirect' interference with inter-state commerce, the High Court managed to restore to the States a large area of competence without ostensibly introducing the 'police power' concept.[82] This approach on the Part of the majority reflecting

78. *Australian Steamships Ltd. v. Malcolm* (1914) 19 C.L.R. 298.
79. Gavit, The Commerce Clause, at pp. 17-19.
80. (1928) 42 C.L.R. 162, 179 *per* Knox, C.J.; 194-97; *per* Higgins, J., Issacs, J. dissented.
81. *Id.* at p. 209.
82. (1936) 55 C.L.R. 1.

the general retreat from Issacs, J. in *McArthur's* remained a nine days wonder. The majority of the High Court consistently upheld State regulation of intra-state trade provided it could be justified with reference to some purpose, which the Court considered to be legitimate concern of the State.

In the circumstances the nature of the freedom, which Sec. 92 protected, became obscure. The High Court had little difficulty in cases where a State indulged in obvious discrimination against the produce of a sister State, as was the case in *Tasmania v. Victoria.*[83] Nor would it tolerate attempts to divert produce from the local Australian market for export.[84] But these decisions failed to make clear whether Sec. 92 preserved a constitutional right of the individual to trade across State lines or whether the test was a purely economic one designed to preserve the unity of the common market. The dominant view, on the Bench of that period, was that of Evatt., J. He came probably closest to the intentions of the Founding Fathers. He argued in *R. v. Vizzard*[85] that Sec. 92 was not inserted to preserve an exclusive area of power to the Federal Parliament or to preserve the economic freedom of the individual trader; its purpose was to preserve the economic unity of the Nation. 'Absolute freedom is ascribed to trade, to commerce and to intercourse, and is not ascribed to traders or to travellers, considered merely as individuals'.

The forbidden purpose therefore is not the destruction of the right of the individual trader, but the discrimination against the commerce of a sister state, whether this is done by direct means or by an elaborate scheme, the purpose of which can only become clear with the aid of extrinsic evidence.[86] Thus, Evatt, J. and Issacs, J. were at two extremes. His approach would involve the Court in avowed statesmanship in striking a balance between State autonomy, including the right to experiment with new forms of social and economic organization, and the preservation of the free-trade area created by the Constitution.

The only true dissenter in this period was Dixon, J. Alone among his brethren he continued the search for a logical formula. To Dixon, J. it seemed irrelevant to inquire into the 'scope, object and purpose of the challenged law'. Nor may the Court, like the United States Supreme Court, consider the question of 'reasonableness' of the State legislation having regard to the legitimate interests of the State.[87] The protection of Sec. 92 is absolute and not to be qualified. The test is purely conceptual:

> "Free must at least mean free of a restriction or burden placed upon an act because it is commerce, or trade, or intercourse, or because it involves movement into or out of the State. By this

83. (1935) 52 C.L.R. 157.
84. *Peanut Board v. Rockhampton Harbour Board* (1933) 48 C.L.R. 266.
85. (1933) 50 C.L.R. 30.
86. *Vacuum Oil Co. Pty. Ltd. v. Queensland* (1934) 51 C.L.R. 108, at pp. 135, 136.
87. *Willard v. Rawson* (1933) 48 C.L.R. 316, 332.

> one means that the application of the restriction or burden to the act cannot be made the consequence of that act being of a commercial or trading character, or of its involving intercourse between two places, or of its involving movement of persons or things into or out of the state."

In essence, this formula represents a more elaborate version of the test favoured by Issacs, J. In this, as in so many other respects, Dixon, J. appears as Issacs, J.'s intellectual heir and the only Justice willing or able to understand him. However, whilst Dixon, J. shared many of Issacs, J.'s logical propositions, he did not seek to relate them to a comprehensive interpretation of the constitution, as Issacs, J. had done. In other words, Dixon, J. agreed with Issacs, J.'s logical reasoning, but not necessarily with the motivation which lay behind such reasoning. Thus, Dixon, J. together with his brethren on the Bench came to share a growing belief that Issacs, J. had been wrong in excluding the Commonwealth from the operation of Sec. 92.[88] As a matter of logical inference such a conclusion seemed to him unjustified. To his brethren, of course, the exclusion of the Commonwealth seemed of little use now Federal exclusiveness had been effectively destroyed.

Evatt, J.'s 'economic' interpretation received its apotheosis in Lord Wright's opinion on behalf of the Privy Council in *James v. Commonwealth.*[89] Not only did the Board demolish the logical structure of Issacs, J.'s judgment in *McArthur's Case,*[90] their Lordships also accepted the view that Sec. 92 was mainly directed at discrimination against the trade of other States, however indirect and however disguised. Their disapproval of *McArthur's Case* and the express approval they gave to passages from Evatt, J.'s judgment in *Vizzard's Case*[91] all indicate their indebtedness to the reasoning of that Justice. On the facts the Board had little difficulty in rejecting a Federal statute which prohibited inter-state traffic in dried fruits except by licence, such licence only being obtainable on evidence that the majority of the grower's produce was intended for overseas export. The freedom of passage, which was vindicated, was that of the dried fruit, not the constitutional right of James to conduct inter-state trade. Their Lordship, like the Founding Fathers, thought in terms of *laisser-passer*, not *laisser-faire.*

The High Court accepted the Privy Council decision as a vindication of Evatt's position and therefore in the succeeding years allowed the states and the Commonwealth fairly wide scope in arranging the economic affairs

88. *O'Gilpin Ltd. v. Commissioner for Road Transport (N.S.W.)* (1935) 52 C.L.R. 189, 205.
89. (1936)55 C.L.R. 1; *R. v. Vizzard,* (1933) 50 C.L.R. 30, at p. 88 and 95 per Evatt, J.; *O'Gilpin Ltd. v. Comm. for Road Transport,* (1935) 52 C.L.R., at p. 212 per Dixon, J.
90. (1936) 55 C.L.R. 1.
91. *Id.* at pp. 50-51.

of the Nation.[92] Indeed the High Court upheld marketing legislation which forced all trade into a particular channel, depriving individual producers of the right to market their produce inter-state as they pleased, provided the scheme did not result in a diminution of the flow of trade across the border.[93] Socialism and Sec. 92 were clearly considered to be compatible.

The *Bank Nationalisation Case*[94] raised a question of quite a different order. The nationalisation of all private trading banks in Australia by the Commonwealth had on the face of it nothing whatever to do with State borders. Nor was it enacted by way of subterfuge to discourage inter-state trade. As Latham, C.J. pointed out in his dissent, the legislation could only offend against Sec. 92, if the Court were prepared to return to *McArthur's Case*[95] and hold that any law, however general in its application, could not apply so as to restrict or burden the conduct of inter-state communication.[96]

However, the majority proceeded to emasculate *James v. Commonwealth*[97] just as the earlier High Court had emasculated *McArthur's Case*. The approach of Rich, J. with whom most of the majority agreed, was to stipulate a constitutional right of the individual to conduct his business across State lines. Legislation, which restricted this right, could only be justified by reference to some 'legitimate' object of the Commonwealth or State.[98] Since the prohibition to the private trading banks to carry on their business in Australia had no such redeeming feature, it failed in his Honour's opinion.

Dixon, J. was equally consistent, but in this case his reasoning was negative rather than positive. His Honour found it necessary to concede that 'Juristically it is doubtless true that Sec. 92 does not confer private rights upon individuals'. But if the effect of Section 92 can better be described as an immunity, it is an immunity enjoyed not by inter-state commerce considered as an *economic phenomenon*, but as an activity and 'as such ... free for people to engage in'.

His Honour also accepted Lord Wright's condemnation of Issacs, J.'s statements in *McArthur's Case*,[99] but he toned down the effect thereof :

> "What, as it seems to me, the judgment in *James v. Commonwealth*[100] has corrected is the error of applying the

---

92. *Riverina Transport Pty. Ltd. v. Victoria* (1937) 57 C.L.R. 327; *Hartley v. Walsh* (1937) 57 C.L.R. 372.
93. *Milk Board (N.S.W.) v. Metropolitan Cream Pty. Ltd.* (1939) 62 C.L.R. 116, 130-135; *Andrews v. Howell* (1941) 65 C.L.R. 255.
94. *Bank of New South Wales v. Commonwealth* (1948) 76 C.L.R. 1.
95. (1920) 28 C.L.R. 530.
96. (1948) 76 C.L.R. 1, 235-40.
97. (1936) 55 C.L.R. 1.
98. (1948) 76 C.L.R. 1, 293-95 per Rich and Williams, JJ., at p. 324 per Starke, J. However Dixon, J. condemned any reference to 'legislative mens res'.
99. (1936) 55 C.L.R. 1.
100. *Ibid.*

conception of freedom where there was no real burden upon and no real obstruction to passing from one State to another or dealing across State lines and in addition the failure to recognize that regulation of trade, commerce and intercourse is compatible with freedom of inter-State passage or converse."

With this statement even Evatt, J. might have agreed. The terms 'burden' and 'regulation' are capable of many meanings. To Evatt, J. this meaning was *largely economic in character*. But Dixon, J. dismissed the economic test :

"To take the volume or flow of inter-state banking business independently of the freedom of private banks to transact it, and make the inquiry whether the law closing them has a purpose or a necessary tendency to reduce the volume or flow, is, I think, to raise an irrelevant consideration. It is, moreover, a consideration of an economic and not a legal character."

From Dixon, J.'s reasoning it is clear that the question is whether the impugned legislation 'burdens' inter-state trade including the activities of those engaged in such trade. The test of 'burden' must be one, which involves only 'legal' considerations. With this his Honour clearly refers to his analytical test as enunciated in *Gilpin's Case*.[101] But for the moment his Honour sufficed by saying that prohibition of all private banking was a *fortiori* such a 'burden'.[102]

The opinion of the Privy Council on appeal[103] betrays the influence of Dixon, J. in much the same measure as Lord Wright had been influenced by Evatt, J.. Not only did the Board agree with all the 'disagreements' of Dixon, J. in the High Court, it gave strong impetus to his analytical test by agreeing that the 'object' or 'purpose' of the legislation was irrelevant. With Dixon, J. the Board agreed that Sec. 92 conferred an immunity upon which individuals could rely.

However, their Lordships were unable to give much positive guidance. The best they could do, was to paraphrase the passage from the judgment of Dixon, J. referred to earlier :

". . . it seems that two general propositions may be accepted: (1) that regulation of trade, commerce and intercourse among the States is compatible with its absolute freedom, and (2) that Section 92 is violated only when a legislative or executive act operates to restrict such trade, commerce and intercourse directly and immediately as distinct from creating some indirect

101. *O'Gilpin Ltd. v. Commissioner for Road Transport (N.S.W.)* (1935) 52 C.L.R. 189, 205.
102. (1948) 76 C.L.R. 1, 387-388.
103. (1949) 79 C.L.R. 497.

or consequential impediment which may fairly be regarded as remote."[104]

It was only on his elevation to the Chief Justiceship, that Dixon, J. achieved predominance on the Bench and set out to give the words 'regulation', 'burden' (or 'impediment') and 'direct' interpretations in accordance with his own analytical approach.

This took place in a very gradual fashion. In the first few cases the High Court concentrated exclusively on the question whether the activities which the impugned legislation seeks to restrain fall within the concept of inter-state trade, commerce and intercourse.[105] A transaction, which falls outside this conception, is *prima facie* outside the protection of Section 92.[106]

5. INFLUENCE OF THE INDIAN "COMMERCE CLAUSE" ON THE ECONOMIC DOMAIN

A. Impediment to Economic Unity

Prof. Jariwala is of the opinion that "the main impediment to economic unity has been the policy of isolationism followed by the Indian States."[107] To strengthen his this view he cites recommendation of the Simon Commission in this regard:

> "Economic forces are such that the States and British India must stand or fall together . . . The increasing importance of industry brings problems that must be faced by both together. In such vital matters as communications (rail, road or postal), customs, monetary policy and labour regulation, co-operation is becoming essential. The fact that the majority of States are land-locked places them in a position of reliance on British India and the outside world, while the existence of parts in some other States has already caused complications."[108]

(a) Rigour of Impediment Mitigated

However, discussions made in subsequent chapters would reveal that the rigour of aforesaid impediment has to a great extent been mitigated by construing strictly the 'exception' provisions contained in Part XIII of our Constitution.

---

104. *Id.* at p. 639.
105. *Fergusson v. Stevenson* (1951) 84 C.L.R. 421; *Cam and Son Pty. Ltd. v. Chief Secretary of New South Wales* (1951) 84 C.L.R. 442; *Reg. v. Wilkinson* (1952) 85 C.L.R. 467.
106. *Carter v. Potato Marketing Board* (1951) 84 C.L.R. 460; *Wilcox Mofflin Ltd. v. New South Wales* (1952) 85 C.L.R, 488, 519; *Wragg v. New South Wales* (1953) 88 C.L.R. 353; *Grannall v. Kelloway and Son Pty. Ltd.* (1955) 93 C.L.R. 36, 52; *Grannall v. Marrickville Margarine Pty. Ltd.* (1955) 93 C.L..R.55.
107. Jariwala, The Freedom of Inter-state Trade in India, Sterling Publishers (1975), Delhi.
108. The Report of The Indian Statutory Commission (1930), Vol. II, para 17.

Undoubtedly, there are far greater impediments to the pace of economic development in India than inter-state barriers to trade and commerce. But the successful creation of an interdependent national territorial area, within which individuals, trade and industry may operate freely without regard to state boundary lines, is a factor of considerable and probably increasing significance to the rapid development of the national economy. Certainly the fact that the American states in the eighteenth century were joined in a federal free trade unit, protected by the negative implications of the "Commerce Clause" against local burdens and repressions by the individual states, has been considered an important component of the favourable climate within which the American economy has grown so rapidly. In mid-twentieth century, the framers of the Indian federation, as well as those moving in the general direction of federalism in Western Europe, have recognized the long-run correlation between economic growth and the curtailment of inter-state barriers. The Indian constitutional draftsmen also considered the mitigation of inter-state preferences as they relate to individual persons, an essential step in the development of national political stability and unity.[109]

Thus, the Indian Constitution, like other federal Constitutions, contains provisions for curbing state discrimination against persons and economic interests that have headquarters, in one sense or another, in another state.

The Indian Constitution envisages basically a federal state with a central government having competence over the whole of the territory of India and regional governments having competence over defined areas known as states. The constitution-makers were aware of the working of other leading federations such as Australia, Canada and the United States, and they attempted to prevent the occurrence of some of the difficulties encountered there. This was equally true in the area of trade, commerce and intercourse, which presents a formidable problem in a federation. Besides, there were problems, which were peculiar to the Indian context, such as removing the disparities between underdeveloped, developed and highly developed areas from the point of view of industry, communication, etc. and the fostering of economic or fiscal integration throughout the territory of India.[110]

There were also the Indian princely states, which though merged and integrated with the rest of the country, had raised tariff barriers. Such problems, which *create economic or fiscal imbalances between various regions in a country*, assume importance in a federation where regional governments enjoy an autonomous status and compete on equal terms with central government in the governance of the country. Thus, one of the tasks of

109. Lawrence F. Ebb, Inter-state Barriers in India and American Constitutional Experience, Stanford L. Rev., Vol. 11, 1958-59 at pp. 38-39.

110. D.K. Singh : Trade, Commerce and Intercourse in India : A Reappraisal of some Constitutional Problems, J.I.L.J, Vol. 14, 1972, at p. 40.

Constitution-makers was to achieve a *fiscal or economic integration* creating a 'common market' throughout the territory of India and yet maintaining a reasonable degree of autonomy for the states within their prescribed competence. This was sought to be achieved in the area of trade, commerce and intercourse by providing Part XIII in the Constitution. While construing the provisions of Part XIII, it has, therefore, to be remembered that the Constitution provides for essentially a federal set-up, and Part XIII found a place in the Constitution primarily for that reason. The desirability of having such a provision would not have arisen otherwise as in a unitary set-up matters such as inter-regional trade barriers, the creation of discrimination between the various regions, or the giving of preference to one region over another are of little importance in the constitutional sense. In the *Atiabari* case,[111] Gajendragadkar, J. appreciated that economic unity was absolutely essential for the stability and progress for the country in the face of different political parties believing in different economic theories and ideologies coming into power in the several constituent units of the union, and emphasised that the object of Part XIII was to preserve national unity by discouraging local and regional pulls and pressures in economic matters. Das, J. also observed to the same effect in the *Automobile case*[112] when he posed the problem of economic integration in the Union and identified the enactment of Part XIII as a corollary essential to a federal or quasi-federal set-up. In this context Part XIII should concern itself only with inter-regional trade, commerce and intercourse. The aforesaid thinking is in consonance with Sec. 297 of the Government of India Act, 1935 which provided that:

"(1) No Provincial Legislature or Government shall—

(a) by virtue of the entry in the Provincial Legislative list relating to trade and commerce within the Province, or the entry in that list relating to the production, supply, and distribution of commodities, have power to pass any law or take any executive action prohibiting or restricting the entry into, or export from, the Province of goods of any class or description; and

(b) by virtue of anything in this Act have power to impose any tax, cess, toll, or due which, as between goods manufactured or produced in the province and similar goods not so manufactured or produced, discriminates in favour of the former, or which, in the case of goods manufactured or produced outside the Province discriminates between goods manufactured or produced in one locality and similar goods manufactured or produced in another locality.

111. *Atiabari Tea Co. v. State of Assam*, A.I.R. (1961) S. C. 232.

112. *Automobile Transport Ltd. v. State of Rajasthan*, A.I.R. (1962) S.C. 1406.

(2) Any law passed in contravention of this section shall, to the extent of the contravention, be invalid."

(b) Another Version

The *politico-economic purpose* of Sec. 92 and of Art. 301 was to ensure the free flow of trade and commerce in general and not to confer primary rights on individuals. This has been recognised in many cases.[113] But when it is sought to achieve that purpose by legal instrument (Art. 301) a new factor is introduced—the legal operation of the instrument chosen, which may or may not be well designed to achieve the purpose. The result of ignoring this may well be paradoxical. Thus, if it is said that Art. 301 is aimed at preventing restrictions on the volume of trade flowing and that therefore the effect of a law on individuals is irrelevant, then the result will be that the primary purpose of Article 301 will be defeated.

This is because courts, if they are wise, will avoid deciding questions about the *calculated economic effect of laws.* As Lord Porter pointed out in the *Bank Nationalization*, the application of Sec. 92 did not involve calculations as to the actual present or possible future effect upon the total volume of inter-state trade—the difficulty in applying such a criterion being too obvious.[114] Unless courts were to venture into that area of speculation the result is that, if the test for the operation of Art. 301 were, "Does the challenged law diminish the total volume of trade?", very few laws that did not on their face limit that volume could be questioned successfully in the courts. Who would argue that it is beyond the skill of a draftsman to destroy inter-State trade, or trade generally, without inviting such a challenge on the face of the Act? However, Derham suggests that the 'volume of trade' theory is not the way to resolve the question.

B. Economic Unity of the Country: An Aspiration of our Constitution-Makers

If one goes through the debates of the Constituent Assembly he finds that Pt. Thakur Das Bhargava was not in favour of giving much power to the states to regulate trade, commerce and inter course. As, according to him, this might impair the unity of the whole India. He was of the opinion that ". . . the powers given to the State, according to me, should never in any case be allowed, because that would mean that every state shall be able to raise barriers against the rest of India and people living in other States and they will constitute a state of things, which I feel, will not conduce to the unity of the whole of India."[115] Emphasising upon general economic improvement of India as a whole, Mr. B.P. Jhunjhunwala added that 'whatever State legislature or the Parliament may pass law or order putting any restriction

113. e.g. in India *Sri Motilal v. State of Uttar Pradesh*, A.I.R. 1951 All. 257 at p. 270, 313 and 314; *Saghir Ahmad v. State of Uttar Pradesh*, A.I.R. 1954, All. 257 at p. 274 and 288.

114. (1950) A.C. at pp. 304-05. Approved by the Supreme Court in *Saghir Ahamad's* case.

115. C.A.D., Vol. IX, 1949 at p. 1130.

regarding trade and commerce between one state and another, that should not be inconsistent with the general economic unity of India as a whole'.[116] On the other hand, Mr. T.T. Krishnamachari[117] argued for the powers given to the states.

C. Object of Protecting Freedom of Trade in a Two-Tier Polity

The *Sarkaria Commission* feels that free flow of trade, commerce and intercourse within and across inter-State borders is an important pre-requisite for ensuring economic unity, stability and prosperity of a country having a two-tier polity. Most federal constitutions contain special provisions to protect this freedom. The Indian Constitution also contains provisions guaranteeing freedom of commerce, trade and intercourse throughout the territory of India. However, no freedom can be absolute. Limitations for the common good are inherent in such freedom, lest it should degenerate into a self-defeating licence. That is why, legitimate regulatory measures are not considered to constitute restrictions on this freedom.[118]

D. Sarkaria Commission's Satisfaction over Judicial Thinking Regarding Economic Unity of the Country Expressed in '*Atiabari*' and '*Automobile*' Cases

The Sarkaria Commission appears to be more than satisfied with the judicial handling of the Indian "Commerce Clause" for strengthening the economic unity of the country, besides the political unity. It has quoted[119] with approval the majority view expressed by Gajendragadkar, Wanchoo and Das Gupta, JJ. that:

> "In drafting the relevant Articles of Part XIII the makers of the Constitution were fully conscious that economic unity was absolutely essential for the stability and progress of the federal policy which had been adopted by the Constitution for the governance of the country. Political freedom has been won, and political unity which had been accomplished by the Constitution, had to be sustained and strengthened by the bond of economic unity. It was realised that in course of the time different political parties believing in different economic theories of ideologies may come in power in the several constituent units of the Union and that may conceivably give rise to local and regional pulls and pressures in economic matters. Local or regional fears or apprehensions raised by local or regional problems may persuade the State legislatures to adopt remedial measures intended solely for the protection of

116. *Id.* at pp. 1134-35.
117. *Id.* at p. 1140.
118. The Sarkaria Commission's Report at p. 499.
119. *Id.* at p. 501.

regional interests without due regard to their effect on the economy of the nation as a whole. The object of Part XIII was to avoid such a possibility. Free movement and exchange of goods throughout the territory of India is essential for the economy of the nation and for sustaining and improving living standards of the country. The provision contained in Article 301 guaranteeing the freedom of trade, commerce and intercourse is not a declaration of a mere platitude, or the expression of a pious hope of a declaratory character; it is not also a mere statement of a Directive Principle of State policy; it embodies and enshrines a principle of paramount importance that the economic unity of the country will provide the main sustaining force for the stability and progress of the political and cultural unity of the country. In appreciating the significance of these general considerations we may profitably refer to the observations made by Cardozo, J. in *Charles H. Baldwin v. G.A.F. Seeling*[120] while he was dealing with the "Commerce Clause" contained in Article 1, Sec. 8, Cl. 3 of the American Constitution. 'This Part of the Constitution', observed Cardozo, J., 'was framed under the dominion of a political philosophy less parochial in range. It was framed upon the theory that the people of the several states must sink or swim together and that in the long-run prosperity and salvation are in union and not division'."[121]

Elucidating the objectives and importance of the Indian "Commerce Clause" for the economic integrity of the nation, what was stated by the Supreme Court in *Automobile Transport* was heartly appreciated by the Sarkaria Commission. The Supreme Court in this case had made the following observation :

The first thing to be noticed in this connection is that the Constitution-makers were not writing on a clean slate. They had the Government of India Act, 1935 and they also had the administrative set-up, which that Act, envisaged. India then consisted of various administrative units known as provinces, each with its own administrative setup. *There were differences of language, religion, etc. Some of the provinces were economically more developed than the others. Even inside the same province, there were underdeveloped, developed and highly developed areas from the point of view of industries, communications, etc. The problem of economic integration with which constitution-makers were faced was a problem with many facets. Two questions, however, stood out; one question was how to achieve a federal, economic and fiscal integration, show that economic policies affecting the interest of India as a whole could be carried out without putting an ever increasing strain on the unity of India, particularly in the context on a developing*

120. (1934) 294 U.S. 511 at p. 523; 79 L.Ed 1032 at p. 1033.

121. *Atiabari Tea Co. v. State of Assam*, A.I.R. 1961, S. C. 232, at p. 247.

economy. The second question was how to foster the development of areas which were underdeveloped without creating too many preferential of discriminative barriers. Beside the provinces, there were the Indian States also known as Indian India. After India attained political freedom in 1947 and before the Constitution was adopted, the process of merger and integration of the Indian States with the rest of the country had been accomplished so that when the Constitution first passed in territory of India consisted of Part A States, which broadly represented the Provinces in British India, and Part B States, which were made-up of Indian states. There were trade barriers raised by the Indian states in the exercise of their legislative power and constitution-maker had to make provision with regard to those trade barriers as well. The evolution of a federal structure or a quasi-federal structure necessarily involved, in the context of the conditions then prevailing, a distribution of powers and a basic Part of our Constitution relates to that distribution with the three legislative lists in the Seventh Schedule. The Constitution itself says by Art. 1 that India is a union of states and in interpreting the Constitution one must keep in view the essential structure of a federal or quasi-federal Constitution, namely that the units of the union have also certain power as has the union itself. One of the grievances made on behalf of the intervening states before the Supreme Court was that the majority view in the *Atiabari Tea Co. case*[122] did not give sufficient importance to the power of the states under the Indian Constitution to raise revenue by taxes under the legislative head entrusted to them, in interpreting the series of Articles relating to trade, commerce and intercourse in Part XIII of the Constitution. It has been often stated that freedom of inter-state trade and commerce in a federation has been a baffling problem to constitutional experts in Australia, in America and in other federal constitutions. In evolving an integrated policy on this subject our constitution-makers seem to have kept in mind three main considerations which may be broadly stated thus: *first*, in the larger interest of India there must be free flow of trade, commerce and intercourse, both inter-state and intra-state; *second*, the regional interest must not be ignored all together; and *third*, there must be a power of intervention by the union in any case of crisis to deal with particular problems that may arise in any Part of India. All these three considerations have played their Part in the series of articles, which one has to consider in Part XIII of the Constitution. Therefore, in interpreting the relevant articles in Part XIII one must have regard to the general scheme of Constitution of India with special reference to Part III (Fundamental Rights), Part XII (Finance, property, etc. containing Art. 276 and 286) and their inter-relation to Part XIII in the context of a federal or quasi-federal Constitutions in which the states have certain powers including the power to raise revenues for their purposes by taxation.

122. *Ibid.*

Recommendation of the Sarkaria Commission Regarding Economic Unity of the Country

The Commission in its report rightly recommends that,

> "Free flow of trade, commerce and intercourse within and across inter-state borders is an important pre-requisite for ensuring economic unity, stability and prosperity of a country having a two-tier polity. Limitations for the common good are inherent in such freedom, least it should de-generate into a self-defeating licence."[123]

E. View of the "National Commission to Review the Working of the Constitution"

The commission is of the view that[124]—

(a) Free flow of trade without geographical barrier is *sine-qua-non* for economic prosperity nationally as well as internationally. Therefore, progressive removal of such barriers has been a general phenomenon in social evolution in the modern world. Today, we are vigorously pursuing the goal of free flow of trade among the nations of the world under the banner of globalisation through, for example, the WTO among the nations of the world. Regionally, member states of the European Community, for example, have already achieved that goal almost fully.

(b) As economy is the most important source of power and identity in the world of today, the nations or regions that constitute the federation do not want to lose their hold on economic power. Nor do the economically strong states want the economically weak states to become parasites on them. Therefore, an arrangement must be devised which will ensure free flow of trade, encourage fair competition and simultaneously remain capable of discouraging and regulating unfair trade practices.

F. Sugarcane, Tea, Coffee, Mint and Like Products—The Pillars of Indian Economy—Require Special Attention

Since, Sugarcane, Tea, Coffee, Mint, Cotton and like products are formidable source of Indian Economy therefore they require special judicial attention if their transportation, export and import across trade barriers (state boundaries), etc. are attempted to be regulated by law. It is humbly submitted that while examining the vires of regulations of these products the judiciary must adopt a strict approach.

The state sugarcane marketing regulation was found not to compete with any central legislation or regulations adopted. A closer scrutiny of the

123. The Sarkaria Commission's Report, at p. 504.

124. Report of the National Commission to Review the Working of the Constitution, Vol. 1 Chap. 8C at pp. 11 of 30.

history of Central and State relationship in regulating the sugarcane industry might reveal some affirmative indications of Central Government approval of these marketing regulations as consistent with a uniform national distribution programme. Thus, it appears from the courts recital of the history of legislation concerning sugar and sugarcane that, starting in the early 1930's, the central legislature of British India provided for both central and provincial regulation. The Indian tariff board, in a 1938 report, commended the advantages of a zonal system to regulate the supply of sugarcane to the sugar industries. This is a major characteristic of the production programmes adopted by Uttar Pradesh and Bihar, which produce 85 percent of India's sugar. Even at this later stage in India's development, the Central Government may still be more concerned about assuring stability in the sugar processing industries and minimizing use of India's overburdened inter-state transportation facilities than about increasing the mobility of capital invested in the sugar industries and increasing inter-state competition for the national market.

The economic importance of this pattern of state production and marketing control is indicated by the fact that India produces 35 percent of the world's sugarcane crop and is reportedly the largest sugar producing country in the world. It is estimated that 20 million farmers are engaged in the production of the sugarcane in India, and the sugar industry is considered one of India's largest industries, second only to cotton textiles.[125]

From the above it is clear that the sugarcane plays an important role in the Indian economy and therefore this fact must be taken into consideration by the judiciary while interpreting the Indian "Commerce Clause." One thing must also be borne into mind that because of regulation leading to slow movement of sugarcane, the Juice product of the same may get decreased, leading to reduction in production of the sugar.

Tea has been one of the major exportable commodities of India and is one of the few products in which the country enjoys the status of a world leader. But its export performance has not been particularly impressive, specially in 1980 and started loosing its share in world tea market. Besides this, due to falling exports in volume terms, the export product ratio has consistently fallen for all tea. The average export production ratio was 43 percent in triennia 1971-73, which fell to 40 percent in triennia 1978-80 and more steeply to only 30 percent in 1988-90. The steep decline in export-production ratio in the 1980s is attributed to a fall in bulk tea exports during the 1980s while in the 1970s bulk tea exports were stagnant.

India has also lost its market share in almost all major tea importing countries. In UK, Indian tea accounted for nearly 33 percent of total tea export in the early 1970s, and its share declined to around 16 percent by the late 1980s. In case of former USSR also its share declined from 100 percent to around 71 percent during the same period. This has been the case in respect

125. Times of India Directory and Year Book 100 (Moraes ed., 156-57).

of almost all the major importing countries of Indian tea. The overall tea export declined from an average of 208.1 million kg. in the triennia 1988-90 to 202.9 million kg. in 1991 and further to 174.66 million kg. in 1992. This assertion gets support from the following tables:

TABLE (I)[126]

Share of Indian Tea in Total Tea Imports of Various Countries

(percentages)

Year	*UK*	*USSR*	*USA*	*Canada*	*Iraq*	*Egypt*	*Afghani-stan*
1972	33.3	100.0	10.0	1.3	25.9	95.0	—
1977	35.7	79.7	10.9	4.0	18.4	53.0	66.0
1982	30.9	92.6	3.3	2.3	3.2	23.7	65.0
1987	15.9	71.9	2.3	5.6	5.4	12.0	—
1991	10.3	64.5	2.1	5.0	0.0	11.3	11.7

TABLE (II)[127]

Export-Production Ratio

Year	*Packet tea*	*Period*	*All tea*
1983	12.07	1971-73	43.21
1985	20.63	1976-78	39.28
1989	30.48	1983-85	34.22
1991	30.44	1988-90	29.61

No body claims that only unnecessary and unusual trade regulations are responsible for such a decline; there are many more other factors responsible for it. But one thing is certain, that is that regulations under the 'Exception Clauses' of the Indian "Commerce Clause" are to a great responsible for such a decline leading to loss of Indian revenue. Therefore, it is humbly submitted that the judiciary must take into account this fact and must perform its creative role while examining the vires of regulations or restrictions under the 'Exception Clause' of the "Commerce Clause".

The Indian economy is in the process of being integrated with the world economy. For a country, like India, which is a price-taker in the world market, a distinct feature of globalisation is the impact of changes in world economic situation on the domestic economic situation and on the performance of external sectors. In the recent past, such an impact seems to

126. *Source*: Calculated from Tea Statistics, cited in Indian Tea Exports : An analysis of performance and constraints by Alok Kumar and Ramani Kumar published in *Foreign Trade Review* (1994).

127. *Source*: Calculated from Tea Digest, cited in Indian Tea Exports : An analysis of performance and constraints by Alok Kumar and Ramani Kumar published in *Foreign Trade Review* (1994).

have been strongly felt in the marketing, pricing and exporting of coffee in India.[128]

TABLE (III)[129]

Annual Export of Coffee From India : 1981-82 to 1993-94

Year	*Total Exports (Rs. lakh)*	*Export of Coffee (Rs. lakh)*	*(3) as a % of (2)*	*Coffee exports ('000 tonnes)*
(1)	*(2)*	*(3)*	*(4)*	*(5)*
1981-82	780590	14629	1.87	7.4
1984-85	1174368	21022	1.79	6.76
1988-89	2023200	34300	1.70	98.3
1990-91	3252728	25238	0.78	85.9
1991-92	4382803	31007	0.71	90.8
1992-93	5368826	37625	0.70	114.1
1993-94	6954679	49695	0.71	120.6
1994-95 (April-June)	1761022	2409527	1.37	44.3

It is important to note that the export taxes on coffee by the Union Government of India are in the form of export duties and export cess.

From the above it is clear that coffee is a formidable source of Indian economy. Therefore, it needs special protection of the "Commerce Clause" for which the judiciary can prove a balance wheel.

Cultivation of mint crop has recently been introduced in India. India has adequate agricultural resources for production of mint oil but it is still confined to only some parts of Utter Pradesh, Punjab and Haryana due to lack of education about the crop and extension work for propagation of this highly commercial and valuable commodity. Its use in the form of flavour and fragrance shows its importance both in the domestic market as well as in the International market. The primary market for mint oil includes soft drink companies, food companies, perfumery companies, cosmetics and pharmaceutical, which are growing at a rate of 18.23 percent in terms of sales value and 17.93 percent in terms of market size. The following graph on next page explains the story.

This is a new area, which needs supportive policy framework for enhancing its production and diversifying its markets by organising this industry in a scientific manner for better economy of India. This would also require judicial support in the formal liberal interpretation of freedom of trade in the area of mint oil.

---

128. See Table (iii).

129. Cited by M.R. Narayana, Marketing, Pricing and Exporting of Coffee in India : Recent changes and implications, *Foreign Trade Review*, 1994, at p. 147.

TABLE (IV)[130]

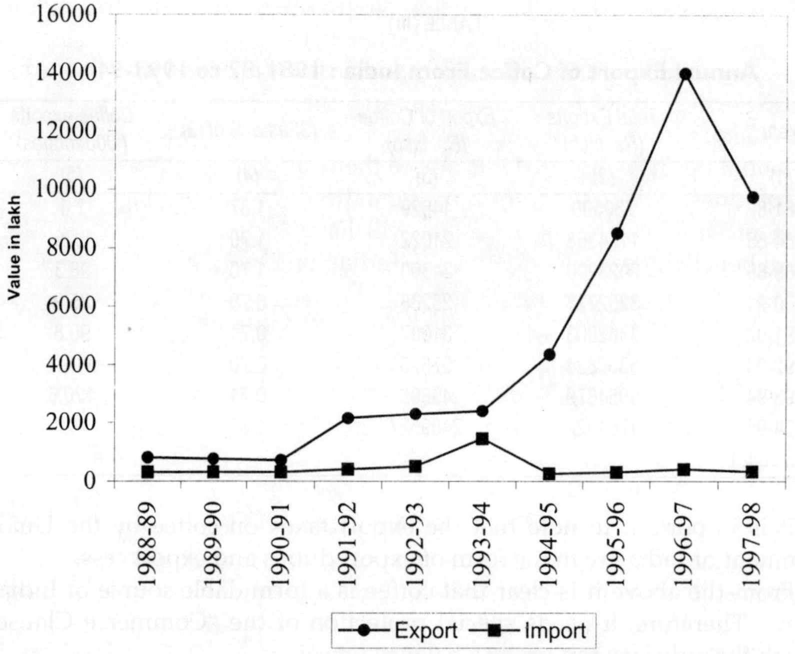

G. A Judicial Indication

In *M/S Video Electronics Pvt. Ltd. v. State of Punjab*,[131] it was pointed out by the Supreme Court that the concept of economic barrier must be adopted in a dynamic sense with changing conditions. What constitutes an economic barrier at one point of time often cease to be so at another point of time.[132]

H. Electronic Commerce *v.* Indian Economy

E-commerce in India is currently centered on business-to-business users who have international market dealings. The Indian Market Research Bureau (I.M.R.B.) conducted a comprehensive survey key issues that of the E-commerce in India to solve key issues that are likely to act as motivators and barriers to the spread of E-commerce. The Survey has great relevance to the creative sector as it captures information on whether companies are considering E-commerce in a big way. The survey also estimates the likely potential of E-commerce in India.

To sum up, Indian businesses are very optimistic about the use of the E-commerce and a large proportion considers it as critical to organization

130. *Ibid*
130. A.I.R. (1990) S.C. at p. 821.
132. Jabir Ali : Export Potential of Indian Mint Oil Industry, *Foreign Trade Review*, 2000 at p. 55.

strategy. On an average, organizations expect that around 12% of their turnover will be contributed through the E-commerce in the next two years. It is currently perceived as a new selling environment that would allow them to axis new international markets. It is expected to benefit them in terms of improved customers' service and increased productivity efficiency. Marketing/sales, operations, corporate and finance and the key functions that are seen to benefit from E-commerce. However, they are not clear about the potential benefits that could accrue to them. This translates to lower level of preparedness with respect to implementation of E-commerce. Technology solution providers and policy-makers will have to focus more to highlight potential benefits more appropriately to Indian businesses.[133]

133. Indian Market Research Bureau (I.M.R.B.).

6

Regulation *versus* Restriction: Rate Fixing

While discussing the extent to which the Centre and States can interfere with freedom of trade, commerce and intercourse, it becomes necessary to examine the extent of regulation in this area. More important than this is to examine whether the power to regulate includes the power to prohibit. Though there are various modes of permissible regulations yet at present only regulations through rate fixing and taxation are being discussed. Rate fixing as a method to regulate commerce is being discussed in this chapter whereas the concept and extent of regulatory and compensatory taxes are being discussed in the next chapter.

I. REGULATION *V.* RESTRICTION

The question out set arises whether regulation includes prohibition? The answer to this question is clear under the Marshall conception of regulation. The power to prescribe the rule by which commerce is to be governed certainly appears to comprehend the authority to determine whether or not particular articles should be barred from inter-state commerce. The power to limit and restrain commerce at pleasure should embrace within its bounds a power to exclude persons and commodities from commerce when that is deemed necessary.

It was not until almost a century after *Gibbbons v. Ogden*[1] that the Supreme Court was squarely confronted with the question of whether or not a power of prohibition is included in the power to regulate commerce. In *Champion v. Ames (Lottery Case 2)*[2] the Court was presented with an attack upon the constitutionality of an Act of Congress prohibiting any person from causing lottery tickets to be carried from one state to another. The law was upheld in a forceful opinion by Justice Harlan, who categorically rejected the

1. (1824) Wheat. 1.
2. 188 U.S. 321 (1903).

view that the power to regulate could not be understood to give the power to exclude. "If lottery traffic, carried on through inter-state commerce, is a matter of which Congress may take cognizance and over which its power may be exerted," asks Harlan's opinion, "Can it be possible that it must tolerate the traffic, and simply regulate the manner in which it may be carried on? Or may not Congress, for the protection of the people of all the states, and under the power to regulate inter-state commerce, devise such means, within the scope of the Constitution, and not prohibited by it, as will drive that traffic out of commerce among the states?"[3]

While the *Lotterry Case* holds that regulation may appropriately assume the form of prohibition, it is far from recognising a general plenary power in the Congress to close the channels of inter-state commerce, whenever, it chooses, to any person, article, or commodity of whatever kind or nature. The Lottary case turns upon the noxious nature of the articles involved and Justice Harlan was most careful to limit his opinion to such commodities. What clause of the Constitution, he inquired, "can be cited which in any degree, countenances the suggestion that one may, of right, carry or cause to be carried from one state to another that which will harm the public morals?"[4]

The commerce power may be exerted to prevent the pollution of commerce by articles confessedly injurious to the public morals. As the *Lottery Case* expressed it, "as a state may, for the purpose of guarding the morals of its own people, forbid all sales of lottery tickets within its limits, so Congress, for the purpose of guarding the people of the United States against the 'widespread pestilence of lotteries' and to protect the commerce which concerns all the States, may prohibit the carrying of lottery tickets from one state to another."[5]

Even though the High Court in the *Lottery Case* limited its decision to traffic in articles like lottery tickets which no one can be entitled to pursue as of right, the case is still a landmark one. It renders explicit what had been implicit since *Gibbons*, that the authority to control includes the authority to supress. The power to regulate must, since the *Lottery decision,* clearly be understood as embracing the power to destroy.

Since the *Lottery Case,* the Supreme Court has repeatedly applied its holding to federal laws closing the channels of commerce to commodities which are themselves dangerous or harmful or which may have an adverse effect upon the public. In Justice Stone's words in an important case[6]: "Congress is free to exclude from inter-state commerce articles whose use in the states for which they are destined it may reasonably conceive to be injurious to the public health, morals, or welfare."[7]

---

3. *Id.* at p. 355.
4. *Id.* at p. 356.
5. *Id.* at p. 357.
6. *United States v. Carolene Products Co.*, 304 U.S. 144 (138).
7. *Ibid.*

Recently in *Camps Newfound/Owatonna v. Harrison*[8] the U.S Supreme Court held that, the constitutionally significant distinction between a state's subsidies of certain charitable activities and tax exemption is applicable to claims that certain state action designed to give residents an advantage in the market place is prohibited by the 'Commerce Clause'. The 'Commerce Clause' does not prohibit all such state action, but only action of that description in connection with the state's regulation of inter-state commerce. While direct subsidisation of domestic industry does not ordinarily run afoul of this prohibition, discriminatory taxation does.

However, in Canada the balance appears to be tilted in favour of the Dominion Parliament. This is evident from *Severn v. The Queen.*[9] In this case the Court examined the American cases in detail, and after carefully discussing *Gibbons* it decided that the commerce power in Canada was much greater than that in the United states. Justice Fournier insisted that the Ontario law was a precise duplicate of the law Marshall had invalidated in *Brown v. Maryland*[10] Fournier, J. said: "Since this is the law in the United States, there is an additional reason why it should be so declared here, where our Constitution does not acknowledge, as in the United States, a division of power as to commerce."[11] Even Justice Strong, who dissented from the majority, did not do so by refusing power to the Dominion, for he contended that "the regulation of trade and commerce in the provinces, domestic and internal as well as foreign and external, is by the British North America Act exclusively conferred upon the Parliament of the Dominion, and calls for no demonstration, for the Language of the Act is explicit."[12]

The very next year a Dominion law imposing jurisdiction on provincial superior courts to settle contested elections to the House of Commons was validated against a charge that the Act invaded the civil rights of the provinces. In *Valin v. Langlois,*[13] Chief Justice Ritchie said that "the terms 'property and civil rights' must necessarily be read in a restricted and limited sense, because many matters involving property and civil rights are expressly reserved to the Dominion Parliament." He pointed out trade and commerce as being among those Dominion powers that most directly affected property and civil rights.

One of the best discussions of the national power over commerce is in *City of Fredericton v. The Queen.*[14] The Canadian Parliament passed a Temperance Act providing for local prohibition after any local referendum. Such an election took place in the City of Fredericton. The election carried, and prohibition took effect. A hotel operator in the city applied to the New

8. (1997) 520 U.S. 564.
9. (1978) 2 S.C.R. 70.
10. 12 Wheaton 419 (1827).
11. *Severn v. The Queen*, (1978) 2 S.C.R. 70 at p. 121.
12. *Id.* at p. 104.
13. (1879) 3 S.C.R. 1 at p. 15.
14. (1979) 3 S.C.R. 505.

Brunswick Supreme Court and obtained a *mandamus nisi* commanding the city officials to issue him a liquor licence. The city officials refused to obey the Court order and cited the Dominion law as controlling. The Supreme Court agreed with the city officials. The contention was that this was not a regulation of trade and commerce as intended in the Constitution, but a Temperance Act—and, of course, dealing with drunkenness and its prevention were within the exclusive powers of the local legislatures. The Chief Justice said :

> "If then, Parliament, in its wisdom, deems it expedient for the peace, order and good government of Canada so to regulate trade and commerce as to restrict or prohibit the importation into, or exportation out of the Dominion, or the trade and traffic in, or dealing with, any articles in respect to which external or internal trade or commerce is carried on, it matters not, as far as we are judicially concerned, nor had we, in my opinion, the right to enquire whether such legislation is prompted by a desire to establish uniformity of legislation with respect to the traffic dealt with, or whether it be to increase or diminish the volume of such traffic, or to encourage native industry, or local manufactures, or with any other object which may, by regulating trade and commerce, or by any other enactments within the scope of the legislative powers confided to Parliament, tend to the peace, order and good government of Canada."[15]

Ritchie was equally certain that the right to regulate trade and commerce was "not to be overridden by any local legislation in reference to any subject over which power is given to the local legislature". In answer to the assertion that the power to regulate did not include the power to prohibit, Justice Taschereau said, "a prohibition is a regulation".

It has been held that though the Dominion Parliament has wide power to regulate trade and commerce',[16] the provincial legislature has power to make police or municipal or sanitary regulations of a merely local character, (e.g.) for the good government of taverns licenced for the sale of liquors in retail;[17] for regulating the importation, manufacture, sale purchase and use of intoxicating liquors, even though such regulation may interfere with manufacturers duly licenced by the Dominion government or they may indirectly affect business operation beyond the limits of the Province.[18] For granting on certain persons an exclusive right to establish a system of electric

15. *City of Fredericton v. The Queen, (1879)* 3 S.C.R. 505 at p. 533.
16. Section 91(2), British North America Act.
17. *Hodge v. Queen* (1883) 9 A.C. 117.
18. *A.G. of Manitoba v. Manitoba Licence-holders*, (1902) A.C. 73.

lighting for a certain term of years in a city[19]. Where regulation of a trade is constitutionally valid, the issuing of licences and the realisation of fees in that connection are also valid.[20]

In Australia the operation of State laws requiring the licencing of vehicles upon persons engaged in inter-state trade has been raised in a number of cases in all of which the State Acts were, by a majority of Court, held to apply, notwithstanding Sec. 92. These decisions have, however, with one exception, been overruled by the Privy Council in *Hughes & Vale Pty. Ltd. v. New South Wales*.[21]

In *Willard v. Rawson*[22] the State legislation in terms applied to all motor vehicles used upon the public highways of the state for purposes of carriage and it was held to apply to a carrier in respect of his driving a motor truck upon a continuos inter-state journey.

In *R. v. Vizzard; ex parte Hill*[23] the State Act set-up a licencing system for motor vehicles which acted as common carriers or otherwise engaged in the carriage of goods, its object being to regulate, co-ordinate and improve, the means of transport and to prevent competition. The Act was held to apply in relation to a carrier who conveyed goods inter-state in motor lorry which was used exclusively in transporting goods upon the journey in question.

In *Gilpin v. Commissioner of Road Transport*[24] another section of same Act was attacked. That section imposed a liability upon persons operating motor vehicles for the carriage of their own goods or goods sold by them other than goods not intended for sale immediately or ultimately; it was held to apply to a company which transported its own goods from Victoria to New South Wales for delivery to and sale in its retail stores in the second state.

In *Bessell v. Dayman*[25] the State Act made it unlawful to operate a motor vehicle for the conveyance of passengers or goods for hire without a licence or permit from the authority constituted by the Act; it was held to apply in respect of portion of an inter-state journey. In this case the various Judges of the courts only referred to their judgments in the previous cases.

The last three cases differ from the first in that the Act in *Willard* was not directed to transport. On this ground Starke, J. agreed with the majority in that case, but dissented with Dixon, J. in the others. The judgements of the majority in all four cases proceeded upon the ground that the real object of the legislation was to facilitate inter-state trade and provide and protect state highways. *It did not suppress or retard but materially assisted trade, commerce and intercourse.* As Evatt, J. expressed it in *Vizzard*[26] "a state does not infringe

19. *Hull v. Ottawa Electric Co.* (1902) A.C. 237.
20. *Shannon v. Dairy Products Board*, A.I.R. 1939 P.C. 36 at p. 38.
21. (1954) 93 C.L.R. 1.
22. (1932-33) 48 C.L.R. 316.
23. (1933) 50 C.L.R. 30.
24. (1934-35) 52 C.L.R. 189.
25. (1934-35) 52 C.L.R.
26. 50 C.L.R. at p. 82.

Sec. 92, if having no concern interest or object in restricting or prohibiting trade between states, or commerce between states, or intercourse between states, it chooses to organise, regulate and co-ordinate those facilities and services which are provided and conducted within the state as the essential instruments of all trade, commerce and intercourse." The learned Judge was of the view that, "the predominant object of Sec. 92 was to secure free trade and free intercourse among the states to give effect to the known economic doctrine and ideal which was one of the chief motive forces of federation. This view was opposed to that which analysed the words of Sec. 92 separately and subsequently put together the resulting definitions; the section should be read as a whole and broadly as referring of the flow of Australian trade by and large, as one abstract thing.[27] In other words, the concept of trade, commerce and intercourse was an integral unit and not the sum of its differentiated components.

In *Duncan and Green Star Trading Co. Pty. Ltd. v. Vizzard,*[28] the foregoing cases except *Willard v. Rawson*[29] were followed. However, Strake, J. dissented. The application of the New South Wales State Transport (Co-ordination) Act, 1931, the regulations thereunder and the administration of the Act as disclosed by the evidence and the terms of the licence in question were upheld. It was sought to distinguish the earlier cases on the ground that in the present case a barrier to the free passage of inter-state goods had been imposed by the limitation of the authority to operate the vehicle to a distance of fifty miles from the border where the journey was competitive with the railways but the argument was rejected on the broad ground that the limitation was non-discriminatory and regulatory.

Application to the Privy Council for special leave to appeal from these decisions were refused and it was in some quarters taken from this that the Privy Council had approved of the principle of the Transport cases, an assumption which, was incorrect, as Dixon, J. observed in a number of cases until the matter was settled in the decision of the Board in the *Hughes and Vale case.*[30]

Two further cases must be noticed. In *Riverina Transport Pty. Ltd. v. Victoria,*[31] a State Act considered by Latham C.J. as being indistinguishable from the legislation involved in *R. v. Vizzard,*[32] was upheld by the whole Court, on the basis of the previous decisions. Dixon, J., who felt bound to apply those decisions, said that, while it was "neither safe nor useful for a mind that denies the correctness of reasoning to proceed to expound its meaning and implications," one important step in the reasoning was

27. *Id.*, at p. 86. See also the judgment of Evatt and McTiernan, JJ. in *James v. The Commonwealth* (1934-1935) 52 C.L.R. at p. 600.
28. (1935) 53 C.L.R. 493.
29. (1933) 48 C.L.R. 316.
30. (1954) 93 C.L.R. 1.
31. (1937) 57 C.L.R. 327.
32. (1933) 50 C.L.R. 30.

adoption of the view that the use of motor vehicles for inter-state carriage of goods, though an incident of trade, commerce and intercourse among the states, was not in itself within the protection of Sec. 92 and that in consequence "a general prohibition subject to a discretion to allow exceptions is valid".[33] It was alleged in the present case that there had been discrimination. As to this point, Latham, C.J. came to some what curious conclusion that discrimination in the terms of a State Act or in the mode of its administration would not in itself infringe Sec. 92, a proposition which Evatt, J. emphatically rejected and which was not accepted by the other members of the Court who found no discrimination in fact. In *McCarter v. Brodie*[34] the Privy Council had in the interval since the *Riverina* delivered its judgment in the *Banking Case*. It was sought to have the *Transport, Hartley* and the *Milk Board Cases*, overruled and, as Latham, C.J. put it "minority judgments throughout have been right".[35] The Learned Chief Justice proceeded to consider in detail the decision of the Privy Council in the *Banking Case* and concluded, after a survey of that case and others that the *Banking Case* had "finally decided that laws directly operating upon persons engaging in inter-state trade and commerce are not infringements of Sec. 92 if they are what can fairly be described as 'regulation'. If, however, they are laws which directly deal with the subject matter of trade and commerce and exceed regulation and pass into prohibition they are invalid." The legislation in the present case was, described as "Regulation Act".[36] Not dissimilar reasoning was used by McTiernan and Webb, JJ. Williams, J. while admitting that the *Banking Case* had thrown new light on the operation of Sec. 92 and had made it plain that the freedom guaranteed by the section was the freedom of the individual, nevertheless considered that that decision had expressly preserved the principle that regulation was compatible with that freedom, even though the regulation placed restrictions upon the right of individuals to engage in inter-state trade, commerce and intercourse, it was clearly said that regulation of trade included the enactment of "all conditions reasonably necessary for its safety and preservation, and of the imposition of reasonable charges for the administration of its regulation, so that a state could enact all legislation reasonably required for the safety maintenance and preservation of the public roads and could make a reasonable charge for their use."[37] *Willard v. Rawson*[38] which went no further than this, was rightly decided, but the acts involved in the other cases went further and it was a question of fact whether such Acts were, as they professed to be, regulatory or something more; the solution of this question raised social and economic problems. But

33. 57 C.L.R. 363.
34. (1950) 80 C.L.R. 432.
35. 80 C.L.R. 446.
36. *Id.*, at p. 463.
37. *Id.*, at p. 476.
38. (1933) 48 C.L.R. 316.

after careful consideration, the Learned Judge was unable to see sufficient reason to overrule the *Transport Cases*.

Dixon and Fullagar, JJ. dissented. Recalling his analysis of the *Transport Cases* in the *Airlines Case*,[39] Dixon, J. said that the Privy Council in the *Banking Case*[40] had clearly rejected three propositions that had been put forward as the basis of those cases. These were *firstly*, that Sec. 92 did not guarantee the freedom of individuals, *secondly*, that the freedom prescribed by Sec. 92 remained unimpaired if the "same volume of trade flowed from state to state before as after the interference with the individual trader," and *thirdly*, that discrimination was the test. Additionally, the *Banking Case* had rejected both the theory that ulterior social or economic effects were relevant to the question of object and purpose of the impugned legislation and the "pith and substance" doctrine in cases where any question of regulation as distinct from prohibition could not fairly arise. There was another element in the *Transport Cases* which was not considered by the Privy Council, i.e. the distinction taken between motor vehicles as "integers of traffic" on the one hand and the trade of carrying by motor vehicle as part of commerce on the other. He had never understood this distinction. It would not suffice as a separate reason for retaining the *Transport Cases* and thus the combination of ideas upon which these cases rested consisted of no element upon which they could survive. As to whether they could be supported on independent grounds, he agreed with the reasons for judgment of Fullagar, J., adding that he adhered to his remarks in *R. v. Vizzard*[41] (in which he had dissented) and that, while his attempt to formulate a general principle in *Gilpin*[42] had not been addressed particularly to the *Transport Cases*, as perhaps it ought to have been, there was not much in it greatly inconsistent with what had been said in the *Banking Case* by the Privy Council and some things which their judgment had confirmed. He was unable to regard the Transport Acts as in any sense regulatory—in the present case the Act prohibited the inter-state carriage of goods unless the Executive Government in the exercise of an uncontrollable discretion saw fit to grant a licence for the purpose.

Fullagar, J. said that *Vizzard* appeared to rest upon three conceptions : (i) that transport was not trade and commerce in itself, but a means thereto, an incident thereof, (ii) that the words "trade and commerce" in Sec. 92 referred to the totality of trade and commerce subsisting between the states, and (iii) that the individual trader was not protected by Sec. 92. The first of these conceptions had been rejected in the *Airlines Case*[43] and the other two had been rejected clearly in the *Banking Case* and the learned Judge was unable to accept the view that the Privy Council had accepted *Vizzard* as

39. (1945) 71 C.L.R. 29.
40. (1949) 79 C.L.R. 497.
41. (1933) 50 C.L.R. 30.
42. (1934-35) 52 C.L.R. 204.
43. (1932-33) 48 C.L.R. 316.

sound either in the *James Case*[44] or the *Banking Case*. But the *Banking Case* had asserted that regulation of trade and commerce and intercourse among the States was compatible with its absolute freedom, as had been argued in the present case and it remained to be decided whether the present Act merely regulated trade and commerce. As to the distinction between permitted regulation and interference, a question of some difficulty, such matters as reasonable rules of the road could not be said to constitute a burden upon traders or to deter them from trading, because commonsense suggested the answer and although rules of this kind could be made to operate as a burden or deterrent in a high degree, it did not seem likely that any very difficult question would arise in the sphere of practical politics. "The real and truly baffling, difficulties of Sec. 92 appear to lie outside the field of transportation where the very nature of the subject matter seems to lend itself to the application of a quite simple test, which will rarely, if ever, be productive of any real difficulty".[45] Charges for the use of facilities, such as bridges and aerodromes provided by the state could, of course, be made and whether a charge was really so great as to constitute a burden on somebody's freedom to engage in trade, commerce or intercourse, was a question which would be resolvable by the application of simple principles of commonsense in human affairs. *Simple prohibition was, at least, not regulation*. So much was clear and the present case was one, in His Lordship opinion, indistinguishable from simple prohibition. It was a prohibition subject to an absolute discretion to exempt. As to the argument that efficient regulation required a system of licencing, no right was given in the present case to the issue of a licence upon compliance with any conditions and the legislation was in any event not concerned with public safety, but with restriction of the development of road transport at the expense of the railways, and one of its supposed advantages was that the discretion to withhold licences could be used to protect the trade of one state at the expense of another.

Prior to *McCarter v. Brodie*[46], there had occurred two other cases affecting transport, but cases of a different order from any of those considered above. In the first of these, *Gratwick v. Johnson*,[47] the whole Court had held to be invalid the provisions of an Order made under National Security Regulations, providing that no person should travel by rail or commercial passenger vehicle inter-state without a permit, which could be granted or refused by the Director General of Land Transport. This was a clear case of what the Chief Justice described as "a mere prohibition of inter-state intercourse"[48] Rich and McTiernan, JJ., distinguished the *Transport Cases*. Starke, J. said that the *Transport Cases* had all recognized that

---

44. (1936) 55 C.L.R. 1.
45. 80 C.L.R., at p. 497 as to regulation, see *Attorney-General for Ontario v. Winner* (1954) A.C. 542.
46. (1950) 80 C.L.R. 432.
47. (1945) 70 C.L.R. 1.
48. 70 C.L.R. 14.

legislation pointed directly at inter-state trade, commerce or intercourse contravened Sec. 92, although the converse was not necessarily true; the present Order, however, was so pointed. Starke, J. took the opportunity to deny the suggestion that the Privy Council had approved the decision in *R. v. Vizzard.*[49] Dixon, J. confined himself to the facts of the particular case and applied the test of "freedom as at the frontier" in *James v. The Commonweath*[50]. The more important argument in this case was, however, based on the *maxim salus populi suprema lex* and is dealt with below.

The other case was that of *Australian National Airways Pty. Ltd v. the Commonwealth*[51] in which an attempt by the commonwealth to confer upon a body corporate, created by it to conduct inter-state services for the transport by air for reward of passengers and goods, a monopoly in respect of inter-state services was held invalid. All of the Justices referred to the *Transport Cases* which were distinguished on the grounds that there was a great difference between co-ordination and regulation on the one hand and simple prohibition on the other. To this distinction Dixon, J. added another. He said that the feature of the *Transport Cases* which was material was "the sharp differentiation between commercial dealings, or perhaps commercial and other intercourse, on the one hand, and, on the other hand, motor vehicles as means or implements used for that purpose and no more".[52] From this differentiation, it itself lie within the concept of trade, commerce and intercourse among the states, although it might in some respects be regulated under the commerce power as being conducive to commerce. His Lordship concluded that the *Transport Cases* did not decide such a proposition but were based upon a number of considerations—in particular, the consideration that it was the undifferentiated transport of the state that was regulated on non-discriminatory basis. The present legislation, however, provided for the elimination of the business of inter-state transportation as such in favour of a state undertaking, and was plainly repugnant to Sec. 92 on Lord Wright's test, for "it was because the business involved crossing the frontier that it eliminated."[53]

The last of these cases was that of *Hughes and Vale Pty. Ltd. v. State of New South Wales*[54] in which the New South Wales legislation previously upheld in *R. v. Vizzard*[55] was again attacked and the plaintiff company succeeded in its claim on appeal to the Privy Council. The results and implications of this pronouncement of the Privy Council, which are not limited in application to matters of transport, have yet to be considered, but

49. 70 C.L.R. at pp. 18-19.
50. (1934-35) 52 C.L.R. at p. 600.
51. (1945) 71 C.L.R. 29.
52. 71 C.L.R. 89.
53. *Id.* at p. 90.
54. (1954) 93 C.L.R. 1.
55. (1933) 50 C.L.R. 30.

it is necessary first to deal with the *Banking Case*, the judgment in which was adopted by the Board as part of the *ratio decidendi* in the *Hughes and Vale Case.*

Conceding that no doubt trade and commerce could be regulated "at all events until regulation is pressed to the point of impairing true freedom of inter-state commerce"[56] and that a regulation of some other subject would not collide with Sec. 92 merely because inter-state trade or commerce might be affected consequentially, e.g. directions for the orderly and proper conduct of commerce, or, again, laws relating to capacity or professional qualification. Dixon, J. summed up his conclusion by saying that he could not see how to close up every bank but a government bank leaves inter-state banking free."[57]

Dealing with *James v. The Commonwealth*[58] and the test there laid down of freedom at state boundaries, it was said that freedom might be impaired by a prohibition, restriction or burden, the application of which was not at the border but at some prior or subsequent stage in the course of inter-state trade, commerce and intercourse. Freedom as at state boundaries had no narrower meaning than that there should not be imposed prohibitions, restrictions and burdens preventing, impeding or prejudicing the passing from state to state of what amounted to trade, commerce and intercourse.

Discrimination was not the test and there were objections to the use of such figurative expressions as that a law, to offend Sec. 92, must be "pointed at" "direct against" "inimical to"or "hostile to" or "antagonistic to" or "hit at" inter-state commerce. Further, the test of "volume" or "flow" of inter-state banking independently of the freedom of private banks was irrelevant, a consideration of an economic and not of a legal character and in any case had no basis of fact. Sec. 92 treated inter-state traffic and intercourse, not as a mere economic phenomenon, but as an activity, and as such set it free for people to engage in *James v. The Commonwealth*[59] showed that a compulsory marketing scheme under a government board restricting the freedom of action of producers involved an impairment of the freedom from which it followed that "the transfer of the marketing of the commodity, that is to say, of the whole trade in the commodity, from the ordinary channels used by individuals to a government board" was an interference with the freedom.[60] Moreover, the view taken by the Privy Council did not appear to give room for the contention that Sec. 92 left it always open to the legislatures to determine by whom operations of inter-State trade might lawfully be conducted. Thus, regulation of trade, commerce and intercourse among the states is compatible with its absolute freedom and Sec. 92 is violated only when a legislative or executive act operates to restrict such trade, commerce and intercourse directly and immediately as distinct from creating some

56. 76 C.L.R., at p. 389.
57. *Id.* at p. 388.
58. (1936) 55 C.L.R. 1.
59. *Ibid.*
60. 76 C.L.R. at pp. 384-89.

indirect or consequential impediment which may fairly be regarded as remote.

However, there is difficulty in applying the test of direct and remote restriction, *The Airlines case* was one in which the "direct and immediate result of the Act" was to restrict the freedom of trade, commerce and intercourse among the states. It was held that this test was analogous to the "pith and substance" doctrine as applied in cases of subject matter in relation to scope of defined legislative powers and might serve a useful purpose in deciding whether an interference was outside Sec. 92 because it was essentially regulatory in character, but neither test could be applied where, as in the present case, no question of regulatory legislation could fairly be said to arise. And, while adding that it was beyond hope that "the area of dispute should be eliminated," it was said that it could be considerably narrowed by the application of two tests: (i) "whether the effect of the Act is in a particular respect direct or remote", and (ii) "whether in its true character it is regulatory."[61]

In *Hughes and Vale Case*[62], the legislation attacked was that (with minor amendments) which had been upheld in *R. v. Vizzard*[63] and it was substantially similar to that upheld in *McCarter v. Brodie.*[64] Thus, in order to succeed, it was necessary for the plaintiff to have *McCarter* and the *Transport Cases,* upon which it was based, overruled and this in turn involved not merely the actual decisions, but the reasoning upon which they had been based. In the High Court[65] Dixon, C.J., Fullagar and Kitto, JJ. held that the *Transport Cases,* including *McCarter* had been wrongly decided as being inconsistent with the *Banking Case.* Fullagar and Kitto, JJ. considered that they were also inconsistent with *James v. Cowan* and *James v. The Commonwealth.*[66] But Dixon, C.J., felt that the application of the *Transport Cases* might be confined to the particular consideration arising from the fact that the railways and roads formed facilities for carriage for the provision and maintenance of which the state was responsible and that they would have no further application and thought that there were insufficient reasons why they should be reconsidered. Accordingly, the Chief Justice joined with Mc Tiernan, Williams and Webb, JJ. (who did not share the view that the *Transport Cases* were wrongly decided) in upholding the legislation in its application to the plaintiff. But the Learned Judge expressed his personal opinion[67] what the Privy Council on appeal described as a "trenchant passage," stating that provision of the type under review prohibiting transport unless licenced and authorising the imposition of a levy could not

61. 79 C.L.R. 642.
62. *Hughes and Vale Pty Ltd. v. State of N.S.W. (No. 1),* (1952-53) 87 C.L.R. 49.
63. (1933) 50 C.L.R. 30.
64. (1950) 80 C.L.R. 432.
65. 87 C.L.R. 49.
66. (1936) 55 C.L.R. 1.
67. 87 C.L.R., p. 67.

be considered to be consistent with Sec. 92 'The carriage of goods by road, which forms the most important part of this very thing (inter-state commerce), is made the subject of heavy imposts and of a definite prohibition except in so far as a branch of the Executive Government of the state thinks fit to permit particular persons to carry goods by specified vehicles. No conditions are laid down by the fulfilment of which a man may become entitled to a licence. It lies entirely within the discretion of the Director of Transport and Highways acting under the direction of the Minister. The refusal of an application for a licence on grounds that are arbitrary or fanciful or that no man could be regarded as lying within the scope or policy of the legislation would not suffice, but the discretion otherwise is absolute and in no circumstances has anyone an enforeable title to a licence.

On appeal,[68] the Privy Council reversed the decision of the High Court, overruled the *Transport Cases* (except *Williard v. Rawson*) and adopted its own the judgments of Dixon and Fullagar, JJ. in *Mc Carter v. Brodie*[69] and the "personal opinion" of Dixon, C.J. in the *Hughes and Vale Case* in the High Court.

Armstrong v. State of Victoria and Another[70] differed slightly from the other cases in that, while as in the South Australian cases special permits were required in respect of specified journeys (unless a vehicle was licenced under the general provisions of the Act, which could have no application since the Privy Council decision in the *Hughes and Vale Case, No. 1*), undefined conditions could be attached, no uniformity of treatment was contemplated—indeed in the presence of other general traffic regulations, this legislation served as a means of imposing particular obligations and restrictions in individual cases—charges undefined were authorised and generally in its practical effects the legislation was considered to be clearly inconsistent with freedom of inter-state trade. "A general administrative control involving the exercise of a discretion with respect to each integer of the particular variety of inter-state transport separately and as an individual case is at variance with the general conception of the kind of regulation which is consistent with freedom."[71]

In India, Art. 302 empowers Parliament to impose restrictions on the freedom of trade, commerce and intercourse between one state and another, or within any part of the territory of India, in the public interest. The reference in Art. 302 to restriction on the freedom of trade between one state and another clearly indicates that the freedom granted by Art. 301 covers both intra-state and inter-state commerce and trade, as Art. 302 is in the nature of an exception to Art. 301. The requirement of 'public interest' in Art. 302 would not present any serious problem in the way of Parliament

68. (1954) 93 C.L.R. 1.
69. (1950) 80 C.L.R. 432.
70. (1955) 93 C.L.R. 264.
71. *Id.* at p. 277.

regulating trade and commerce because of the strong presumption in favour of Parliamentary Legislation being in public interest. The majority judgment in *'Atiabari'* even suggested that *prima facie* the question of public interest underlying a parliamentary law imposing restrictions on the freedom of trade 'may not be justiciable'. If this be the correct approach, then Parliament's power to decide what restrictions need be imposed under Art. 302 may be said to be practically unlimited. However, the correctness of this view was doubted later by the Court in *'Kheyerbari'*.

2. RESTRICTION DISTINGUISHED FROM REGULATION

Anything which directly hinders the free flow of trade, commerce and intercourse between any two parts of India, constitutes a 'restriction' within the meaning of Arts. 302 and 304, e.g., prohibition of any class of commercial or financial transactions relating to any goods, such as forward contracts.[72]

It is now established that even apart from the specific provisions in Arts. 302 and 305 the Union as well as state legislatures have the power to exercise legitimate regulatory control over the freedom of trade and commerce which does not amount to a 'restriction'. In fact, legitimate regulation does not infringe the freedom declared by Art. 301.[73]

It is therefore necessary to distinguish a regulation from 'Restriction' which term is used in 'Arts. 302 and 304 (b). While restrictions obstruct the freedom of movement of inter-state transactions, regulations promote it. 'Restriction' is to be distinguished from 'regulation' because neither Art. 19(1)(g) nor 302[74] is offended if it is a law which is merely regulatory, as distinguished from imposing a restriction upon the exercise of the freedom of trade or business.

The object of regulation is to ensure the orderly conduct of a business. Even though regulations, to ensure some public interest, e.g., public safety,[75] or elimination of middleman from business or control of excess stock or prevention of hoarding of, an essential commodity, involve restraint. Such restraints do not restricts the flow of trade or commerce, but in reality facilitate such flow; hence, it does not violate Art. 301.

Such a regulation may be made by means of a tax or non-tax law. For example, the following measures have been held to be regulatory:

(i) Police regulations, such as provisions for lighting, rules of the road, etc., which facilitate the movement rather than retard it.

(ii) Licencing provisions with compensatory fees.

---

72. *Koteshwar v. K.R.B. Co.*, A.I.R. 1969 S.C. 504.

73. *Automobile Transport v. State of Rajasthan*, A.I.R. 1962 S.C. 1406 at p. 1436; *Malwa Bus Service v. State of Haryana*, A.I.R. 1983 S.C. 634; *Meenakshi v. State of Karnataka*, A.I.R. 1983 S.C. 1283.

74. *Bishamber v. State of U.P.*, A.I.R. 1982 S.C. 33.

75. *Krishnan v. State of T.N.*, A.I.R. 1975 S.C. 583.

(iii) Provision for necessary services to enable the free movement, whether charged for or not.

On the other hand, the following have been held to be 'restriction' rather than regulation:

(i) A rule which totally prohibits movement of certain goods during a specified period.[76]
(ii) Anything which directly hinders the free flow of trade, commerce and intercourse between any two parts of India, constitutes a 'restriction' within the meaning of Arts. 302 and 304, e.g., prohibition of any class of commercial or financial transactions relating to any goods, such as forward contracts.

Though the power to impose a restriction will not include the power to impose a 'simple prohibition', it may include the power of total prohibition or extinction if the commerce in question spreads an evil which is irresistible in nature[77] or where the traffic or commerce is unlawful, e.g. carrying liquor in a public carriage for the use of passengers.[78]

3. WHEN MAY TOTAL PROHIBITION AMOUNT TO REGULATION

The reasonable restriction under Arts. 302 and 304, imposed by the parliament and State legislatures respectively and Art. 305 provide for state monopoly in any trade or business. And monopoly means total or partial exclusion of others from that trade or business. The question is whether a purely regulatory law may create prohibition.

In *G.K. Krishna v. State of Tamil Nadu,*[79] Mathew, J. said that the word 'regulation' has no fixed connotation. Its meaning differs according to the nature of the thing to which it is applied. The Supreme Court of India has preferred flexible meaning of regulation and shown an inclination, to accept the view of the Privy Council expressed in *Commonwealth of Australia v. Bank of New South Wales*[80] that in certain circumstances prohibition might be the only practical and reasonable manner of regulation.[81]

In *State of Tamil Nadu v. M/s Sanjeetha Trading Co.,*[82] the Supreme Court held that the matter may be different where total prohibition has been imposed on the movement of goods or article from one state to another which have not been declared to be essential commodities or article. In those

76. *State of Mysore v. Sanjeviah*, A.I.R. 1967 S.C. 1190.
77. *Reid v. Colorado* (1913) 187 U.S. 137.
78. *U.S. v. Hill* (1919) 248 U.S. 420.
79. (1975) 2 S.C.R. 715.
80. (1950) A.C. 235.
81. *State of Tamil Nadu v. Hind Stone* (1981) 32 S.C.C. 2005.
82. A.I.R. 1993 S.C. 237 at p. 243.

cases the State, which has imposed such ban, has to satisfy the Court that in spite of total prohibition it amounts only to regulation of the trade in such articles or that even if it was a restriction it was reasonable within the meaning of Art. 304(b) of the Constitution and has been imposed by law as required by Art. 304(b).

4. REGULATION THROUGH RATE FIXING

Let us now discuss the extent to which the freedom of trade and commerce may be regulated through rate or price fixing. There is no doubt that the reasonableness of such restrictions is a justiceable issue and the same can be judged either in the garb of due process or otherwise but there are many other considerations, apart from reasonableness, which compel courts to consider the permissible limits of such regulation. Here below, those permissible limits are being examined in the perspective of few notable decisions in different federal set up.

In America the *Cooley*[83] test has been applied most frequently to determine the validity of state regulations of transportation by land. The important cases in this area arose out of state laws regulating railroads. In *Munn v. Illinois*[84] one of the true landmarks of American Constitutional Law[85] the substantive authority of the states to regulate Railroads was sustained. State power was expressly held to include the authority to prescribe *Railroad rates.*[86] But this did not settle the question whether state rate control was valid for transportation within the states which constitute a part of inter-state commerce.[87]

That question was directly presented to the High Court in the 1886 case of *Wabash, St. Louis & Pacific Railway v. Illionis.*[88] The issue there was the validity of a state statute which sought to regulate railroad rates for transportation whose origin or destination was beyond the boundaries of the state. To decide that issue, the Court relied squarely on the *Cooley* test. "It is one thing", said Justice Miller, for a state to fix the rates for carriage entirely within its borders. It is quite another for it to regulate fares and charges within its limits for transportation which constitutes a part of commerce among the states."

As far as inter-state rates are concerned, if there is to be regulation at all, there is a manifest need for uniformity. If one state may fix inter-state rates, all other states may do so, and they need not prescribe the same rates. Unless all the states were to reach identical conclusions with regard to what rates were proper, a uniform standard of rates would be impossible, as the

83. *Cooley v. Board of Wardens* (1851)12 How. 299.
84. 94 U.S. 113 (1877).
85. Schwartz, An introduction to American Administrative Law, 10 (2d. 1962).
86. 94 U.S. 155 (1877).
87. 94 U.S. 164 (1877).
88. 118 U.S. 557 (1886).

standard would fluctuate and vary, dependent upon the divergent conclusions reached by the various states. In the words of the *Wabash* opinion: "If each one of the states through whose territories these goods are transported can fix its own rules for prices, for modes of transit, for times and modes of delivery, and all the other incidents of transportation to which the word 'regulation' can be applied, it is readily seen that the embarrassments upon inter-state transportation, as an element of inter-state commerce, might be too oppressive to be submitted to."[89]

Inter-state railroad rates, if regulated at all, must be regulated by one national body, to ensure that they are uniform from state to state. As the *Wabash* opinion stated, "this species of regulation is one which must be, if established at all, of a general and national character, and cannot be safely and wisely remitted to local rules and local regulations."[90] Rate regulation must be uniform and the states have no power over inter-state rates, even in the absence of any federal legislation on the subject.

As a practical matter, the *Wabash* decision laid the issue of effective railroad rate regulation directly up to the Congress. Since some three-fourths of the country's railroad tonnage was inter-state in character, Congress was expected to act under its commerce power if railroad rates were really to be regulated. *Wabash* did, indeed, result directly in the passage with a few months of the Inter-state Commerce Act of 1887—the first great regulatory law enacted under the federal commerce power. Under that statute, Inter-state rail rates are now regulated by the INTER-STATE Commerce Commission, though the states still retain their authority over purely intra-state rates.[91]

States may control the price which local sellers charge out-of-state buyers only to the extent that such regulation of the inter-state market is an incidental consequence of regulation of the local market. For example, in *Milk Control Board v. Eisenberg Farm Products*,[92] the Supreme Court held that Pennsylvania could fix the price charged by local dealers selling to a Pennsylvania-based processing company that subsequently shipped the milk it purchased to New York. The Court noted that the regulated transaction took place entirely within Pennsylvania; that the state could not effectively control the price paid for milk eventually consumed in Pennsylvania if it were not permitted incidentally to fix the price of milk purchased in Pennsylvania but later shipped out-of-state; and that "only a small fraction of the milk produced in Pennsylvania is shipped out of the Commonwealth."[93] In earlier cases, this last factor had been absent. Thus, for example, in *Lemke v. Farmers Grain Co.*,[94] a North Dakota attempt to fix the price paid by inter-

89. *Id.* at p. 572.
90. *Id.* at p. 577.
91. *Minnesota Rate Case*, 230 U.S. 352 (1913).
92. 306 U.S. 346 (1939).
93. *Id.* at p. 353.
94. 258 U.S. 50 (1922).

state dealers for local grain was found by the Supreme Court to be unconstitutional, given the absence of any significant local market for the regulated commodity.[95]

In *Cities Service Gas Co. v. Peerless Oil and Gas Co.*,[96] the substantial state interest in natural gas conservation substituted for the incidental character of the inter-state agricultural price regulations affirmed in Eisenberg, as the Supreme Court approved an Oklahoma programme attempting to reduce economic waste by fixing the price paid by pipeline monopoly for natural gas produced by local suppliers, even though the gas was destined almost exclusively for out-of-state users.[97] The decision in *Cities Service* seems dubious in light of the major concern of the Commerce Clause with avoiding any state's exploitation of its geographical or resource position to the disadvantage and displeasure of its less strategically situated neighbours.

In *West Lynn Creamery v. Healy*[98], a states pricing order which was designed to aid only in state milk producers by imposing an assessment on all fluid milk sold by dealers to in-state retailers was held to be discriminatory and violate of Commerce Clause. The reasons for such holding were put by the Supreme Court as under :

(i) The avowed purpose and undisputed effect of the order were to enable higher-cost dairy farmers in the state to compete with lower cast dairy farmers in other states.

(ii) The assessment was effectively a tax which makes milk produced out of state more expensive.

(iii) The tax, like an ordinary tariff was effectively imposed only on out-of-state products.

(iv) The order will almost certainly cause local goods to constitute a larger share, and goods with an out-of-state source to constitute a smaller share, of the total sales in the market, which in effect renders the order unconstitutional, since the order, like a tariff, neutralises advantages belonging to the place of origin.

(v) Inclusion in the distribution to in-state dairy farmers of the portion of the fund derives from assessments paid on the sale of milk produced out-of-state exacerbates the dangar to the national market posed by tariff-like barriers, by giving domestic producers an additional tool with which to share up their competitive position.

(vi) By distributing monies directly to in-state dairy farmers, the order ensures that in-state producers will benefit.

---

95. See also *Shafer v. Framers Grain Co.*, 268 U.S. 189 (1925).
96. 340 U.S. 179 (1950).
97. *Id.* at p. 187.
98. (1994) 129 L.Ed. 2d 157.

(vii) Even if each component of the programme imposed under the order, the tax on milk sales and the subsidy to in-state dairy farmers would be unconstitutional.

(viii) Even if the dealers who pay the tax are not competitors of the farmers who receive disbursements from the fund, the order impasses a discriminatory burden on commerce.

(ix) Even if the costs of the porgramme are borne by only in-state dealers and consumers, the order was unconstitutional.

(x) The order's burden on commerce, where about two-thirds of the milk sold to the state's retailers was produced out of state was not justified by the local benefit of preserving the state's dairy industry.

The Supreme Court in the aforesaid case quoted with approval *United State v. Darby,*[99] *Wickard v. Filburn*[100] and *Mandeville Island Farms, Inc. v. American Crystal Sugar Co.*[101] and held that the Commerce Clause vests Congress with ample power to enact legislation providing for the regulation of prices paid to farmers for their products.[102]

In Canada, the doctrine of indirect taxation has been invoked to adjudge the validity of price fixing. If it is a colourable attempt the same has not been honoured by the courts. *Lower Mainland Dairy Products Board v. Turner's Dairy Ltd.*[103] is the best example of this assertion. In this case, British Columbia sought to avoid the tax pitfall of the *Lower Mainland Dairy Products Sales Adjustment Committee v. Crystal Dairy Ltd.,*[104] through a new scheme of milk marketing involving the establishment of a central agency with exclusive power to buy from producers and sell to dairies. A cardinal feature of the scheme was price-fixing authority which was exercised to fix the price payable to producers for fluid milk and the price payable by dairies. The scheme was held to be invalid as falling within the *Crystal Dairy Doctrine;* it was "colourable" attempt to use provincial marketing and price-fixing authority to carry out an equalisation policy which amounted to indirect taxation. However, in *Prince George Gas Co. Ltd. and Prince George v. Inland Natural Gas Ltd. (No. 2)*[105] Darey, J. refused to apply the *Crystal Dairy* doctrine "to a process of rate fixing in the quite different field of public utility regulation, a process which in this respect contains no element of taxation."

In Australia *Mc Arthurs's Case*[106] was generally supposed to have established the proposition that it was incompetent for the states to fix prices

99. 312 U.S. 100; 85 L.Ed. 609 (1941).
100. 317 U.S. 111; 87 L. Ed. 122 (1942).
101. 334 U.S. 219; 92 L. Ed. 1328.
102. *West Lynn Creamery v. Healy* (1994), 129 L. Ed. 2d 157.
103. 1941 S.C.R. 573.
104. (1933) 1 D.L.R. 82.
105. (1958) 1 C.L.R. (2d.) 247.
106. (1920) 28 C.L.R. 530.

in respect of goods in relation to inter-State trade and commerce and this view of the decision appears to have been accepted in *James v. The Commonwealth*,[107] for the Board said of it that it "deprived Queensland of its soverign right to regulate its internal prices". The question was raised in *Graham v. Paterson*[108], but it was unnecessary to decide it, since in the case there was a "Severability" Clause and the transaction in question was not of an inter-state character. In *Wragg v. State of New South Wales*,[109] it was raised again and, at all events, a partial answer given. The state law purported to fix a maximum price in respect of the sale of potatoes in the state. Whether imported or not, at every stage of the trade until they reached the consumer. The plaintiffs consisted of growers in Tasmania, merchant dealers in that state and merchant dealers in the state of New South Wales, who dealt, *inter alia*, in potatoes grown in Tasmania and imported into New South Wales. They sought declarations as to the validity of the law. The matter came before the full Court on a case stated by Fullagar, J. and, as in all such cases, the judgment must be read in the light of the facts stated. In holding that none of the plaintiffs were entitled to the relief claimed, the Court pointed out that some of the sales of the imported potatoes were made by importer while other sales were made by other persons. The latter sales were clearly not part of inter-state trade, but sales by primary wholesalers who were importers might conceivably come within Sec. 92; as to these, however, it had not been established that some of those sales would be made in the course of inter-state trade and the facts stated showed no more than a course of business in which it was convenient to make the first inter-state sale from the wharf. It was sought to establish that Sec. 92 would be infringed if it could be shown that Tasmanian growers had received for crops exported to New South Wales a price less than cost of production. Many had substituted less choice varieties for varieties previously grown. Many Growers had planted reduced acreage and the total acreage planted in Tasmania had been seriously reduced, all by reason of the price fixing in New South Wales. This contention was not accepted. It was held that these disadvantages were the indeterminate and variable product of economic factors and not a necessary legal effect of the law. The Chief Justice pointed out, it was necessary to preserve the distinction made by the Constitution between inter-state and inter-state trade and "the economic interdependence of trade and commerce among the states with the domestic trade of a State cannot lead to a weakening of this legal distinction."[110] Some closer connection with inter-state importation was than the mere interdependence of domestic transaction within a state must be shown in order to attract Sec. 92. It was a difficult question to determine when inter-state importation complete what was

107. (1936) 55 C.L.R.1.

108. (1950) 81 C.L.R. 1.

109. (1953) 88 C.L.R. 353.

110. 88 C.L.R. 386; See also *Williams v. Metropolitan and Export Abattoirs Board*, (1953) 89 C.L.R. 66 at p. 75.

indispensable to the completion of the actual importation was which within the protection of Sec. 92. An illustration was supplied by the decision in *Fergusson v. Stevenson,*[111] where possession of an article was penalised and it had been held that that possession was an inseparable concomitant or consequence of the inter-state transaction. In the present case, however, the law governing prices was not one "operating in reference to or in consequence of any matter or thing itself forming part of trade, commerce or inter-course among the states."[112]

But it was Taylor, J. who delivered the main judgment in this case, a judgment concurred in by the Chief Justice, Mc Tiernan, Williams, Fullagar and Kitto, JJ. His Lordship dealt exhaustively with *Mc Arthur's Case* which upon examination, did not lay down any such wide proposition as appeared to have been commonly supposed, even by the Privy Council in the *James Case.*[113] It was an express decision to the contrary, excepting only sales made "in the course of trade, commerce and intercourse among the states." The *James Case* had not thrown any doubts upon the power of the state to fix prices, nor did it impugn the validity of the proposition in *McArthur's Case* that where a contract of sale or a delivery of goods to be sold might, at the option of the vendor, be consummated entirely within the state, it could not be said that the transaction was of an inter-state character. And this proposition did not conflict with either the *South Australian Petrol Case*[114] or the reasoning in the *Vacuum Oil Co's Case*[115] in both of which cases the invalidity of the legislation had resulted, "not because the affected transactions were themselves necessarily part of inter-state trade and commerce but because the particular burdens imposed were, in the circumstances, considered to be burdens directly imposed upon inter-state trade as such"[116] and on this view immaterial whether the burden was imposed at a stage when the goods themselves might have ceased to be the subject of inter-state trade, for, as Dixon, C.J. had observed in the *Field Peas Case,*[117] the restriction prohibited by Sec. 92 might be "a proper restraint or subsequent burden." In the *Field Peas Case*[118] the restriction did not result "in the levying of a tax upon goods or importers"(as in the *Petrol Case*), "nor in the imposition of an impost or burden upon a person because he has introduced goods from one state into another"(as in the *Vacuum Oil Case*)[119]

In India, the validity of restrictions imposed upon the inter-state export and hoarding of food grains, by the Rajasthan Wheat (Export Control)

111. (1951) 84 C.L.R.421.
112. 88 C.L.R., p. 387.
113. *James v. The Commonwealth* (1936) 55 C.L.R. 1.
114. *Common Oil Refineries Ltd. v. South Australia* (1926) 38 C.L.R. 408.
115. *Vacuum Oil Co. Pvt. Ltd. v. Queensland* (1934) 51 C.L.R. 108.
116. 88 C.L.R. at p. 397.
117. 76 C.L.R. at p. 423.
118. *Ibid.*
119. 88 C.L.R. at p. 398; Lurye, Price Control and the Constitution, 21 A.L.J. 250.

Order, 1981 and the Rajasthan Trade Articles (Licencing and Control) Order, 1980, have been upheld in the public interest requiring distribution of essential commodity to the people of the state, at a reasonable price.[120] So also, the U.P. Foodgrains (Procurement and Regulation of Trade) Order, 1978[121] and Punjab Food Grains Dealers Licencing and Price Control Order, 1980 have been upheld on the same ground of public interest.[122]

Trades in certain commodities (designated as essential commodities) may be more drastically regulated than trade in other commodities. To assess the reasonableness of a restriction, the nature of the business and conditions prevailing therein are important factors to be considered. As these factors differ from trade to trade, no hard and fast rules concerning all trades can be laid down. The result of this approach is that courts may hold drastic restrictions on certain trades in certain circumstances as reasonable. As for example, fixation of a ceiling of 200 quintals on wheat stocks possessed by a dealer at any times is valid to obviate black-marketing and hoarding in essential commodities.[123] A similar embargo on sugar stocks has been held valid.[124] A notification under the Essential Commodities Act imposed a levy on sugar manufacturers. They were required to hand over to the government 50 per cent of their production at a *fixed price*. They could sell the rest in free market. The notification was challenged on the ground that the price of levy sugar was not sufficient to cover their manufacturing cost. The Court rejected the argument on the following grounds :

(i) Interest of the consumers must prevail over that of manufacturers. The dominant object of the price control policy was to ensure equitable distribution and make the commodity available at fair price so as to benefit the consumers. Thus, individual interests must yield to the larger interests of the community.

(ii) Even if the petitioners had to bear some loss, that would not make the restriction unreasonable.[125] The determining factor was the interest of the consumer and not that of the producer.

(iii) Since the petitioners could sell 50 per cent of their production in the open market, the loss to them, if any, would be minimal.[126]

---

120. *Krishnan v. State of Rajasthan*, A.I.R. 1982 S.C. 2.
121. *Bishamber v. State of U.P.*, A.I.R. 1982 S.C. 33.
122. *Sukhwinder v. State of Punjab*, A.I.R. 1982 S.C. 65.
123. *Sura] Mal Kailash Chand v. Union of India*, A.I.R. 1982 S.C. 130.
124. *P.P. Enterprises v. India*, A.I.R. 1982 S.C. 1016.
125. *Meenakshi v. State of Karnataka*, A.I.R. 1983 S.C. 1283; *Prag Ice and Oil Mills v. Union of India*, A.I.R. 1978 S.C. 1296.
126. *New India Sugar Works v. State of U.P.*, A.I.R. 1981 S.C. 998.

In *S.I. Syndicate Ltd. v. Union of India*[127] clause of the Sugar (Control) Order (1996) was challenged. In this case one of the contentions on behalf of the petitioners was that prices should not have been determined on the basis of 22 joins but should have determined either on all All India scale or for five zones as recommended by the Sugar Enquiry Commission. Costs of production for purposes of price fixation, can only be determined on the basis of averages from data collected from each particular region and conditions which affect factories in general in that region. It may be that on particular items, the Government may have reasons to regard data collected in one region to be unreliable. Other data collected in another region may be considered good enough for a more general use of it. The results of price fixation are actually given separately in an annexed table for each factory in each state and are not uniform. One can read into clause 7 (2) an obligation to fix the price on an All India basis of five region basis. It is enough if the basis adopted is not shown to be patently unreasonable as to be in excess of the power to fix price. This power is confined to fixation for the purposes mentioned in Essential Commodities Act, 1955. In any case, the appellants objections could form the subject-matter of representation which could have been made to the Government by each of the parties affected. If their case had substance, they ought to have made a demand for a more just fixation on what they considered to be more appropriate and reasonable basis before going to court. They had not done so.

In this case, the petitioners did not challenge the price fixation on the ground that a quasi-Judicial procedure had to be adopted before prices are fixed even if such price fixation affects, as it must, each factory. Price fixation is more in the nature of a legislative measure even though it may be based upon objective criteria found in a report or other material. It could not, therefore, give rise to a complaint that a rule of natural justice has not been followed in fixing the price. Nevertheless, the criterion adopted must be reasonable. Reasonableness, for purposes of judging whether there was an 'excess of power' or an 'arbitrary exercise of it' is really the demonstration of a reasonable nexus between the matters which are taken into account in exercising a power and the purpose of exercise of that power. This was made clear by the Supreme Court in the two cases cited on behalf of the appellants *Meenakshi Mill Ltd. v. Union of India*[128] and *Panipat Co-operative Sugar Mills v. Union of India.*[129]

Meenakshi Mill case related to price fixation under the provisions of Cotton Textile (Control) Order, 1948. There, Court observed that the case of *Premier Automobile Ltd. v. Union of India*[130] does not consider that concept of fair prices varies with cirumstances in which and the purposes for which the

---

127. A.I.R. 1975 S.C. 460 at p. 462.
128. A.I.R. 1974 S.C. 366.
129. A.I.R. 1978 S.C. 537.
130. A.I.R. 1972 S.C. 1690.

price control is sought to be imposed, and it indicated that the decision in that case was based on a 'special agreement ' involved there.

The question of fair price with reference to the dominant object and purpose of the legislation claiming equitable distribution and availability at fair price is completely lost sight of its profit and the producer's return are in the forefront. The maintenance or increase of supplies of the commodity or the equitable distribution and availability at fair prices are the fundamental purposes of the Act. If the prices of yarn or cloth are fixed in such a way to enable the manufacturer or producer to recover his cost of production and secure a reasonable margin of profit, no aspect of infringement of fundamental right can be said to arise. The same view was reiterated in *Panipat case* also.

In *Bishamber Dayal Chandra Mohan v. State of U.P.*[131], Supreme Court has held that regulatory measure to prevent price rise in wheat was in the public interest and hence constitutional.

131. A.I.R. 1982 S.C. 32.

7

Regulation of Trade, Commerce and Intercourse through Taxation: The Permissible Limits

I. REGULATION THROUGH TAXATION IN DIFFERENT FEDERAL SET-UP

The power to regulate inter-state commerce in a non-discriminatory manner and thus to break down and to eliminate barriers to trade among the states is a necessary power of the Central Government in a federation.[1] The achievement of economic union, of a single market, while obviously contributing to essential united defence also improves material peacetime welfare.[2] In the absence of such a power "local interests exerting powerful influences in state legislatures would, in the long-run, prefer home industries over those that are out of state, establish tariff barriers, or employ other means tending to Balkanize the nation into hostile trade areas".[3] Since the elimination of state tariff barriers is one of the chief motives[4] in the formation of federal union, the question arises what is a trade barriers ? A trade barrier may be defined as one which operates in a nation of many territorial units usually called states to the disadvantage of persons, products or services coming from sister states of the advantage of local residents, products or enterprises.[5]

The federations of the world have tried to achieve this object through different methods. One method is to confer the power to regulate inter-state

1. Marshall, C.J. in *Brown v. Maryland*, (1827) 12 Wheat. 419, 445.
2. Bowie and Frederich, Studies in Federalism (1954) at p. 297.
3. William O. Douglas, From Marshall To Mukherjea, Tagore Law Lectures, 1956 at p. 297.
4. *James v. Commonwealth*, 1936 A.C. 578 at p. 630.
5. Paul T. Truitt, Inter-state barriers in the United States, 8 Law and Cont. Problems 209 (1941).

commerce on the federal government and to deny such power to the regional governments. In the U.S.A. the Constitution confers power upon the Congress "to regulate commerce with foreign nations, and among the several states, and with the Indian Tribes."[6] These sixteen words, generally known as "Commerce Clause", as such do not deal with any of the rights of the citizen to do inter-state business. In the U.S.A., the states are not wholly powerless to regulate inter-state business.[7] Sec. 91(2) of the Canadian Constitution is another example of this type of "Commerce Clause." In Canada the courts have given a very narrow interpretation[8] to the word's 'trade and commerce' and the extent of power exercised by the federal legislature is comparatively very limited in there. A second mode of providing for free commerce is to guarantee the freedom of commerce by the Constitution itself. In such a case the power of both[9] the federal and the state legislatures to interfere with the right[10] of citizens to engage to inter-state activities is restricted. The Australian Commerce Clause has played only comparatively insignificant[11] role in contrast to its counterpart in the U.S.A.

A. Position under American Commerce Clause

Possibly the area of greatest agreement at the Constitutional Convention was that the federal government must have the capacity to tax and to compel payment of those taxes. In fact, the very first power listed in Sec. 8 of the Constitution reads: "The Congress shall have power to lay and Collect Taxes, Duties, Imposts and Excises."

There are four constitutional restrictions on the federal tax power. *First,* Art. I, Sec. 9, prohibits the imposition of export taxes and, *Second,* it provides that all direct taxes must be in proportion to the population of each state. *Third,* Sec. 8 of the same article says that "duties, Imposts and excises shall be uniform throughout the United State" and, *Forth,* that the "Taxes, Duties, Imports and Excises" must be used to "pay the Debts and provide for the common defence and General Welfare of the United States." Under the Constitution, the states continued to exercise the same broad tax powers they had before federation, subject to Art. I, Sec. 10 provision that they might not, without the consent of Congress, tax imports or exports or levy tonnage duties. This restriction had little effect on the tax capacities of the American states, in contrast to the experience of Canadian and Australian local governments which had depended upon such taxation for most of their income before federation.

---

6. Article 1, Section 8, Clause 3 of the United States Constitution.
7. *Colley v. Board of Wardens*, 53 U.S. 299 (1851).
8. Section 92 reads "On the imposition of Uniforms duties of customs, trade commerce and intercourse among the states, whether by means of internal carriage of ocean, navigation shall be absolutely free.
9. *James v. Commonwealth*, 1936 A.C. 578 at p. 633.
10. *Commonwealth v. Bank of N.S.W*, 1950 A.C. 235.
11. Baily, Fifty years of the Australian Constitution, 25 A.L.R. 314 at pp. 322-23 (1951).

The division of tax power in Canada and Australia has had a very adverse effect upon the fiscal independence of the provinces and states. American states have claimed this to be true in the United States but the argument has not been completely convincing. In the earliest days the states insisted that the national government should limit its taxation to imports and leave to the states all forms of internal taxation, but the argument was refused by Hamilton who imposed such taxes merely to establish the precedent in case such taxes were ever needed".[12]

The financial needs of all governments were relatively simple at the time the American Constitution was written, and during the latter part of the eighteenth and all of the nineteenth centuries the financial demands of the national government were largely met by customs duties and the sale of land, while the states were virtually alone in imposing internal taxes; indeed even state budget needs were usually met easily with only very low property taxes.

The doctrine that a state cannot directly tax foreign or inter-state commerce is derived from a judicial interpretation of the Commerce Clause. That Clause, as we have observed, vests in Congress plenary powers over the regulation of foreign and inter-state commerce. *As taxation is only a form of regulation,* it is argued, no state could tax foreign or inter-state commerce directly without trenching upon the powers which are confided to Congress under the Commerce 'Clause'. Nor should this line of argument be any matter for surprise. One of the main reasons which impelled the framers of the Constitution to vest in Congress the control over foreign and inter-state commerce was to free such commerce from the burdens and restrictions which the states in pursuit of their own selfish ends were wont to lay upon them in the confederation days. And if the courts had, by their interpretation of the 'Commerce Clause', countenanced the direct state taxation of such commerce, they would, in large measure, have restored the very condition which it was the purpose of the 'Commerce Clause' to terminate. But it is not every taxing measure which in any wise impinges upon or affects foreign or inter-state commerce that could be regarded as a regulation of such commerce. So broad a conception of the inhibitions supposed to be immanent in the Commerce Clause to the exercise of state taxing power would spell disaster to the states and all but bring their governmental machinery to halt. The motive power which keeps the wheels of government in motion is finance. And if foreign and inter-state commerce cannot be taxed in any form whatever, the plight to which the states would be reduced to finance their everyday activities is easily imagined.

However, the Supreme Court has taken up no such extreme stand. When the validity of state taxing measure is in issue, the Supreme Court balances the inconvenience to foreign or inter-state commerce against the

12. J.A. Maxwell, The Fiscal impact of Federalism in the United States (Cambridge, Mass., 1946) 8.

reasonable claims of the state for revenue and determines on practical considerations where the line has to be drawn.

The doctrine that a state may not tax foreign or inter-state commerce directly may be illustrated by a few examples. For instance, it has been held that a state can not tax the act or privilege of engaging in foreign or inter-state commerce or the gross receipts derived therefrom as, so to do would be to put a restraint or burden on such commerce and be an invasion of the powers of regulation confided to Congress by the Constitution.[13]

Nor may a state tax goods or persons carried in inter-state commerce as that would also amount to a regulation of such commerce and be an invasion of the congressional field. Such a tax would be restraint on the privilege to have the subjects of commerce pass freely from one state to another without being obstructed by the intervention of state lines.[14]

But it was surely not the purpose of the 'Commerce Clause' to exempt those engaged in foreign or inter-state commerce from bearing their just share of the burdens of taxation, on the mere ground that a consequential effect of a tax levy would be to add to the cost of conducting such business. No proposition could be more reasonable than that every foreign or inter-state business which is conducted under the protective care of a state should make a proper contribution to its public exchequer. It has been held that property employed as an instrument of foreign or inter-state commerce and having its situs in a particular state is liable to property taxation of that state. And it is clear that if such property were permitted to escape state taxation, then, this would result in the conferring upon it of a bounty not shared by similar property employed in intra-state commerce. The controversies that have arisen in connection with the taxation of property employed in inter-state or foreign commerce—their amenability to state taxation being quite well-settled—are mainly concerned with the propriety of the methods of assessment adopted.[15] Where property devoted to inter-state transportation is used both within the state and without the state, a tax fairly apportioned to its views within the state will be sustained.[16] And it is also well established that whatever may be the objections to a tax on gross income, persons and corporations otherwise subject to the jurisdiction of the states are not exempted from paying state taxes on net incomes simply because they happen to be engaged in foreign or inter-state commerce. Even foreign and inter-state businesses must pay their way and when a state tax is levied on net incomes derived there from no burden is cast on them and it is but a

---

13. *Fisher's Blend Station v. Tax Commission* (1936) 297 U.S. 650.
14. *State Freight Tax case* (1873) 15 Wall. 232; *Philadelphia & S. Mail Steamship Co. v. Pennsylvania* (1887) 122 U.S. 326.
15. *Western Union Telegraph Co. v. Taggart* (1896) 163 U.S. 1; *Postal Telegraph Co. v. Adams (1895)* 155 U.S. 688; *Admas Express Co. v. Ohio State Auditor* (1897) 165 U.S. 194.
16. *Cudahy Packing Co. v. Minnesota* (1918) 246 U.S. 450.

method of distributing the cost of government like a tax upon property or upon franchises treated as property.[17]

The Supreme Court has also held that a state franchise tax upon corporations exercising their corporate franchises within the state, measured by that portion of their net income from inter-state, intra-state or foreign commerce, which is derived from business done within the state, does not violate the Commerce Clause.[18]

As commerce succeeds production or manufacture a state tax upon production or manufacture is a legitimate exercise of the state taxing power.[19] And in certain cases it has been held that although production and the beginning of the journey in inter-state commerce are physically inseparable, the two operations can be separated, at least in the eye of law, so as to enable the state to collect its toll upon production, which is after all an essentially local activity.[20] Most Art, before their shipment in inter-state commerce, have had work done upon them which adapts them to the needs of commerce and prepares them for safe and convenient tranportation, but that fact has never been considered to immunise from local taxation either the articles themselves or those who have manufactured or otherwise prepared them for transportation.[21] The principle involved in such cases is clear because the privilege taxed is exercised before inter-state commerce begins, and the burden of the tax upon commerce is too indirect and remote to offend against constitutional limitations. If the movement of goods in inter-state commerce has been interrupted between the point of origin and of final destination, then those goods become subject to local taxation at the point of interruption. The reason is that, unless the interruption is incidental to and solely in furtherance of the intended transportation, the continuity of transit is broken and goods which have come to rest in a state enjoy its protection and are amenable to its taxing laws.[22] And goods which have reached their ultimate destination after the end of their inter-state journey or after importation from foreign countries become amenable to state taxing laws in the same way as other property in the state. Nice questions arise as to when the inter-state transit or importation is over in the case of such goods so as to subject them to state taxation as part of the general mass of property in the state. It is in this connection that we encounter the famous *original package doctrine* which was first formulated by Marshall, C.J. in *Brown v. Maryland*.[23] A state may not demand a licence or occupation tax from importers of foreign articles or commodities for the selling of the same in the original

17. *United States Glue Co. v. Oak Creek* (1918) 247 U.S. 321; *Shaffer v. Carter* (1920) 252 U.S. 37.
18. *Matson Navigation Co. v. State Board of Equalization* (1936) 297 U.S. 441.
19. *Oliver Iron Mining Co. v. Lord* (1923) 262 U.S. 172; *Crescent Oil Co. v. Mississippi* (1921) 257 U.S. 129.
20. *Utah Power & Light Co. v. Pfast* (1932) 286 U.S. 165.
21. *Hope Natural Gas Co. v. Hali* (1927) 274 U.S. 284.
22. *Florida Compress & Warehouse Co. v. McClean* (1934) 291 U.S. 17.
23. (1827) 12 Wheat. 419.

packages in which they are imported Marshall, C.J. pointed out in that case that there was no difference in substance between a duty on an article and a duty on a person for the sale of the article and if the former was repugnant to the Constitution, the latter was equally so. It was contended on behalf of the taxing state of Maryland that the licence tax was a tax on occupations and was within its competence. Thus, the original package doctrine, bars a state from taxing imports from abroad while in the hands of the importer in their original package.

In *Oklahoma Tax Commission v. Jefferson Lines, Inc.*[24] the American Supreme Court has laid down the following proposition regarding state's taxing power :

A state imposition of a sales tax on the full price of a ticket for bus travel form that state to another state is consistent with the Commerce Clause, the sale of inter-state transportation services has a sufficient nexus to the taxing state, since the sale is where the ticket is purchased and the service originates. The tax is properly apportioned, since the tax is (a) internally consistent, in that if every state were to impose a tax on ticket sales within the state for travel originating there, no sale would be subject to more than one state's tax, and (b) externally consistent, in that it reaches only the taxing state, that is the sale of the transportation service. The tax does not discriminate against inter-state commerce, since only the taxing state can tax a sale or transportation to begin there and the state imposes the same duty on equally valued purchases regardless of whether the purchase prompts inter-state or only intra-state movement and the tax is fairly related to the services provided by the state, since, police and fire protection, along with the usual advantages covered by the state's maintenance of a civilized society, are enough justification for the state's imposition of the tax, and the tax falls on a state that takes place wholly inside the state and is measured by the value of the service purchased.

The Commerce Clause reflects a central concern of the framers that in order to succeed, the new union would have to avoid the tendencies toward economic bulkanisation that had plagued relations among the colonies and later among the states under the 'Articles of Confederation.'

A state tax does not violate the Commerce Clause, if such tax is applied to an activity with a substantial nexus within the taxing state and if it is fairly apportioned; does not discriminate against inter-state commerce and is fairly related to the services provided by the state. For purposes of determining the validity of a state tax under the Commerce Clause, a sale of tangible goods has sufficient nexus to the state in which the sale is consummated to be treated as local transaction taxable by that state.

In order to determine whether a state tax is properly apportioned so as not to violate the Commerce Clause, the state tax must be both internally and externally consistent. A failure of internal consistency shows, as a matter of

24. (1994) 514 U.S. 131 L.Ed. 2d 261 at pp. 262-63.

law that the state is attempting to take more than its fair share of taxes from an inter-state transaction. External inconsistency looks to the economic justification for the state's claim upon the value taxed to discover whether the tax reaches beyond that portion of value that is fairly attributable to economic activity within the state.

The Commerce Clause does not forbid the actual assessment of a succession of taxes by different states on distinct events as the same tangible object flows along in commerce. Thus, a sales tax to the buyer does not preclude a tax to the seller upon the income earned from a sale, and there is no constitutional trouble inherent in the imposition of a sales tax in the state of delivery to the customer, even though the state of origin of the thing sold may have assessed a property or severance tax on it.

Under the Commerce Clause a business performing service upon tangible items retrieved from and delivered to out-of-state customers may be taxed on the full gross receipts from the services, because such services were performed wholly within the taxing state; and sales with at least partial performance in the taxing state justify that state's taxation of the transaction's entire gross receipts in the hands of the seller.

A state's imposition of a sales tax on the full price of a ticket for bus travel from that state to another state is not invalid under the Commerce Clause on the ground that the tax subjects taxpayers to double taxation, because: (i) the tax falls on the buyer of the transportation services, who is no more subject to double taxation than the buyer of goods would be; and (ii) the taxable event comprises agreement, payment, and delivery of some of the services in the taxing state, and no other state can claim to be the site of the same combination.

Again, the Commerce Clause does not require that a state must use a particular apportionment formula in imposing a tax simply because it would be possible to use such formula. When a state has chosen an apportionment formula, an objecting taxpayer has the burden to demonstrate by clear and cogent evidence that the income attributed to the state is out of appropriate proportions to the business transacted in that state or has led to a grossly distorted result. Under the Commerce Clause a state may not impose a tax which discriminates against inter-state commerce by providing a direct commercial advantage to local business.

Further, in *Associated Industries v. Lohman,*[25] the Court explained the ambit of state's taxing power. It said that a state's imposition of a uniform state wide use tax, on all goods purchased outside the state and stored, used or consumed within the state discriminates against inter-state commerce, in violation of the Commerce Clause, where such use tax exceeds the sales tax imposed by such local jurisdictions on sales of goods in the state—even though the local sales taxes across the state may, in the aggregate, place a greater burden on intra-state trade than that which the uniform use tax

25. (1994) 511 U.S. 128 L.Ed. 2d 639, at p. 640.

places on inter-state trade. This is so because of two reasons. *Firstly*, the state's tax use tax scheme runs afoul of the basic requirement that, for a tax system to be valid under the Commerce Clause as compensatory, the burdens imposed on inter-state and intra-state commerce must be equal. Whether the use tax is equal to or lower than the local sales tax is a matter of fortuity, depending entirely upon the locality in which the purchaser happens to reside. Also, where the use tax exceeds the sales tax, the discrepancy imposes a discriminatory burden on inter-state commerce. And, *secondly*, discrimination against inter-state commerce in violation of the Commerce Clause is appropriately assessed with reference to the specific political sub-division in which applicable laws reveal differential treatment. It further said that the Commerce Clause embodies a negative command forbidding the states to discriminate against inter-state trade. The Commerce Clause prohibits regulatory measures designed to benefit in state economic interest by burdening out of state competitors. A fundamental command of the Commerce Clause is that a state may not tax a transaction or incident more heavily when it crosses state lines than when it occurs entirely within the state. Again, it was pointed out that a state use tax which exempts from its scope all sales of goods occurring within the state, while appearing to violate the cardinal rule of non-discrimination against inter-state commerce under the Commerce Clause may be saved from constitutional infirmity if the use tax is a valid compensatory tax designed simply to make inter-state commerce bear a burden already borne by intra-state commerce.

Recently, In *General Motor's Corporation v. Tracy,*[26] sales and use taxes were examined in the light of equal protection and discriminatory behaviour. The American Supreme Court in this case held as under :

A state's application to a company that buys from independent out-of-state marketers virtually all the natural gas for the company's plants in the state of a regime under which purchases of natural gas by state-regulated local public utilities are exempt from the state's general sales and use taxes that are applied to purchases of natural gas by other in-state and out-of-state sellers does not violate the 'Equal Protection Clause' of the 'Federal Constitution's Fourteenth Amendment'. The Supreme Court held that such application did not violate the Commerce Clause because *firstly*, although in some circumstances state tax classifications facially discriminating against inter-state commerce may violate the 'Equal Protection Clause' even when they pass muster under the 'Commerce Clause', the state's differential tax treatment of public utility and independent marketer sales does not facially discriminate against inter-state commerce; and, *secondly*, in any event, there is a rational basis for the state's distinction between these two kinds of entities. A company that buys from out of state marketers virtually all the natural gas for the company's plants in a state has standing to raise in the United States Supreme Court a challenge under the Commerce Clause to the

26. (1997) 519 U.S. 278. 136 L.Ed. 2d. 761, at p. 763.

state's regime under which sales of natural gas by state regulated local public utilities are exempt from the state's general sales and use taxes that are applied to sales of natural gas by other in state and out-of-state sellers, because, although the company is not one of the sellers said to suffer discrimination under the challenged tax laws. Cognizable injury from unconstitutional discrimination against inter-state commerce does not stop at members of the class against whom a state ultimately discriminates, as customers of that class may also be injured, as in the case at hand, where the customer is liable for payment of the tax and as a result presumably pays more for the gas it gets from out-of-state producers and marketers. Consumers who suffer this sort of injury from regulation forbidden under the Commerce Clause satisfy the standing requirements of the Constitution's Art. III.

In *Camps Newfound/Owatonna v. Harrison,*[27] the Supreme Court of United States gives an idea about tax on real estate. The Court held that a state tax on real estate, like any other tax, may impermissibly burden inter-state commerce, for to allow a state to avoid the strictures of the 'Dormant Commerce Clause' by the simple device of labeling discriminatory tax as a levy on real, estate would destroy the barriers against protectionism that the Constitution provides. It is impermissible, as violative of the 'Dormant Commerce Clause' for a state to use a tax exemption as a means of encouraging non-profit institutions to favour local citizens, notwithstanding any possible adverse impact on the larger markets in which those institutions participate, or to use discriminatory tax exemptions as a means of encouraging the growth of local trade.

B. Position under Canadian Commerce Clause

It will be convenient to list at the outset those provisions of the B.N.A. Act, which confer upon the Dominion and the provinces authority to raise money and which conversely, limit that authority. The Dominion's powers are in Sec. 91(3) i.e., "the raising of money by any mode or system of taxation" and Sec. 122 i.e., "the customs and excise laws of each province shall subject to the provisions of this Act, continue in force until altered by the Parliament of Canada." Thus, Sec. 122 is now spent and customs and excise laws are, independently of Sec. 122, within the competence of the Dominion under Sec. 91(2) and Sec. 91(3).[28] In any event, Sec. 122 may be regarded as confirmatory of some of the things covered by Sec. 91(3).[29] The Provincial powers are in Sec. 92(2), i.e., "direct taxation within the province in order to the raising of a revenue for provincial purposes" and Sec. 92(9), i.e., "shop, saloon, tavern, auctioneer and other licences in order to the raising of a revenue for provincial, local or municipal purposes". Two

27. (1997) 520 U.S., 564.
28. Mac Donald, taxation power in Canada, (1941) 19 Can. Bar Rev. 75 at p. 95; *A.G.B.C. v. Kingcome Navigations Co. Ltd.* (1934) A.C. 45.
29. *P.A.T.A. v A.G. Canada,* (1931) A.C. 310.

limiting provisions are Sec. 121, i.e. "all articles of the growth, produce or manufacture of any one of the provinces shall from and after the Union be admitted free into each of the other provinces" and Sec. 125 i.e., "no lands or property belonging to Canada or any province shall be liable to taxation".

In the context of legal aspects of federal and provincial revenue powers, the issues raised and considered in conjunction with the various subsidy arrangements, *first,* under Sec. 118,[30] and *later,* under the B.N.A. Act, 1907 (U.K), Cl. 11 and also under federal legislation and transcend legalism and go to the heart of a working federalism.[31] It has become a truism of Canadian Constitutional Law that judicial interpretation of the B.N.A. Act, has given the provinces substantive legislative authority that far exceeds their money-raising power, while it has left the Dominion an ample taxing power overshadowing its regulatory authority. Having regard to this result of the legal division of powers, and to the disparate economic strength of the various provinces *interse,* it is understandable why the financial relations of Dominion and provinces have become a central issue in Canadian Federalism an issue in which the strict legal position is of secondary importance.[32]

B.N.A. Act, delegates power to the provinces, and reserves power to the Dominion. This inversion of the American-Australian practice means that the provinces in Canada have only the tax power mentioned in Sec. 92 of the Constitution. British Legal theory insists that there are no areas of anarchy in Canadian law and that all governmental power belongs either at one level of government or the other. This means that all other taxes belong to the Dominion as reserved power.[33] Even without this theory, the Constitution verifies the fact through Sec. 91 of the Constitution.

In *Caron v. The King*[34] suggests that the Dominion could not impose a direct tax within a province in order to the raising of a revenue for provincial purposes, as this is the exclusive right of the province.

But there is no question of the Dominion's power to tax directly within the province for Dominion purposes and no question of the Dominion's indirect tax power at all, or of its power to impose customs and excise duties. Taxation does not have to be uniform, either intrinsically or geographically, nor does it have to be raised for 'national purposes ' or for 'general welfare'. In fact, it has been stated that the 'Parliament of Canada may adopt any mode or system of taxation it chooses, be it direct or indirect, progressive or regressive, fair or discriminatory'.[35] It may be remembered that Sec. 92

30. Repealed by 1950 (U.K.), Cl. 6.
31. Maxwell, A Flaxible Portion of the B.N.A. Act, (1933) 11 Can. Bar Rev. 149.
32. Laskin's Canadian Constitution Law, 975, at p. 637.
33. Johnston, The effect of Judicial Review on Federal-State Relations in Australia, Canada and the United States, 1969 at p. 120.
34. (1924) A.C. 999.
35. F.R. Scott, The Constitutional Background of Taxation Agreements, *McGill Law Journal,* II *(1955),* 2.

reserves the field of Criminal Law to the Dominion, in contrast to the American-Australian pattern. This means that the Dominion legislature has never had to adopt tax devices to attempt to regulate or eliminate undesirable behaviour, or to prohibit behaviour that is illegal in provinces through regulation attached to tax measures.

As a matter of fact most of the tax questions that arise in Canada relate to the provision that provincial taxation must be direct. While this is an interesting and highly controversial field of law in Canada, it has had relatively little to do with federal-provincial relations for while the Court's view of the provincial power has been generous, it has never interpreted that power in a manner that denied federal tax power.

In *Lawson v. Interior Tree Fruit and Vegetable Committee,*[36] the Supreme Court of Canada invalidated the British Columbia produce Marketing Act, 1927, on the principal ground that it invaded federal legislative power in relation to trade and commerce: Cannon, J. in a concurring Judgment said that by the Produce Marketing Act of 1927, the province of British Columbia imposed levies on the fruits or vegetables grown or produced in a large area, including appellants farm, and obliged all shippers to secure a licence to market and sell products of the province any where within the Dominion under a penalty for each contravention. Even leaving aside the licence, and considering only the levy, that such imposts on commodities or on trade in commodities, have always been regarded as indirect taxes for a public purpose and come under the head of 'taxation'—which is dealt with in Part VIII of the B.N.A. Act, where is found Art. 121. It may be considered as an excise tax which necessarily has a tendency to affect, and affects, the price of the product to the customer in another province. As said Mac Millan, J. in *Attorney General for British Columbia v. McDonald Murphy Lumber Co.,*[37] the levy in question 'is an export tax falling within the category of duties of customs and excise, and as such, as well as by reason of its inherent nature as an indirect tax, could not competently be imposed by the provincial legislature.' Therefore, this legislation is an attempt to impose by indirect taxation and regulations an obstacle to one of the main purposes of confederations, which was, ultimately, to form an economic unit of all the provinces in British. North America with absolute freedom of trade between its constituent parts.[38]

C. Position under Australian Commerce Clause

The Commonwealth of Australia Constitution Act, delegates power to the federal government and reserves power to the states as is in the American model, Cl. 51, which enumerates Dominion powers, says that the Parliament shall have power to make laws for the peace, order and good government of the Commonwealth with respect to 'Taxation'; but so as not

36. (1931)2 D.L.R. 193. See also *Texada Mines Ltd. v. A.G.B.C.* (1960) 24 D.L.R. 2D 81.
37. (1930) A.C. 357 at p. 363.
38. *Re The Farm Products Marketing Act, R.S.O.* 1950 C. 131 as Amended (1957) S.C.R. 198.

to discriminate between states or parts of states. Sec. 90 of the Constitution says : "On the imposition of uniform duties of customs the power of the Parliament to impose duties of customs and excise shall become exclusive". Because all powers not delegated to the Commonwealth are reserved to the states, the state power of taxation is limited only by the exclusive nature of the federal customs and excise power and by Sec. 109 which provides for the supremacy of federal law over conflicting state law. The federal power seems to be limited only by the requirement that federal taxes not discriminate between states or parts of state. The only other restriction is in Sec. 114 preventing either level of government from taxing the property of the other government. But in Australia, as in Canada, the financial relationship developed between the Commonwealth and the states is so complex that some discussion of it is necessary before the evaluation of the legal problems.

Although, the High Court has usually been generous in its treatment of the Commonwealth tax power, the cases prior to the 1920 *Engineers' Case* are exceptions. The effort of the High Court to protect the states from the actions of the Commonwealth Parliament in regard to inter-governmental immunities was only one aspect of the legal process by which a general derogation of federal power was accomplished. The first attempt of the Commonwealth to use its newly granted exclusive power over excise duties was rebuffed by the Court on state "reserved power" grounds. In *Peterswald v. Bartley*[39] the Court held that the Commonwealth's exclusive power over excise duties did not extent to brewer's licence fees, although the Court admitted that traditional American and British legal definitions of excise duties included such licence fees, and in addition that Australian state legislation imposing such fees spoke of them as "duties of excise".

Griffith in Peterswald said that : "In considering the validity of laws of this kind we must look at the substance and not the form. In this instance the subject matter is one which the legislature of New South Wales has the power to regulate, that is to say the carrying on of any business in the exercise of the police power of the state." The astonishing fact is that the High Court had to reverse the State Supreme Court to arrive at this decision, but it did so, with the result that the express power of the Commonwealth Parliament was limited by the reserved power of the state. This principle was to receive even wider application. The first time the Commonwealth tried to use its tax power to accomplish an objective otherwise beyond its competence. The Commonwealth Excise Tariff Act, of 1906 imposed duties on certain agricultural implements manufactured in Australia, but it contained a provision exempting goods manufactured in accordance with labour conditions as specified in the law. The Act was tied together with another Act, which increased the protective duties imposed on the importation of such articles, and the objective of the two laws was clear : to

39. (1904) 1 C.L.R. 497.

bring prosperity to Australian manufacturers and to guarantee that such prosperity would be shared to some degree with the labouring force.

Rex v. Barger[40] is possibly the best example furnished in Australian law of the Court's effort to measure the extent of federal power by determining the degree of power reserved to the state. Barger was taxed for paying "sub-standard" wages, and in the High Court suit which followed he claimed that the Excise Tariff Act, invaded the reserved power of the states to regulate labour conditions.

The Australian Courts were to look at the Constitution as a whole, and the extent of the delegated power to the nation was to be measured in context with, and subject to, the restrictions implied by the reservation of certain powers to the state, including labour relations. C.J Griffith continued, saying : "even if the term 'taxation' uncontrolled by any context, were capable of including the indirect regulation of the internal affairs of a State by means of taxation, its meaning in the Constitution is limited by the implied prohibition against direct interference with matters reserved exclusively to the states".

This was too much for Justice Higgins and Isaacs, who were moved to dissent. Higgins, J. said that totally different constitutional powers—one state and one national—could be exercised in such a manner as to effect the same object, but this did not mean that because the state could have accomplished the object by the use of its power to regulate labour conditions, the nation was denied the right to accomplish the same object through its own constitutional, but different, power. Further, insisted Higgins, J., "The truth is that, where two law-making powers operate over the same territory and the same people, the laws of one authority must necessarily touch, at every point, the subjects committed to the other authority, and must frequently affect the conduct of persons with regard to those subjects." When this happens, said Higgins, J.:

> "To say that the Federal Parliament cannot make a law because legislation on the object belongs to the states is rather to invert the true position. The Commonwealth has certain powers, and as to those powers it is supreme ; the state has the rest. We must find what the Commonwealth powers are before we can say what the state powers are. The Federal Parliament has certain specific gifts; the states have the residue. We have to find out the extent of the specific gifts before we make assertion as to the residue. The question, then, is merely what is the extent of this power of taxation given to the Federal Parliament?"

Justice Higgins did not see that this posed much of a problem. He said that because the Constitution specifically granted the plenary power to

40. (1908) 6 C.L.R. 41.

Parliament to make laws with respect to taxation, "if the Act, is within the ambit of the power, and if it does not discriminate between states or parts of state, the motives of the Parliament in passing the Act, are immaterial, and the Act, is valid." If one accepts Justice Higgins' arguments, it does not matter that the Parliament claimed that this was an "Excise Tax" and thus an exclusive parliamentary power. What he is saying is that at any rate it is a tax and that Commonwealth tax power is limited only by the prohibition against discrimination. And Sec. 109 validates any federal tax law when it is in conflict with an inconsistent state tax law.

D. Position under Indian Commerce Clause

The framers of Indian Constitution had these two examples before them in addition to the provisions contained in Sec. 297 of the Government of India Act, 1935. The scheme of Part XIII of the Constitution seems to be a synthesis of the "Commerce Clause" of the United States and Australian Constitutions. As in Australia (Sec. 92) the general freedom of commerce is declared by Art. 301 as "Subject to the other provisions of this part, trade, commerce and intercourse throughout the territory of India shall be free".[41] Art. 302,[42] which gives the Central Legislature power to impose restrictions on commerce, both intra-state and inter-state in public interest, it is submitted, embodies the law in U.S.A. But the courts have permitted[43] Parliament to delegate the power of regulation under Art. 302 to the executive governments of the states, and this device has undermined much of the efficacy of a provision like Art. 302 resulting in inaction by Parliament and also overactive erections of trade barriers by states under such delegated power. Such delegation of the very power to the states, which the Constitution has withheld from them is, it is humbly submitted, not proper.

Neither the Parliament nor the state legislatures should give *preference* to one state over another or make any discrimination between one state and another except in a case where the Parliament makes a law to meet situation of scarcity[44] in any part of the country. The states are permitted to impose reasonable restrictions in the interests of general public on the freedom of trade, commerce intercourse through legislative action with the sanction of the President of India obtained for the introduction of such a bill in the state legislatures.[45]

41. It is to be said that apart from this, Part XIII has no resemblance to the Australian Constitution and the heavy reliance on Australian law by our courts is clearly misconceive (Shah, J. in *Dist. Collector v. Ibrahim & Co.*, A.I.R. 1970 S.C. 1275 at p. 1279.
42. It has been held that prevention of evasion of tax is a measure in the public interest in *State of Tamilnadu v. Sitolakshmi Mills*, A.I.R. 1974 S.C. 1505 at p. 1509.
43. *Krishan Lal Praveen Kumar v. State of Rajasthan*, A.I.R. 1982 S.C. 29 at pp. 30-31.
44. Article 303 (2) of Indian Constitution.
45. Article 304(b) of the Indian Constitution.

Art. 303(1) does not control the power of taxation as the article specifically refers only to the legislative power[46] relating to trade and commerce. The article is similar in words to Sec. 99 of the Australian Constitution and there it has been held[47] that the Sec. 99 applies only to laws, which can be made under the powers conferred upon Parliament to make laws with respect to trade and commerce under Sec. 51(1) of the Australian Constitution. The terms 'preference' and 'discrimination' are the two sides of the same coin because where a thing is being preferred it can be done only by discriminating against another. The preference may be any 'tangible advantage'[48] or even 'impediment'[49] in the course of trade or commercial operations. Sec. 8 of the Central Sales Tax Act, 1956 dealing with the rate of sales tax on inter-state sales, has been challenged under Art. 303 unsuccessfully. The section prescribed different rates of taxes.

In *State of Madras v. Nataraja Mudaliar,*[50] the Supreme Court rejected the contention as the prevalence of different rates in various states did not amount to giving preference to one over another. The contention was again raised before the Supreme Court in *State of Tamil Nadu v. Sitolakshmi Mills*[51] and the Court again held that the rates had been so fixed to discourage sales to non-registered dealers. The maximum that could be said about the section is that it may enable a state to decrease the rate of tax and help its goods to be sold more in different states. But that is not preference or discrimination against goods coming from other states.

In *Automobile Transport Ltd. v. State of Rajasthan,*[52] Subba Rao, J. observed that reference to Art. 303 in the opening non-obstante clause of Art. 304 was irrelevant. Theoretically, it follows that under Art. 304(b) if President assents to a bill, the state legislature can impose any restriction on the freedom of commerce provided that it is not unreasonable. Such laws are subject to judicial security regarding reasonableness and public interest. The purpose behind the insistence on presidential sanction is to ensure uniformity among state laws. This is a deviation from the law available in the United States of America,[53] because in India a limited field is expressly left for state regulation and the authority to decide whether such field is amenable to state regulation is the federal executive. The states are prohibited from imposing taxes on goods imported from the other states so

46. *State of Madras v. Nataraja Mudaliar,* A.I.R. 1969 S.C. 147 at p. 156.
47. *Morgan v. Commonwealth* (1947) 74 C.L.R. 421, 455.
48. Dixon, J. in *Crowe v. Commonwealth* (1935) 54 C.L.R., 69 at. p. 92.
49. Starke, J. at p. 86.
50. A.I.R. 1969 S.C. 147, Justice Hedge (concurring) correctly pointed out that the provision aimed at evasion of tax by sales effected to non-registered dealers.
51. A.I.R. 1974 S.C. 1505 at p. 1509.
52. A.I.R. 1962 S.C. 1406 at p. 1434.
53. In U.S.A. only the Federal Legislature can authorise such states regulation. See *Wilkerson v. Rahrer,* 140 U.S. 545 (1891), where a law of Congress provided that all shipments of liquor into any state where to be subject to state laws and such delegation was upheld.

as to discriminate between goods so imported and goods produced or manufactured inside the state.

Art. 305 provides that nothing in Art. 301 or 303 shall affect the provisions of any existing law except insofar as President may otherwise direct and thus protects all pre-constitutional laws from the operation of Arts. 301 and 303. In *Bangalore W. C. & S. Mills Co. v. Corporation of Bangalore,*[54] an octroi duty was levied by the respondent Corporation in 1954 under the Bangalore Municipal Corporation Act, which was a pre-constitutional legislation of 1949. Rejecting the contention of the appellant, it was held that all the articles on which octroi was leviable were intended to be included in the parent statute itself, and that there was no alternation or modification of the existing law in 1954 so as to divest the protection under Art. 305. The decision appears to lay down the law that where a statute authorises the levy of a tax or a restriction, it would not matter even if such levy or restriction was imposed after the commencement of the Constitution.[55] But the position of law is not so simple as it appears and *Kalyani Stores v. State of Orissa*[56] may be mentioned here. The Court by a majority held[57] that the increase of levy was hit by Art. 301. The Court held that only the pre-constitutional rate would be saved by virtue of Art. 305. However, it is really difficult to appreciate the difference between the imposition of a fresh duty and the increase of the rate of an existing duty.

Art. 305 has been made use of in upholding taxes imposed on goods from sister states in *Chobe v. Palnitkar.*[58] It is submitted that the decision is incorrect as Art. 305 refers only to Arts. 301 and 303 and not to Art. 304. Since no import duty could be levied on indigenous goods the levy was hit by Art. 304(a). The view that Art. 305 was enacted not to save existing discriminatory taxes or tax barriers is evident from the exclusion of Art. 304 from the, operation of Art. 305. Art. 303 refers to discrimination and preferences by Parliament and state legislatures other than by way of taxation[59] and by excluding Art. 304 from the operation of Art. 305 the Constitution-makers intended to do away with tax barriers wholly and to preserve other restrictions till federal scrutiny is done. The view finds support from the fact that Sec. 297 of the Government of India Act, 1935 also prohibited discriminatory taxes on out-of-state goods. It has been held[60] that Art. 305 would not protect the extension of an existing law to a new area

54. Article 304(a) of the Indian Constitution.
55. *Surajmal Bal v. State of Rajasthan,* A.I.R. 1954 Raj. 260.
56. AIR 1966 S.C. 1686.
57. *Id.* at p. 1692.
58. A.I.R. 1954 Hyd. 207 (a duty on sweets, brought from Lucknow, Imposed under Hyderabad Customs Act).
59. That is "by Virtue of any entry relating to trade and commerce in any of the Lists in the Seventh Schedule." It is clear that entries could not mean entries dealing with taxation.
60. *Vallabhadas Kunji v. S.T. Officer,* A.I.R. 1963 Ker. 202 at p. 209.

after the commencement of the Constitution. In *State of Mysore v. Sanjeeviah*[61] it was held that rules framed after the commencement of the Constitution under a pre-constitutional law would not get the protection of Art. 305. Hence, it might be said that the present position of law is that though all existing laws are protected by Art. 305 any fresh action taken under such laws is not protected.

In *Atiabari Tea Co. v. State of Assam*,[62] the Court found the tax to be violative of Art. 301, and held that it could not be upheld under Art. 304(b). Similarly, in *Kalyani Stores v. State of Orissa*,[63] the majority held the tax infringed the freedom under Art. 301 and might be saved only if it fell within the exceptions contained in Arts. 302, 303 and 304.

Justice Hidayatullah, who dissented, observed : "Art. 304(a) imposes no ban but lifts the ban imposed by Arts. 301 and 303 subject to one condition." The use of the word 'ban' appears to make the power of the state to legislate and impose tax the highest good and not the economic unity of the nation. *In State of Kerala v. Abdul Kadir*[64], the Court held that only on a finding that the tax offended Art. 301, the questions whether it was saved by Art. 304(a) arose. It is to be admitted that defective drafting has also crept into the provision of Part XIII. For example,[65] though Art. 301 is expressly made subject to other provisions of Part XIII, Art. 301 is referred to in the non-obstinate clauses of Arts. 304 and 305. Again, the Court has treated Art. 304 prospective and enabling provision. Since it is the law that legislative power flows from the entries in the legislative lists, how Art. 304 could be viewed as an enabling provision is difficult to understand. By the term prospective also, what was intended is not clear, since it is no new provision and Sec. 297(1)(b) of Government of India Act, 1935 provided for the same.

(a) Does the Freedom Guaranteed by Article 301 Extend to Tax Laws

After a long-drawn controversy in the high courts as well as in the Supreme Court, it has been settled[66] that tax laws are not outside the purview of Part XIII of the Constitution. The main ground advanced by the Supreme Court in coming to conclusion is that the power to levy taxes is ultimately based on Art. 245 and the said power in terms is subject to the provisions of the Constitution including those in Part XIII.[67]

The impact of the above conclusion is, however, primarily on the state legislature and very little on Parliament, for, by reason of Art. 302, a tax law cannot be challenged on any ground other than that it is not 'in the public

---

61. A.I.R. 1967 S.C. 1189 at p. 1192.
62. A.I.R. 1961 S.C. 232 at p. 254.
63. A.I.R. 1966 S.C. 1686 at p. 1692.
64. A.I.R. 1970 S.C. 1912 at p. 1918 and in *A.B. Abdul Kadir v. State of Kerala*, A.I.R. 1976 S.C. 182.
65. Subba Rao, J., in *Automobile Transport Ltd v. State of Rajasthan*, A.I.R. 1962.
66. *Atiabari Tea Co. v. State of Assam* (1961) S.C.R. 809 at p. 860.
67. *Automobile Transport v. State of Rajasthan*, A.I.R. 1962 S.C. 1406 at p. 1422.

interest', which it would be well-nigh impossible to establish so far as a taxing measure is concerned. The other bar against preference and discrimination under Cl. (1) of Art. 303 may be avoided by Parliament by making a declaration as to scarcity under Cl. (2) of that article. But, in a case of a state legislature, a tax law which, not being purely compensatory, has for its direct object an activity or instrumentality of trade, commerce and intercourse, shall have to be justified either under Art. 304, or under Art. 305.

Of course, in a sense, every tax imposed by a state legislature may have an indirect effect on the flow of trade or commerce. But if the power of the state legislature to make any tax laws be held to be subject to the limitation under Art. 301, the legislative power of the state legislature would be rendered hollow, and, the federal scheme would be rendered meaningless.[68] The Supreme Court has, accordingly laid down certain conditions for the application of Art. 301, i.e., every tax does not interfere with the freedom of trade guaranteed by Art. 301; it does so only if it directly and immediately restricts or hampers the free flow of trade, commerce or intercourse.[69]

In determining whether a tax directly offends against Art. 301, it is the movement of the goods, which are the subject of the trade that has to be borne in mind. Thus, if a tax is imposed solely on the basis that the goods are carried or transported, that directly affects the freedom of trade as contemplated by Art. 301, a terminal tax or octroi duty.[70] If a law directly and immediately imposes a tax for general revenue proposes on the movement of trade, it would be violating the freedom. On the other hand, the imposition of a licence fee on the sale of tobacco within a state would not constitute a violation of Art. 301, in the absence of a finding that it operated directly and immediately to restrict the flow of tobacco from other states.[71]

Nor does the imposition of a case upon lands held for carrying on mining operations come within the purview of Art. 301.[72] It is evident that taxes which facilitate trade or commerce cannot be said to offend against Art. 301. Taxes of this nature are compensatory taxes for the use of trading facilities or services rendered.[73]

Though it is not possible *a priori* to draw a dividing line between that which would really be a charge for a facility provided and which would be a deterrent to the trade, so long a particular tax remains compensatory, it cannot operate as a hindrance to the freedom of trade and commerce.[74]

---

68. *Ibid.*
69. *State of Kerala v. Abdul*, A.I.R. 1970 S.C. 1913 (Para. 9); *State of Karnataka v. Hansa Corp.*, A.I.R. 1981 S.C. 425 (Para. 32).
70. *Bangalore Weaving Mill v. Bangalore Corpn.*, A.I.R. 1962 S.C. 562 at p. 565.
71. *State of Kerala v. Abdul*, A.I.R. 1970 S.C. 1912.
72. *Laxmi Narayan v. State*, A.I.R. 1983.
73. Automobile, A.I.R. 1962 S.C. 1406.
74. *Atiabari*, 1961, 1 S.C.R. 809.

Thus, a tax for the use of a road or a bridge is a compensatory tax for the use of the road or bridge which facilitates trade and intercourse instead of interfering with its freedom. A licencing system would also come within this category.[75]

In *M/s Sharma Transport v. Government of A.P.*,[76] Supreme Court held that imposition of tax does not in every case infringe Art. 301. It has to be seen whether the impugned provision amounts to a restriction directly and immediately on the movement of trade or commerce, so long as a tax remains compensatory it can not operate as hindrance.

In *Shree Digvijay Cement Co. Ltd. v. State of Rajasthan*,[77] notification reducing sales tax on inter-state sale of cement by any dealer from that state, to 40% was not violative of Art. 301 of Constitution on ground that it had effect or preventing or hindering free movement of goods from one state to other.

(b) Article 304(a) and Taxation

Art. 304(a) being a provision which deals specifically with taxation, a brief discussion of its scope is necessary. It places goods imported from sister states on a *par* with similar goods manufactured or produced within the state in regard to state taxation within the allocated field.[78] The object of Art. 304(a) was to limit the power of taxation by states so as to prevent discrimination against imported goods by imposing taxes on such goods at a higher rate than is borne by indigenous goods. The exact connotation of the words has not been hitherto considered by the courts. But this provision has been hitherto considered by the courts. But this provision has been expressly referred to in the case of a tax on sale[79] of goods, excise duty[80] and may cover octroi; but toll[81] or tax on vehicles may not be called so. Even though it is verbal law making, the tax has to be on 'goods' and hence a tax on vehicle may not be within the ambit of the provision. Even if such goods are apparently taxed alike the law may be bad for discrimination if some secret advantage is given to domestic goods over out-of-state goods.

Patanjali Sastri, C.J. in *State of Bombay v. United Motors*[82] observed that the commercial unity of India was made to give way before the state power of imposing 'any' non-discriminatory tax on goods imported from sister states. The statement of law, it is submitted, is too wide. The fact that home-made goods are subject to similar tax burden is *prima facie* proof of non-

---

75. *Automobile*, A.I.R. 1962 S.C. 1406.
76. A.I.R. 2002 S.C. 322.
77. A.I.R. 2000 S.C. 680.
78. Subba Rao, J. in *Automobile Transport Ltd. v. State of Rajasthan*, A.I.R. 1962. S.C. 1406 at p. 1436.
79. *Hajee Abdul Shukoor v. State of Madras*, A.I.R. 1964 S.C. 1729.
80. *Kalyani Stores v. State of Orissa*, A.I.R. 1964 S.C. 1729.
81. *Girdharilal Anand v. State of Jammu & Kasmir*, A.I.R. 1969 J&K 113 at p. 120.
82. A.I.R. 1953 S.C. 252 at p. 257.

discrimination. At one time it was thought[83] that such absence of indigenous goods would result in arbitrary exercise of taxation and consequent destruction of the trade of such imported commodity. In *Kalyani Stores*, Shah, J. observed: "As no foreign liquor is produced or manufactured in Orissa the power to legislate given by Art. 304 is not available and the restriction which is declared on the freedom of trade, commerce or intercourse by Art. 304 of the Constitution remains unfettered." *In State of Kerala v. Abdul Kadir*[84], Justice Ramaswami held that the correct approach was to see whether the impugned tax impeded the free flow of commerce under Art. 301 and only if a court came to the conclusion that it infringed Art. 301, the question whether it was saved by Art. 304(a) as a non-discriminatory tax could arise. *Kalyani Stores* was explained away as a non-application of Art. 304(a) as there was no indigenous production of foreign liquor. The view that *Kalyani Stores* is related to the power of state legislatures to impose countervailing duty under Entry 51, List II of the Seventh Schedule to the Constitution is clear from *M.M. Breweries v. E & T Commr.*[85] and *Sat Pal & Co. v. Lt. Governor of Delhi.*[86]

The problem remains whether protection is necessary for goods coming from other states when similar goods are not manufactured inside the state. It is true that though there are chances of hostile taxation of such goods, a blanket protection from taxation is not warranted. Any heavy taxation of such goods may be examined by courts under Art. 301 to see whether it infringes the freedom of inter-state trade and commerce. This has to be done objectively and not in a superficial way of labelling as 'direct or indirect' restriction.

The term 'goods imported' in Art. 304(a) would certainly cover cases of goods brought by traders from other states for sale inside the state. So the term is wider than the term inter-state sale. For example, if a businessman goes to another state, purchases goods there and brings it to the first state, or if a trader from one state takes his goods to another state and sells there, such transaction would not be inter-state sales. Art. 304(a) would cover such cases as here the test is whether the goods are of local origin or out-of-state origin.

Art. 304(a) apparently ensures only equal rate of tax for incoming goods. So if such goods are taxed at a higher rate or where they are taxed at any rate when indigenous goods are exempt, Art. 304(a) is attracted. These are simple cases of hostile discrimination[87] as evidenced in *State of Madhya Pradesh v. Bhailal Bhai.*[88] In *Lakshman v. State of Madhya Pradesh*[89] the petitioner was a nomad grazier belonging to Gujarat who wandered from place to

83. *State of Bombay v. R.M D.C.*, A.I.R. 1956 Bom.1 at p. 16.
84. A.I.R. 1966 S.C. 1686 at p. 1697.
85. A.I.R. 1976 S.C. 2020.
86. A.I.R. 1979 S.C. 1550.
87. *Henneford v. Silas Mason Co.*, 300 U.S. 577 (1937).
88. A.I.R. 1964 S.C. 1006.
89. A.I.R. 1983 S.C. 656.

place with his cattle. State of Madhya Pradesh did not like this and imposed a higher duty for out-of-state cattle owners. The levy was found invalid by the Court. In *Laxmi Paper Mart v. State of Uttar Pradesh,*[90] the sale of exercise books made with paper purchased inside Uttar Pradesh was exempt from tax while books made with paper purchased out side the state was taxed at 5%. The levy was invalidated. Art. 304(a) does not inhibit the power of a state to impose tax on out-of-state goods non-discriminatory. In *Rattan Lal & Co. v. Assessing Authority*[91], the tax on sale of declared goods was on the last dealer inside the state. It was argued that the tax would be heavier on the imported goods. It was held that the rate was same and the slight burden was owing to the fact that the tax was *ad volorem.* Similarly, in *Suryalal Makand Lal v. State of Uttar Pradesh*[92] the tax on imported vanaspati on first sale by importer, and on that produced within the state on first sale by the manufacturer was upheld. However, cases may arise where through the rate of tax is similar both on indigenous and out of state goods, discrimination may result owing to other non-apparent factors.

In *Hajee Abdul Shukoor & Co. v. State of Madras*[93] this defect was attempted to be rectified by providing a rate of tax of two percent on the turnover of hides and skins purchased in the untamed condition from outside the state for the years 1955 to 1959 from the first seller inside the state. This was invalidated as the rate was higher because three price per rupee was the rate of tax for untanned hides. A later amendment in 1964 providing for the tax to be calculated on the purchase price of untanned skins and hides rectified this and was upheld in *Appellate Asst. Comm. v. L.M.S. Sadak Tamby & Co.*[94]

It has to be noted that in *Mehtab Majid & Co.* the rate of tax for indigenous goods and imported goods was same. But later in *State of Madras v. Nataraja Mudaliar*[95], it was wrongly observed that the defect in *Mehtab Majid & Co.* was of different rates and that where rates were same there was no defect under Art. 304(a). The observation was later approved by the Supreme Court in *Rattan Lal & Co. v. Assessing Authority.*[96] The Andhra Pradesh High Court has held that by these later pronouncements *Mehtab Majid & Co.* was not good law in *Abdul Samad & Co. v. C.T.O.,*[97] and *Associated Tanners v. C.T.O.*[98] It is humbly submitted that the view of the Andhra Pradesh High Court is wrong in this matter.

90. 1975 Tax L.R. 1303 (All.)
91. A.I.R. 1984 S.C. 1542.
92. A.I.R.1970 S.C. 1742 at p. 1750.
93. A.I.R. 1964 S.C. 1729 at p. 1733.
94. A.I.R. 1974 S.C. 2344.
95. A.I.R. 1969 S.C. 147 at p. 158.
96. A.I.R. 1970 S.C. 1742 at p. 1750.
97. 1976 Tax L.R. 1885 (A.P.).
98. 1973 Tax. L.R. 2590 (A.P.)

Art. 304(a) can apply to a tax only if two conditions are satisfied, viz., the tax should be on goods coming from outside the state, and such tax should be discriminatory in nature. It is true that the term tax on goods should be given a liberal interpretation and should not be construed in narrow sense. Cases may arise where the tax levied is not on goods but discriminatory in nature and also where the tax levied is on goods which though not discriminatory is really a curtailment of the freedom of commerce. To Illustrate the point, if dealers in out-of-state goods are required to take out licence on payment of high fee,[99] or a tax is levied only on non-resident sellers[100] it will be difficult to bring such cases under Art. 304(a). Further, it seems that Art. 304(a) has no application if a state imposes a tax on goods sent outside it.[101]

In *Western Electronics v. State of Gujarat*,[102] it was held that sales tax which has the effect of discriminating between goods of one state and goods of another, may affect the free flow of trade and it will then offend against Art. 301 and will be valid only if it comes within the terms of Art. 304(a). The effect of the sales tax on tanned hides or skins imported from outside is that the latter becomes subject to a higher tax by the application of the proviso to sub-rule (2) of R. 16 of the Rules, then the tax is discriminatory and unconstitutional and must be struck down.

In *State of Bihar v. Bihar Chamber of Commerce*,[103] the Supreme Court held that the requirement of prior consent of President has been satisfied in the case of the impugned Act. Further, an additional levy of 3 per cent by virtue of the impugned Act, on tobacco could not be said to be impeding the trade, commerce or intercourse in tobacco products directly and immediately or to any appreciable degree. In this connection, it is not relevant to take into consideration the harmful nature of the tabacco products. The extraordinary high level of excise duties on tobacco is meant precisely to discourage its consumption. Therefore, it can not be said that the addition of three percent is either an unreasonable restriction on the freedom of trade and commerce or that it is not required in public interest. Thus, it could be said that the requirements of Art. 304(b) have been satisfied and the challenge upon the validity of the impugned Act, on the ground of violation of Art. 301 would not be tenable.

In M/s Video Electronics Pty. Ltd. v. State of Punjab,[104] the Supreme Court has held that the imposition of a rates of sales tax is influenced by various political, economic and social factors. Prevalence of differential rate of tax on sales of the same commodity can not be regarded in isolation as determinative of the object to discriminate between one state and another.

99. *Robbins v. Shelby County Trading Dist.*, 120 U.S. 489 (1887).
100. *Best & Co. v. Maxwell*, 311 U.S. 454 (1940).
101. *Morvi Vegatable Products v. M.C. Padia*, 1976 Tax L.R. 1277 (Guj.).
102. A.I.R. 1988 S.C. 2038 at p. 2040.
103. A.I.R. 1996 S.C. 2344.
104. A.I.R. 1990 S.C. 820.

Where the general rate applicable to the goods locally made and on those imported from other states is the same nothing more normally and generally is to be shown by the state to dispel the argument of discrimination under Art. 304(a), even though the resultant tax amount on imported goods may be different.

It can not be disputed that it is open to the states to release tax and there after remit the same or pay back to the local manufactures in the shape of subsidies and that would neither discriminate nor be hit by Art. 304(a) of the Constitution. The taxes which do not directly or immediately restrict or interfere with trade, commerce and intercourse throughout the territory of India, would therefore be excluded from the ambit of Art. 301 of the Constitution. It has to be born in mind that sales tax has only on indirect effect on trade and commerce.

In *M/s Andhra Steel Corp. v. Commissioner of Commercial Taxes in Karnataka,*[105] Sec. 5(4) of the Karnataka Sales Tax Act was held to be violative of Art. 304(a). It was held by the Supreme Court that Sec. 5(4) of the Act, in so far as it pertains to Item 2 in the IVth Schedule read with the Explanation II is violative of Art. 304(a) of the Constitution as under that provision the sale of finished goods manufactured out of imported raw material is taxed but the sale of finished goods manufactured out of locally purchased raw material is not taxed and that amounts to hostile discrimination in the rate of tax or quantum of tax. In the instant case the assess purchased iron scrap both from local registered dealers and also from the dealers outsides the state of Karnataka and manufactured ingots and sold the same mostly within the state of Karnataka. In view of the provisions of Sec. 5(4) read with Item 2 of Sec. IV and Explain. II thereto while the assessee's sale of ingots manufactured out of locally purchased scrap would not be subjected to tax, the assessee's sale of ingots manufactured out of scrap purchased from outside the state of Karnataka would be subjected to tax. This would be violative of Art. 304(a).

Recently in *M.P. Cement Manufacturers Asson. v. State of M.P.,*[106] the Madhya Pradesh High Court held that the M.P. State Electricity Board is the principle distributor of electrical energy in the state. It has to provide electricity to all sections of society residing at different distant locations irrespective of the fact whether the execution of such society-oriented schemes are profitable or not. Therefore, such organisations stand apart and cannot be equated with the petitioners, industries who produce electrical energy by their Captive Power unit or Diesel generator set. The power generation by petitioners is limited to their industries. The petitioners do not suggest initiation of schemes for common welfare nor can they do since the generation of electrical energy by them is for self use. With this background, levy of energy development cess at *different rates* on producers and

105. A.I.R. 1990 S.C. 1912.
106. A.I.R. 2002 M.P. 62.

distributors is not discriminatory and such classification is constitutionally permissible.

(c) Tax on Sales or Purchase of Goods Outside a State and in Inter-state Trade and Commerce

A federation, although divided into several constituent units, nevertheless, constantly strives to promote freedom of trade and commerce within the country in order to weld it into one economic unit. It therefore, becomes necessary to regulate taxation of inter-state sale or purchase *lest* indiscriminate state taxation may hamper free flow of trade and commerce from one state to another and thus, jeopardise the economic unity of the country. The Indian Constitution seeks to regulate taxation of inter-state sale or purchase in two ways: negatively, by prohibiting a state from levying, and, positively, by empowering the Center to levy, a tax on such sale or purchase.

Before 1956, Art. 286 sought to avoid multiple taxation of sales by stipulation that a state could not tax a sale taking place outside the state or in the course of inter-state trade and commerce. A sale was regarded as falling within the state in which goods under it were delivered for consumption.

Interpreting Art. 286, in *Bombay v. United Motor's*[107], the Supreme Court adopted the "outside consumption" test and held that the exporting state could not tax a sale under which goods went to another state, and that it could be taxed only by the state in which the goods were actually delivered for consumption. The word 'consumption' was interpreted broadly so as to envisage not only consumption by the actual purchaser himself but also distribution for eventual consumption within the state. No other state except that of consumption[108], could tax a sale touching several states and thus, multiple taxation of such a sale was avoided. States resorted to the practice of taxing inter-state sales under which goods come to them for consumption, but placed the liability to pay the tax on out-of-the-state dealers. This was done because of convenience of tax collection, but it was very inconvenient to a trader spending goods to several states as he could be taxed by all the states. He had, therefore, to acquaint himself with the taxing laws of all the states, produce his account books and file returns before all the taxing jurisdictions. Consequently, the matter was reagitated in *Bengal Immunity Co. v. State of Bihar.*[109] A company in Calcutta accepted orders there and then sent goods to Bihar. Bihar sought to tax the company's sales to Bihar dealers, but the company objected to it. The Supreme Court overruling its view in the *Uniter Motors*, now held that it was an inter-state sale which could not be taxed by any state, not even by the state of consumption, because of the bar imposed by Art. 286 on taxation of a sale in the course of inter-state trade and commerce. Inter-state sale thus became immune from all state taxation.

107. (1953) S.C.R. 1069.

108. M.P. Jain, Justice Bhagwati and Constitutional Law, 2 J.I.L.I. at p. 3.

109. AIR 1955 S.C. 661.

To ensure that the inter-state trade and commerce does not go absolutely tax-free and pays tax at least once, the Constitution (Sixth Amendment) Act, 1956, modified Art. 286, and gave it its present form, Entry 92A was also added to List I. The effect of these modifications is that the power to tax inter-state sale or purchase now belongs to the Center and not to be states which are also debarred from taxing an 'outside' sale and what is an 'outside' sale or inter-state sale are matters for Parliament to define under Art. 286 (2) and 269 (3) respectively.

By giving power of assessment to the exporting state, the difficulties created by the *United Motors*, are avoided as dealers exporting goods to other states can be assessed by their own state. The Central Act, also lays down the test to determine what is an 'outside' sale. It defines a sale inside a state and characterises the same as being outside all other states. Only an inside sale can be taxed by a state and not an outside sale. The test to ascertain an inside sale is the existence of goods within the state.[110] In this way, a sale or purchase the different ingredients of which occur in different states is now located, by a fiction of law, in one state only i.e., the state where goods exist and thus multiple taxation of such a sale is avoided.

The problem of multiple taxation of inter-state sale or purchase does not arise in Australia as only the Center and not the states can levy sales tax. In Canada, the provinces can levy a sales tax payable by the ultimate consumer and the problem of multiple taxation does not arise[111]. The problem is rather acute in the U.S.A. the judiciary has made some attempts to avoid multiple taxation of inter-state commerce by invoking the Commerce Clause and the Due Process Clause[112] of the Constitution, but the problem is too complicated to be solved only by the judiciary.

(d) Export and Import

Foreign trade being of great importance to the national economy, it become necessary to protect it from indiscriminate taxation. Consequently, Art. 286(1)(b) bars a state from imposing a tax on sale or purchase of goods which takes place in the course of import of goods into, or export of goods out of India. Under Art. 286(2), Parliament may by law formulate the principle for determining when a sale or purchase of goods takes place in the course of export or import. Accordingly, under section 5 of the Central Sales Tax Act, 1956, a sale or purchase is in the course of export or import if it occasions the export or import of goods out of or into India, or the sale is effected by a transfer of documents of title of the goods; (i) in case of export, after the goods cross, and (ii) in case of import, before the goods cross, the customs frontiers of India. Purchases in a state by an exporter for the purpose of export, as well as sales in the state by an importer after the goods

110. Inter-state Trade Barriers & Sales Tax Law in India, I.L.I. (1962).

111. *Atlantic Smoke Shops Ltd v. Conlon*, 1943 A.C. 550.

112. This provision has been used to invalidate state attempts to tax an object outside the state borders.

have crossed the customs barrier, are not within the exemption. But sale in the state by an exporter or importer by transfer of shipping documents while the goods are beyond the customs barrier are within the exemption.

Art. 286 (3) lays down that a state law imposing a tax on the sale or purchase of goods declared by Parliament by law to be of special importance (ii) inter-state trade or commerce, is to be subject to such restrictions and conditions in regard to tax so levied as Parliament may specify.

In *Steel Authority of India Ltd. v. State of Orissa,*[113] the Court pointed out that Art. 286(1) of the Constitution states that no law of a state shall impose, or authorise the imposition of, a tax on the sale or purchase of goods where such sale or purchase takes place outside the state or in the course of the import of goods into, or export of goods out of the territory of India. Art. 286(2) authorises Parliament by law to formulate principles for determining when a sale or purchase of goods takes place in any of the ways mentioned in sub-Art. (1). Acting upon this power, Parliament has set out in sections 3, 4 and 5 of the Central Sales Tax Act, 1956, principles for determining when a sale or purchase of goods can be said to take place in the course of inter-state trade or commerce, when a sale or purchase of goods can be said to take place outside the state and when a sale or purchase of goods can be said to take place in the course of import or export.

In *M/s Gannon Dunkerley and Co. v. State of Rajasthan,*[114] the Supreme Court has held that it is necessary to exclude from the value of a works contract the value of goods which are not taxable by a state in view of Sections 3, 4 and 5 of the Central Sales Tax Act, 1956. It was contended that this requirement proceeded on the assumption that half of the amount was not liable to tax being in respect of inter-state sales, outside sales and export sales. No such assumption based on the rate of tax at any given point of time can be made.

In *20th Century Finance Corp. Ltd. v. State of Maharashtra,*[115] the Court held that by virtue of clause (1) of Art. 286 the state legislature is precluded to make law imposing tax on the transactions of transfer of right to use any goods where such deemed sales takes place (a) outside the state, and (b) in the course of import of goods into the territory of India. Yet, there are other limitations on the taxing power of the state legislature by virtue of Cl. (3) of Art. 286. Although Parliament has enacted law under Cl. (3)(a) of Art. 286 but no law so far has been enacted by Parliament under Cl (3)(b) of Art. 286. When such law is enacted by Parliament, the state legislature would be required to exercise its legislative power in conformity with such law. Thus, what has been stated above, are the limitations on the powers of state legislatures on levy of sales tax on deemed sales envisaged under sub-clause (d) of clause (29-a) of Art. 366 of the Constitution.

---

113. A.I.R. 2000 S.C.946.
114. (1993) A.I.R. S.C.W. 2621.
115. A.I.R. 2000 S.C. 2436.

2. THE CONCEPT OF COMPENSATORY TAXES AND REGULATORY MEASURES

The concept of compensatory tax has been borrowed from Australia where it has been evolved to dilute somewhat the rigours of Sec. 92. Now there is one basic difference between the Indian and the foreign models. In Australia, Sec. 92[116] admits of no exception: If a law imposes a restriction on trade it is just unconstitutional. In this context, the courts have evolved the test of compensatory tax to loosen the rigours of Sec. 92. Similarly, in the U.S.A. the states have conceded some power to tax inter-state commerce as against the constitutional protection given to such commerce to help them to raise some funds to maintain roads, etc. Therefore, the concept of compensatory tax has been adopted to make inter-state commerce pay it way.[117] But in India, Art. 301 is not absolute in the sense that Arts. 302 to 304 provide exceptions to it. A state wishing to restrict freedom of trade has only to follow the conditions laid down in Art. 304(b). The question, therefore, arises; when the Constitution itself provides a mechanism to impose restrictions on freedom of trade, is it necessary to adopt other concepts for the same purpose from foreign systems which operate in a very different context? The basic reason for propounding the theory of compensatory taxes appears to be to free the states, to some extent, from the restraints of Art. 304(b). One of these requirements their laws restricting trade and commerce. This has been done on the ground is to have Central consent than otherwise state autonomy would be greatly compromised. This is, therefore, a judicial attempt to make the Indian Constitution more federal that what its framers had envisaged it to be.

The Supreme Court of United States has explained compensatory tax doctrine in different cases.

In *Associated Industries v. Lohman*[118], the Court explaining the doctrine of compensatory tax held that the compensatory tax is a facially discriminatory tax that imposes on inter-state commerce. It does not offend the negative aspect of the Commerce Clause. For the purpose of such doctrine, the taxes on inter-state and intra-state to ensure that the state is merely imposing countervailing burdens on comparable commerce must be imposed on substantially equivalent events transactions, to justify any levy as a compensatory tax, a state must, as a threshold matter, identify the intra-state tax burden for which the state is attempting to compensate. In *Oregon Waste Sys. v. Deptt. of Env.*,[119] the Court said that in order to justify a charge on inter-state commerce as a compensatory tax, a state must as a threshold matter, identify the inter-state tax burden for which the state is attempting to compensate, The tax on inter-state commerce must be shown roughly to

---

116. *Freightlines and Construction Holding Ltd. v. New South Wales*, 1968 A.C. 625.
117. *Aero Mayflower Transit Co. v. Board of R.R. Commrs.*, 332 U.S. 197 (1942).
118. (1994) 128 L.Ed. 2d 639.
119. (1994) 128 L.Ed. 2d. 13.

approximate, but should not exceed, the amount of the tax on intra-state commerce, and the events on which the inter-state and intra-state taxes are imposed must be substantially similar, that is must be sufficiently similar in substance to serve as mutually exclusive proxies for each other.

In *Fulton Corp. v. Faulkner,*[120] Court identified the nature of compensatory tax. It is a state tax which is on its face discriminatory, but may still survive scrutiny under the Commerce Clause, if it is a truly compensatory tax, that is, a tax designed simply to make inter-state commerce bear a burden already borne by intra-state commerce. A valid compensatory tax may be found where the state, as a threshold matter, identifies the intra-state tax burden for which the state is attempting to compensate. The tax on inter-state commerce is shown roughly to approximate, but not exceed, the amount of the tax on intra-state commerce, and the events on which the inter-state and intra-state taxes are imposed are substantially equivalent, that is, sufficiently similar in substance to serve as mutually exclusive proxies for each other.

In *South Central Bell Telephone Co. v. Alabama*[121] the issue was "foreign franchise tax a compensatory tax ?" In connection of this issue the Court held that a state franchise tax on foreign corporations discriminates against inter-state commerce in violation of the Commerce Clause, where the tax facially discriminates against foreign corporations by allowing domestic corporations to reduce their franchise tax liability simply by reducing the par value of their stock, while denying foreign corporations the same ability. Such discrimination is borne out in practice, as the average domestic corporation pays substantially less franchise tax than it would pay if treated as a foreign corporations, and the state cannot justify the discrimination on the ground that the foreign franchise tax is complementary or compensatory tax that offsets the tax burden which other state taxes impose on domestic corporations, because the tax burdens are neither roughly approximate nor similar in substance.

The position of law available in India is that a tax may be a hindrance on the freedom of commerce apart from the provisions of Art. 304(a). The matter arose directly for consideration in *Atiabari Tea Co. v. State of Assam,*[122] and it was held that such tax laws should satisfy the conditions laid down in the proviso to Art. 304(b), viz. previous assent of the President of India to the bill and that such tax should be reasonable restriction in the public interest. In the above decision the validity of Assam Taxation (on Goods carried by Road or Inland Waterways) Act, 1961 was challenged. The Act had imposed a tax on tea carried through inland waters. The appellants before the court were of two types The *first* category grew tea in West Bengal and while sending it to the port of Calcutta (situated in West Bangal) had to travel partly through the rivers in Assam, and the *second* category grew tea in

---

120. (1996) 123 L.Ed. 2d 796.
121. (1996) 526 L.Ed. 2d U.S. 160.
122. A.I.R. 1961 S.C. 232.

Assam and sent it to the port of Calcutta. Justice Gajendragadkar, who spoke on behalf of the majority, held[123] that the test was whether such restriction directly and immediately restricted[124] and impeded the free flow and movement of trade.

A tax on the transport or movement of goods solely on the basis that the goods are thus carried or transported was held to affect directly the freedom of trade contemplated by Art. 301[125] Justice Shah, who concurred with the majority, observed that movement was not an essential ingredient of trade and commerce. According to him[126] the guarantee was addressed to tariffs, licences, marketing regulations, price control, nationalisation, economic or social planning, discriminatory tariffs, compulsory appropriation of goods, freezing and standstill orders and other orders affecting the freedom directly and immediately. Thus, it was held that all taxation touching the above matters were hit by Art. 301.

The view of the *Majority in Atiabari Tea Co.*, it could be seen, would have put the taxing power of states at a disadvantage as President sanction was required for imposing such a tax. As the learned Chief Justice pointed out, taxation in every case could not be an impediment. For example, a cess imposed on sugarcane growers for making transport facilities to reach the cane to the factory makes it feasible for opening new means of communication or for improving old ones. According to him, the public purpose is implicit in every taxation except where it imposes a high tariff wall, or prevents import into or export out of a state. Hence, the question really boils down to whether the tax in its true nature and effect is an impediment to the free flow of goods and commodities between one State and other. It was also pointed out that the Assam legislation was a simple taxing statute and also that it would not be in the interest of Assam to put any such impediment as Assam was a tea producing state which had to send the goods to Calcutta for export.

Keeping in view the impact of *Atiabari decision* on federal set-up and reaction of states, the matter became subject of another decision in *Automobile Transport Ltd. v. State of Rajasthan.*[127] The appellants carried on the business of plying stage carriages intra-state and inter-state. Regarding both these routes the appellant's Vehicles had to travel through a portion of the roads in the State of Rajasthan. The appellants were asked to pay tax under the Rajasthan Motor Vehicles Taxation Act, 1951. Justice S.K. Das, on behalf of the majority, examined the three lines of views propounded in *Atiabari Tea Co.* in detail. The view of Shah, J. was rejected as its adoption, it was held, would result for

123. *Id.* at p. 245, Wanchoo and Das Gupta, JJ. along with him Shah, J. concurred Sinha, C.J. dissented.
124. Wynes, Legislative, Executive and Judicial powers in Australia, 1970 at p. 248.
125. A.I.R. 1961 S.C. 232 at p. 253.
126. *Id* at p. 260 and Krishna Iyer, J. in *Fatehchand v. State of Maharashtra*, A.I.R. 1977 S.C. 1825 at p. 1834.
127. AIR 1962 S.C. 1406.

all practical purposes in "an end of state autonomy even within the fields allotted to them under the distribution of powers by our Constitution ". All laws whether dealing with taxation or not which had only an indirect effect on trade and commerce were held to be beyond the reach of Article 304(b). The majority also rejected the other view characterized as the narrow interpretation by Sinha, C.J. The majority view in *Atiabari Tea Co.* was adopted with a clarification that regulatory measures and measures imposing compensatory taxes did not fall within the provision to Article 301 and hence need not comply with the proviso to Article 304(b). The Rajasthan statute was found to be compensatory as the tax was found not at all heavy[128] and the State was found to spend more for the upkeep and maintenance of the roads than it received by way of tax.

Justice Subba Rao, who concurred with the majority, held that restrictions obstructed the freedom while regulations promoted it. Regulations such as provision for lighting, speed, good condition of vehicles, timings, rules of the road and similar others really facilitate the freedom of movement rather than retard it. Regarding the application of this part to taxation statutes, the Learned Judge observed that in case where such taxes had only an indirect effect, as in where vehicles were taxed as property the tax would be valid. Even in such cases if the burden is very heavy, it may be considered a direct burden.

The minority Judgment was delivered by Hidayatullah, J. who reviewed the constitutional history with regard to Part XIII of the Constitution. According to him the only taxes which are outside the purview of Article 301 are general taxes[129] which fall on all persons including those engaged in trade and commerce. Regarding trade barriers it was observed that restrictions might be diverse, subtle and disguised and the nature of tax and its effect on trade and commerce were held to be the things to be considered. Regarding the Australian concept of regulatory and compensatory measures the Learned Judge observed that the detailed provisions of Part XIII rendered the importation of the concept unnecessary and impermissible. It was also held that so far as out-of-state vehicles were concerned, as in the present case, their entry into the state was barred unless the tax was paid. The Learned Judge also pointed out that the particular tax involved would not have been regarded as compensatory or regulatory even in Australia.[130] The Tax was held bad not being incidental to trade but directly on it and on its movement.

From the above discussion it is clear that the majority accepted the general principle that the compensatory or regulatory provisions, whether by

128. *Automobile Transport. Ltd v. State of Rajasthan,* A.I.R. 1958 Raj. 114 at p. 117.

129. In an Australian case *Commonwealth Freighter Pty. Ltd. v. Sneddon* (1959) 102. C.L.R. 280 at p. 289. Dixon, C.J. observed that the incidents of inter-state commerce which were "on premises occupied by a carrier carrying on an inter-state business, his profits may be taxed, so may his petrol".

130. Dixon, C.J. in *Hughes & Vale Pty. Ltd. v. New South Wales* (1955) 93 C.L.R. 127 at p. 182.

way of a tax or not, would not attract the proviso to Article 304(b). Hence, *first*, the states are free to impose such restrictions without the concurrence of the federal executive and *secondly*, such measures may also pass the test of 'reasonableness in the interest of public' easily. The latter part of the statement only means that a regulatory or compensatory provision usually would be viewed by courts as a reasonable restriction on the freedom of commerce and this initial presumption may be rebutted by persons who allege the contrary.

In other federations like the U.S.A. and Australia also it is an accepted principle that the inter-state business must pay its way. The term tax barrier applies the U.S.A. only to those taxes which tend to place inter-state business at a disadvantage[131] in competing with local business. Apart from these general principles the law in U.S.A. on this point is for from clear and it has been observed "seizing both horns of the dilemma, one horn playing the melody that inter-state commerce must be free of taxation and the other that even inter-state commerce must pay its way, the Court has scarcely resolved the dissonance."[132] In Australia the matter was considered by the Privy Council in *Freightlines and Construction Holding Ltd. v. New South Wales*,[133] and it was held that if a state fixed a charge for the convenience or service provided by it or its agency and imposed it upon those who chose to avail themselves of it, the freedom of commerce under Section 92 might well be considered unimpaired. In Australia, it has been held that[134] the cost incurred in enforcement of a law against pillaging of cargo could not be raised by a tax upon goods discharged from inter-state ships or that a tax could not be imposed upon transport of goods or passengers by road in order to meet the cost of enforcing the traffic laws. The exact frontiers of such taxation are bound to remain unclear even in the face of the attempt by eminent judges to fix them precisely.

The majority view in the *Automobile Transport Ltd*. that a compensatory tax or regulatory measure is not within the purview of the proviso to Article 304(b) seems to have been accepted as the law on the point, though Gajendragadkar, J. was not ready to agree[135] on the same. That a compensatory tax also can be a reasonable rèstriction under Article 304(b) seems to be clear from *Khyerbari Tea Co. v. State of Assam*.[136] The case was concerned with the validity of Assam Taxation (On Goods Carried by Road or on Inland Waterways) Act, 1961. The Assam Act, which was struck down in *Atiabari Tea Co.*[137] was re-enacted and received the assent of the President of India. The only question remained to be considered was whether the tax

131. *Bode v. Barrett*, 344 U.S. 583 (1953).
132. Poul A. Freund, "Umpiring the Federal system, 54 Col. L. Rev. 561, at pp. 569-70 (1954).
133. (1967) 116 C.L.R. 1 at p. 5.
134. *Hughes & Vale Pty. Ltd v. New South Wales* (1955) 93 C.L.R.127 at p 176-77.
135. *Rai Ramakrishna v. State of Bihar*, A.I.R. 1963 S.C. 1667 at 1677.
136. A.I.R. 1964 S.C. 925 at p. 940.
137. A.I.R. 1961 S.C. 232.

was reasonable restriction under Art. 304(b). The majority Judgment was delivered by Gajendragadkar, J. and it was assumed[138] that the tax was not compensatory in character.[139] The Court held that the tax was levied not merely to raise general revenue for the state (which itself was a public purpose)[140] but utilized for keeping the waterways and the roads in good condition and that would render the tax a reasonable restriction on inter-state trade. The state of Assam had filed an affidavit in which it was stated that tea and jute were the main products of the state, and in order to have an easy and regular flow of trade it had to maintain good roads. The trade through water was cheaper and the state also had to incur large sums for maintaining the waterways. The affidavit also showed that every year the expenditure incurred was much more than the revenue received from tax. It was held that this fact was sufficient to uphold the tax as reasonable restriction.

It is true that the majority held that the tax here was not compensatory in character. But applying the test of the majority in *Automobile Transport Ltd.*, viz. whether a state needs the collection of the tax to maintain or construct new facilities for the flow of trade and commerce, the tax could have been upheld compensatory in character. In *Assam v. Labanya Probha Devi* [141], Assam Motor Vehicles Tax Amendment Acts of 1963 and 1966, which added new schedules to the Act, prescribing new rates of tax of vehicles, were challenged. The Acts were held to be "only regulatory measures improving compensatory taxes for facilitating trade, commerce and intercourse". In *Nazeeria Motor Service v. State of Andhra Pradesh*[142] the State did not attempt to justify the tax as compensatory or regulatory measure and hence the Court examined the reasonableness or the levy under Art. 304(b). The tax was sustained on the ground that the operators were permitted to increase the fares and freight charges and the burden of tax would not fall upon the operators but only[143] on the passengers and goods. In *Malwa Bus Service (P) Ltd. v. State of Punjab*[144] the tax on stage carriage operators was upheld after verifying that the receipt of revenue and expenditure on road maintenance was proportionate.

In *Meenakshi v. State of Karnataka,*[145] the state had abolished octroi and to compensate the loss of revenue increased the tax on stage carriages. The abolition of octroi was a measure which facilitated commerce but why the stage carriage buses should shoulder the burden instead of goods vehicles

138. A.I.R. 1964 S.C. 925 at p 933.
139. *Khyerbari Tea Co. v. State of Assam,* A.I.R. 1964 S.C. 925.
140. *Id.* at p. 940.
141. A.I.R. 1967 S.C. 1575.
142. A.I.R. 1970 S.C. 1864.
143. *Id.* at p. 581.
144. A.I.R. 1983 S.C. 634.
145. A.I.R. 1983 S.C. 1283.

was difficult to understand. While upholding the levy as compensatory the Court did not give any valid reason.

In most of the decisions the tax, whether on motor vehicles or on passengers and goods, had been challenged by residents[146] of the state concerned. It has to be remembered that in such cases the grievance cannot be serious as they are taxed by their own representatives. In this respect *International Tourist Corpn. v. State of Haryana*[147] is important and needs to be analysed. Here out-of-the-State vehicles, operating on national highways, were bound to pay tax while merely passing through Haryana. Justice Chinnappa Reddy did not refer to the figures in budget and only referred to the various responsibilities the State had to meet. The tax was upheld as it was only proportionate to the fare and freight of the distance travelled in Haryana. The decision correctly brings out the consideration to be applied in cases where out-of-State operators were involved.

A tax may be imposed for regulatory purposes, for revenue purpose, as a compensatory measure to defray the whole or part of the expenses incurred or as protective tariff on inter-state goods. The last one, if on goods is prohibited under Article 304(a). The regulatory taxes and compensatory taxes are outside the purview of the freedom guaranteed under Part XIII of the Constitution. If that be the case, then the only remaining category of tax is one imposed for revenue purpose, that is to say, taxation simpliciter in the language of Sinha, C.J. in *Atiabari Tea Co.* in *State of Madras v. Nataraja Mudaliar*[148], the challenge against the Central Sales Tax Act, was that different rates of tax prevailed in various exporting states and that resulted in discrimination and obstruction of the free flow of inter-state trade in similar goods. Repelling the contention, the Court held that the flow of trade did not necessarily depend upon rates of Sales Tax, but did depend upon a variety of circumstances such as source of supply, place of consumption, existence of trade channels, etc.

It is clear from the above discussion that a tax imposed for revenue purpose also is beyond the challenge under Articles 301 and 304(b). If so the only tax which seems to have been hit by Part XIII is a discriminatory tax, or better still a tax in the nature of a barrier on free trade or commerce, which is expressly prohibited under Article 304(a).

In the case of all-India tourist permits, several states had agreed to exempt vehicles if they had paid tax in the state where they were registered and on a reciprocal basis. The facility was misused by operators by getting their vehicles registered in one State and operating them elsewhere. The State of Karnataka later withdrew the exemption and this was challenged in *B.A. Jayaram v. Union of India.*[149] The Court refused to interfere on the ground

146. *Misrilal Jain v. State of Orissa* (1977) 3 S.C.C. 212.
147. A.I.R. 1981 S.C. 774.
148. A.I.R. 1969 S.C. 147 at p. 155 followed in *State of Tamil Nadu v. Sitolakshmi Mills,* A.I.R. 1975 S.C. 1505, at p. 1509.
149. A.I.R. 1983 S.C. 1005.

that, *"Not to pat on the back is not to stab on the back."* The withdrawal of exemption was certainly a retrograde step and the Court did not even examine whether the burden of tax was proportionate to the use of roads inside the state.

Where such taxes affect inter-state trade they should contain special provision alleviating the burden on inter-state commerce. For example, in the leading case of *Sainik Motors v. State of Rajasthan*[150]. The court assumed[151] that such a route would be an inter-state route. The petitioners were doing intra-state business and neither it was alleged[152] that any inter-state route existed nor that substantial part of such a route lay in another state.

In *Khyerbari Tea Co. v. State of Assam*[153], Ganendragadkar, J. observed that the law of taxation was in the ultimate analysis the result of balancing of several complex considerations and it would be unreasonable to insist that a flat rate must always be treated as unreasonable.

Mere data reading amounts collected by way of tax being below the actual expenses of the State for maintaining roads, should not be sufficient or conclusive regarding the compensatory nature of the tax.

Regarding correlation between the tax recovered and the cost incurred in *Malwa Bus Service (P) Ltd. v. State of Punjab*[154], Venkataramiah observed:

> "Courts, however, cannot insists upon an exact correlation between the tax recovered and the cost so incurred because such exact correlation is in the very nature of things impossible to attain. There may be in some cases a little excess recovery by way of taxes. That by itself should not result in the nullification of the law imposing the tax if the extent of such excess is marginal having regard to the total cost involved."

In *Western Electronics v. State of Gujarat,*[155] it was held that it is therefore now well settled that taxing laws can be restrictions on trade, commerce and intercourse, if they hamper the flow of trade and if they are not what can be termed to be compensatory taxes or regulatory measures. Sales tax of the kind under consideration here, was not said to be a measure regulating any trade nor was it a compensatory tax levied for the use of trading facilities.

In *State of Bihar v. Bihar Chamber of Commerce,*[156] the Supreme Court held that it is not and it can not be stipulated that for the purpose of establishing the compensatory nature of the tax, it is necessary to establish that every rupee collected on account of the entry tax should be shown to be spent on

---

150. A.I.R. 1961 S.C. 1480.
151. *Central Greyhound Lines v. Mealey*, 334 U.S. 653 (1947).
152. *Sainik Motors v. State of Rajasthan*, A.I.R. 1961 S.C. 1480 at p. 1486.
153. A.I.R. 1964 S.C. 925 at p. 940.
154. A.I.R. 1983 S.C. 634 at p. 640.
155. A.I.R. 1988 S.C. 2038 at pp. 2039-40.
156. A.I.R. 1996 S.C. 2344.

providing the trading facilities. It is enough if some connection is established between the tax and the trading facilities provided : The connection can be a direct one or an indirect one. Thus, the entire state is divided into local areas when no part of the state is left uncovered by a local area and when the impugned tax is levied for the purposes of the welfare schemes being undertaken, the tax cannot but be compensatory in nature. The impugned tax will help the state in providing and improving the trading facilities since the interest of the state lies in promoting trade and commerce in goods and commodities with and within the state of Bihar. Therefore, it can be said that the impugned tax is compensatory in nature. This finding is by itself sufficient to negative the attack based on Art. 301 but even if it is assumed that the state has not established the said fact, the result is not different.

However, *Ashok Nagar Welfare Association v. R.K. Sharma*[157] overruled *Jayaram*[158] and stated that a mere claim that tax is compensatory would not suffice. Whether a tax is commendatory or not cannot be made to depend on the preamble of the stature imposing it. A tax cannot also be said not to be compensatory because the precise or specific amount collected is not actually used to providing any facilities.

Thus, in relation to state taxing power on inter-state transportation the Courts have upheld state laws even though it was found to provide for no fair recompense, if the rate of tax was not excessive or prohibitive and if amount collected from the tax was more than the expenditure incurred on maintenance and construction of roads. The Courts have allowed taxes on spared buses merely kept or use; they have ignored the fact that the tax collected has been kept in a separate fund; they have not insisted upon separate assessment on the basis of the types of vehicles, their weight, mileage covered by them and nature of road used. And when such a differentation has been done by the states, the Court have allowed the law repelling the charge of discrimination.[159] They have also ignored if the income was lightly more than expenditure incurred and when the income has been much more than expenditure incurred by the state on maintenance and construction of roads, bridges, etc. state taxation has been allowed by taking into account the expenditure in earlier years. The validity of taxes like octroi and tolls have been upheld in view of their compensatory nature.

3. REGULATION OF E-COMMERCE THROUGH TAXATION

A. Rationale behind Taxing E-Commerce

It should not come as surprise to anybody that the question of how the Internet and E-commerce will affect taxes has received such early and intense policy attention. Most analyses of E-Commerce and tax tend to focus on the specifics of how to implement existing regimes given the changing

157. A.I.R. 2002 S.C. 322 at pp. 334-35.

158. *B.A. Jayaram v. Union of India*, A.I.R. 1983 S.C. 1005.

159. *Shyam Sunder Roy v. State of Bihar*, A.I.R. (1983) Pat. 14.

environment. This understandable since business tax accountants and government revenue authorities have to deal right now with the very real questions of, on the one side, what taxes do I owe to whom, and, on the other side, how much revenue are we likely to receive into government coffers. Taxation should be viewed in terms of its effect on the economy as a whole and fiscal policy as the major policy tool of governments. Taxation is clearly part of a political economy. Tax principles naturally involve ethical and political question. Taxation is the principle means by which governments can attempt to redistribute wealth and bring about social change through various social policies. There are several reasons why E-commerce should be taxed. It's only fair-taxes should not depend on the way you buy it. As E-Commerce stands right now, a local music store has to collect 5% sales tax on a CD when it is purchased, while you could buy the same exact CD over the phone or on the Internet from CDnow.com directly, and by doing so avoid any sales tax. Taxes are very important for the state governments, who heavily rely on sales taxes to fund schools, pay state salaries, and repair roads. States are worried that if E-commerce continues to grow, business will shift more to tax-free Internet shopping, taking business away from the normal methods of shopping. By doing so, the states will lose valuable revenue. States are already losing Rs. 90 to Rs. 120 billion a year on mail-order sales.

B. Taxes on Internet Transaction in United States

The Internet Tax Freedom Act ("ITFA") has placed a moratorium until October of 2001 on new discriminatory state sales taxes on E-commerce and the levying of new internet access taxes.[160] Significantly, the ITFA "prohibits state and local governments from requiring remote electronic merchants to collect sales tax based solely on the ability of a consumer to access that merchant's computer server" and "prevents states from imposing taxes solely because a remote seller displays content on or processes orders through an Internet service provider's out-of-state computer server.[161]

The ITFA has been highly controversial. State and local officials remain greatly concerned that the Act will become permanent, resulting in a loss of revenues.[162] Advocates of E-commerce feel that an electronic tax will burden on-line transactions, discourage E-commerce, and violate the Commerce Clause. However, the Advisory Commission on Electronic Commerce has noted the need to "be respectful of sovereignty of state and local jurisdictions".[163] While Congress has addressed taxes and indecent

160. Internet Tax Freedom Act, Pub. I, No. 105-277, Title XI, Codified at 47 USCA 151 (West 1998), cited by Melissa G. Liazas, Can States Impose Registration on Online Charitable Solicitors? Uni. Chi Rev. (2000) Vol. 67 at p. 1379.

161. Lisa I. Fries, Internet Taxation: An Advisory Committee is Embroiled in Debate, NY, L.J. 5 (Sept. 23, 1999).

162. *Ibid.*

163. Advisory Commission on Electronic Commerce, Issues and Policy options paper: Final Draft submitted to the Commission from Drafting Sub-committee, 12-03-99.

content on the Internet, it has not passed legislation providing for comprehensive federal control of the Internet. It has not addressed many aspects of the internet, including solicitation laws. Thus, there has been no preemption of state solicitation laws as applied to the internet.

In the context of taxes on Internet transactions, the Advisory Commission on Electronic Commerce, created by the Internet Tax Freedom Act, has recognized the need to for state and local governments to make every effort to simplify current sales and use tax systems. Similarly, which most states and some localities requiring solicitors to register, simplification in registration could ease the burden for charities while still encouraging charitable giving and protection legitimate state interests. Further moves toward uniform requirement could do so, as could a coordinated database.

C. Taxing E-Commerce in India

(a) Direct Taxes

Indian residents are taxed on their world-wide income. Non-residents are taxed on their Indian source income.

(i) Residence

A company is considered resident in India in any previous year, if it is an Indian Company; or during that year, the control and management of its affairs is situated wholly in India.[164] Every Indian company is deemed to be resident in India even if its control and management is situated wholly or partly abroad, while a non-Indian company is deemed to be resident only if its control and management is situated wholly in India. Thus, most foreign companies fall under the non-resident category.

(ii) The Source Rule in India

Section 9 of the Income Tax Act, 1961 (ITA) specifies various types of income which would be regarded as deemed to accrue or arise in India and therefore become taxable in India. The income is covered under this section when it is not chargeable on the basis of its receipt. This principle is applicable to both residents as well as non-residents.

Any income, though directly or indirectly, which is derived through or from any property in India, or business connection in India, or any asset or source of income in India, or transfer of capital asset situated in India, is deemed to accrue or arise in India.

However, in case of a business of which not all operations are carried out in India, only such part of income as is attributable to Indian operations would be regarded as income accrued or arisen in India.

Business connection: The expression 'business connection' has a wide but uncertain meaning. It has no precise definition. A business connection involves a relation between business carried on by a non-resident which

164. Section 6(3) of the Income Tax Act, 1961.

yields profits or gains and some activity in India, which contributes directly or indirectly to the earning of those profits or gains. Thus, to establish business connection, there should exist an element of continuity between the business of the non-resident and the activity in India. The concept of 'business connection' is similar to but much wider in meaning as compared to PE. If it were established that a non-resident has a business connection in India, then his income would be subject to Indian taxation under Sec. 9 of the ITA. However, the tax would apply only on such income which is attributable to business in India.

Royalty/Fee for technical services: Section 9(vi) of the ITA deals with the source rule in respect or royalty income. Royalty income is deemed to accrue or arise in India if it is paid either by a resident or a non-resident in respect of any right, property, information or services utilized for carrying on a business in India if it is paid either by a resident or a non-resident in respect of any services utilized for carrying on business in India.

(iii) Withholding Provision

Any person responsible for making any payment to a non-resident of a sum chargeable to tax in India is required to deduct income-tax at source. This can be done at the time of credit of such income to the account of the payee or at the times of payment, whichever is earlier.

(iv) The Treaty-Domestic Law Interface

Section 90(2) of the ITA provides that Act, will apply to an assessee only to the extent that it is more beneficial to the assessee as compared to the relevant Double Taxation Avoidance Agreement (DTAA). In the case of a conflict, the more beneficial provision will prevail.

(b) Indirect Tax

(i) Sales Tax

In India, sales tax is levied by the respective states under the state Sales Tax Laws and also by the centre under the Central Sales Tax Act, 1956. A state levies sales tax on the sales that take place inside the state. Sales in the course of inter-state trade and commerce are taxed by the centre under the Central Sales Tax Act, 1956. The state from which movement of goods commences collects these taxes on behalf of the centre and retains the proceeds of the taxes. Where the sale takes place in the course of import into India, or export out of India, no tax is leviable under the Central Sales Tax Act, or the State Sales Tax Laws.

The specific issue that EC would give rise to is sites of a sale. In the case of corporeal or tangible goods, which are specific or ascertained, their sale is deemed to take place in the state in which they are at time the contract of sale is made. In the case of unascertained or future goods, the sale is deemed to take place in the state in which the goods are at the time of their appropriation to the contract of sale by the seller or by the buyer (Section 4(2) of the Central Sales Tax Act). Therefore, the time of conclusion of the contract is of critical importance to the question of situs. The situs of intangibles depends on where the contract of sale can be said to be concluded. Such sales cannot be in the course of inter-state trade or commerce or in the course of import or export as there is no movement of goods from one state to another or from one country to another.

(ii) Customs Duties

The only significant charge introduced by e-commerce would be taxation on the on-line transfer of goods. Where the transaction is concluded on-line, and the goods are delivered physically, there is no issue regarding the tracing and taxation of such transactions. However, when the goods are delivered on-line, tracing of the delivery of such goods for the impositions of tax continues to be a significant issue facing tax authorities, and remains to be sorted out. The present taxation regime is not wholly equipped to face such challenges and is dependant on voluntary disclosures by the persons engaged in these transactions.

8

Regulation of Trade, Commerce and Intercourse through 'VAT'

I. TOWARDS AN APPROPRIATE VAT SYSTEM FOR A FEDERAL ECONOMY

Let us now analyse the current division of responsibility between the Centre and the States with regard to commodity taxation and the efforts initiated during the last few years to introduce the VAT in place of union-excise duty at the central and the sales taxes at the state levels. The VAT is a tax on supplies of goods and services applied at all stages of the production process. If is charged by the supplier and then credited by the users of the inputs in the course of doing business. Each transaction leaves on invoice path, so the VAT system essentially relies on 'double-entry' book-keeping by VAT-registered businesses on both sides of a transaction. The final consumer is not a VAT registered entity, so ultimately pays the tax. The Indian sales tax system is different in that final users (usually retail) pay the taxes, principally only on tangible property (with exceptions) and usually not on services. Business inputs generally are exempt from the tax. Several federal countries—Argentina, Austria, Brazil, Canada, Columbia, the Federal Republic of Germany, and Mexico—levy a VAT. The VATs of Argentina, Austria, Germany and Mexico, are all centrally-controlled with revenue-sharing arrangements between the federal and provincial governments. It has been the experience that the VAT in federal economy presents several difficult issues, which have their repercussions on the sensitive federal-state political relations. That the only three OECD countries which still have not switched over to the VAT, i.e. Australia, Switzerland and the US which are all federations is also significant. While there do not seem to be any legal proscriptions against the federal government adopting a VAT despite the fact that to date general sales taxes have typically been the domain of the states, there could be difficulties in administering a federal VAT in conjunction with the states' Retail Sales Tax Systems (RSTSs). The simplest solution, according to Tait[1], is to entrust the administration and collection of the VAT either with the states or with the federal government and then use a formula to share the revenue between the central government and the states. If this is unacceptable owing to the loss of fiscal autonomy, then a federal VAT might have a state VAT 'piggybacked' on it. Tait[2] holds that as a model for other federal countries, the German VAT illustrates the need for agreed federal and state legislation. Base, structure and rates once established, the formula for splitting the proceeds may be the most clear and least contentious method of revenue distribution. He, however, hastens to add that even the limited flexibility in recent years of the federal state split from 68/32 to about 70/30 in Germany was not achieved without considerable disagreement and concludes that in a federal system.

Where the states try to retain more discretion over their own exemptions, rates and revenues, the system would not work. While the system may be working satisfactorily in Germany, it should be appreciated that fiscal federalism issues still stand in the way of a smooth switch over to a national VAT even in an industrial country like Canada, not to speak of the problems associated with introduction of the VAT in developing country federations.

2. PERMISSIBLE LIMITS OF TAXATION AND THE VAT SYSTEM

A. Commodity Taxation

In the field of commodity taxation, the Constitution of India has assigned the powers of customs and excise taxation to the Central Government with the exception of excise on alcoholic liquor, while the states have been given the powers of sales taxation. It is necessary to elaborate the nature and import of these two levies, namely, the union-excise duty by the centre and the sales-tax by the states, while there is no essential difference between the two from the angle of incidence on the consumer, it has to be recognised that the two taxes are neither identical nor interchangeable and that there are some basic differences between the two different levies. In the first place, an excise is a levy at the production point whereas a sales tax is levied on a commodity at one or more points of sale or purchase between the stages of production and final consumption. If there is only one stage at which any particular commodity completes its production process, the incidence of an excise duty should theoretically be only at one point. Since, however, the component parts of the commodity could have themselves been subject to excise duty, an excise duty on the final product could in practice involve a multiple duty on the components unless the duty is based on the value-added components only. It was with a view to eliminate cascading in the incidence of excise duty that the government of India

1. Tait, Alan A. (1988): Value Added Tax, International Practice and Problems, International Monetary Fund, Washington, D.C. at p. 155.
2. *Id.* at p. 156.

introduced the MODVAT some time in 1985.[3] In case of sales, the same commodity might pass through various stages of sales, making itself susceptible to sales tax at more than one point, depending upon the system of the sales tax levy. While an excise duty ends at the production point and does not take into account, can indirectly, elements of cost that are incurred after the production stage, namely, freight, insurance, distribution charges and the like, a sales tax is on a much more comprehensive concept of cost and touches not merely the cost at the production point, but also subsequent elements including profits and the excise duty itself.

The excise duty in India, being a union levy, does not differentiate between one region and another and is uniform throughout the country while the sales tax structure and the rates of sales taxes differ from state to state. Again, while most of the excise duties are specific, sales tax are *ad valorem* levies with the result that during a period of high inflation, the sales tax yield automatically goes up, other things remaining the same. In certain countries where excise duties are exclusively reserved for the Centre, the levy of sales tax by states has been held to be unconstitutional on the ground that they are substantially the same as excise duties. Similarly, the question has also been raised whether the *ad valorem* excise duties are not really sales taxes. Despite all these similarities, both taxes have "distinguishing features" and both have "positive place in a comprehensive system of taxation and are expressly mentioned in our Constitution".

In order to minimise the cascading effects of excise taxation of inputs, the Government of India, in 1985, introduced a modified form or excise duty called the MODVAT. Shome[4] points out that unlike in almost all countries which have introduced the VAT—where the conversion of a turnover tax regime into a VAT was preceded by a year or longer of administrative preparation, computerisation and taxpayer education—in India the process has been one of iteration towards a VAT, both in terms of tax structure and tax administration.[5] For example, the credit mechanism was introduced for a few commodities at the beginning, and its coverage was slowly extended to other commodities. In the following two or three years, the MODVAT was extended to cover practically all chapters of the Central excise tariff except petroleum products, textile products, tobacco, cinematogrphic films and matches. This practice, according to Shome, is quite different from the usual model of including all goods under the VAT with a few exemptions and excluding small business under a threshold based on turnover. The fact, however, remains that MODVAT is not a value added tax in the real sense of the term: The so-called Indian MODVAT is not a VAT at all, but rather a form of modified excise duty. The MODVAT is essentially manufacturing excise tax with credit allowed for excise duty and customs in a limited

3. Chakraborty, A.: The Idea Behind MODVAT: Capital (Calcutta), Vol. 196.
4. Shome Parthasarathi, VAT: Structural Aspects and Experience in Value Added Tax in India: A Progress Report (1997).
5. *Ibid.*

number of industries, introduced mainly with a view to eliminate the cascading effect of multi-point excise levies.

Under the MODVAT scheme, union excise duties on most manufacturing goods have been converted to incorporate a credit mechanism for taxes paid on inputs. Apart from reduction in the number of tax rates, credit is available for tax on raw materials as well as capital goods. Further the earlier requirment of matching inputs with particular output has been eliminated

B. Cross Border Trade

(a) European Union Experience

The main reason why the VAT was originally adopted as the required form for general sales taxation in the European Union was its advantage in implementing the destination principle with respect to cross-border trade. As observed by *Bird and Genderon*[6] only with the value added form of sales tax could member countries be sure that imports were fairly treated in comparison to domestic products, and that exports were not subsidized by over-generous rebates at the border. "It is thus somewhat ironic that the best way to apply VAT to cross-border trade within the EU has been a matter of considerable debate since the beginning. This issue has not yet been resolved."

According to Keen and Smith[7], the destination method is both more compatible with independent taxation of consumption and, in practice, less likely to result in important economic distortions. At present, The EU applies the destination principle using "the deferred payment" method. Exports by firms in one member country A to registered traders in other member countries are zero-rated in A without border clearance being required. Such sales are therefore treated in the same way are all sales outside the EU: In contrast to imports from non-EU countries, however, imports by registered traders in A from firms in other EU member countries are not taxed at the border. Instead, importers in A in effect pay the VAT on imports at country A's rates on their own sales since they have no input tax credits to offset against the tax due. The system works on a self-assessment basis; importers are supposed to declare their imports compute the VAT that would be due, and claim credit for that VAT, all in the same return. The effect is that the VAT is collected on imports only when they are resold or incorporated in goods sold by the importing firm, since imported inputs, unlike domestic inputs, will not generate offsetting input tax credits at that time.

---

6. Bird Richard M. and Genderon, Pierre Pascal : Dual VATs and Cross Border Trade: Two Problems and One Solution? International Trade and Public Finance, 5, Kluwer Academic Public Boston at pp. 429-42.
7. Keen, M. and S. Smith: The Future of Value Added Tax in the European Union, Economic Policy, 23 at p. 375.

The system may be contrasted with the 'clearing house' method under which the VAT would be charged on exports by the exporting state, with a credit allowed for this VAT by the importing state as for any other input VAT, but at the tax rate imposed by the exporting state. Revenue accounts would then be balanced between states either on a transaction basis or more likely, as in the recent European Commission proposal, in accordance with consumption statistics. The deferred payment system, which in effect puts reliance on private sector accounting subject to VAT audits, appears to work as well as or better than explicit public offsetting of accounts. This is particularly so because, since 1993, exporters who zero-rate sales to other member countries have been required to quote the VAT registration number of the buyer. Keen and Smith[8] see at least three problems with the deferred payment system as it now operates in the EU : (i) the sustainability of revenues in the face of cross-border shopping, (ii) the asymmetrical treatment of trade within and between member states, and (iii) problems in cross-border audits, which must rely on the inevitably weak reed of inter-jurisdictional information exchange.

(b) Canadian Experience

At the present time, as Bird[9] notes, Canada may be most interesting country in the world for sales tax aficionados. The Country has ten provinces, with five distinct sales tax systems. There is a federal VAT, the Goods and Services Tax (GST), that applies throughout the Country. In one province (Alberta), the GST is the only sales tax. In four provinces, namely, British Columbia, Saskatchewan, Manitoba, and Ontario, in addition to the GST there is a separate Retail Sales Tax (RST) applied to the GST-exclusive tax base. In one province, Prince Edward Island, the provincial RST is applied to the GST-inclusive tax base. In three provinces, namely, Newfoundland, Nova Scotia, and New Brunswick, there is a joint federal-provincial VAT, called the Harmonised Sales Tax (HST) and administered by the federal government at a uniform rate of 15%. Finally, in one province, Quebec there is a provincial VAT the Quebec Sales Tax (QST), applied to the GST-inclusive tax base. The QST is administered by the provincial government, which also administers the GST in the province on behalf of the federal government.

Canada thus presents a variety of interesting situation: separate federal and provincial VATs administered provincially, joint federal and provincial VATs administers federal, and a federal VAT and provincial RSTs administered separately.

8. *Ibid.*
9. Bird, Richard M., Cost and Complexity of Canada's VAT: The GST in International Perspective, Tax Note International, Vol. 8 (1994).

C. Exploring the Indian Possibilities

While introducing a VAT model in federal India what appears to the most intractable among the various problems that face the states is the one relating to inter-state trade.[10]

(a) The Kelkar Committee

The Kelkar Committee has submitted two reports. One is on direct taxes, levied on incomes and wealth, e.g. income tax, corporate tax, wealth tax). The other is on indirect taxes levied on goods and services (e.g. excise duty, sales tax). The world over, countries are replacing excise duties and sales taxes by Value Added Tax (VAT). We have been moving towards this in India too for years. Hopefully the technical and Jurisdictional problems will be overcome in coming years.

Why are all countries shifting from excise duties to VAT? There are two major reasons. *First*, excise duties have an unwitting cascading effect. For instance, plastic toys are made from petrochemicals, which are made from petroleum products, which are made from crude oil. If excise duty and sales tax are high on crude oil, petrochemicals and petroleum, plastic toys will bear a cascade of taxes even if no tax at all is levied on toys. VAT avoids such cascading. It taxes the difference between the value of output and the value of inputs of every producer. Let us consider a uniform VAT of 20 percent.

The plastic toy manufacturer will pay 20 percent VAT on his sales, but get a VAT refund of 20 percent on the process of petrochemicals and other inputs used in manufacturing. This will avoid cascading, and tax incidence will be consistent 20 percent across all activity. *Second*, VAT will check tax evasion through by providing powerful incentives for honesty. Today, manufacturers may file false returns or none at all. Tax evasion is rampant at every stage.

But a comprehensive VAT, covering all goods and services, will make tax evasion unprofitable. The plastic toy manufacturer may want to escape paying VAT by not declaring his output. But able to claim a refund of the VAT already levied on his purchased inputs. He may not be able to compete with rivals that declare their full production and get VAT refunds. Thus, VAT can induce tax honesty. Let us now take a closer look at what value added really is. It is the difference between our earning and costs, whether we are businessmen or anybody earning wages, rents, interest or professional income.

Apart from physical inputs, what are the other expenses of the toy manufacturer? He pays salaries and wages. He pays rent for hired premises. He pays interest on loans. And he makes a profit. So, the value added by him is the total of four items—wages, rents, interest and profits. The 20 per cent VAT on toys is actually a 20 per cent tax on the wages, rents, interest and

---

10. Sukumar Mukhopadhyay, VAT Options for Inter-state Trade in Federal India, Ex. Law Times, Vol. 139 (2002) 194.

profits of his company. We started with the idea that VAT is a tax on products and services, like toys. Now we suddenly discover that VAT is in fact a tax on different sorts of income wages, rents interest and profits.

VAT is an alchemist converting indirect taxes into direct taxes. It obliges us to confront a basic economic truth : The value of a product is simply the total of incomes of participants in its production.

So, a foolproof VAT will capture all income. Even those who seek to evade VAT will not really succeed. A manufacturer who refuses to declare his production will pay no VAT on his output and no income tax either. But he has already paid VAT on his purchased inputs, and will not be able to claim a refund. However, he is in the tax net.

There remain political and technical problems in extending VAT to every activity. There is great resistance from services. But if we succeed in creating a full-fledged VAT, we will already be taxing all forms of income. In that case, some will ask, why have a separate income tax or corporate tax ? Why not abolish them ?

The middle class and small businessmen will be delighted if the government abolishes direct taxes on income, interest, dividends, and pensions. However, totally abolishing direct taxes will be inequitable. Income tax is progressive the rich pay most, the poor pay nothing. But VAT taxes the rich and poor at the same rate. So, equity requires more than just VAT.

The distinction between direct and indirect taxes is blurred one. We will do well to get the vast bulk of our tax revenue from a comprehensive VAT, and relatively little from income tax.

(b) Comparison with Other Federations

It should, however, be appreciated that giving the power to the states to levy the surcharge on income tax alone would not be enough to compensate the states for agreeing to surrender their powers of sales taxation. This takes us to have a look at the possibility of allowing the states to exploit the corporate income tax base on the lines of the system prevailing in countries like Canada and the US. According to Norregaard,[11] there is almost universal agreement that the taxation of larger business, and in particular corporate profit taxes, should be left to the national government and to provinces or states only where these are very large as in Canada.

The current experience with allocation is found in the U.S., Canada, and Switzerland. In the US, the 46 states that levy corporate income taxes use a factor formula to apportion income to its jurisdiction. Non-business income such as capital gains, royalties, dividends, interest, and rents may be taxed separately by the state if the income is earned in the jurisdiction.

However, some states apportion all sources of business and non-business income. The factors generally include sales, property, and payroll

11. Norregaard John : Tax Assignment in Teresa Ter Minnession (ed.), Fiscal Federalism in Theory and Practices, International Monetary Fund, Washington, DC at p. 66 (1977).

factors but they vary from state to state. Many states use an equally weighted average of payroll, sales, and property but almost half of the states use some other variant, most often by putting twice the weight on the sales factor. Corporate income is measured by adjusting the federal definition for specific state provisions. Maximum rates of corporate income tax at the state level vary from 3.4 per cent in Indiana to 12.25 per cent in Pennsylvania, the average being about 7 per cent.[12] State taxes are deductible from the federal corporate income tax. Though 46 states in the US impose corporate income taxes, the share of corporate income tax in total revenues of the states has declined in the recent years. In fact, Michigan has replace its corporate income tax with a value added tax, which differs from the value added tax, elsewhere in the sense that it is based on the additive method. Under this method, the tax base is determined by adding wages and profits before taxes and debt service with certain adjustments.

In contrast, the Canadian system is based on a more harmonised approach for determining the amount of corporate income allocated to provinces. Partly this is driven by the tax collection agreements which the federal agreement has with seven provinces where by the federal government collects provincial corporate income taxes at no charge and the provinces agree to use the federal corporate base for determining income. The provinces are free to set their own rates of tax and the federal government collects provincial corporate income taxes at no charge and the provinces agree to use the federal corporate base for determining income. The provinces are free to set their own rates of tax and the federal government will administer on their behalf tax credits, namely, investment tax credits for manufacturing equipment or research and development, which reduce the amount of provincial tax owing to the province. Three provinces, Ontario, Quebec and Alberta, collect their own corporate income tax. In fact, these three provinces account for nearly 75 percent of the provincial corporate income tax base in Canada.

All provinces, including those that collect their own corporate income tax, use a common factor formula where equal weights on sales and payroll to determine the shares. Even those provinces which collect their own tax, use a base similar to federal base except for a few adjustments. The federal government provides a 10 per cent tax credit to make room for the provincial corporate income tax. In Switzerland, the cantons levy corporate income taxes on a progressive basis subject to minimum and maximum rates. The Swiss cantons may use their own factor formula and there is no consolidation of returns in Switzerland.[13] In Brazil, the states can levy a 5 per cent surcharge on the corporate income tax. The argument put forward by some of these countries is that the economy could benefit from state and

---

12. S. Gurumurthi, Fiscal Federalism Towards An Appropriate VAT System For a Federal Economy, *Eco. & Pol. Weekly*, Vol. 34 (1999) 2875.
13. Mintz Jack M., The Role of Allocation in a Globalised Corporate Income Tax, WP/98/134, IMF Working Paper, International Monetary Fund, Washington, DC (1998).

local governments competing for industrial development, that local governments are entitled to recoup the cost of public services used by business, and that, in any case, many companies do most of their production and sales within a single jurisdiction.[14]

If one is serious about introducing and implementing a value added tax in its true letter and spirit in India, the system of commodity taxation in vague at present has to undergo a sea change into 'something rich and strange': the union excise duties of the Centre and the sales taxes of the states have to be merged, the central sales tax abolished and the powers of commodity taxation fully vested in the central government to facilitate the transformation of the existing cascading taxes, namely, the union excise duties and sales taxes into a full-fledged value added tax. This has to be invariably accompanied by giving the powers to the states to exploit personal income tax by 'piggybacking' the central income tax base on the one hand and allowing the states to levy corporate income tax on the lines of the system prevailing in Canada and the US. Since the sales tax revenue accounts for as high 20 per cent of the combined tax revenue of the centre and the states, even the above dispensation alone may not be adequate to compensate the states for the loss of revenue which the stands are likely to suffer. Therefore, the shortfall has to be complimented by the traditional revenue sharing mechanism or the revenue from new VAT. In order to ensure a fair share to the states, it would also be necessary to assign suitable weight, say 10 to 15 percent, to the 'contribution' factor in the scheme of horizontal redistribution of the revenue from the new VAT among the states. In other words, part of the divisible pool of the new VAT revenue will have to be made available to the states on a derivation basin. This would be necessary since the loss of revenue of the states on surrendering the powers of sales tax to the centre will be directly proportional to the quantum of the revenue from the first-point sales tax bulk of which comes from the excisable commodities. Fine-tuning of the vertical as well as horizontal sharing of the new VAT revenue will have to be done carefully in consultation with the states and the mechanism of the Finance Commission will be best suited for this purpose. While the above model has been specifically designed for India, the rationale of the model and the principles on which it has been formulated apply in equal measure to other federal economies which suffer from the system of dual level of commodity taxation and wish to implement a VAT.

For instance, we could apply the above principle to another federal economy, Canada, which is keen to replace the state retail sales taxes by a nationally administered integrated VAT. Canada has been finding it extremely difficult to secure the co-operation of the provinces to implement the national VAT. While three smaller provinces have introduced the H.S.T., Quebec is the only province which has harmonised its general sales tax with

14. Bahl Roy: Revenues and Revenue Assignment: Inter-governmental Fiscal Relations in The Russian Federation Christine Wallace (ed.), Russia and the Challenge of Fiscal Federalism, World Bank, Washington, DC (1994) at p. 133.

the federal VAT, other provinces still levy a general sales tax, which is single stage tax collected at the retail level. These states not only have varying tax rates, but in the case of Alberta, there is no provincial sales tax at all. The existence of two widely different sales taxes imposes collection costs on business firms which are quite high and clearly unnecessary.

In the first place, it should be noted that on a national accounts basis as of 1993, federal government own source revenues in Canada, were almost equal to own account expenditures just 1.1 per cent, while the provincial local governments had own source revenues 23.2 per cent below own account expenditure.[15] This vertical imbalance is a clear pointed just not towards the need for federal transfers to the sub-national governments in Canada but also the need for the provinces to be provided with additional sources of resources.

In Canada, natural resources belong to the provinces as per the Constitution and therefore the provinces have access to royalties was well as tax revenues. The provinces derive large revenues for levies on natural resources, to capture their economic rents. Such revenues are rather unevenly distributed, going largely to the three western provinces. Eighty-five per cent of all oil and gas is produced in one western province. Alberta and the natural resources are largely responsible for the differences in the fiscal capacity of provinces. At the same time, under the Canadian Constitution, the federal governments also has the authority to tax natural resources and the federal government's main source of revenue from Oil and Gas has been the corporate income tax. This division of powers, namely, provincial ownership and federal regulation, has been a source of inter-governmental conflicts in Canada.[16] The Canadian authorities may consider negotiating with the provinces by offering them powers of taxation of natural resources in exchange for their agreeing to implement the national VAT.

In the final analysis, the experience gained in several federal economies, irrespective of the fact whether they are developed or developing, has established fairly beyond doubt the undesirability of subjecting commodity taxation to two levels, the federal and provincial, particularly in the context of introducing the VAT. While it is considered necessary to entrust the entire field of commodity taxation to the national government which is best equipped to implement the VAT, the redistribution of the power of taxation between the central or federal government and the states will depend on the situation and circumstances prevailing in each country and that no generalisation may be possible with regard to assignment of specific taxes to the states. International experience has shown that both personal and corporate income taxes are good

15. Clark Douglas H: The Fiscal Transfer System in Canada in Ethisham Ahmad (ed.) Financing Decentralised Expenditures : An International Comparison of Grants, Aldershot, the United Kingdom and Brookfield, Edward Elgar, US (1996).

16. *Ibid.*

candidates for partial assignment, particularly in large federations but the same cannot be said about a tax like the one on natural resources. Similarly, while property taxes have been traditionally assigned only to the sub-national government, the system is somewhat different in Brazil, where urban property is taxed at the municipal level, while the federal government levies and administers the tax on rural property. This may be a possible reform in the event of Brazil wishing to develop a model based on the above principles. Therefore, it may be necessary for each federal country to evolve its own system by applying the above principles.

3. E-COMMERCE CHALLENGES TO INDIRECT TAXATION

Fifty years ago, VAT was a simple system to administer and audit. Its popularity is know for a simplified tax system. However, times have changed, and by and large, VAT has not. In India, it is a country spread debate as to implementation of VAT. Services Transactions unreveal the clarity and simplicity of the VAT system, and it is instructive to examine this more closely for the difficulties that E-commerce, when it grown more significant, will create for a VAT system.

For many services, the supplier under the presumption that the customer for the services needs to be relatively geographically close to receiving the services collects VAT. However, for intangible or intellectual services (copyright, licences, advertising, professional and consultant services and financial transactions) the customer already pay VAT. If the customer is not VAT registered, he is supposed to declare the transaction and pay the tax. Certain types of service firms, including financial intermediaries, and looking forward, possibly Internet service provider, often cannot recover VAT and end up paying it as if they were final consumers.

If digitalised products are treated as services, the inconsistencies created by the VAT increase. Some products, such as book and music, when they are purchased as tangible goods have lower VAT than if they are digitised and therefore treated as services. On the other hand, a digitalised product that is downloaded from a site outside European Union often generates no tax revenue unless the customer declares and pays it. In this simple example, a single product yields three possible tax rates depending on the form and geography of the transaction—hardly the OECD goal of neutrality, efficiency, certainty and simplicity, effectiveness and fairness, and flexibility.

Under these circumstances, it is not surprising that businesses expend time and effort tax strategizing. For example, Internet Service Providers (ISPs) are the 'portal' or starting point for many activities on the Internet. Looking forward, ISPs could end up playing the role of tax collector (as the delivery man does with flowers) or might have to pay the service VAT themselves (as in the case of financial intermediaries). The clear incentive is to move the ISP activity offshore so as to blur responsibility for paying or collecting VAT, and indeed some European ISPs have been set-up in low-tax-jurisdictions.

The issue facing the US *vis-a-vis* sales taxes offers similar examples of tax strategizing. For example, 'BarnesandNoble.com' is incorporated as a separate business entity from the parent stores so as to avoid 'nexus' (or physical presence) and the requirement to apply sales taxes on all purchases through the Internet. However, because these entities must remain separate, business synergies and brand-extension cannot be exploited. For example, someone who prefers to shop and buy a book on-line (because they like the additional features of book reviews available on-line) cannot go and pick up the book at a local store branch.

The Internet market place characterised by cross-border trade in information-rich products will increasingly strain systems of indirect tax both because of diminishing coverage and because myriad tax rates are costly to administer and invite strategizing. In particular, economic transactions created from various international and domestic locations make it increasingly difficult to make sense or to apply the credit—invoice method of accounting for VAT at each stage of the value-chain; there is not a value-chain but a network creating value. Because governments do need to raise revenues, they need to look at other ways of doing so.

Many tax system depend on indirect taxes, such as sales taxes, Value-Added Taxes (VAT) or Goods and Services Taxes (GST) to raise a substantial share of government revenues. Both the United States and the European Union have been struggling with how to apply sales tax and VAT to E-Commerce transactions, both within and across borders. Neither body fully recognizes that decisions taken in the domestic arena have implications for cross-border application of these types of taxes. Inconsistent tax treatment of transaction between the US and the EU and within each country as well, already has surfaced.

In the US, when the Congress passed the Internet Tax Freedom Act in 1998.[17] It mandated review of the implication of E-commerce for domestic sales taxes. A majority of members or the Gilmore Commission proposed (they could not formally recommend to Congress, because no super-majority view was agreed to) that digital products downloaded over the Internet (including software, books, or music) should not be taxed. Moreover, in the interests of tax neutrality, their tangible equivalents also would be tax exempt. This represents a "harmonising down" approach, which could generate inconsistent treatment of purchases over the Internet via and through other means for products not explicitly exempted. While still being reviewed, one objective of this proposal was to encourage states and localities to harmonise their own rates and reduce the myriad state and local taxes (some 30,000 within the United States) which are both administratively cumbersome and encourage tax-strategizing behaviour.

17. Which kept domestic Internet transactions free from any new taxes for three years but did not revoke existion sales or use taxes.

In contrast, to the US, the EU tax authorities are drawing a bright line between goods and services purchased over the Internet, and to a greater extent than the US already have captured these transactions in their tax orbit. All electronic transmissions[18] have been deemed services and, therefore, should be taxed at the appropriate VAT rate.

In June 2000, the European Commission proposed rules that would have forced online sellers from around the world to collect VAT on sales of digital products and services location and rates for taxing to European customers. The main goal of these rules was to protect European sellers, who must collect VAT, from competition by foreign sellers who do not. US sellers targeted for tax collection declared the proposals unacceptable by many. Late in 2000, Europeans found the proposals. The EC is now rethinking ways to protect European sellers of digital products, while maintaining a workable VAT system.

The original proposals were made in June 2000. The proposed legislation would have required non-EU sellers to collect VAT on sales of digital products and services to non-business customers in Europe. Only those sellers with more than 100,000 Euro in sales from Europe would have been subject to these rules. The types of sales that would have been subject to the tax included, among other things, downloaded products, like software and music, and online entertainment services, such as pay-for-use video broadcasting.

The reason for the proposed laws was summarised in statement by Frits Bolkestein European Commissioner for taxation :

> "Today European producers of digital products, such as computer games and software, are at a competitive disadvantage compared with non-European producers because they have to apply VAT to their products within Europe. US competitors, by contrast, can export to Europe free of VAT. Similarly, European exporters to the US are now obliged to pay European VAT, whereas US producers are not faced with the same obligation. It is proposed to put European producers of digital products on an equal footing with US and Japanese competitors by applying VAT to digital imports into the EU and exempting digital exports form the EU. This would create a global level playing-field for European and non-European Companies".

The attempt by the EU to impose VAT collection on sellers outside the EU was seen as overreaching in many countries. However, it was a logical solution to a real problem. The ease of selling digital products across

18. Those under the general term 'soft goods' such as software, books, or architectural drawings.

international borders gives vendors from non-European countries, especially the US, a competitive advantage over those in Europe.

However, the proposals encountered far to many complaints. For instance, there was considerable doubt whether the EU could enforce compliance on sellers with no presence in Europe. Backers of the proposals felt that non-EU sellers, especially well known ones, would be hesitant to build up a large unpaid VAT liability in the EU. Supporters of the proposals suggested that the EU could withhold protection of the intellectual property rights of non-complaint sellers. This threat was seen by some as fairly ill conceived, because:

(i) The seller may not be the holder of the intellectual property rights, so punishment would be misplaced; and

(ii). The tax authorities may not have the power to affect enforcement of intellectual property rights, which are the subject of international agreements.

A more serious complaint came from inside the EU itself. The proposals allowed non-EU vendors to register in only one EU country, and collect and remit only that country's VAT countries such as Denmark, with a 25% VAT rate, did not like this part of the proposal. Most agreed that non-EU vendors would pick a country like Luxembourg, with its 15% rate, in which to register. For Denmark, non-EU vendors would still enjoy a VAT advantage. Not only that, but VAT from non-EU vendors would flow into only a few countries.

Some European countries would have non-EU vendors' register to collect VAT in all 15 EU member states. While this solves the problems presented by allowing vendors to register in only one country. It presents a worst-case scenario for sellers. Tax compliance would be very difficult and many vendors would simply not comply. The advantage of one-country registration is that it makes collecting and remitting VAT fairly simple. The simpler the process, the more likely a foreign seller will comply.

So, the June 2000 proposals have pretty much been rejected. The final blow was the ECOFIN meeting on November 27, 2000, where the EC was asked to rework the proposals. This means that non-EU sellers of digital products need not worry about new rules requiring them to collect VAT on digital product or service sales to European customers, at least not for now.

In India, the fate of VAT itself is uncertain and therefore nothing can be said about VAT's application in relation to Internet transactions. But once the VAT system is implemented, problems of its implication to electronic commerce, as mentioned above would be inevitable.

9

Conclusion and Suggestions

CONCLUSIONS

A federation is a compromise between regional autonomy and national integration. But as seen[1], it takes one step in advance of other loose forms of alliances between independent states in that it creates a National Government apart from the State Governments. Both the national and the state Government owe their existence and derive their powers from the Federal Constitution and both are separate legal entities known to the law. In the words of Prof. Wheare:

> "There is a single independent authority for the whole area in respect of some matters and there are independent regional for other matters."

A federal state is a union of several states into a central or federal government. After the federation is formed, both the federal and the state governments owe their existence to and authority from the Federal Constitution which distributes governmental powers between the federal and the state governments which are to be exercised by them, according to the constitutional distribution, independently of each other.

The principle that our economic unit is the Nation, which alone has the gamut of powers necessary to control of the economy, including the vital power of erecting customs barriers against foreign competition, has as its corollary that the states are not separable economic units. What is ultimate is the principle that one state in its dealings with another may not place itself in a position of economic isolation.

The great problem of any federal structure is to prevent the growth of sectional and local interests which are inimical to the interests of the nation

1. See Chapter 1, Federalism and the Commerce Clause.

as a whole. The strength of the Union may be achieved only by minimising inter-state barriers as much as possible, so that the people may feel that they are the members of one nation, though they may, for the time being, be residents of particular geographical divisions of the country. One of the means to achieve this object is to guarantee to every citizen the freedom of movement throughout the territory of the Union, and also to reside and settle in any part thereof. No less important is the applied freedom of every citizen to trade with any part of the country. On principle, thus, it comprises both inter-state and intra-state freedom of trade, commerce and intercourse. From the federal standpoint we are concerned with the former, i.e., freedom of trade, commerce and intercourse as between the several states of the Union, which might raise economic barriers against each other, in the absence of any constitutional prohibitions in this behalf.

I

The American Constitution in its Art. 1, Sec. 8, Clause 3 contains Commerce Clause which vests in Congress the power "to regulate commerce with foreign nations and among the several states . . ." has functioned, *firstly*, as a great workshop for the federal Centre to fashion a wide range of powerful instruments for regulating, in the country's larger interests, the countless activities which are comprehended in foreign and inter-state commerce, and *secondly*, as a brake upon the action of the constituent states of the federation which in any wise obstructed, burdened or discriminated against the free operations of foreign and inter-state commerce. An almost identical provision contained in Sec. 51(i) of the Commonwealth of Australia Constitution Act, 1900, gives the Commonwealth Parliament the power to enact laws with respect to "trade and commerce with other countries, and among the states."[2]

The "Commerce Clause" has a negative as well as a positive aspect. The Clause not only serves to augment federal authority. By its own force it also cuts down the power of the constituent state in its exercise of what would normally be a part of its residual police power.[3] If there were no "Commerce Clause," each state could shut out the products of other states or admit them only on conditions. It is consequently clear that the "Commerce Clause," in and of itself, affords protection from state legislation inimical to national commerce.

Thus, the "Commerce Clause", by necessary negative inference, limits the authority of the states. In actuality, despite Justice Story's statement to the contrary, the Marshall view of the commerce power was not that of unequivocal federal exclusiveness. In *Gibbons v. Ogden*,[4] referring to the argument that the commerce power was an indivisible whole, vested

2. See Chapter 2.
3. Schwartz, A Commentary on the Constitution of the United States, Ed. 1977 at p. 238.
4. 9 Wheat. 1 (1824).

exclusively in the Congress, it was stated that there is great force in the argument and the court is not satisfied that it has been refuted. But this is only passing a qualified judgment on a point not relevant to the decision in the case. More significant was Marshall's express recognition that the states did, in fact, possess powers, which might be exercised over commerce. As *Gibbons* acknowledged, "Inspection laws, quarantine laws, health laws of every description, as well as laws for regulating the internal commerce of a state, and those which respect turnpike-roads, ferries, etc., are component parts of this mass" i.e., of state legislation which may, in Marshall's words, have a considerable influence on commerce. The *Wilson*[5] opinion indicates that the Marshall interpretation of the negative aspect of the "Commerce Clause" was not as far from that of his successor, Taney, C.J., as is generally believed. Both Marshall and Taney refused to follow the notion of complete exclusiveness of federal power, under which the "Commerce Clause," of its own force, removed from the states any and all power over inter-state and foreign commerce.

In *Gibbons*, Danial Webster had presented to the highest Court a theory, which, like the Marshall approach just discussed, is somewhere in between the notion of complete exclusiveness and concurrent power. In his argument, Webster contended that the power of Congress to regulate commerce was complete and entire, and to a certain extent necessarily exclusive. He meant by this that this proposition was, not that all the commercial powers are exclusive, but that those powers being separated, there are some which are exclusive in their nature.

Not only this, it has been held that congressional legislation can confer legitimacy on a State law which is passed even in the exclusive congressional field and Congress can also evidence an intention to stop state Legislatures even from legislation in the concurrent area. This has led Johnston to observe as below:

> "The Court, in finding the balance between state and National interest in commercial regulation, is not exercising its constitutional function of judicial review, but rather is acting as a non-judicial mediatory body. The power of Congress in this area is co-extensive with the will of Congress, and the Court's job is to determine what that will is."[6]

The 'Commerce Clause' of the Constitution of the United States limits the power of Congress in relation to commerce with foreign countries, commerce with Indian Tribes and commerce among several states. It was left to the Supreme Court of the United States to demarcate the respective jurisdictions of the Congress and States because while Congress could

5. *Wilson v. Black Bird Creek Marsh Co.*, 2 Pet. 245 U.S. (1829).
6. Johnston, The effect of Judicial Review on Federal State Relations in Australia, Canada and the United State (Louisiana State University Press) 1969, at p. 223.

regulate commerce among states, the states themselves had with them the police powers. It is another matter that in the ultimate analysis the congressional power has come to be construed so broadly as to embrace the entire economic life of the nation.

However, the framers of the Canadian Constitution did not leave it to the Courts to enlarge the federal power over commerce. In Canada, Sec. 91(2) of the B.N.A. Act, 1867, gives the power to regulate commerce in its entirety to the Dominion Parliament and does not limit it to anything like commerce with foreign countries and commerce among the provinces. The courts in their interpretation of the Canadian Constitution have given the narrowest meaning to the federal commerce power. This restrictive interpretation of Dominion's Commerce power continued and judicial interpretation continued to encourage provincial autonomy in matters of trade and commerce.[7]

In the Australian Constitution Sec. 51(i) confers on the Commonwealth Parliament "power to make laws for the peace, order and good governments of the Commonwealth with respect to trade and commerce with other countries, and among the states". Thus, it will be seen that on the pattern of the American Constitution and differing from the Canadian pattern, the text of the Australian Constitution has limited the Commonwealth Parliament's power in the field to commerce with other countries and among the federating states.

The Australian Constitution goes into more detail regarding trade and commerce than either the American or Canadian Constitution. Parliament is given power to make laws with respect to "trade and commerce with other countries, and among the states."[8] Sec. 98 specifically authorises extending this power to navigation and shipping, and to state-owned railways. Parliament is forbidden to give preference to one state over another by such regulation, or to use this power in such a manner as to deny states or residents therein the "reasonable" use of the river waters for conservation or irrigation. In contrast to the American Constitution, the Australian Constitution additionally grants federal legislative power over a number of specific subjects of trade and commerce, such as banking and the incorporation of banks, insurance, foreign corporations, and trading or financial corporations formed within the Commonwealth, the nationalisation of any property from any state or person for any purpose in respect of which the Parliament has power to legislate, and the conciliation and arbitration of Industrial disputes extending beyond the limits of any one state.

Thus, what is called as intra-state commerce is clearly excluded from Central Government's jurisdiction and is left to remain with the states as part of their reserved powers. In addition, the commerce power of the

7. Mackinnon, Victor, Comparative Federalism—A Study in Judicial Interpretation (Hague Martinus Nijhoff), 1964 at p. 7.
8. Lumb, R.D. and Ryam, K.W., The Constitution of the Commonwealth of Australia—Annotated (Butterworths) 1974 at p. 67.

Commonwealth Parliament under Sec. 51(i) itself has not been treated to be exclusive; states have a concurrent jurisdiction in the matter. Consequently, even in the field of inter-state trade and commerce. Parliamentary view can prevail over the state law only by taking the recourse to Sec. 109 which makes the Central law prevail over a state law in the case of conflicts between the two.

When the Constitution-makers of India wanted to make a distribution of legislative powers between the Union and the constituent states on the topic of trade and commerce they had before them not only the Australian and American constitutional models on this topic but also the rich storehouse of experience garnered by America and to a lesser degree by Australia in the course of the working of those models in the myriad situations of life over a long stretch of time. It is true that the two provisions, the one contained in the first part of Entry 41 of List 1 of the Seventh Schedule which runs as "Trade and commerce with foreign countries" and the other embodied in Entry 42 of List 1 of the same Schedule which is worded as "Inter-state trade and commerce", if read together, practically reproduce the language of the Australian and American Commerce Clauses.[9] List II of the Seventh Schedule contains an entry, Entry 26 which is worded like this, "Trade and commerce within the state subject to the provisions of Entry 33 of List III." If these three entries alone are read shutting one's eyes to the other entries bearing on the subject of trade and commerce in the three legislative lists, as also the related provisions contained in Art. 286 and Part XIII of the Constitution, the impression is likely to be created that the Indian Commerce Clause which would be the result of the joining up of the first part of Entry 41 with Entry 42 of the Seventh Schedule will have an influence on the economy of the country comparable to the one exerted on the American economy by the American Commerce Clause. Definitely the Australian Commerce Clause as compared with its American counterpart has played relatively insignificant role. The Indian Commerce Clause is likely to play an even less significant role in the Indian economy than what the Australian Commerce Clause contained in Sec. 51(i) of the Commonwealth of Australia Constitution Act, 1900, has played in the economic life of Australia.

The control over intra-state trade, subject to certain qualifications, vested in the states under Entry 26 of List II of the Seventh Schedule of the Indian Constitution, resembles to the control over intra-state trade and commerce exercised by the constituent states of the Australian and American federations as part of their residual sovereignty. Both under the Australian and American Constitutions, there is only one legislative list enumerating the matters which come within the legislative competence of the federal

9. M. Ramaswamy, Indian Constitutional Provisions against Barrier to Trade and Commerce Examined in the Light of Australian and American Experienced, J.I.L.I. at p. 327 (1959-60).

centre while the residue of authority lying outside the area of federal action comes within the field of the constituent units.

We have seen that in the United States of America the Supreme Court has so interpreted the Commerce Clause that the responsibility for adjusting the conflicting demands of uniformity and diversity has come to be vested in the congressional hands. It is the Congress, which determines the respective claims of commercial unity and local autonomy. The Courts play their role but that is more in the nature of mediation rather than judicial review. On the other hand, in Australia it is the Courts, which play the vital role to see that the mandate of Sec. 92 is observed. Our Constitution-makers have entrusted the responsibility to both the Courts and the Central Government subject to one limitation that it shall not discriminate between one state and another or that it shall not give preference to one state over another, Parliament has been given the power to restrict the freedom of trade, commerce and intercourse in the public interest.

The difference between Indian Constitution and Constitutions of United States and Canada is in as much as our Constitution specifically and elaborately defines the respective jurisdictions of Central and State Legislatures in the field of trade and commerce and thereby attempts to avoid difficulties which were faced in Canada and the United States.

II

Extensive linguistic and historical study reveals that "Commerce" means the voluntary sale or exchange of property or services and all accompanying market-oriented activities, enterprises, relationships and interests. Thus, "Commerce" covers a wide range of subjects, which can roughly be grouped into three categories:

The *first* includes buying and selling goods; the production of such merchandise through activities as manufacturing, farming and mining; and incidents of that production, such as environmental and safety effects. The *second* encompasses the compensated provision of services (such as labour, insurance, and banking), which have long been regarded as "Commercial", and which form a vital element of our modern economy. The *third* consists of the means by which Commerce is transacted—for example, the documents used to facilitate commerce (contracts, negotiable instruments, securities, letters of credit, security interests in property, etc.).

Commercial transportation cuts across all three categories. It is integral to the sale and production of goods; it is a service provided for a fee; and it is a means of transacting commerce. Yet the definition includes transportation only if it is undertaken for business purposes or provided by a common carrier. Therefore, the Court's "channels" and "instrumentalities" theories, which equate all transportation with commerce and thus permit Congress to exert plenary control over any person or thing that moves across state lines for any reason, deserve to be resected.

The foregoing definition is broad but not unlimited. Most significantly, the historical understanding has been that "Commerce", as used in Art. 1, referred solely to market-based activities and enterprises. Thus, there is no need to equate "Commerce" with modern "economics", which covers virtually all human endeavors and interactions, including areas such as crime[10] and religion.[11] Although all conduct has economic consequences, it does not thereby become "commercial" in nature. Similarly, the economists find artificial effort to distinguish production and services for the marketplace from similar activities undertaken for personal or home use. Rather, they treat all such actions as an integrated whole because of the effect of home-oriented economic activities on market supply, demand and price.[12] Again defining "Commerce" to include all economic impacts would enable Congress to regulate everything, and thereby drain the 'Commerce Clause' of any meaningful content.

In short, Congress has no power to legislate conduct that does not constitute "Commerce", such as gender motivated violence or the possession of guns or drugs for personal use. In such cases, the Court should strike down the statute without reaching the secondary question of whether the activity affects inter-state commerce.

In Canada, from the beginning there has been no distinction between trade and commerce. Trade means the act or business of exchanging commodities by barter, or the business of buying and selling for money. Commerce is only another term for the same thing.[13]

However, in Australia the trade and commerce have been given a narrow meaning. It has been said that "Trade" strictly means the buying and selling of goods. However, it is a specialised meaning of the word. The present primary meaning is much wider, covering the pursuit of a calling or handicraft, and its history emphasises rather use, regularity and course of conduct, than is concerned with commodities. "Intercourse" was doubtlessly added because of the view, now no longer open in the United States that "Commerce" might not extend to "Intercourse" that was not concerned with business profit or pecuniary gain and because of the degree to which the right of the citizen to access to every constituent part of the Union had been rested on implication. It cannot be thought that the essential content of the expression "Trade, Commerce and Intercourse" in Sec. 92 is in any way less than what is included in the conception of "Commerce" in the modern American view of the "Commerce power." One is not speaking of the spread of that power over an immense field of activities that are incident to

10. Richard A. Posner, Economic Analysis of Law, 217-18 (4th Ed., 1992); Gary S. Becker, Crime and Punishment : An Economic Approach, 76 J. Pol. Econ. 169 (1968).
11. Michael W. McConnell & Richard A. Posner, An Economic Approach to Issues of Religious Freedom, 56 Uni. Chi. L.Rev. 1 (1989).
12. Indeed the court adopted this economic theory in *Wickard v. Filburn*, 317 U.S. 111 (1942).
13. See Chapter 3.

"Commerce." It is the central conception expressed in the word to which reference has been made.

The words "Trade, Commerce and Intercourse" are not naturally susceptible of such a reactionary interpretation. The very manner in which they are combined would carry, even to a mind unfamiliar with their background, an intention to include all forms and variety of inter-state transaction whether by way of commercial dealing or of personal converse or passage. An understanding of what lies behind the choice of expression confirms the natural impression produced by the language itself.

The Indian Judiciary has not felt that difficulty, as the American, in ascertaining the ambit of "Commerce" because most of the activities which were included within the scope of "Commerce" by judicial interpretation in America have been specifically enumerated in the Union List giving Parliament exclusive power to legislate with respect to them.[14]

Basu and Seervai are opposed to each other regarding the interpretation of the term 'Intercourse'. Seervai says that 'Intercourse' means 'Commercial Intercourse' and it comprises in commerce whereas Basu, on the other hand, says that intercourse does not include commercial intercourse. But as it has seen in Chapter 3 Seervai has not given any sound justification for his this Conclusion. Therefore, one is left with no option but to accept Basu's assertion. It is thus humbly submitted that Basu appears to be correct in his approach.

We have seen that in the United States of America term 'Commerce' was given a wide meaning and this helped in enlarging the power of Congress over national economy and commerce. In Australia, on the other hand, Sec. 92 was partly used as a guarantee to an individual in matters of trade and business. These compulsions do not exist in India. Indian Parliament has very wide powers with respect to economic and commercial matters.

(a) In America, the Court sustained New Deal Legislation under the 'Commerce Clause' in *three* key cases. *First,* in *NLRB v. Jones & Laughlin Steel Corp.,*[15] the court upheld the National Labour Relations Act ("NLRA") despite the finding that the steel workers involved were engaged in "manufacture" (not commerce) within a state. Although activities may be intra-state in character when separately considered, if they have such a close and substantial relation to inter-state commerce that their control is essential or appropriate to protect that commerce from burdens and obstructions. Congress cannot be denied the power to exercise that control. The fact that the employees here concerned were engaged in production is not determinative. The question remains as to the effect upon inter-state

---

14. For example, posts and telegraphs, telephones, wireless, broadcasting and other like forms of communication have been mentioned at Entry 31, List I. Similarly, inter-state quarantine has been mentioned at Entry 81, List I.
15. 301 U.S. 1 (1937).

commerce of the labour practice involved.[16] The Court concluded that labour relations at the plant of a national manufacturer had the requisite substantial effect.[17]

Second, United States v. Darby[18] sustained the application of two provisions of the Fair Labour Standards Act of 1938 ("FLSA") to a lumber manufacturer. Following *Jones & Laughlin*,[19] and invoking *McCulloch v. Maryland*[20], the Court held that Congress may regulate intra-state non-commercial activities (such as the manufacturing involved here) if they had a substantial effect on inter-state commerce.[21] Although the Court acknowledged that the Commerce power could not be exercised in violation of a specific constitutional prohibition,[22] it ruled that the Tenth Amendment imposed no such independent bar.

Third, Wickard v. Filburn[23] upheld the Agricultural Adjustment Act of 1938 ("AAA"), which sought to lessen fluctuations in wheat prices by authorizing the Secretary of Agriculture to set quotas for wheat production and to penalise farmers who exceeded them, even if their surplus was not intended for sale.[24]

Wickard transformed the 'Commerce Clause' by declaring that it not only included "commerce" (i.e., market-oriented activities), but also "economics" (i.e., anything that affects the quantity or price of goods and services).[25] Because virtually everything has an economic effect, Wickard enabled Congress to regulate whatever it pleased—a point well understood by Justice Jackson, who wrote the Court's opinion.

More generally, the New Deal Court could have invoked *McCulloch* to support the modest proposition that Congress can regulate the production of goods as reasonably related to its Commerce Clause power of governing the inter-state sale of those commodities. Instead, the Court twisted *McCulloch* and *Gibbons* to justify its far broader holdings that (1) Congress can regulate activities that are not "commerce" as long as they "substantially affect" the inter-state economy, and (2) the latter determination constitutes a political question. This distorted, and unnecessary, reasoning emboldened Congress to expand its regulatory empire immensely. The definition of "commerce" should also include all production of commodities and articles for the marketplace.[26] Therefore, one should agree with the Court's repudiation of its

---

16. *United States v. Lopez*, 514 U.S. 549, 558-59 (1995).
17. *Jones & Laughlin*, 301 U.S. at 30, 37.
18. 312 U.S. 100 (1941).
19. *NLRB v. Jones & Laughlin Steel Corp.*, 301, U.S. 1 (1937), cited in Darby, 312 U.S. at 119.
20. 17 U.S. (4 Wheat.) 316(1819), cited in Darby, 312 U.S. at 118-19, 124.
21. Darby, 312 U.S. at 118-19.
22. *Id.* at 115-16.
23. 317 U.S. 111 (1942).
24. *Id.* at 115-19, 128 (citing statute).
25. Wickard, 317 U.S. at p. 125.
26. See Chapter 4.

pre-1937 precedent prohibiting Congress from regulating activities such as manufacturing, mining, and agriculture. One should immunise only production intended for personal use.

The case that best illustrates this "commercial *versus* personal" distinction is *Wickard's* case, which upheld a statutory penalty on a farmer for exceeding his government-mandated wheat quota, even though some of that surplus was used for his family's own consumption. *Wickard* affords Congress a judicial carte blanche under the Commerce Clause to regulate virtually every aspect of agricultural production.

From this it may be concluded that production of goods for the market, whether in a factory or on a farm, is commerce. Thus, to the extent that Filburn planted wheat for sale or to feed poultry or cattle held for sale, his activity constitutes commerce. As such, a rational Congress surely may conclude that the cumulative impact of planting wheat by all farmers for such a commercial purpose has the requisite inter-state effect. Indeed, one would permit Congress to regulate most wheat production in the country. On the other hand, the test would prohibit penalising Filburn for any of the wheat used for consumption in his household, because growing for one's own use without the intent to sell is simply not commerce.

Some may argue that this analysis represents intellectual hairsplitting at its worst. After all, is it practical for the federal government to determine which part of Filburn's wheat is "commercial" to create a formula based on Filburn's past practice? What possible benefit to Filburn justifies the administrative burden on the government?

Manufacture is not of itself inter-state commerce, the shipment of manufactured goods inter-state is such commerce and the prohibition of such shipment by Congress is indubitably a regulation of the commerce. Is this a proposition which applies in Canada? If so may the prohibition of shipment be accompanied by regulations that permit such shipment on due compliance?

May it be said, in view of the *Margarine case,* that prohibition of manufacture and, indeed, the regulation of production, is open only to the Province, save in situations which may be brought within the *Russell case,* and that, absent competent federal legislation, it is no answer to such provincial legislation that it will remove goods from inter-provincial or foreign trade?[27]

Australia had its *Grannall's case,* where an allegation was made that Sec. 92 of the Constitution was infringed by a State statute prohibiting the manufacture of margarine unless under licence. While it was appreciated that the restriction was in the interests of the dairy industry, the Court found that there was no unconstitutional interference with inter-state trade. The issue here, however, differs from the problem as it arose under the B.N.A. Act.

27. *Mugler v. Kansas* (1887) 123 U.S. 623.

In United States, mines and mills, factories and farms—all engaged in production rather than commerce in the literal sense—have been brought within the sweep of the 'Commerce Clause' provided only that they exert some economic effect upon inter-state commerce.

In Canada, there is judicial insistence upon the observance of the rule that if in a trade activity, including manufacture or production, there is involved a matter of extra-provincial interest or concern its regulation thereafter in the aspect of trade is by that fact put beyond provincial power.

In Australia, the courts has consistently held that production even when earmarked for inter-state trade is not a part of inter-state trade and commerce. Inter-state trade in manufactured products only begins, the court has said, with the inter-state *movement* of the products; the production is a mere inter-state preparation for a proposed act of inter-state trade in manufactured goods and is not itself a part of inter-state trade. However, production or manufacturing when linked with an export market comes within the ambit of commerce.[28]

The Indian position in this respect is quite different from that of other federations. Indian judiciary has not faced the problem whether production, mining, manufacturing or other like operations comes within the ambit of "Commerce" or not. This is, as observed earlier because of detailed provisions made under the Constitution. Constitution through three lists demarcates the legislative competence of Central and State Legislatures. Manufacture, mining, agriculture and other productive activities have been mentioned at one Entry or the other in any of the three lists. Not only this, if one goes through Art. 304(a) it can be seen that words "manufactured" or "produced" are there. This strengthens the view that manufacturing is definitely an aspect of "Commerce". This dimension of argument gets support from different judicial decisions[29] which though not directly involving the issue whether manufacturing is comprised in "Commerce" or not, yet talk about manufacturing in the perspective of the "Commerce Code".

(b) In U.S.A. before June 5, 1944 the court in a series of cases commencing from *Paul's case* had consistently maintained the view that insurance was not commerce. This anomalous situation was removed in *South Eastern Underwriters' Association*. In this case, court held that 'Insurance is Commerce'. The business of insurance conducted across state lines constitutes inter-state commerce. This would have created grave dislocation in an important segment of the national economy but for passing of the McCarran Act by Congress. The object of this Act was broadly to give support to the existing and future state's systems for the regulating as well as the taxing of the business of the insurance.

28. See Chapter 4.
29. *Ibid*.

In Canada, the question whether insurance was a trade for purposes of Sec. 91(2) was lost in a generalized assertion that federal power was unequal to the regulation by licencing of particular trades carried on in the provinces.

In Australia, insurance is not considered as a part of inter-state trade; whereas in India "Insurance" is mentioned at Entry 47, List I and thus Parliament has power to make laws including regulation regarding insurance. Therefore, in India it should not be a debatable issue whether insurance is included within "trade and commerce" or not.

The Indian position is not similar to that of Australia. Assuming that transactions in insurance are concluded it one place, it would make no difference for the Indian Judiciary.[30] Also, it is humbly submitted that though in most of the insurance transaction the philosophy is of social security and the element of gain is either zero or negligible, the same may be put within the ambit of intercourse.

(c) In India, the examination of cases on the inter-state trade and commerce shows that the Courts have given a restricted meaning to the scope of Art. 301 and thereby have saved many state laws from falling within the purview of the article and fulfilling the requirements of Art. 304(b). This they did by giving a restricted meaning to the expression "trade, commerce and intercourse" so as to exclude activities *res extra commercium.*[31] Thus, they have refused to include business activities in prize competitions, business in intoxicants and business in money lending within the meaning of commerce. The Supreme Court has also upheld the power of the states to derecognise certain trade activities in the interest of socio-economic justice.

What constitutes "Trade" and "Commerce" is a question of fact to be determined in the light of contemporary social values and practices.[32] In the words of McTiernan, J. whether an activity is trade or commerce "is a matter of social opinion rather than jurisprudence."[33] But all kinds of organised activities with a view to earning profits cannot *ipso facto* acquire the status of "Trade" or "Commerce." Only legitimate profit-oriented activities can acquire the status of trade and commerce. What activities are legitimate is a question to be answered in terms of social opinion, values and realities. In India, the *doctrine of extra-commercium,* which took birth in *State of Bombay v. R.M.D. Chamarbaugwala,*[34] has been applied in the areas of gambling, lottery and money lending.

In *Chamarbaugwala,*[35] the Court derived the doctrine of *res extra commercium* from the observations in certain *Australian* cases, in preference to American decisions in which even deleterious activities in course of inter-

30. *Ibid.*

31. *Ibid.*

32. M.P. Singh: Is Money Lending Extra Commercium? Some Thoughts on *Fatehchand v. State of Maharashtra* (1978) 2 S.C.C. 1.

33. *The King v. Connare,* 61 C.L.R. 596, 631 (1939).

34. A.I.R. 1957 S.C. 699.

35. *State of Bombay v. Chamarbaugwala,* A.I.R. 1957 S.C. 699 at pp. 718-21.

state trade were held to be included within the ambit of the "Commerce Clause", but they were subject to regulation which could go to the extent of prohibition in more dangerous cases, e.g. importation of adulterated food[36]; inter-state transportation of women for immoral purposes.[37]

The American view was discarded on the ground that there was nothing in the American Constitution corresponding to Sec. 92 of the Australian Constitution and the only relevant provision in this behalf was the "Commerce Power" of Congress[38] so that unless every activity of inter-state trading or intercourse were brought within the ambit of this power, no Legislature would be competent to control or suppress such inherently dangerous activities.[39] In *M/s B.R. Enterprises,* though the Supreme Court laboured a much but its resultant was nothing more than the mere restamping of the *Chamarbaugwala* verdict. Therefore, the *Chamarbaugwala* still stands as a pointer with respect to what should be treated as *res extra commercium.*

III

In America, the Framers of the Commerce Clause intended to authorise Congress to prevent states from pursuing protectionist economic policies and to promote national commerce, and the Constitution's Ratifiers shared this understanding. The clause was part of a systematic plan to resolve a severe economic crisis.

Several related problems had plunged the economy into an abyss. Most obviously, the break from England ruptured America's umbilical commercial connection to the mother country, with special harm flowing from the loss of colonial subsidies and preferences.[40] American enterprises that had emerged during the war could not compete with those of established and well-financed European countries.[41] Consequently, the balance of trade became skewed towards imports, thereby draining specie and creating a financial crisis. Furthermore, Great Britain and other nations pursued hostile commercial policies and refused to execute treaties that would open up foreign markets to the United States.[42] America's weak national government under the Articles of Confederation could not pass retaliatory measures or raise revenues to meet the mounting debt.

36. *Hipolite v. U.S.* (1911) 220 U.S. 45.
37. *Hoke v. U.S.* (1913) 227 U.S. 308.
38. American Constitution, Art. I, Sec. 8, Cl. 3.
39. As Das, C.J. observed in *Chamarbaugwala's case,* A.I.R. 1957 S.C. 699, the American Congress would have no power to control gambling and like spurious transactions under its power over 'inter-state commerce' if they were not held to be 'commerce.'
40. Max Farrand, The Framing of the Constitution of the United States, 6 (1913).
41. Hamilton & Adair, The Power to Govern, 179, 191-92 (1937).
42. Elliot, The Debates In The Several State Conventions on the Adoption of the Federal Constitution, 106-08 (1901).

Independent state governments filled the political vacuum. They were usually dominated by radically democratic legislatures, which pursued disastrous commercial policies. Especially pernicious were debtor relief laws, which enabled borrowers to avoid their contractual obligations and authorised the emission of worthless paper money. These pro-debtor laws led to retaliation by states, which had a large number of creditors. States also engaged in economic warfare by enacting protectionist trade laws, taxes, and port fees. Of particular importance, states with excellent harbours, such as New York and Virginia, took advantage of their neighbours without good ports. Border quarrels erupted and regional economic tensions grew, especially between North and South. Finally, the confederation government could neither stop the states from impeding commerce nor affirmatively regulate commerce among them. Various reform efforts in the mid-1780s failed, and America faced economic and political disintegration.[43] The Constitutional Convention met in June 1787 to resolve these problems. The delegates agreed that the National government required greatly enhanced commercial powers, but had to be radically restructured to exercise such authority effectively and safely.

One of the overarching goals of the Founders was to repair America's economy by granting the Federal government control over all commercial matters affecting the nation. To achieve this aim, they balanced many competing economic interests: (i) the agricultural and merchant classes, especially the slave-based agrarian, South and the Northern economy featuring an increasingly influential class of traders and manufacturers, (ii) maritime and non-maritime states; and (iii) small and large states. The Framers sought to enable each state and region to exploit its particular advantages, thereby enriching the entire United States.

Many Constitutional provisions reflect the delegates' economic concerns. For example, to protect creditors and the financial system, the Framers authorised Congress to coin and regulate the value of money and to punish counterfeiting, and they provided that no state shall coin money; emit Bills of credit; make any thing but gold and silver Coin a Tender in payment of Debts; or pass any Law impairing the Obligation of Contracts. To encourage and facilitate commerce, the Constitution allowed Congress to "fix the Standard of Weights and Measures, create a postal system, secure patents and copyrights, and establish uniform laws concerning bankruptcy."[44] To promote a proper balance of trade and prevent its disruption, Art. 1 prohibits states (absent Congress's consent) from "laying any Imposts or duties on Imports or Exports."[45] Moreover, Congress could levy taxes, duties and imposts, except against "Articles exported from any

43. Grant S. Nelson & Robert J. Pushaw, Jr., Rethinking the Commerce Clause Applying First Principle to Uphold Federal Commercial Regulations But Preserve State Control Over Social Issues, Iowa L. Rev., Vol. 85, No. 1, 1999 at p. 24.

44. United States Constitution Art. 1, Sec. 8 , Cl. 8.

45. United States Constitution Art. 1, Sec. 10, Cl. 2.

state."[46] Finally, Congress could not give a preference to the ports of any state, and vessels bound to or from one state could not be required to pay duties in another.[47] *The centerpiece of the new economic regulatory system, however, was the commerce power.*

In this context it is important to note that there is no corresponding restraining force operating under the United States Constitution on the exercise of the powers of regulation granted to Congress over foreign and inter-state Commerce under the commerce clause. And this power as visualized in some of the decisions of Supreme Court[48] gives the widest amplitude to congressional control of inter-state economic activities. In the words of Murphy, J. the "federal commerce power is as broad as the economic needs of the nation" and the authority resident in that power could be used "to solve national problems directly and realistically." In view of the plenary nature of this commerce power, Congress is deemed to have the authority to regulate, restrict and even prohibit the flow of foreign or inter-state commerce to meet particular situations. It is also an established doctrine of the American Supreme Court that the mere grant of power to Congress over the domain of foreign and inter-state commerce did not, except in regard to subjects in this domain which were national in nature or admitted to only one uniform system or plan of regulation, foreclose the right of the constituent states to regulate matters of local concern, though such regulation may unavoidably involve some measure of regulation of such commerce.[49]

Unlike the American Commerce Clause, its Australian counterpart has played a relatively insignificant role in the economic life of Australia.[50] There are many reasons for this striking difference. *Three* important reasons may be noted.

The *first* springs from the population and economic set-up of Australia.[51] Although, Australia and Continental United States have roughly the same area, the former consists of only six states while the latter comprises fifty states. Australia, moreover, has a population, which approximately is only one-eighteenth of the population of the United States. And Australian industries, comparatively speaking, unlike their American counterparts are organised on a local instead of a national scale. All these factors have produced the resultant effect of making inter-state commerce play a less significant role in the Australian economy as compared to what it does in the

46. United States Constitution Art. 1, Sec. 9, Cl. 5.
47. United States Constitution Art. 1, Sec. 9 , Cl. 6.
48. See Chapter 5.
49. This doctrine which was first enunciated in *Cooley v. Board of Wardens*, 12 How. 299 (1851) has been followed in number of later cases e.g., *South Pacific Co. v. Arizona*, 325 U.S. 761 (1945); *Morgan v. Virginia*, 328 U.S. 373 (1946).
50. See Chapter 5.
51. M. Ramaswamy, Indian Constitution Provisions against Barriers to Trade and Commerce Examined in the Light of Australian and American Experience, J.I.L.I., Vol. 2 at p. 322 (1959-60).

economic life of the American nation. The *second* reason is to be found in the fact that while the shout and terse but dynamic commerce clause has operated as a rich deposit of economic power for Congress to sustain its legislation on the topic of trade and commerce, in Australia, such legislation is largely grounded upon specific assignments of power made by the more modern Australian Constitution which came upon the scene over a century after the American Constitution began to operate. The *third* reason is to be found in the specific provision contained in Sec. 92 of the Australian Constitution, which declares that "on the imposition of uniform duties of customs, trade, commerce and intercourse among the states, whether by means of internal carriage or ocean, navigation, shall be absolutely free." After the decision of the Privy Council in *James v. The Commonwealth of Australia,*[52] it has been established beyond doubt that this provision in the Australian Constitution binds the Parliament of the Commonwealth equally with the states. How far and in what directions this provision operates as a restraint on Commonwealth and state legislative powers in the realm of the trade and commerce raises many issues of great complexity.

Definitely the Australian Commerce Clause as compared with its American counterpart has played relatively insignificant role. The Indian Commerce Clause is likely to play an even less significant role in the Indian economy than what the Australian Commerce Clause contained in Sec. 51(1) of the Commonwealth of Australia Constitution Act, 1900, has played in the economic life of Australia.

In India as seen in Chapters 5 and 7, the concept of regulatory and compensatory taxes imported by the judiciary in the Indian Commerce Clause has positively influenced the Indian economy. It, on one hand, has given an opportunity to the states to collect revenue for maintaining wear and tear and on the other hand has given an opportunity to the traders to get better services which would have a positive impact upon their trade freedom leading to strengthening of country's economy.

IV

As no freedom is absolute, the freedom of trade, commerce and intercourse can and should not also be absolute. A restriction is to be distinguished from regulation in that regulations do not restrict the flow of trade or commerce rather they facilitate it. Restrictions may be imposed subject to *three* riders. *Firstly,* they should be on permissible grounds, e.g. on the ground of public interest, *secondly,* they should be non-discriminatory and *thirdly,* it should be within the legislative competence of the Legislature imposing it i.e., which legislature—federal or state is competent to regulate should be clear.

52. (1936) A. C. 578.

In America, it was not until almost a century after *Gibbons v. Ogden*[53] that the Supreme Court was squarely confronted with the question whether or not a power of prohibition is included in the power to regulate commerce. In *Champion v. Ames (Lottery Case)*[54] the Court was presented with an attack upon the constitutionality of an Act of Congress prohibiting any person from causing lottery tickets to be carried from one state to another. The law was upheld in a forceful opinion by Justice Harlan, who categorically rejected the view that the power to regulate could not be understood to give the power to exclude. "If lottery traffic, carried on through inter-state commerce, is a matter of which Congress may take cognizance and over which its power may be exerted," asks Harlan's opinion, "Can it be possible that it must tolerate the traffic, and simply regulate the manner in which it may be carried on? Or may not Congress, for the protection of the people of all the states, and under the power to regulate inter-state commerce, devise such means, within the scope of the Constitution, and not prohibited by it, as will drive that traffic out of commerce among the states?"[55] However, there it has been the judicial thinking that the commerce power may be exerted to prevent the pollution of commerce by articles confusedly injurious to the public morals. .

But in Canada, the balance appears to be titled in favour of the Dominion Parliament. There the judicial thinking has been that the commerce power was much greater than that in the United States. If one analyses *Ritchie's* views, he would find that in Canada right to regulate trade and commerce should not be over ridden by any local legislation in reference to any subject over which power is given to the local legislature. There, the judicial philosophy is that a prohibition is regulation.[56]

In Australia, the position in this regard may be summarised as under:

Absolute prohibition of inter-state trade, commerce or intercourse is not regulation and appears to be clearly contrary to Sec. 92. But for the qualification mentioned by the Privy Council in the *Banking Case* and unreservedly reaffirmed in the *Hughes and Vale Case,* this statement might have been made unequivocally. It remains to consider the qualification that there might be circumstances under which some economic activities might be prohibited (e.g., "with a view to state monopoly") as the "only practical and reasonable manner of regulation." It appears to be straining language somewhat to say that inter-state trade, commerce and intercourse "thus prohibited and thus monopolised" nevertheless remained "absolutely free." It is conceived that the Board may well have had in mind activities such as those of the Post Office, which, as Dixon, J. had previously observed in the *Airlines Case,* undertakes as exclusive function independently of state boundaries and are a traditional function of government dealt with as such

53. (1824) 9 Wheat. 1.
54. 188 U.S. 321 (1903).
55. *Id.* at p. 355.
56. See Chapter 6.

in the Constitution and nowhere forming a business. But it is conceived that the qualification was enunciated as an *abundans cautela* designed to guard against the application of Sec. 92 in very special circumstances which the Board was unable or unwilling (for very good reasons) to define.

But, while absolute prohibition; or prohibition subject to an absolute discretion (which comes to the same thing) involves a collision with Sec. 92, regulation does not and it becomes necessary to decide what constitutes 'regulation." In the *Hughes and Vale Case;* as has been seen, the Privy Council accepted the principle enunciated by Taylor, J. in the High Court. The principle is that prohibition *sub modo* may well be legitimate, and that there may be licencing. But where the discretion is limited to or confined within the ambit constituted by those matters which can properly be regarded as regulatory of the particular transaction concerned, the legislation may be valid. In other words, the regulation of a subject matter of trade, commerce or intercourse among the states will not necessarily be invalidated and will probably be upheld where the regulation does not permit of arbitrary conditions being prescribed, conditions which are not essentially regulatory in character-regulatory in the sense contemplated by the legislation in question. Further, as Fullagar, J. observed in the High Court, what is or is not a regulation as distinct from a conditional prohibition is in the last resort a question of fact.[57]

However, as the *Transport Cases* have shown "regulation" is a necessarily vague term, conveniently used to mark the distinction between permissible and prohibited forms of control. That the legislation in question, taken as a whole and having regard to its legal operation, was anything but "regulatory", is clear enough. Basically, the objection was that it was too vague, indeterminate and arbitrary to be capable of being described as "regulation" in short, it was unreasonable. But from the judgments a clear principle emerges. While each case must be viewed in the light of its own circumstances and it would be impossible to define inclusively and exclusively what is comprehended in the term "regulation" consistently with the freedom which Sec. 92 prescribes. There is a basic distinction between *essentialia* and *incidentalia:* "direct control of the former will generally be invalid; the latter, comprising the manner of doing something which is merely incidental to the actual trading or commercial activity,"[58] may, generally speaking, be subjected to regulation, provided that the regulation is not used, or does not in fact (e.g., by reason of *ad hoc* conditions imposed at discretion) operate, to impede or restrict the activity itself. This will be a question of degree.

As seen in Chapter 6, there are many modes of regulating trade and commerce, taxation and rate fixing being more important amongst them.

57. *Attorney General for Ontario v. Winner* (1954) A.C. 542, pp. 556-79.

58. Fullagar J. in *Hughes and Vale v. State of New South Wales* (No. 2) (1955) 93 C.L.R. at p. 206.

(a) In America, rate regulations have been held to be uniform and the states have no power over inter-state rates even in the absence of any federal legislation on the subject. In Canada a process of rate fixing in the quite different field of public utility regulation is a process which in this respect contains no element of taxation.[59] In Australia *McArthur's* case was generally supposed to have established the proposition that it was incompetent for the states to fix prices in respect of goods in relation to inter-state trade and commerce. Under Indian Constitution, the price control is a concurrent power and thus in India power to fix rates or prices has been conceded both to the Centre as well as the states subject to the rider of reasonableness. However, it is humbly suggested that whenever Centre fixes the rates or prices it should be on an all India basis and no discrimination should be made between sates *interse* except than those which are unavoidable because of regional imbalances or because of other compelling circumstances. Where states are to fix rates or prices within their states it would be proper if there is some all India based regulatory body having been given power to monitor the states to insist upon uniformity in the rates and prices, of course keeping in view the existing local variations.

(b) In *Atiabari*,[60] the Court found the tax to be violative of Art. 301, and held that it could not be upheld under Art. 304(b). Similarly in *Kalyani Stores*,[61] the majority held that the tax infringed the freedom under Art. 301 and might be saved only if it fell within the exceptions contained in Arts. 302, 303 and 304.

After a long-drawn controversy in the high courts as well as in the Supreme Court, it has been settled[62] that tax laws are not outside the purview of Part XIII of the Constitution. The main ground advanced by the Supreme Court in coming to this conclusion is that the power to levy taxes is ultimately based on Art. 245 and the said power in terms is subject to the provisions of the Constitution including those in Part XIII.[63]

In a sense, every tax imposed by a state legislature may have an indirect effect on the flow of trade or commerce. But if the power of the state legislature to make any tax law be held to be subject to the limitation under Art. 301, the legislative power of the state legislature would be rendered hollow, and, the federal scheme would be rendered meaningless.[64] The Supreme Court has, accordingly laid down certain conditions for the application of Art. 301, i.e., every tax does not interfere with the freedom of

59. *Ibid.*
60. A.I.R. 1961 S.C. 232, at p. 254.
61. A.I.R. 1966 S.C. 1686 at p. 1692.
62. *Atiabari Tea Co. v. State of Assam* (1961) S.C.R. 809 at p. 860
63. *Automobile Transport v. State of Rajasthan*, A.I.R. 1962 S.C. 1406 at p. 1422
64. *Ibid.*

trade guaranteed by Art. 301; it does so only if it directly and immediately restricts or hampers the free flow of trade, commerce or intercourse.[65]

To ensure that the inter-state trade and commerce does not go absolutely tax-free and pays tax at least once, the Constitution (Sixth Amendment) Act, 1956, modified Art. 286, and gave it its present form, Entry 92A was also added to List I. The effect of these modifications is that the power to tax inter-state sale or purchase now belongs to the Centre and not to be states which are also debarred from taxing an 'outside' sale and what is an 'outside' sale or inter-state sale are matters for Parliament to define under Art. 286(2) and 269(3) respectively.

In America, it is well-established doctrine that a state cannot directly tax foreign or inter-state commerce. This doctrine is derived from the judicial interpretation of the Commerce Clause. That Clause, as we have observed, vests in Congress plenary powers over the regulation of foreign and inter-state commerce. As taxation is only a form of regulation, it is argued, no state can tax foreign or inter-state commerce directly without trenching upon the powers, which are confided to Congress under the 'Commerce Clause'.

The division of tax power in Canada and Australia has had a very adverse effect upon the fiscal independence of the provinces and states. American states have claimed this to be true in the United States but the argument has not been completely convincing. In the earliest days the states insisted that the national government should limit its taxation to imports and leave to the states all forms of internal taxation, but the argument was refused by Hamilton who imposed such taxes merely to establish the precedent in case such taxes were ever needed.[66]

The problem of multiple taxation of inter-state sale or purchase does not arise in Australia as only the Centre and not the states can levy sales tax. In Canada, the provinces can levy a sales tax payable by the ultimate consumer and the problem of multiple taxation does not arise.[67] The problem is rather acute in the U.S.A. the judiciary has made some attempts to avoid multiple taxation of inter-state commerce by invoking the Commerce Clause and the Due Process Clause[68] of the Constitution, but the problem is too complicated to be solved only by the judiciary.

(c) The concept of compensatory tax has been borrowed from Australia where it has been evolved to dilute somewhat the rigours of Sec. 92. Now there is one basic difference between the Indian and the foreign models. In Australia, Sec. 92[69] admits no exception. If a law imposes a

65. *State of Kerala v. Abdul*, A.I.R. 1970 S.C. 1913; *State of Karnataka v. Hansa Corpn.*, A.I.R. 1981 S.C. 425.
66. J.A. Maxwell, The Fiscal Impact of Federalism in the United States (Cambridge, Mass., 1946), 8.
67. *Atlantic Smoke Shops Ltd. v. Conlon*, 1943 A.C. 550.
68. This provision has been used to invalidate state attempts to tax an object outside the state borders.
69. *Freightlines and Construction Holding Ltd. v. New South Wales* (1968) A.C. 625.

restriction on trade it is just unconstitutional. In this context, the courts have evolved the test of compensatory tax to loosen the rigours of Sec. 92.

Like the American Supreme Court, the High Court of Australia has taken the view that compensatory taxes do not amount to restriction on the freedom of inter-state trade and commerce. In *Hughes & Vale (No. 2)*, Dixon, C.J. and Mc Tiernan, Williams, Webb and Fullagar, JJ. took the view that the states were entitled to impose fair and reasonable charge for the use made of roads by vehicles engaged in inter-state trade. In Australia, it is possible to reconcile with the freedom postulated by Sec. 92 the extraction from commerce using the roads, whether the journey be inter-state or not, of some special contribution to their maintenance and upkeep in relief of the general revenues of the state drawn from the public at large.

The American phrase is that inter-state commerce must pay its way. In the U.S.A. the states have conceded some power to tax inter-state commerce as against the constitutional protection given to such commerce to help them to raise some funds to maintain roads, etc. Therefore, the concept of compensatory tax has been adopted to make inter-state commerce pay it way.[70]

In America, a tax might be explained in terms of its regulatory impact, as licence taxes some times are. Taxes thus justified raise the same issues as do state regulations. Taxes have at times been branded regulatory or compensatory depending upon how directly they bore upon inter-state commerce. The more common arguments however, is that the tax is a bill presented to inter-state commerce for services rendered by the taxing state. The Supreme Court has recognised that the states have a legitimate interest in compensatory taxation of inter-state commerce: "It was not purpose of the commerce clause to relieve those engaged in inter-state commerce from their just share of state tax burden even though it increases the cost of doing the business. Even inter-state business must pay its way."[71]

It does not follow from the 'Compensatory Taxation' argument, however, that taxes collected from inter-state commerce are valid only to the extent that the resulting revenues are ultimately used in a way that can be related to local activities of the multistage enterprise taxed. In America, the test may be summarised as 'state taxation falling on inter-state commerce can only be justified as designated to make such commerce bear a fair share of cost of the local government whose protection it enjoys. Thus, there the test is of fair share.'[72]

The degree of 'connection', 'contact' or 'nexus' between the taxing state and the inter-state commerce taxed is also the fundamental measure of whether or not a state tax violates the commerce and due process clauses.

---

70. *Aero Mayflower Transit Co. v. Board of R.R. Commrs.*, 332 U.S. 497 (1942).
71. *Western Livestock v. Bureau of Revenue*, 303 U.S. 250, 254 (1938); *Freeman v. Hewit*, 329 U.S. 249, 253 (1946).
72. *Evansvile Vanderburg Airport Authority District v. Delta Airlines*, 405 U.S. 707 (1972); *Colonial Pipeline Co. v. Traigle*, 421 U.S. 100, 108 (1975).

The Supreme Court of United States has explained compensatory tax doctrine in different cases. In order to justify a charge on inter-state commerce as a compensatory tax, a state must as a threshold matter, identify the inter-state tax burden for which the state is attempting to compensate.[73] Identifying the nature of compensatory taxes the American Judiciary has said that it is a tax, which is on its face discriminatory, but may still survive scrutiny under the Commerce Clause, if it is a truly compensatory tax, that is, a tax designed simply to make inter-state commerce bear a burden already borne by intra-state commerce.[74] In United States, compensatory taxes have also been described as complementary taxes.[75]

Indian Judiciary have favoured a restrictive interpretation of limitations, both constitutional and statutory on the taxing powers of the Union and the States. Since states have been put under severe restrictions, they have been the main beneficiaries of this judicial approach. The examination of cases on the regulation of inter-state trade and commerce show that the courts have preferred to take a restricted view of the scope of freedom guaranteed by Art. 301. Only those laws have been declared to have been affected by Art. 301 which directly and immediately impede the free flow of trade and commerce. This direct and immediate effect test is subject to clarification by test of compensatory taxes and regulatory law. The Courts have pointed out that compensatory taxes and regulatory measures do not fall within the purview of Art. 301.[76] The Judicial decision on the point show that Indian Courts have gone a long way to save state measures by giving a very wide meaning to the concept of compensatory taxes and regulatory measures. In doing so they have gone beyond not only what was comprehended in the concept in Australia but even in America. Thus, in relation to state taxing power on inter-state transportation the Courts have upheld state laws even though it was found to provide for no fair recompense, if the rate of tax was not excessive or prohibitive and if amount collected from the tax was more than the expenditure incurred on maintenance and construction of roads. The Courts have allowed taxes on spared buses merely kept for use; they have ignored the fact that the tax collected has not been kept in a separate fund; they have not insisted upon separate assessment on the basis of the types of vehicles, their weight, mileage covered by them and nature of road used. And when such a differentiation has been done by the states, the Courts have allowed the law repelling the charge of discrimination.[77] They have also ignored if the income was slightly more than expenditure incurrred and when the income has been much more than expenditure incurred by the state on maintenance and construction of roads, bridges, etc., state taxation has been allowed by taking

73. *Oregon Waste Sys. v. Deptt. of Env.* (1994) 128 L. Ed. 2d 13.
74. *Fulton Corp. v. Faulkner*, (1996) 123 L. Ed. 2d 796.
75. *South Central Bell Telephone Co. v. Alabama* (1999) 526 L. Ed. U.S. 160.
76. See Chapter 7.
77. *Shyam Sunder Roy v. State of Bihar*, A.I.R. (1983) Pat. 14.

into account the expenditure in earlier years. The validity of taxes like octroi and tolls have been upheld in view of their compensatory nature. From the discussion made in Chapter 7 it is clear that the Judiciary has accepted the general principle that the compensatory or regulatory provisions, whether by way of a tax or not, would not attract the proviso to Art. 304(b). Hence, *first*, the states are free to impose such restrictions without the concurrence of the federal executive, and *secondly*, such measures may also pass the test of 'reasonableness in the interest of public' easily.

It is not and it can not be stipulated that for the purpose of establishing the compensatory nature of the tax, it is necessary to establish that every rupee collected on account of the entry tax should be shown to be spent on providing the trading facilities. It is enough if some connection is established between the tax and the trading facilities provided. The connection can be a direct one or an indirect one.[78] However, a mere claim that tax is compensatory would not suffice. Whether a tax is commendatory or not cannot be made to depend on the preamble of the statute imposing it. A tax cannot also be said not to be compensatory because the precise or specific amount collected is not actually used to providing any facilities.[79]

(d) Several federal countries—Argentina, Austria, Brazil, Canada, Columbia, the Federal Republic of Germany, and Mexico—levy a VAT. The VATs of Argentina, Austria, Germany and Mexico, are all centrally-controlled with revenue sharing arrangements between the federal and provincial governments.[80] It is better to entrust the administration and collection of the VAT either with the states or with the federal government and then use a formula to share the revenue between the central Government and the states. If this is unacceptable owing to the loss of fiscal autonomy, then federal VAT might have a state VAT 'piggybacked' on it.

Discussion made in Chapter 8 compels us to conclude that the VAT system by itself would not hamper the freedom of trade, commerce and intercourse, rather it would facilitate the same. Therefore, there is urgent need to implement it throughout the country so as to have an uniform VAT system. This system of taxation would definitely be regulatory measure coming well within the 'Commerce Clause', though there may be practical difficulties in implementing the VAT system to E-commerce but even that too is being attempted to be shorted out.

V

There was a time when horse with its rider, sailing vessels, coach and steamboat, railroads, etc. were treated as different instrumentalities of commerce in different eras. But these instrumentalities also have become

78. *State of Bihar v. Bihar Chamber of Commerce*, A.I.R. 1996 S.C. 2344.
79. *Ashok Nagar Welfare Association v. R.K Sharma*, A.I.R. 2002 S.C. 322 at pp. 334-35; overruling *B.A. Jayaram v. Union of India*, A.I.R. 1983 S.C. 1005.
80. See Chapter 8.

outdated in this modern "high-tech-era". Thus, if by process of interpretation telegraph can be held as an instrumentality of commerce why not the modern Internet system? One should not disagree with the affirmative answer to this question, if two things are kept into mind. *One,* that the E-commerce is processed through Internet system which is based upon *telephone lines, cable lines, wireless connection,* etc. which have been judicially held as instrumentalities of commerce. *Two,* the Internet can function not only within a state (intra-state) or between states (inter-state), rather it can function at global level also facilitating export and import (cross-border trade or international trade). Thus, there is no reason not to include E-commerce within the "Commerce Clause".

In United States, courts have found that the dormant commerce clause applies to Internet also. The Internet like a highway or railroad, may be an instrument of inter-state commerce and analysed accordingly.[81] Justice *Dixon's* observation in *Banking Case* gives ample support to conclude that even in Australia the electronic commerce is well within the comprehension of commerce. However, the Indian situation is slightly different. Indian Courts have not to labour much for bringing E-commerce within the ambit of "Commerce". It has not even to depend upon the "Commerce Clause" contained in the Constitution. The simple reason is that various Entries contained in List I of the Constitution give ample opportunity to the judiciary to bring E-commerce within the scope of "Commerce Clause." For example, Entry 31 of List I mentions "posts and telegraphs, telephones, wireless, broadcasting and *other like means of communication.*" At Entry 41 of the Union List there is mention of "trade, commerce with foreign countries, import and export trade and commerce" and Entry 42 speaks about "inter-state trade and commerce." Internet can safely be interpreted as being included in *other like means of communication* mentioned at Entry 31st of List I. Therefore, is no reason why the *Parliament* can not *regulate E-commerce* and why the *Judiciary* can not *regulate Parliament* if it crosses the limits prescribed by the Indian Commerce Clause.

A general theoretical framework for analysing dormant commerce clause challenges to state Internet regulations can be provided. *Five* points bear emphasis. *First,* the out-of-state costs of state regulation of cross-border externalities are commonplace and often desirable from the efficiency perspective that informs the meaning and scope of the dormant commerce clause. *Second,* the appropriate question about these state regulations is not whether they produce out-of-state costs, but rather whether they are properly calibrated to redress local harms. *Third,* the real concern underlying the extra-territoriality and inconsistent-regulations prongs of dormant commerce clause analysis is not out-of-state effects and non-uniformity *per se,* but rather whether the out-of-state burdens of a regulation outweigh its local benefits. *Fourth,* courts applying the dormant commerce clause to state

81. See Chapter 3.

Internet regulations may commit significant errors in identifying and weighing the regulations' costs and benefits. *Fifth,* as a general matter, the federal political branches may be better suited than the courts to balance and redress the harms and benefits of state Internet regulations.

To date, dormant commerce clause analysis of state Internet regulations has been marked by the same general error that infects much thinking about Internet regulation more broadly. The error is the belief that the Internet is a unique phenomenon that requires suspension of the normal principles that govern cross-border conduct. In the dormant Commerce Clause context, as in other regulatory contexts, this assumption is false. Insight about Internet regulation comes, at least in the first instance, from focusing not on how the Internet is different from other communication systems, but rather in the many ways in which if is similar.[82]

Further, if a commercial activity is prohibited by law in real space, how can it be permitted in cyber space? From this the idea of *'electronic res extra commercium'* developed. Therefore, every regulatory law applying in relation to trade, commerce and intercourse in real space should equally apply to business done through Internet (inter-state, intra-state or cross-border trade).

The development of electronic commerce (E-commerce) has revolutionised the way businesses operate. It has also challenged the adequacy and fundamental validity of principles of international taxation such as physical presence, place of establishment, etc., that have formed the basis for assessing tax liability. With the advent of E-commerce, even smaller corporations and individuals can aspire to have a global presence. Correspondingly E-commerce has also bridged the gap between developed and developing countries. It has therefore become extremely essential to provide a legal and tax environment that is conducive to the growth and development of these technologies. The implications of the growth of E-commerce on domestic and international tax systems has already been felt and considerable work on this subject has already been done by countries like U.S., U.K., Australia, Canada, etc. They have identified the issues arising out of E-commerce and have attempted to lay down the fundamental principles of taxation of E-commerce. Most countries have advocated principles of neutrality, certainty, avoidance of double taxation and low compliance. The physical location of the server and the website would constitute a dependent agent or nexus. It is humbly submitted that India should not lag behind in this direction.

SUGGESTIONS

The study conducted so for, reveals certain shortcoming in the area of the regulation of Trade, Commerce and Intercourse. With a view to make

82. Jack J. Goldsmith and Alan O. Sykes, The Internet and the Dormant Commerce Clause, *Yale Law Journal*, Vol. 110, No. 5, Mar. (2001), p. 785.

commerce clause gives under the Constitutions more fruitful, the following suggestions are preferred:

1. Every activity should be brought within the ambit of commerce unless it is purely for the personal use. From this it is clear that personal use should be segregated from the commercial use. But this suggestion is subject to certain limitations and clarifications. In some cases, it may be impossible, as was in *Wickard case,* to separate personal use from commercial use, i.e., both may be difficult to be segregated. In that case it is suggested that the 'Substantial Effect Test' should be the correct approach. The Court must weigh both the personal use and commercial use and should give way to that which out ways the other.
2. In this commercial age every activity intended to be undertaken with profit-oriented motive should well be brought within the ambit of 'Commerce Clause'. Applying the principle 'Insurance' though having an element of social security, should with no exception be treated as trade or business and should thus be brought within the coverage of 'Commerce Clause'. So, should be the case with 'manufacture' also. Every manufacturing activity intended to be followed for another profit-oriented activity should be given the characteristic of trade or business.
3. As there has been a shift in the principles of morality, the doctrine of *res extra commercium* should be construed strictly. What was at one time being considered as immoral is now being considered as not immoral if not moral (take in case of liquor).
4. As seen in Chapter 8 the VAT system is successfully running in European countries, U.S.A. and Canada therefore, there is urgent need to implement the VAT system throughout India on an uniform basis.
5. An Inter-state Commission on the pattern of U.S.A. and as was mooted in Australia, with such powers of adjudication and administration as the Parliament deems necessary for the execution and maintenance of the provisions of the Constitution relating to Trade and Commerce, should be established. The above suggestion is in consonance with the recommendations of the Sarkaria Commission as contained in para 18.05.05. The Commission recommends that an expert authority should be constituted under Art. 307. Among other things, such an authority may be enabled to:
   (a) Survey and bring out periodically a repon on the restrictions imposed on intra-state and inter-state trade and commerce by different governments and their agencies.
   (b) Recommend measures to rationalise or modify the restrictions imposed to facilitate free trade and commerce.

(c) Examine complaints from the public and the trade in this regard.

(d) Suggest reforms in the matter of imposition, levying and sharing of taxes for purposes of Part XIII of the Constitution.

The National Commission to review the working of the Constitution in Chapter 8 of its report has also recommended for the setting up of an authority as suggested above.

National Commission's Report in this connection recommends:

"For carrying out the objectives of Articles 301, 302, 303 and 304 and other purposes relating to the needs and requirements of inter-state trade and commerce and for purposes of eliminating barriers to inter-state trade and commerce. Parliament should by law establish an authority called the "Inter-state Trade and Commerce Commission" under the Ministry of Industry and Commerce under Art. 307 read with Entry 42 of List I."

6. Where states are to fix rates or prices within their states it would be proper if there is some all India based regulatory body having been given power to monitor the states to insist upon uniformity in the rates and prices, of course keeping in view the existing local variations.

7. Since, Sugarcane, Tea, Coffee, Mint, Cotton and like products are formidable source of Indian Economy therefore, as discussed in Chapter 5, they require special judicial attention if their transportation, export and import across trade barriers (state boundaries), etc. are attempted to be regulated by law. It is humbly submitted that while examining the vires of regulations of these products the judiciary must adopt a strict approach.

List of Cases

Bibliography

A. Mitchall Polinsdy, An Introduction to Law and Economics, 10 (2d ed., 1989).

Abel, The Commerce Clause in the Constitution Convention and in Contemporary Comment (1941), 25, *Minn. L. Rev.* 432.

Advisory Commission on Electronic Commerce, Issues and Policy Options Paper: Final Draft Submitted to the Commission from the Report Drafting Sub-committee, 12-03-1999 (available online).

Alok Kumar and Ramani Kumar, Indian Tea Exports : An analysis of Performance and Constraints, *Foreign Trade Review* (1994).

Annuals of the American Academy of Political Science Federal *versus* State Jurisdiction in American Life, Vol. C XXIX, January 1927.

Bahl, Roy (1994): "Revenues and Revenue Assignment: Inter-governmental Fiscal Relations in the Russian Federation", Christine Wallich (ed.), Russia and the Challenge of Fiscal Federalism, World Bank, Washington, D.C.

Bailey, Fifty Years of the Australian Constitution, 25, *A.L.J.R.* 314 (1951).

Basu, Commentary on the Constitution of India, Vol. L.

Bernard Swartz, A Commentary on the Constitution of the United States (1977).

Bird, Richard, M. and Genderon, Pierre Pascal (1998): Dual VAT's and Cross-Border Trade : Two Problems, One Solution? International Trade and Public Finance, 5, Kluwer Academic Publishers, Boston.

Bird, Richard M. (1994): Cost and Complexity of Canada's VAT: The GST in International Perspective : Tax Note International, Vol. 8.

Bowie and Frederich, Studies in Federalism (1954).

Burk, Federalism in Cyberspace, 28, *Conn. L. Rev.* (1996) at p. 1096.

C.A.D., Vol. IX.

Chakraborty, A. : The Idea Behind Modvat, *Capital* (Calcutta), Vol. 196.

Charles E. Carpentar & Robert Charles Mardian, What is Commerce, 22 S, *Cal. L. Rev.* 398 (1949).

Citizens for a Better Government, 444 U.S. at 636.

Clark, Douglas H.: 'The Fiscal Transfer System in Canada' in Ehthisham Ahmad (ed.), Financing Decentralised Expenditures : An International Comparison of Grants, Albershot, the United Kingdom and Brookfield, Edward Elgar, U.S. (1996).

Clements, Law of the Canadian Constitution, 3rd Edition, 1916.

Commission on Private Philanthropy and Public Needs, Giving in America: Toward a Stronger Voluntary Sector, 117 (Treasure Deptt. 1975): cited in the *Uni. Chi. L. Rev.*, 2000.

Corry, Difficulties of Divided Jurisdiction (Royal Commission Study, Appendix 7).

D.F. Mulla, Principals of Hindu Law (14th ed., 1974).

D.K. Singh : Trade, Commerce and Intercourse in India: A Reappraisal of Some Constitutional Problems, *J.I.L.I.*, Vol. 14, 1972.

David M. Kreps, Game Theory and Electronic Modelling, 26, No. 8 (1990).

David M. Eisenberg, Questions and Answers about Advertising on the Internet, 43, *Prac. Law*, 79, 80 (July 1977).

David R. Johnson & David Post, Law and Borders—The Rise of Law in Cyberspace, 48, *Stan. L. Rev.* 1367 (1996).

Derham, Some Constitutional Problems arising under Part XIII of the Indian Constitution, 1, *J.I.L.I.*, 523.

Dicey, Law of the Constitution, 10th ed., (1962).

Don F. Vacarro, Validity and Application of Governmental Limitation on Permissible Amount or Proportion of Fund-raising Expenses and Administrative Costs of Charitable Organisations, 15, A.I.R. 4th 1163 (1982).

Douglas G. Baird *et. al.*, Game Theory and the Law, 1 (1994).

Ebb, Interstate Barriers in India and American Constitutional Experience, 11, *Stan. L. Rev.*, 37 (1958-59).

Elliot, The Debates in the Several State Conventions on the Federal Constitution (1901).

Eric Rasmuson, Games and Information: An Introduction to Game Theory, 9 (2d ed., 1994).

F.R. Scott, The Constitution Background of Taxation Agreements, *McGill Law Journal*, 11(1955) 2.

Fredrich, Constitutional Government and Democracy, 10th Edition.

Gavit, The Commerce Clause.

Goldsmith, Against Cyberanarchy, 65, *Uni. Chi. L. Rev.* (1998).

Goldsmith, The Internet and the Abiding Significance of Territorial Sovereignty, 5, *Ind. J. Global Legal Studies*, 475 (1998).

Grant S. Nelson & Robert J. Pushaw, Jr., Rethinking the Commerce Clause: Applying First Principle to Uphold Federal Commercial Regulations but Preserve State Control Over Social Issue, *Iowa Law Review*, Vol. 85, No. 1, 1999.

H.M. Seervai, The Freedom of Trade and Commerce in the Indian Constitution (The Atiabari case and after), *Cambridge Law Journal* (1963) 54.

Hamilton & Adair, The Power to Govern, 179 (1937).

Hamilton, The Federalists No. 35, at. 216.

Hicks, Federalism Failure & Success.

Hovenkamp; Judicial Restraint and Constitutional Federalism: The Supreme Court's Lopez and Seminole Tribe Decisions, 96, *Colum. L. Rev.*, 2230.

Ian Ayres, Playing Games with the Law, 42, *Stan. L. Rev.*, 1291 (1990).
Indian Market Research Bureau (I.M.R.B.).
Inter-state Trade Barriers & Sales Tax Law in India, I.L.I. (1962).
Internet Tax Freedom Act, Pub L. No. 105-277, Title XI codified at 47 U.S.C.A. 151 (West, 1998).
J.A. Maxwell, The Fiscal Impact of Federalism in the United States (Cambridge, Mass., 1946) 8.
Jabir Ali, Export Potential of Indian Mint Oil Industry, *Foreign Trade Review*, 2000.
Jack J. Goldsmith and Alan O. Sykes, The Internet and the Dormant Commerce Clause, *Yale Law Journal*, Vol. 110, No. 5 (2001).
James E. Gaylord Note, State Regulatory Jurisdiction and the Internet: Letting the Dormant Commerce Clause Lie, 52 *Vand. L. Rev.* 1095 (1997).
Jariwala, Freedom of Inter-state Trade in India, Delhi, Sterling Publishers (1975).
Johnson and Post, Law and Borders—The rise of Law in Cyberspace, 48, *Stan. L. Rev.*, 1367 (1996).
Joseph Story, Commentaries on the Constitution of the United States (1833).
Julian N. Eule, Laying the Dormant Commerce Clause to Rest, 91, *Yale L.J.*, 425, No. 1 (1982).
Keen, M. and S. Smith (1996): The Future of Value Added Tax in the European Union, Economic Policy, 23.
Keith Aoki, Considering Multiple and Overlapping Sovereignties: Liberalism, Libertarianism, National Sovereignty, "Global" Intellectual Property And the Internet, 5, *Ind. J. Global Legal Studies*, 443 (1998).
Laskin, Peace, Order and Good Government Re-examined.
Laskin's Canadian Constitutional Law, 1975.
Lawrence H. Tribe, American Constitutional Law, 2d ed., 1988.
Lessig, The Law of the Horse: What Cyberlaw Might Teach, l13, *Harv. L. Rev.*, 501 (1999).
Lisa I. Fried, Internet Taxation: An Advisory Committee; Is Embroiled in Debate, *Ny. L.J.*, 5 (Sept. 23, 1999).
Lord Wright of Durby, Sec. 92: A Problem Piece, *The Sydney Law Rev.*, Vol. 1, No. 2, Jan. 1954, 167.
Lumb, R.D. Ryan, K.W., The Constitution of the Commonwealth of Australia—Annotated (Butterworths), 1974.
M.P. Jain, Indian Constitution Law (1999).
M.P. Singh, Some Reflections on Jariwala's Freedom of Inter-state Trade in India, *J.B.C.I.*, 1977, 26.
M.P. Jain, Justice Bhagwati and Constitutional Law, 2, *J.I.L.I.* (1962).
M.P. Singh, Prohibition against Preference on Discrimination in Trade, Commerce and Intercourse in India: A Reappraisal of Constitutional Problems, 14, *J.I.L.I.*, 39 (1972).

M.P. Singh: Is Moneylending Extra Commercium? Some Thoughts on Fatehchand *v.* State of Maharashtra, 1978, 3 S.C.C. 1.

M.R. Narayana, Marketing, Pricing & Exporting of Coffee in India : Recent Changes and Implications, *Foreign Trade Review* (1994).

MacDonald, Taxation Power in Canada (1941) 19, *Can. Bar Rev.*, 149.

MacKinnon Victor, Comparative Federalism—A Study in Judicial Interpretation (Hague : Martinus Nijhuff), 1964.

Max Farrand, The Framing of the Constitution of the United States, 6, (1913).

Mark Seidenfeld, Microeconomic Predicates to Law and Economics 85 (1996).

Mark Tushnet, Rethinking the Commerce Clause, 1979, *Wis. L. Rev.*, 125.

Maxwell, A Flexible Portion of B.N.A. Act (1933) 11, *Can. Bar Rev.*, 149.

Melissa G. Liazos, Can State Impose Registration on Online Charitable Solicitors ? *The Uni. Chi. L Rev.*, Vol. 67, 1379 (2000).

Michael E. Smith, State Discriminations against Inter-state Commerce, 74, Cal 1203 (1986).

Michael W. McConnell & Richard A. Posner, An Economic Approach to Issue of Religious Freedom, 56, *Uni. Chi. L. Rev.*, 1 (1989).

Miller, Lectunes on the Constitution of the United States (1893).

Mintz, Jack, M. (1998): The Role of Allocation in a Globalised Corporate Income Tax, WP/98/134, I.M.F Working Paper, International Monetary Fund, Washington, D.C.

N.C. Sen Gupta, Evolution of Ancient Indian Law (1953).

Neumann, European and Comparative Government (1960).

Norregaard, John (1997): "Tax Assignment" in Teresa Ter-Minassian (ed.), Fiscal Federalism in Theory and Practice, International Monetary Fund, Washington, D.C.

P.E. McGreal, The Flawed Economics of the Dormant Commerce Clause, *Wm. & Mary L. Rev.*, 39, No. 4 (1998).

P.H. Lane, Trade and Commerce Power: Constitution, Sec. 51(I), *The Australian Law Journal*, Vol. 34 (1960) 99.

Paul T. Truitt, Inter-state Barriers in the United States, 8, *Law and Const. Problems*, 209 (1941).

Peter Nygh, Freedom of Inter-state Trade in Australia, *Uni. of Q.L.J.*, 1966-67.

Poul A. Freund, Umpiring the Federal Systems, 54, *Col. L. Rev.*, 561 (1954).

Preserve State Control over Social Issue, *Iowa Law Review*, Vol. 85, No. I, 1999.

Prof. Anirudh Prasad: Centre-State Relations in India, Ed. 1985.

Prof. F.R. Beasley, The Commonwealth Constitution: Sec. 92, Its History in the Federal Conventions (1948)1, *Uni of West Austr. Ann. L. Rev.*, 97.

Ramaswamy, Indian Constitutional Provisions against Barriers to Trade and Commerce, 2, *J.I.L.I.*, 320 (1960).

Ramaswamy, The Commerce Clause in the Constitution of U.S.A.

Rao, The Framing of India's Constitution—A Study, 1968.

Record of the Debates of the Federal Convention, Third Session, Melbourne, 1898.

Report of the National Commission to Review the Working of the Constitution, Vol. 1.

Rice, Division of Powers to Control Commerce, 1, *J.I.L.I.*, 151 (1959).
Richard A. Posner, Economic Analysis of Law, 3, (5th ed., 1998).
Richard E. Johnston, The Effect of Judicial Review on Federal State Relations in Australia, Canada and United States, Ed. 1969.
Robert L. Stern, That Commerce which concerns more states than one, 47, *Harv. L. Rev.*, 1335 (1934).
S. Gurumurthi, Fiscal Federalism: Towards an Appropriate VAT-Systems for a Federal Economy, *Eco. & Pol. Weekly*, Vol. 34 (1999) 2875.
S.N. Jain, Freedom of Trade, Commerce and Restraints on the State Power to Tax Sale in the Course of Inter-state Trade and Commerce, 10, *J.I.L.I.*, 544 (1968).
Sawer, Australian Federation in the Courts (1967).
Schwartz: An Introduction to American Administrative Law, 10 (2d., 1962).
Sherwood, L.R., Sec. 92 in the Federal Conventions--A Fresh Appraisal (1958) 1, *Melb. Uni. L. Rev.*, 331.
Shome, Parthasarathi; VAT : Structural Aspects and Experience in Value Added Tax in India : A Progress Report (1997).
Stern, The Commerce Clause and the National Economy (1946) 59, *Harv. L. Rev.*, 645.
Steven R. Salbu, Who Should Govern the Internet ?: Monitoring and Supporting a New Frontier, 11, *Harv. L.J. & Tech.*, .429 (1998).
Sukumar Mukhopadhyay, VAT-options for Inter-state Trade in Federal India, *Ex. Law Times*, Vol. 139 (2002) 194.
Tait, Alan A. (1988): Value Added Tax, International Practice and Problems, International Monitory Fund, Washington, D.C.
The Lotteries, Revenues and Social Costs: A Historical Examination of State-Sponsored Gambling, It records in *Boston College Law Review*, Vol. 34, 11.
The Report of the Indian Statutory Commission, Vol. II.
The Sarkaria Commission's Report.
Thomas K. Anson & P.M. Schenkhan, Federalism, The Dormant Commerce Clause and State Owned Resources, 59, *Tax. L. Rev.*, 71(1980).
W. Murphy, Law and Poverty, 212(1973).
Wheare, Federal Government (1963).
William O. Douglas, From Marshall to Mukerjea; Tagore Law Lectures, 1956.

Index